CW01669613

Universal Principles of ART

First published in the United States of America in 2015 by
Rockport Publishers, a member of
Quarto Publishing Group USA Inc.
100 Cummings Center
Suite 406-L
Beverly, Massachusetts 01915-6101
Telephone: (978) 282-9590
Fax: (978) 283-2742
www.rockpub.com
Visit RockPaperInk.com to share your opinions, creations, and passion for design.

10 9 8 7 6 5 4 3 2 1

ISBN: 978-1-63159-030-6

Digital edition published in 2015
eISBN: 978-1-62788-223-1

Library of Congress Cataloging-in-Publication Data
Parks, John A., 1952-
Universal principles of art : 100 key concepts for understanding, analyzing, and practicing art / John A A Parks.
pages cm

1. Art--Dictionaries. I. Title.
N33.P38 2014
703--dc23
2014025501

Design: Bryn Freeman

Cover Images: *Grande Odalisque* by Jean Auguste Dominique Ingres; *Portrait of Picasso* by Juan Gris; Noc sculpture, Nigeria; *Nine Jackies* by Andy Warhol (image courtesy of Alamy).

Printed in China

Universal Principles of ART

100 Key Concepts for Understanding, Analyzing, and Practicing Art

John A. Parks

Rockport Publishers
100 Cummings Center, Suite 406L
Beverly, MA 01915

rockpub.com • rockpaperink.com

PREFACE

As a professional artist and a teacher of many years at the School of Visual Arts in New York, I sometimes find myself guiding a group of students around a museum.

They are often bewildered.

In the space of a few minutes we may come across Renaissance angels, fearsome tribal masks, a canvas displaying nothing more than a geometric shape on a white ground, Impressionist views of sunny afternoons, photorealist paintings of Californian diners, and artworks that are simply typewritten sheets of instructions.

How can I begin to explain to my students what these products have in common and how they function as works of art? How can I convey what ideas, techniques, practices, superstitions, stylistic developments, and cultural contexts were in play when they were made? And how can I do it in a way that is simple, direct, and accessible? Then there is the most mysterious question of all: Why is all this stuff here in the first place? What is it that has driven so many people throughout history to keep on making art?

I begin by pointing out the extraordinary fact that every human culture makes art, from the most remote preliterate tribe to the most educated western elites. Our abilities and drive to make art undoubtedly arose from evolutionary necessity. A number of surveys, conducted over many cultures, have identified a marked preference for paintings of savannah-like landscapes, with rolling grassland, trees, and water. Evolutionary psychologists point out that this is an image of the kind of landscapes in Africa in which our forebears lived during the Pleistocene epoch. It is the ideal environment in which hunter-gatherer tribes might expect to prosper. Similarly, qualities such as balance and symmetry, as well as certain ratios related to the human body, may be attractive because they are evidence of fitness traits in humans. The delicate aesthetic senses we deploy today may have emerged from our ability to discern good mating choices in prehistory.

Aesthetic pleasure may have grown from evolutionary pressures to become part of our very nature, but it has also been taken up by the development of our cultures and transformed into something immensely diverse and complex. The history of ideas, religious beliefs, cultural practices, technological advances, and sheer ingenuity have proliferated a dizzying variety of artworks. This book provides a clear and concise account of how a number of key ideas, techniques, cultural contexts, and creative inspiration have combined to bring into being a broad array of artworks. It is the book I would like to put into my students' hands as they wander through the museum or talk earnestly about art in the studio.

Above all, I would like my students to feel that understanding art is not an intellectual exercise, but an introduction to joy. Art is a way of conveying feeling, of relating to other human beings' ways of being in the world, of sharing experience and insights, of manufacturing pleasure. It can be provocative, charming, cathartic, beautiful, deeply moving, sexy, cerebral, humorous, spiritual, or sensational. In fact it can access and transmit the entire range of feelings in ways that are continually fresh and engaging. It is the very best and most extraordinary thing that human beings do.

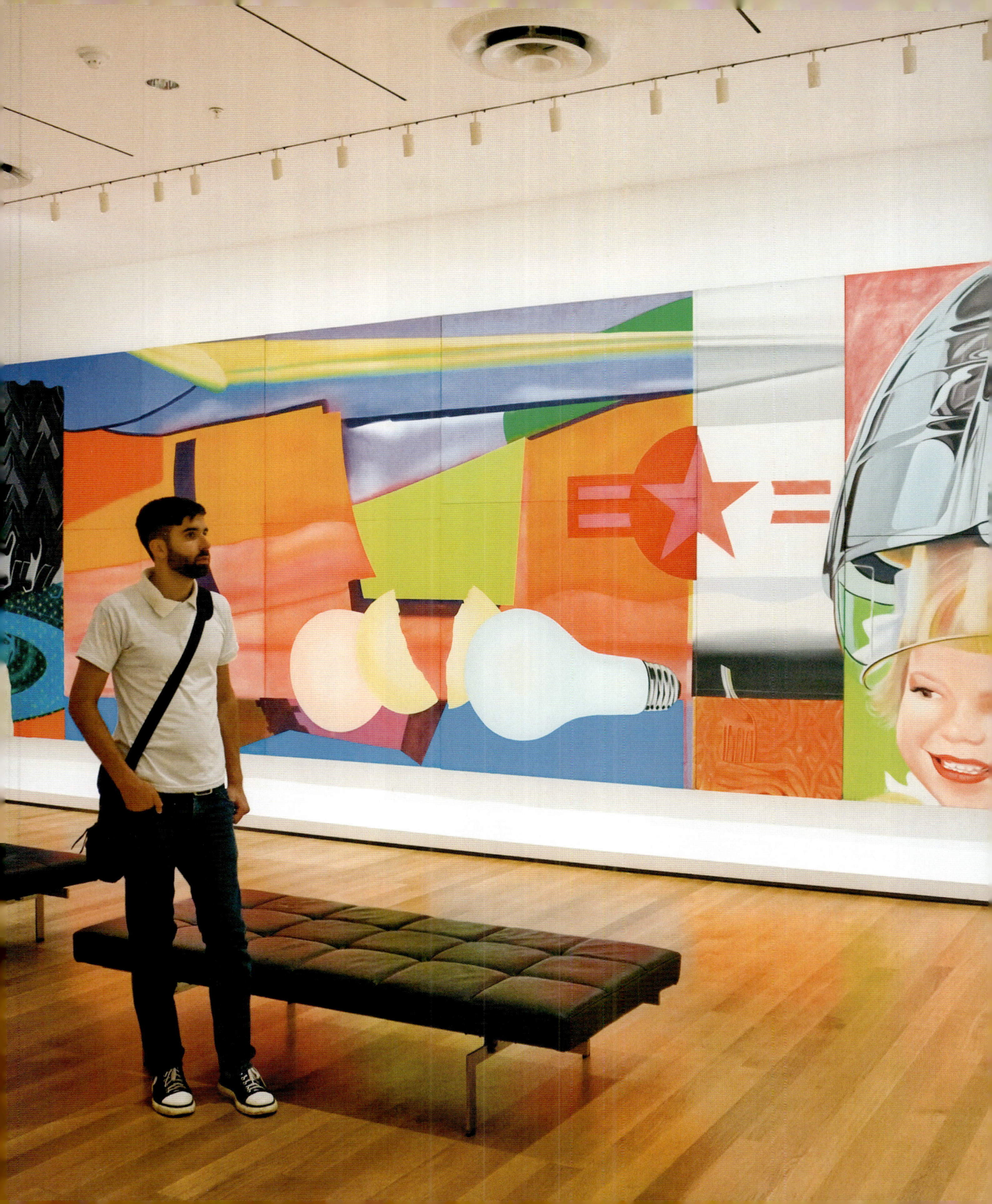

CONTENTS

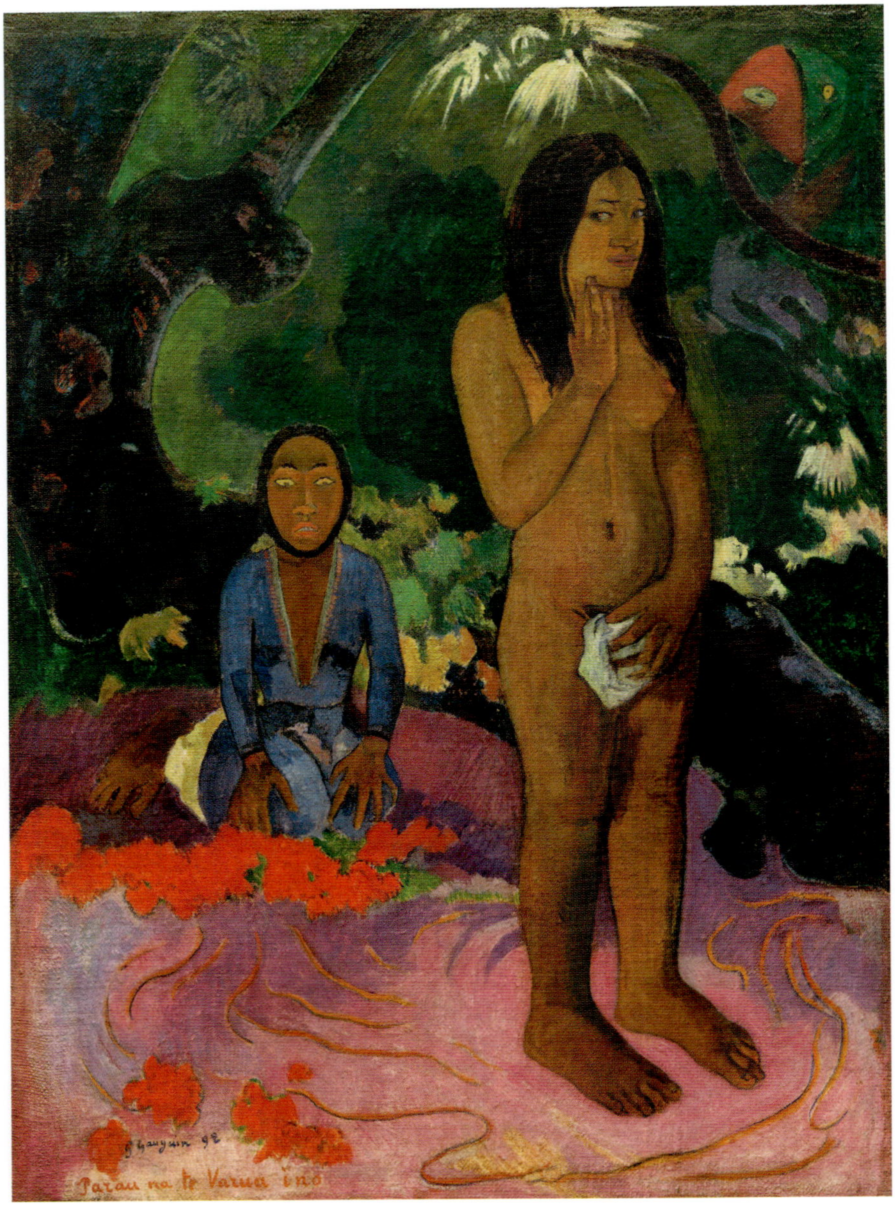

INTRODUCTION

The visual arts are unique in that they form a nexus where craft, technology, philosophy, and the imagination come together to make something that is both wonderful and necessary. This book provides an account of how one hundred powerful ideas and principles intersect with the practice of making art. The number, of course, is not definitive, and many more chapters could be included. The ideas presented range from very broad principles, such as harmony or rhythm, to more precise and local ideas, such as Mannerism or Minimalism. I have given a clear and concise presentation of these ideas and have provided for many of them an account of the strategies that artists have used to bring them into play.

The book will be of considerable use to artists who wish to understand and explore the art of the past and get a sense of what kinds of original enterprises are possible in the future. For the art student, it will provide a rich and varied focus for discussion and learning as well as a stimulating look at how physical work in the studio relates to the play of ideas within the culture at large. For the art lover, it will provide a valuable additional frame of reference and an enjoyable, informative, and provocative companion in exploring the pleasures of art.

The arrangement of the chapters is alphabetical for the purpose of easy access and reference. Most chapters take up two facing pages: The first page explains the subject in succinct and straightforward language. The facing page displays illustrations that demonstrate the principle at work.

Although I have tried to find examples from as broad a range of art as possible, you will quickly note that they are heavily weighted toward Western art. This is the tradition that has generated the most diverse and active change in recent centuries. The principles, however, apply to all cultures. Indeed, one of the fascinating things about art is that, although it emerges from a cultural matrix, it is readily understood across many cultures. French Impressionism is popular in Japan, just as Japanese prints have a ready following in Europe. Tribal art is collected in New York, and Shakespeare is performed in Africa. Art is a universal human utterance, and as we share it around the globe with pleasure and passion, we are all enriched immeasurably.

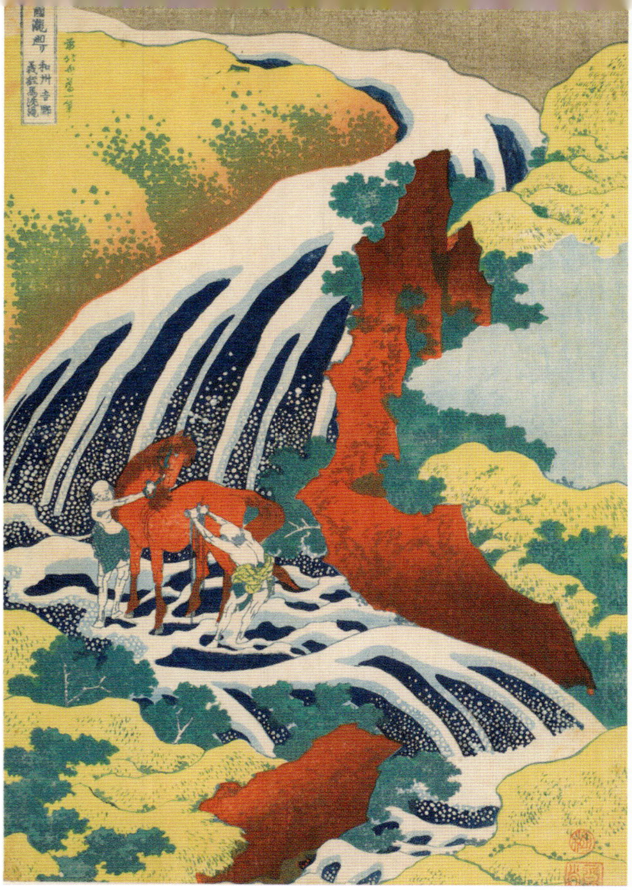

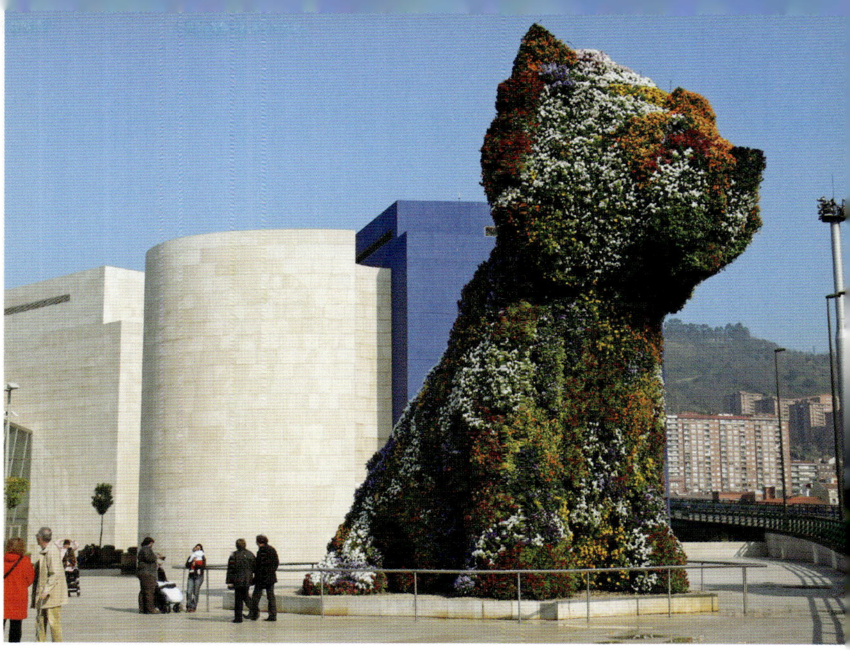

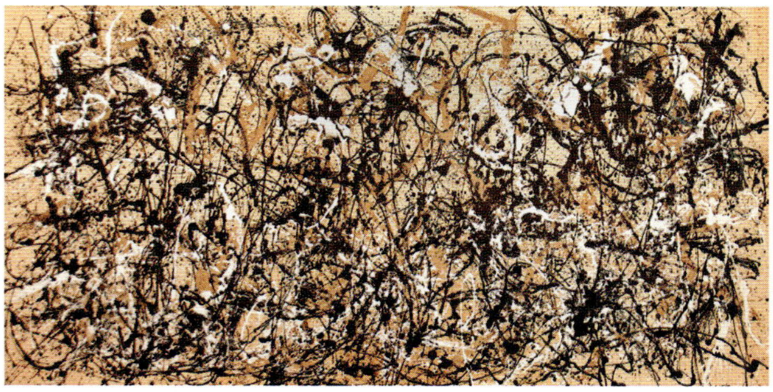

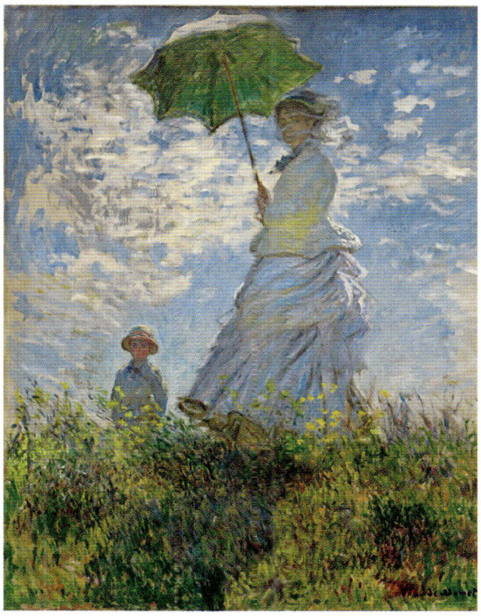

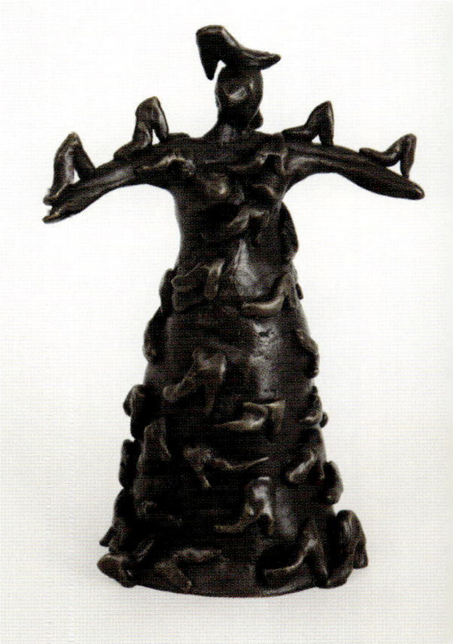

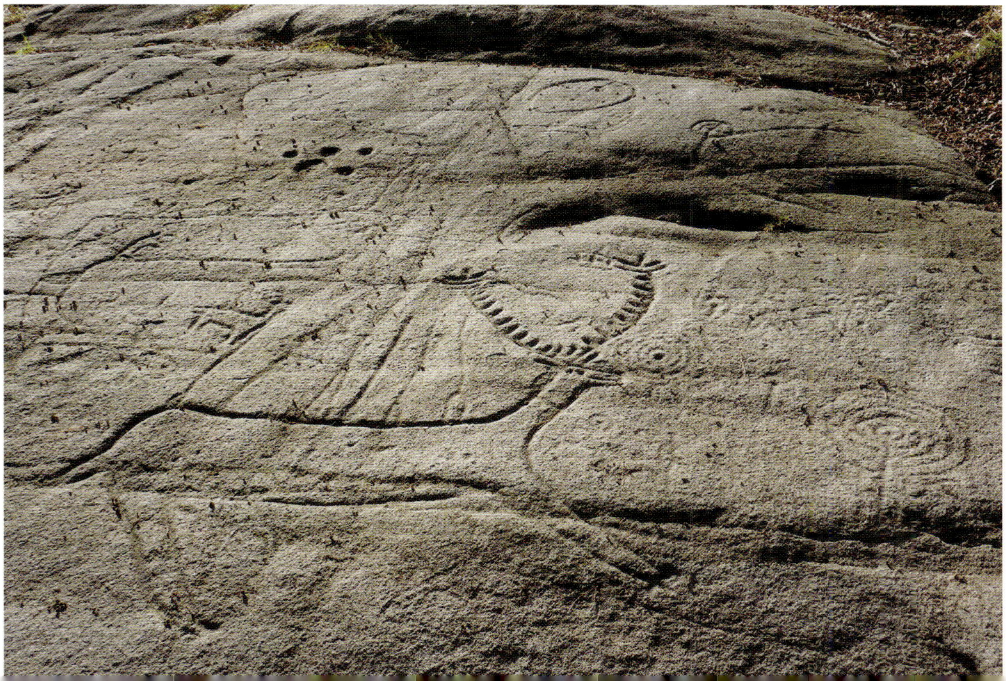

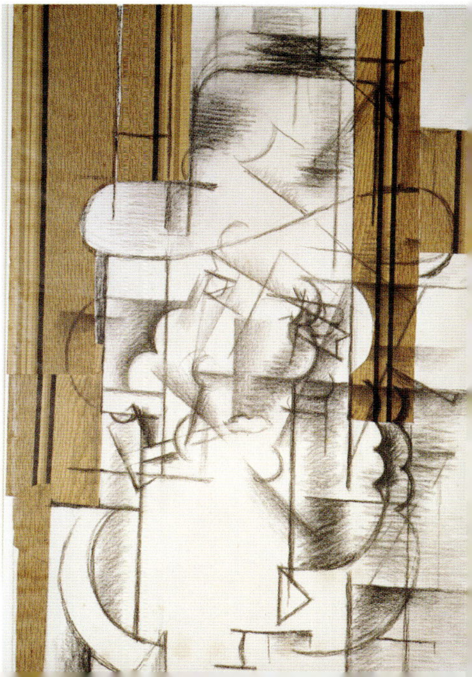

1 ABSTRACTION

THE DISTANCING OF AN IDEA FROM OBJECTIVE REFERENTS

Abstract, or nonrepresentational art, emerged in the early twentieth century as a radical idea. When used in philosophy, the word refers to the distancing of an idea from objective referents so that it becomes a distillation of thought. Abstraction came about in art through a similar process of distancing, as various artists began to present simplified, or distilled, notions of the objective world.

A series of art movements—starting with Impressionism in the 1870s and continuing through Postimpressionism to Cubism in the 1920s—gradually shifted the focus in art away from the task of representation and toward the making of artworks that were entirely autonomous. As early as 1907, the Fauvist artists of Paris were producing works in which the representational subject matter was little more than a motif on which to hang adventurous explorations of non-natural color. By 1910, the Cubists were making paintings in which classical space had been replaced by a shallow pictorial space that suggested multiple viewpoints. During World War I, Dadaist artists in Zurich began making artworks that challenged cultural expectations on all fronts; works by Hans Arp (1886–1966), for example, featured nonobjective sculpted reliefs. Exactly who was the first artist to do entirely abstract works is open to some question. The most popular candidate is Wassily Kandinsky (1866–1944), whose paintings moved away from simplified and flattened allusions to figurative subjects to become compositions of autonomous floating forms by 1912.

Today, abstract art covers a huge range of different kinds of artworks in both two and three dimensions. Some of the abstract or nonobjective qualities that can be manipulated by artists are color, form, space, volume, geometry, texture, weight, balance, presence, scale, decoration, rhythm, and movement.

1 Kasimir Malevich (1879–1935)
Black Square on White Ground, 1915, Oil on linen, 31 5/16 × 31 5/16 in (79.5 × 79.5 cm)

In Russia, the Constructivists, led by Malevich, began to make abstract art of great geometric austerity by 1915.

2 Wassily Kandinsky (1866–1944)
Improvisation 27 (Garden of Love II), 1912, Oil on canvas, 47 3/8 × 55 1/4 in (120.3 × 140.3 cm)

Kandinsky was amongst the first artists to make purely abstract works. This painting was shown at the famous Armory Show in New York in 1913, where new ideas in European art were seen in the Americas for the first time.

1

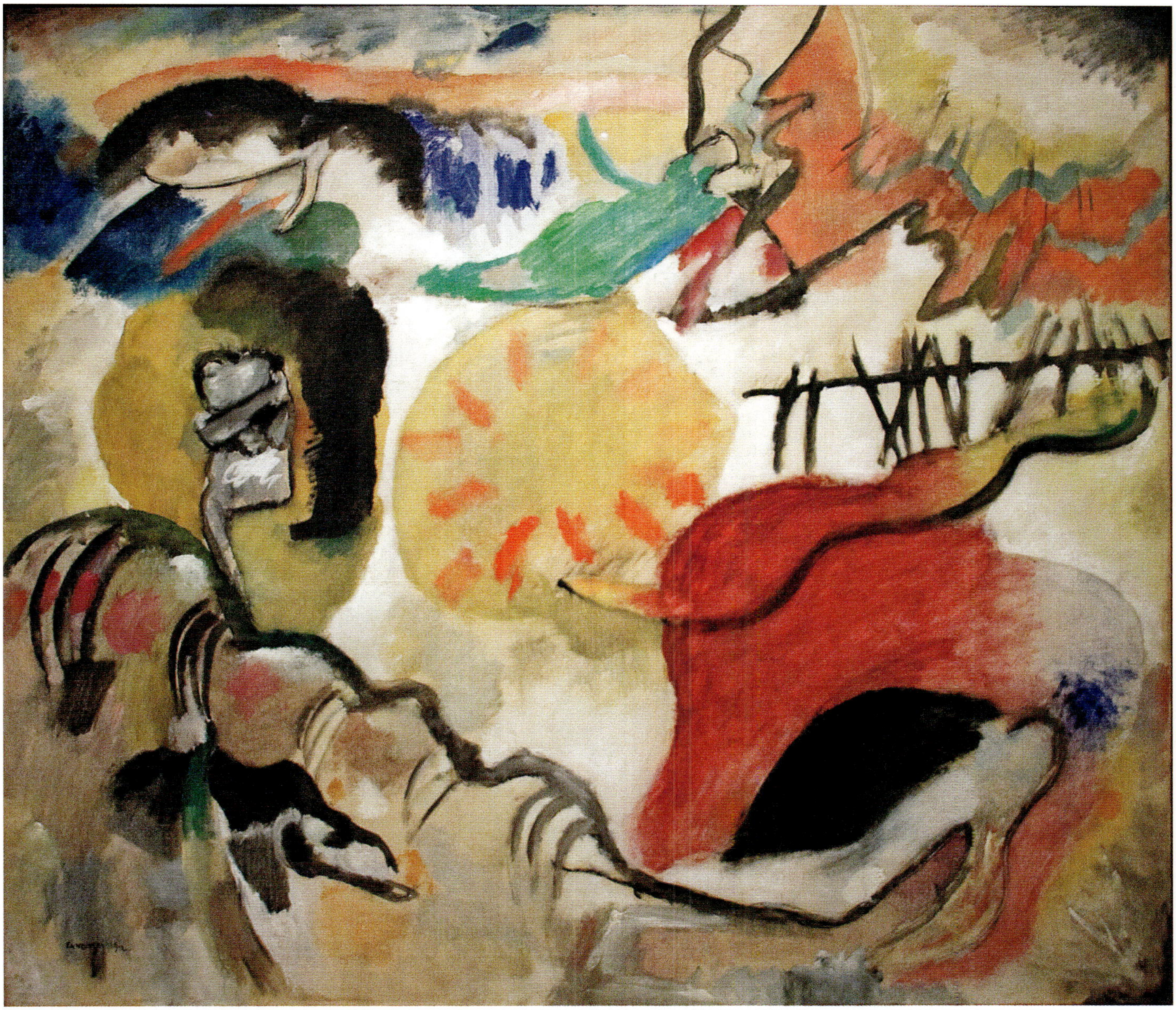

2

2 ALLEGORY

ABSTRACT IDEAS COMMUNICATED WITH CONCRETE IMAGES

Allegory is a device whereby abstract ideas can be communicated using images of the concrete world. Elements, whether figures or objects, in a painting or sculpture are endowed with symbolic meaning. Their relationships and interactions combine to create more complex meanings.

The success of an allegorical work naturally depends on the audience's ability to recognize the identities and corresponding symbolic meanings of each of the elements within the work. A famous example is Titian's *Allegory of Age Governed by Prudence*. Here, the three human heads represent the past, present, and future. They also represent the three ages of man: youth, maturity, and old age. Beneath them three animal heads symbolize the three stages of life and give us new information about them. The head beneath the young man is an eager puppy. Beneath the middle-aged man is a powerful lion, while beneath the old man a large and aging wolf stands with its ears back. Above the figures is an inscription in Latin: EX PRAETERITO/PRAESENS PRUDENTER AGIT/NE FUTURA ACTIONE DETURPET ("From [the experience of] the past, the present acts prudently, lest it spoil future actions").

As in most allegorical paintings, the meaning offered here is complex and open to a number of interpretations. Part of the pleasure of contemplating such a work involves reflecting on the possible multiplicity of meanings. For instance, we know that in this painting the old man is a self-portrait of Titian (c. 1488–1576), while the middle-aged man is his son, and the youth is his nephew. The painting might be seen as a cautionary image in which the artist is telling his family not to make the same mistakes that he did. On the other hand, the painting might just be a general observation about the increase of wisdom and circumspection that so often comes with age. Or again, the painting may refer to the more narrow idea that artistic judgment and discrimination become better with age.

Although allegory was a popular form of painting during the Renaissance and Baroque periods, it has long fallen out of favor and played little role in the development of modern art. This is no doubt because the moderns, with their interest in abstraction and visual purity, found allegory to be too literary.

See also: *Symbols* on page 186

1 Titian (c. 1488–1576)
Allegory of Age Governed by Prudence, 1565–70, Oil on canvas, 30 × 27 in (76.2 × 68.6 cm)

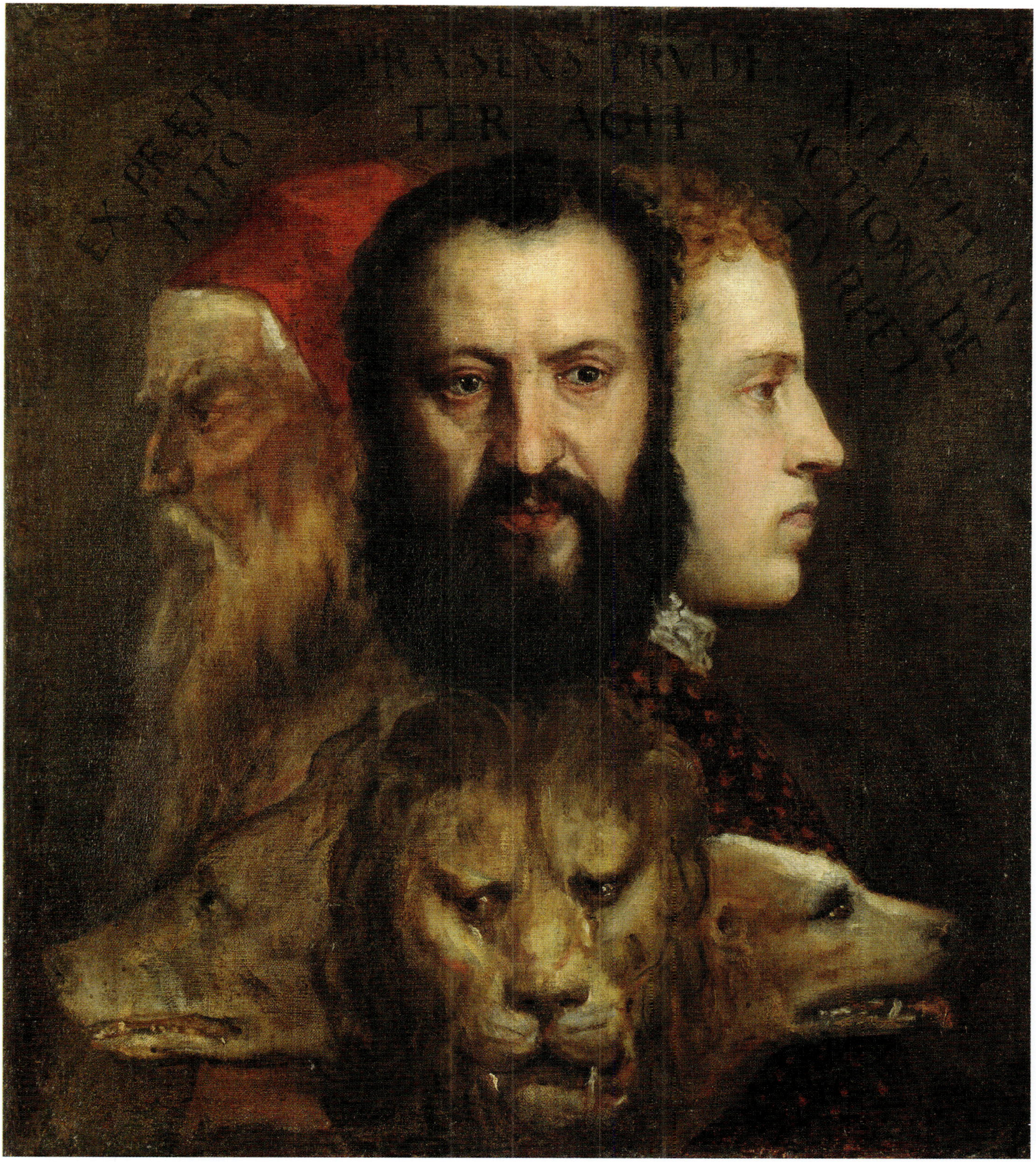

1

3 AMBIGUITY

LEAVING THE WORK OPEN TO DIVERSE INTERPRETATION

Sometimes a work of art acquires strength by projecting a structure or meaning that is ambiguous.

VARIETIES

- **Perceptual ambiguity**
  A representation of a three-dimensional formation that can be interpreted in alternative ways. The classic example is the Necker cube, a drawing of a cube that can be seen as occupying space in two alternative ways. The most notable artist to explore perceptual ambiguity was M. C. Escher (1898–1972). In many of his works, ambiguities of both recognition and spatial construction are presented in endlessly playful and provocative ways.
- **Ambiguity of recognition**
  A representational element has more than one interpretation due to inadequate or confusing cues. A shadowy shape might be a human head or an apple, for instance. The surrealist artist Yves Tanguy (1900–1955) made many paintings in which he rendered forms that had ambiguous and confusing identities, deliberately presenting the viewer with a sense of puzzlement and mystery.
- **Ambiguity of meaning**
  The sense or import of the artwork is ambiguous. The viewer is presented with an ongoing conundrum because symbols, narrative action, or other cues do not coalesce around a clear idea. This was a favorite strategy of the French artist Balthus (1908–2001) whose paintings often present narrative scenarios of indeterminate meaning.

See also: *Surrealism* on page 184; *Allegory* on page 12

1 Necker Cube

The cube can be read as being seen from above or from below. There are insufficient cues to tell the viewer which way is meant.

2 William Hogarth (1697–1764)
False Perspective, c. 1750,
Engraving 8⅛ × 6¹³⁄₁₆ in
(20.6 × 17.3 cm)

The artist plays various amusing games with spatial ambiguity.

3 Balthus (1908–2001)
The Mountain, 1936–37, Oil on canvas, 98 × 144 in (248.9 × 365.8 cm)

The meaning of the painting remains tantalizingly ambiguous.

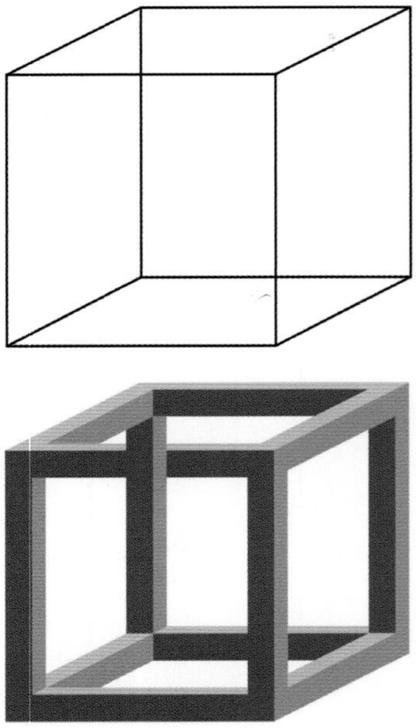

1

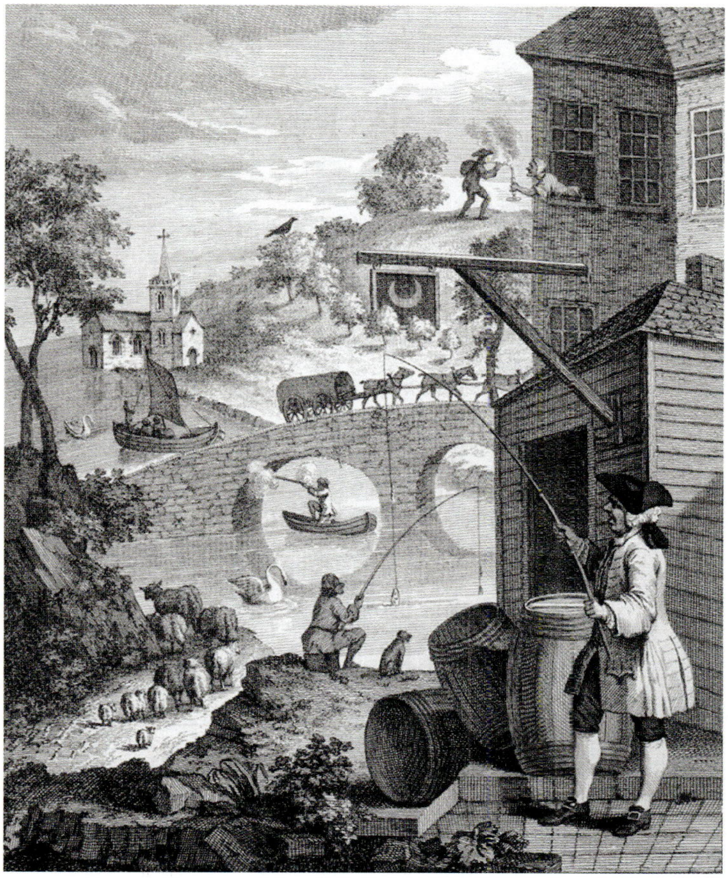

2

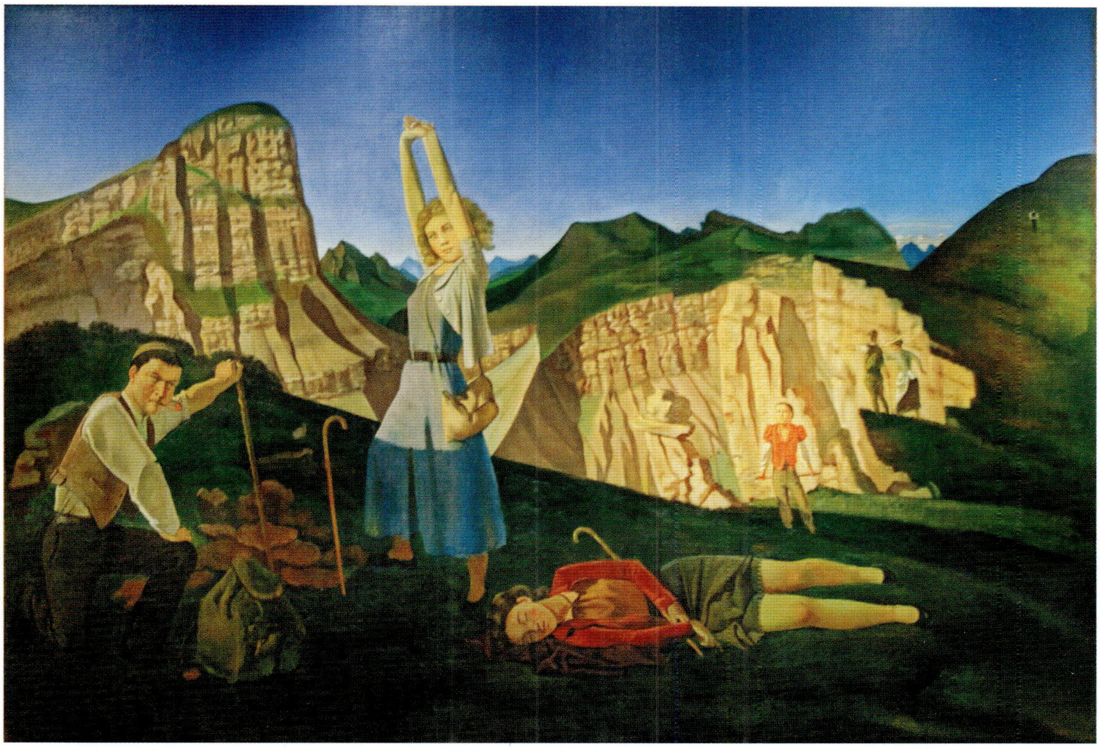

3

4 APPROPRIATION

PRESENTING THE WORK OF OTHERS IN A NEW CONTEXT

Appropriation is the act of taking work by another artist and presenting it in a new context as original. The intention is to highlight the radical idea that art is something whose meaning is as much defined by its context as by anything built into, or contained by, an artwork. This process of appropriation and re-presentation is known as recontexualization. It naturally invites questions about the nature of originality, authorship, authenticity, and uniqueness.

Wholesale appropriation of an artwork is very different from quoting another work of art within a new one, a maneuver that goes back through many centuries. It also differs from the appropriation of other objects or images for use as elements within a work of art, as with collage or in many works of the Pop Art era in which advertising and packaging imagery was imported into painting and sculpture. Appropriation is more closely related to the art of the readymade but is different because it involves the reuse of a work that was intended to be an artwork to begin with.

The foremost exponent of what became known as "appropriation art" was Sherrie Levine (1947–), whose output in the 1980s featured several exhibitions presenting the more or less unaltered work of other artists. In a 1980 exhibition in New York titled *After Walker Evans*, she presented a set of photographs of a printed catalog of photos by Walker Evans, the Depression-era photographer. Other projects by Levine included a series of photographs of images of paintings by Van Gogh and a remake of Marcel Duchamp's readymade *Fountain* (see page 147).

Richard Prince (1949–) made photographs from billboards used to advertise Marlborough cigarettes during the 1970s and '80s. Many other artists made artworks in which appropriation was accompanied by some physical transformation. Jeff Koons (1955–) made a number of works in which he took an image by another photographer and had it made into a sculpture.

Not surprisingly, artists who engage in appropriation have often been sued by the makers of the original image for copyright infringement. The estate of Walker Evans gained possession of Levine's photographs to prevent them from being sold.

See also: *Quoting* on page 144; *Readymades* on page 146; *Collage and Assemblage* on page 36; *Conceptual Art* on page 46

1 Richard Pettibone (1938–)
Andy Warhol. Flowers. 1964, 1965,
Acrylic and silkscreen ink on canvas,
8¼ × 6¼ in (21 × 16 cm)

Pettibone exhibited many miniature versions of famous works of art as his own work.

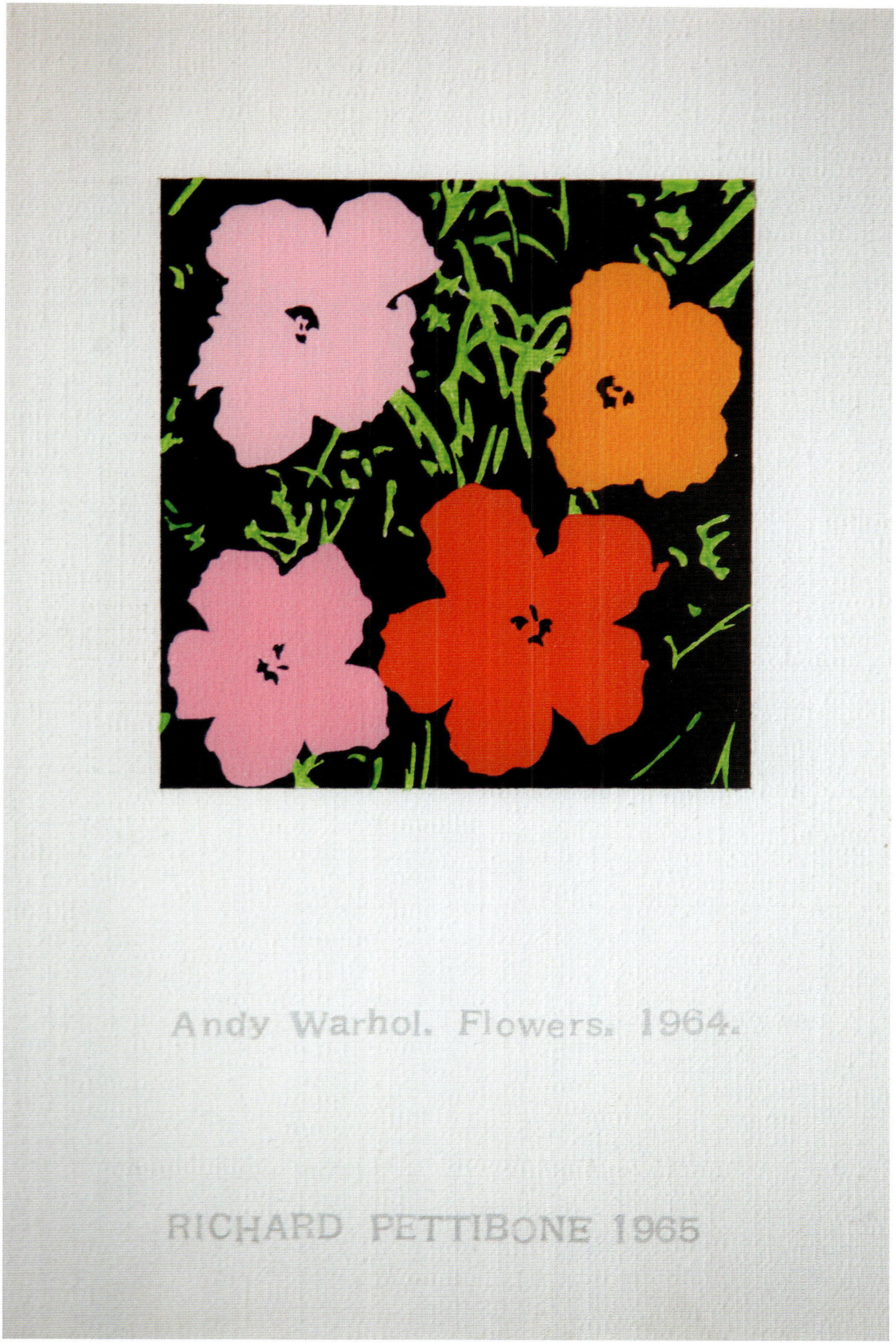

1

5 AREAS OF COMPETENCE

EVERY MEDIUM HAS AREAS IN WHICH IT EXCELS

The "area of competence" is the range of usefulness of a particular medium. The idea is that certain kinds of expression are more suited to one medium than another. Thus, marble is excellent for making sculptures that explore volume and figural representation but is not much good for expressing color relationships. Silverpoint is perfect for making delicate and precise drawings but is not suited to making powerful expressionist works. It follows that the selection of a particular medium for a particular task is an important decision and can greatly affect the success of an artistic enterprise. The decision by Edgar Degas (1834–1917) to abandon oil painting and work in pastel enabled him to transfer the fine qualities of his drawing into a colored medium, obtaining results that would have been impossible in oil.

A poor decision about choice of mediums can lead to disastrous results. The most famous example is the decision by Leonardo da Vinci (1452–1519) to use tempera rather than true fresco for his painting of the Last Supper at Santa Maria delle Grazie in Milan. He wanted to transfer the delicate layered rendering of his easel paintings to the large scale of the wall and didn't want to deal with the fast drying time of fresco. Unfortunately, the paint immediately began to flake and peel.

Sometimes positive results can come from forcing one medium into another area of competence. The photorealist painters of the 1960s and '70s, for example, transferred the ability of the photograph to make a perfect mechanical rendering to the medium of painting. In effect, they spent months doing what the camera can do in less than a second. This brought to light new ideas about what painting is and might be. It also called into question the nature of artistic agency by presenting the artist as merely equivalent to a machine.

1 Edgar Degas (1834–1917)
Woman Bathing, 1886, Pastel on paper, 27½ × 27½ in (70 × 70 cm)

The area of competence of pastel is to allow the combination of linear drawing with the layering of rich color. This perfectly suited Degas's style and needs.

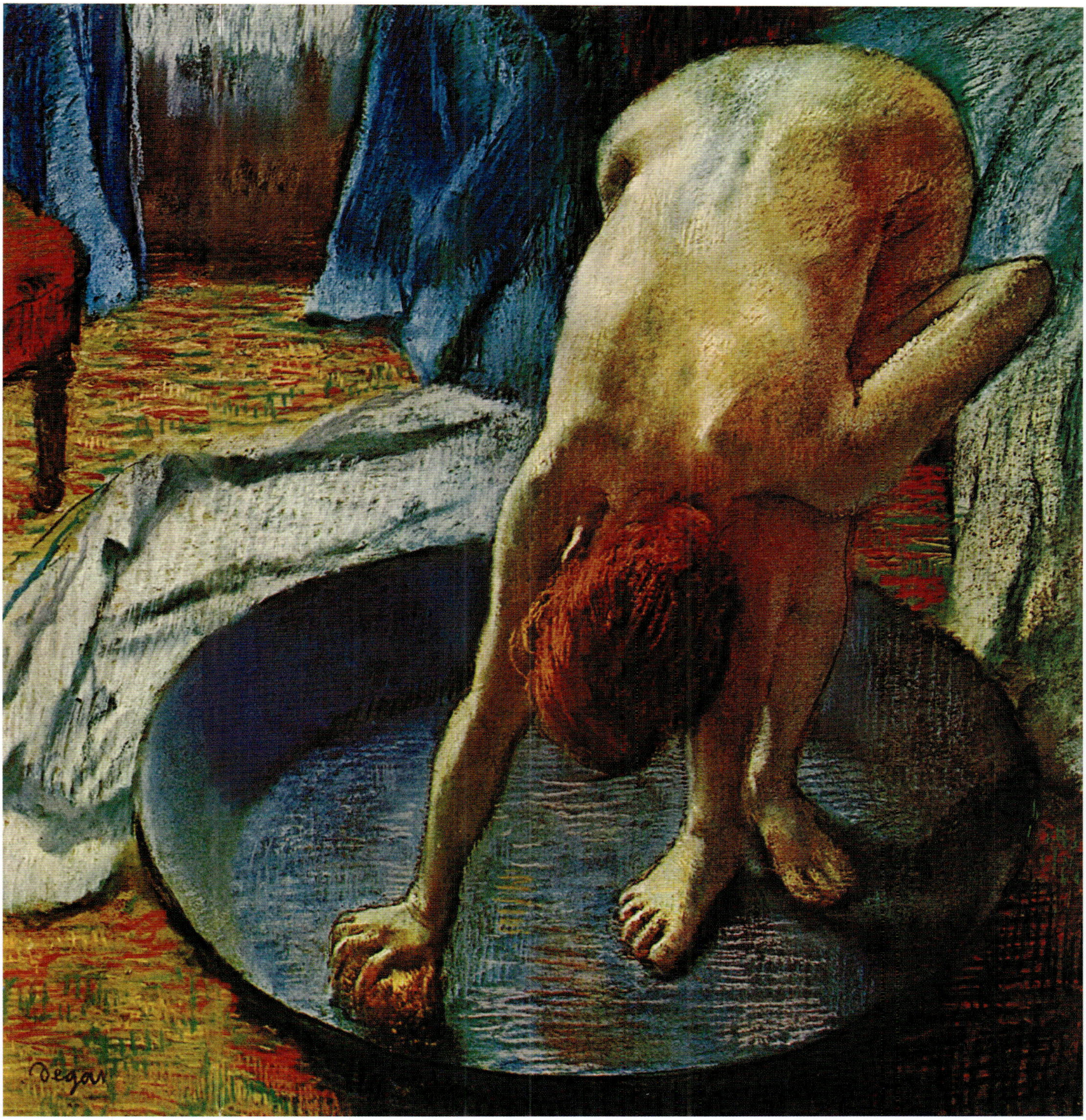

1

6 AUTHENTICITY AND OUTSIDER ART

THE POWER OF ART MADE OUTSIDE THE CULTURAL MAINSTREAM

In 1922, Hans Prinzhorn, a German doctor, published *Bildnerei der Geisteskranken* (*The Artistry of the Insane*), a study of the art of hundreds of mental patients whose work the doctor had collected. This book influenced some of the leading artists of the time, including Franz Marc (1880–1916), Paul Klee (1879–1940), Jean Dubuffet (1901–85), and Max Ernst (1891–1976). Dubuffet was so fascinated that he went on to form a movement called "Art Brut," which championed the art of the insane and other people working in isolation, untouched by the mainstream art world. "Those works created from solitude and from pure and authentic creative impulses—where the worries of competition, acclaim, and social promotion do not interfere—are, because of these very facts, more precious than the productions of professionals," he wrote.

"Outsider art" was coined by the critic Roger Cardinal in 1972, as an English equivalent of "Art Brut." Interest spread, and soon discoveries were made all over the world of individuals whose production matched the criteria. In 1973, for instance, the work of American artist Henry Darger (1892–1973) was unearthed shortly after his death. He had lived in one room for thirty years, producing nearly one hundred large and elaborate drawings showing battles between a violent body of soldiers and a group of brave and stalwart children called "The Vivian Girls." The style was curious, obsessive, and compelling, and continues to attract considerable interest.

The growth in interest in outsider art has led to a lively market for its products and much dispute about what does and does not constitute the authentic outsider. In practice, it is hard to be entirely cut off from the cultural mainstream and the products of most such artists betray at least some external influence. There is also considerable contention about the merits of such art. Much of it tends to be obsessive, repetitive, and aesthetically marginal.

1 Henry Darger (1892–1973)
At Five Norma Catherine. But Are Retaken, Mid-20th century, Watercolor, pencil, carbon tracing, and collage on pieced paper, 23 × 36¾ in (58.4 × 93.4 cm)

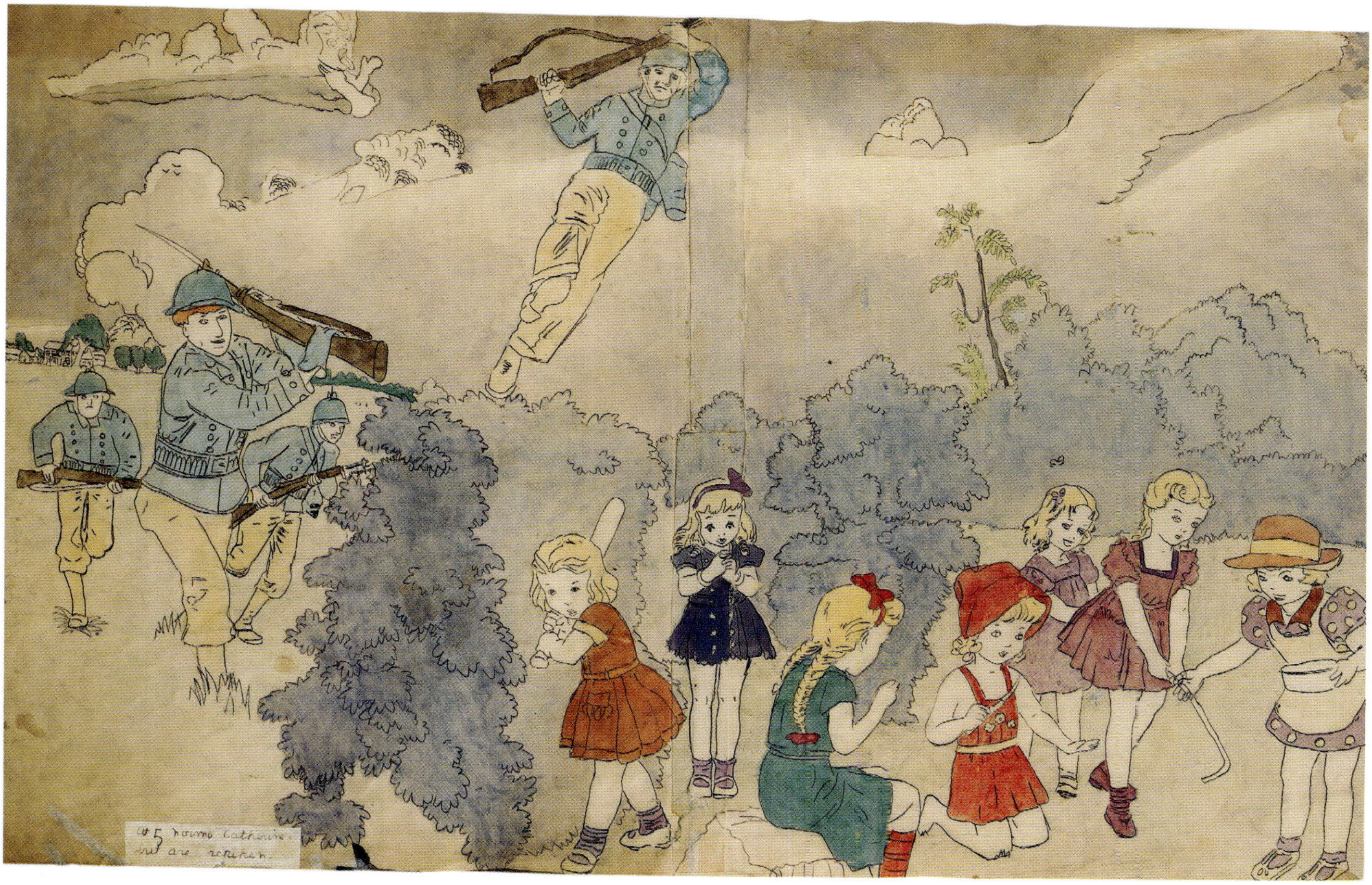

1

7 AUTOBIOGRAPHY

THE ARTIST AS SUBJECT

In the fifteenth century, artists discovered the power of art as an autobiographical record. Painters such as Masaccio (1401–28) and Andrea Mantegna (1431–1506) occasionally slipped their own image into a crowd of figures in a religious painting. The Flemish artist Jan Van Eyck (1395–1441) included a tiny self-portrait in the reflection of a convex mirror in his famous *Arnolfini Wedding*. Entire paintings devoted to self-portraiture were rare. Albrecht Dürer (1471–1528) twice painted himself with great attention to detail, and there are fine self-portrait drawings by Giovanni Bellini (c. 1430–1516) and Leonardo da Vinci (1452–1519).

Rembrandt (1606–79) painted himself more than forty times and made more than thirty etchings of his own image. These works comprise one of the most remarkable visual records of the progress of a single life. The youthful and sensitive face of the early work grows into the confident and successful portrait painter. Later, after many reversals, the stooping, lined visage carries the weight of experience, wisdom, and regret. Rembrandt also plays games with his image, dressing himself up in exotic costumes, adopting strange facial expressions, and generally mugging for the viewer.

Twentieth-century artists tended to concentrate more on manipulating the image of self than on quiet reflection. Pablo Picasso (1881–1973) explored his own presence and behavior in numerous works, taking on roles as matador, Zeus, artist, lover, and many others. In postwar art, the work of the English painter Lucian Freud (1922–2011) provides an almost unbroken record, not only of the artist's own image, but also of a shifting cast of family and friends.

1 Vincent van Gogh (1853–90)
Self-Portrait, 1889, Oil on canvas, 22½ × 17¼ in (57.2 × 43.8 cm)

In his short career, Van Gogh painted himself thirty-seven times, chronicling his stylistic growth from a somewhat clumsy tonal painter to a vibrant and powerful expressionist master.

2 Rembrandt van Rijn (1606–79)
Self-Portrait Frowning, c. 1630, Etching, 2 13/16 × 2 3/8 in (7.2 × 6.1 cm)

3 Egon Schiele (1890–1918)
Self-Portrait with Lampfruit, 1912, Oil on canvas, 12 11/16 × 15 11/16 in (32.2 × 39.8 cm)

The Austrian painter Egon Schiele made numerous drawings and paintings of himself that explored nudity, sexuality, and shifting ideas of self-image.

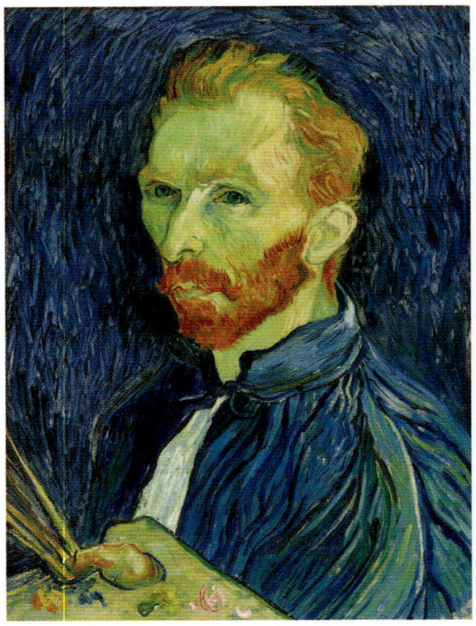

1

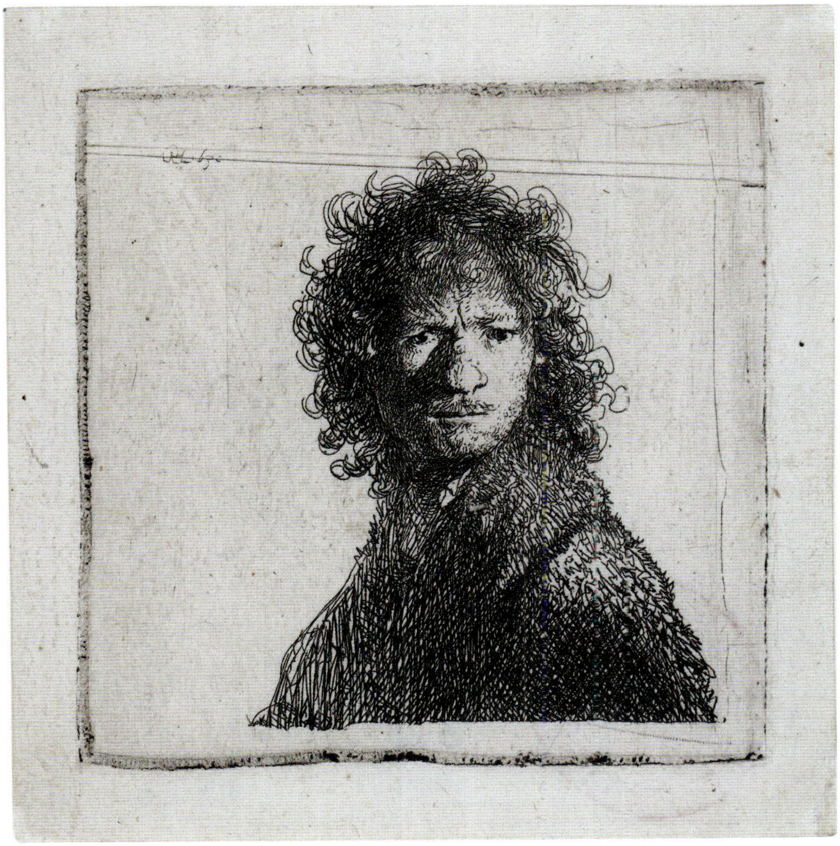

2

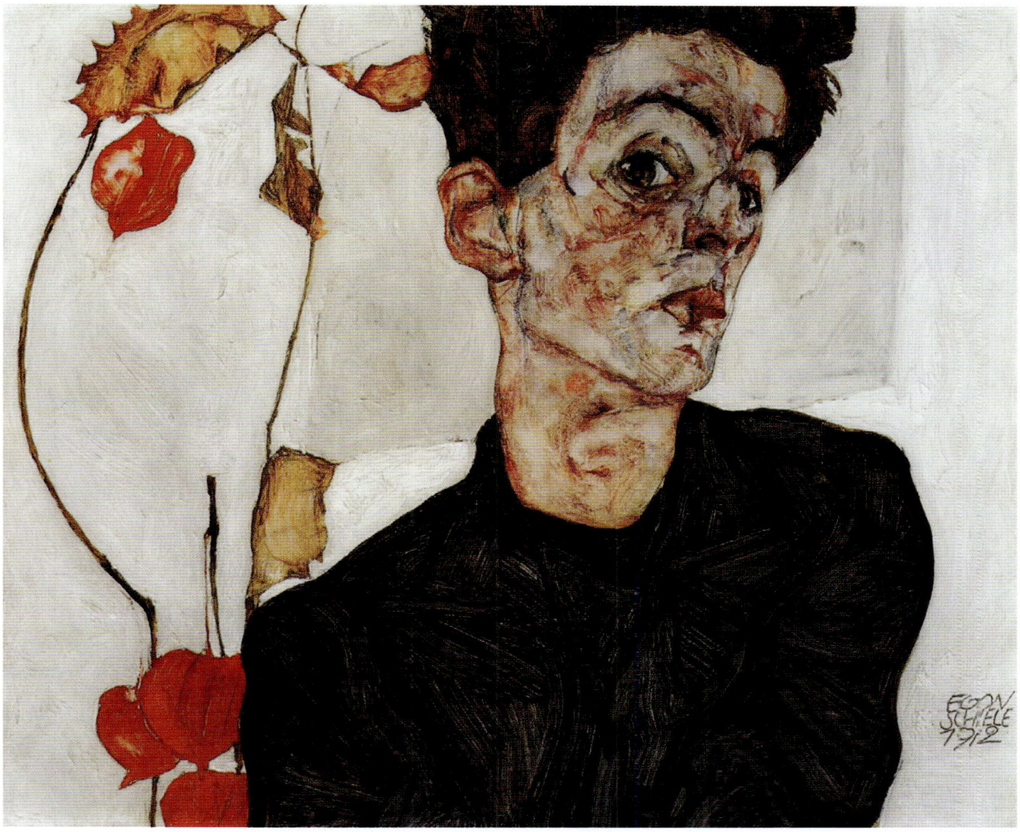

3

8 BALANCE

A COMPOSITIONAL PLEASURE

A sense of balance can be one of the paramount intentions in composing a work of art and a source of pleasure for the viewer. Balance is generally a compositional quality that can be achieved in many different ways. In looking at a painting, the eye tends to assign varying senses of weight to elements within the composition and enjoys a more satisfactory experience when they seem to be balanced across the painting around an axis. Of course, balance can always be achieved by a purely symmetrical composition, but usually this feels less interesting than the possibilities involved in balancing asymmetrical elements.

When elements are dynamic—that is, they feel as though they are in movement—the eye is more satisfied when their strengths and directions balance out within the composition. There will always remain a certain amount of subjective assessment when it comes to judging qualities such as balance, force, tension, or weight in a composition.

The assignment of weight to a particular element can be affected by the following:

- **Scale**
  Larger elements are read as heavier.
- **Color**
  Saturated color is usually read as heavier than unsaturated color.
- **Tone**
  Darker elements generally feel heavier than lighter elements.
- **Strength of shape**
  Assertive shapes generally feel heavier than amorphous shapes.
- **Relationships within the picture**
  The sense of weight attached to an element can be affected by its relationship with other elements within the picture.

In sculpture, balance becomes a real and very physical issue and is often a requirement for a work to stay upright at all. In classical figure sculpture, the consideration of balance was integral to engineering a free-standing figure. Some modern kinetic sculpture, particularly the subgenre of mobiles, is built around the notion of balance. In mobiles, developed most notably by the American artist Alexander Calder (1898–1976), moving elements are arranged around a set of fulcrums so that they float in a circular fashion with any moving air around them. Various games are played with the disparate densities of materials, color, and scale to achieve all manner of variations within the work.

See also: *Composition* on page 44

1 Alexander Calder (1898–1976)
Little Spider, 1940, Sheet metal and wire

In this mobile, one counterweight balances an entire set of elements to create a charming descriptive piece.

2 Johannes Vermeer (1632–75)
Woman Holding a Balance, c. 1664, Oil on Canvas, 15 5/8 × 14 in (39.7 × 35.5 cm)

A woman holds a delicate gold balance while the vertical line of the frame behind her exactly bisects the canvas. The painting celebrates balance both in its composition and subject matter.

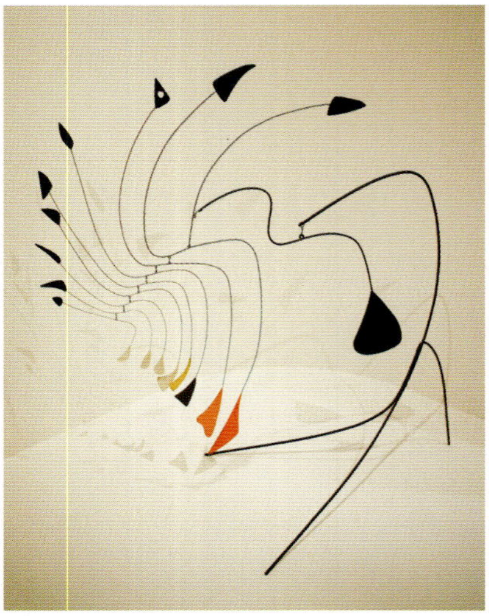

1

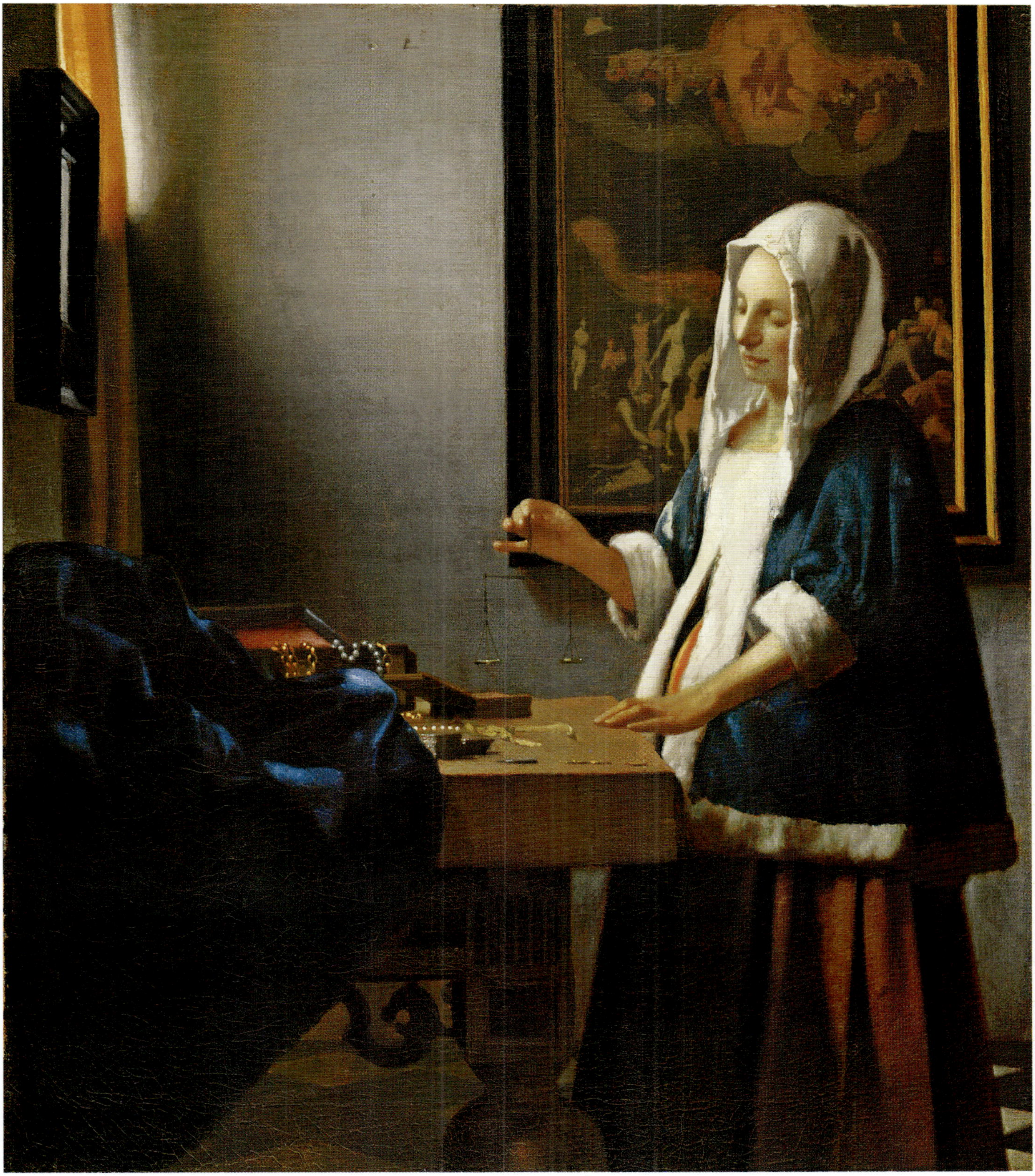

2

9 BEAUTY

THE AESTHETIC RESPONSE

The idea that a work of art should be beautiful or should in some way offer the experience of beauty is widely held. But just exactly what beauty is and what objects and artifacts can or cannot be considered beautiful are questions that have been debated since ancient times. Moreover, we extend the judgment of beauty to a broad array of subjects, including landscapes, physiognomy, and mathematical proofs. We might well ask what it is exactly that all these things share. Is it possible to identify the components of beauty? To what extent is our comprehension of beauty conditioned by the culture in which we are immersed, and to what extent is it an innate response to certain stimuli? And then is beauty, after all, a necessary quality for a successful work of art? Can we have art without beauty?

The ongoing debate is known as aesthetics, a branch of philosophy whose name derives from the Greek *aisthetikos*, meaning esthetic, sensitive, sentient. Here are some of the principal points of view put forward by a few of the world's great minds:

Plato (427–347 BCE) felt that we perceive an object as beautiful because it partakes of an ideal form of beauty that exists in some sort of higher plane. He identified some of the components of beauty as proportion, harmony, and unity of its parts.

Aristotle (387–322 BCE) discusses beauty in his *Metaphysics* and declared that its universal constituents were order, symmetry, and definiteness.

Vitruvius (c. 80–15 BCE) proposed, in his *Ten Works on Architecture*, a theory of beauty based on the idea that nature provides in its designs certain proportions that are universally beautiful. This Roman architect cited in particular the ideal proportions of a human body as the most desirable basis for structuring beautiful buildings and objects. Vitruvius' ideas were rediscovered in the fifteenth century and had a large influence on the Renaissance: Leonardo da Vinci and others reconstructed images of the so-called "Vitruvean Man."

Sigmund Freud (1856–1929) writes in *Civilization and Its Discontents*: "All that seems certain is its derivation from the field of sexual feeling. The love of beauty seems a perfect example of an impulse inhibited in its aim. 'Beauty' and 'attraction' are originally attributes of the sexual object."

A Darwinian theory of beauty has been proposed by evolutionary psychologists, most notably by **Dennis Dutton** (1944–2010). He rejected the idea that beauty is a learned cultural phenomenon citing the fact that many great works of art find favor in diverse cultures. Rather, the appreciation of beauty is an adaptive trait common to all humans. "Beauty," says Dutton, "is nature's way of acting at a distance so to speak. You can't expect to eat an adaptive landscape. It would hardly do to eat a baby or a lover. So nature's trick is to make them beautiful, to have them exert a kind of magnetism, to give you the pleasure of simply looking at them."

See also: *Proportion and Ratio* on page 140

1 Leonardo da Vinci (1452–1519)
Vitruvian Man, c. 1490,
Pen and ink on paper, 14 × 10 in
(35.6 cm × 25.4 cm)

2 Raphael (1483–1520)
Madonna with the Infant Christ and John the Baptist, 1506,
Oil on panel, 44½ × 34⅞ in
(113 cm × 88.5 cm)

Art of the Italian Renaissance was influenced by Aristotle's components of beauty: order, symmetry, and definiteness (clarity). Usually a sense of balance was substituted for symmetry. Here the perfectly rendered forms and highly ordered composition convey a feeling that is both exquisite and serene.

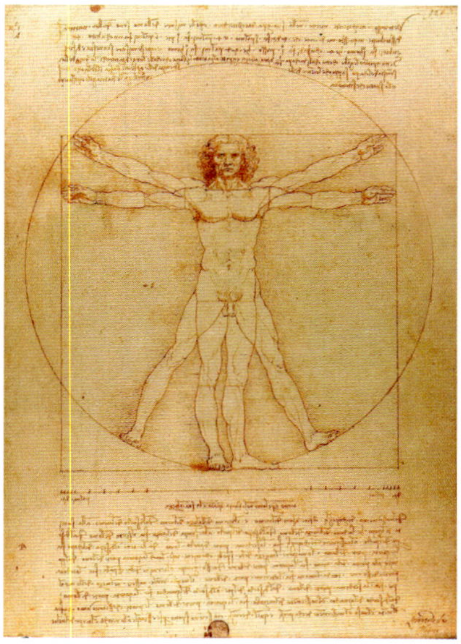

1

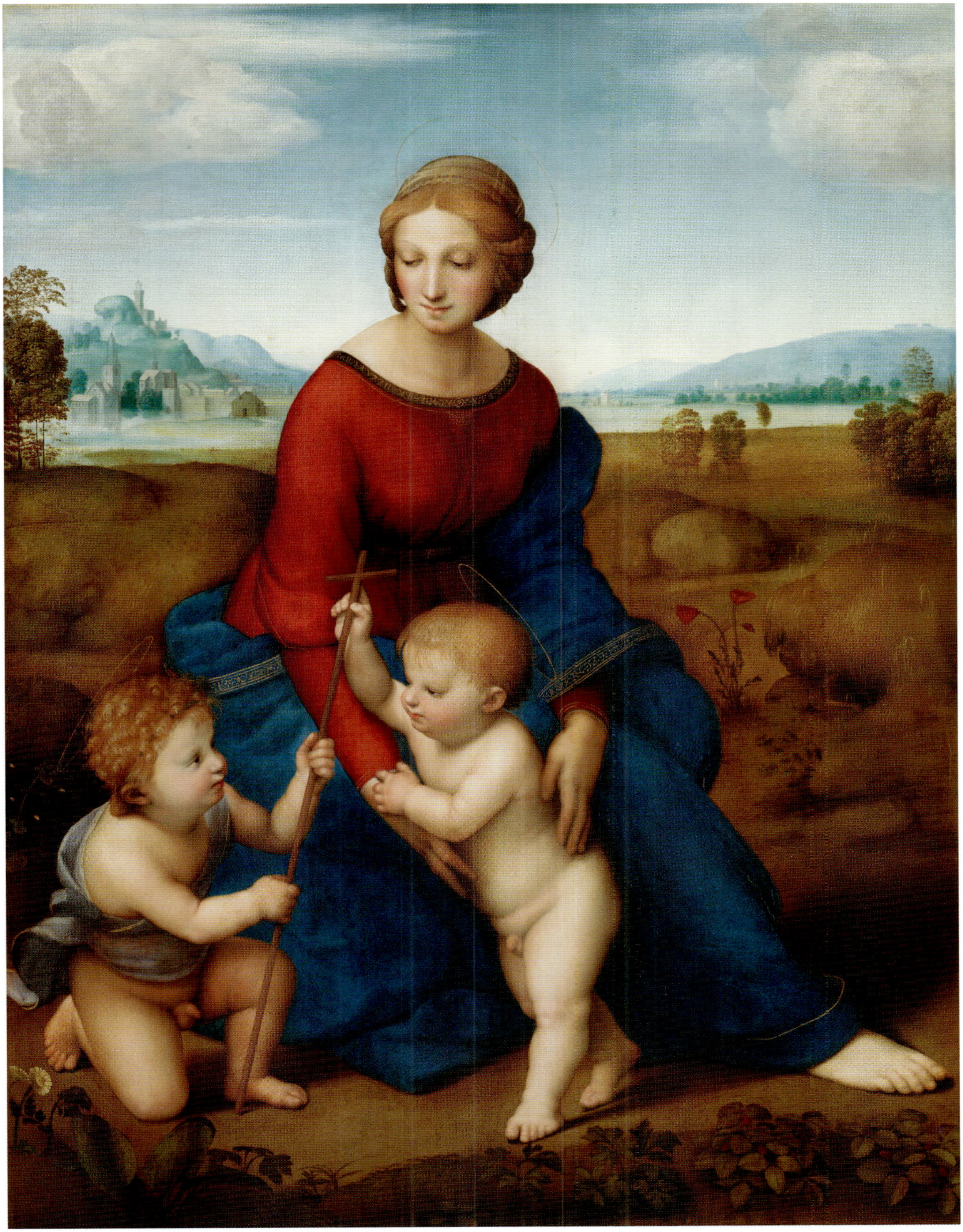

2

10 BOUNDARIES

HOW ART IS SEPARATED FROM THE WORLD

One of the defining characteristics of artworks is that they are separated from the world by an implied or formal boundary. This is true in all cultures. Tribal artworks are usually physical objects or are confined to the objects or structures on which they are painted. In Western painting, the picture frame formalizes the separation of the artwork from its surroundings. Mural painting is necessarily defined by the wall or ceiling space that it takes up, while manuscript paintings are held within the pages of a book. Western sculpture developed the plinth, essentially a formal stage on which the work could be displayed. Sculpture in architectural settings was often contained within niches or was otherwise combined with the fabric of the architecture. In Asian art, the handscroll became formalized over many centuries into a form of display that encourages an almost ceremonial viewing of the artwork. There is also a tradition of resetting artworks into ever-larger handscrolls as the artist's friends or successive owners add comments, poems, or words of appreciation to the area surrounding it.

In the late twentieth century, a number of artists sought to blur or dispense with the boundaries of the artwork. For instance, various kinds of installation art occupy spaces that the audience can walk through. Similarly, in theater and some performance art, there have been attempts at incorporating the audience in the action, negating the usual separation of viewer and artwork. But once again, even these immersive experiences exist within the confines of a theater or gallery space. Modern sculpture rarely uses a plinth but usually projects a clear enough set of boundaries.

It appears that contemplating an artwork requires that we see it as something separate from other parts of life, that it provides a realm set apart in which the imagination and sensibilities might roam. This arrangement is both convenient and salutary. If the artwork were to become too much of the world, the effect might be confusing and destabilizing.

1 ***Carrigagulla Stone Circle, Ireland***
Photo: Cecil @ English Language Wikipedia

Many preliterate cultures demarcate boundaries within which religious rites and magical events take place.

2 Anonymous Artist
Picture Frame Workshop, c. 1900,
Oil on canvas, $116\frac{13}{16} \times 94$ in
(296.7 × 238.7 cm)

1

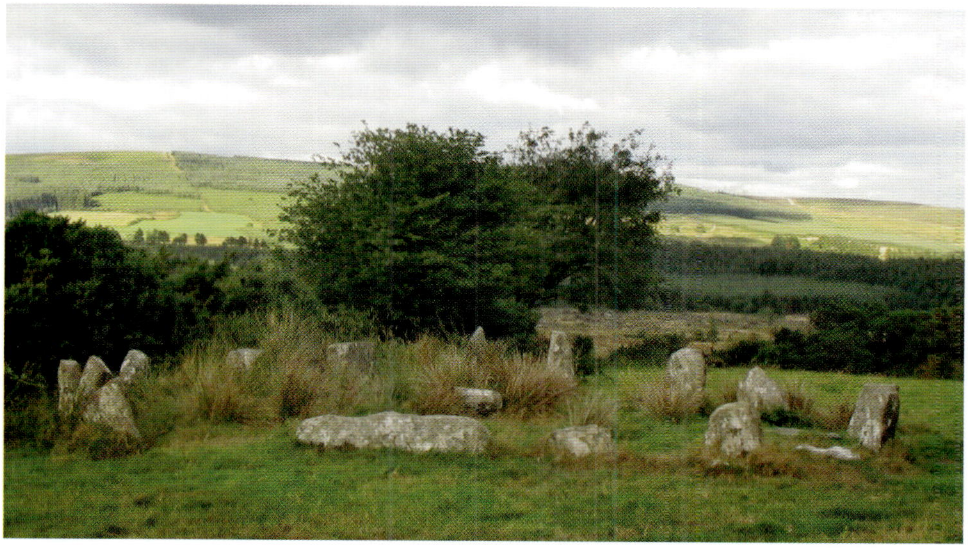

2

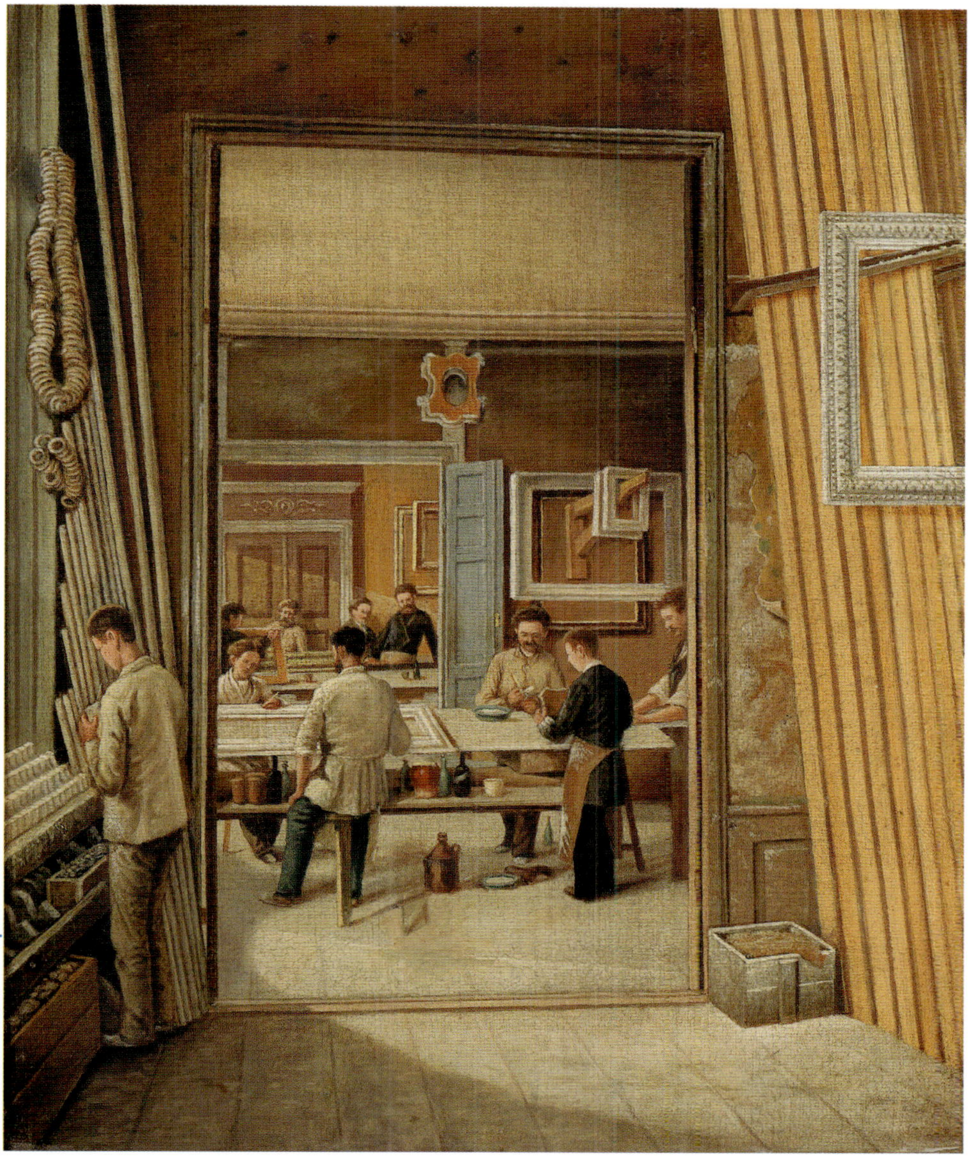

11 BRUSH TECHNIQUES

THE EVOLVED USES OF THE MOST POPULAR ART-MAKING TOOL

Almost all painting in both the Eastern and Western traditions is accomplished with brushes. Over the centuries, a variety of brushing techniques have evolved—ways of handling and delivering paint that give differing results, facilitate a wide variety of expression, and allow a broad selection of finishes.

- **Glazing**
  Paint, usually oil or acrylic, is applied in semitransparent layers. Each layer is allowed to dry before the next is applied, allowing for great depth and richness of tone and color. A soft brush is used and layers can be modified using a fan brush.
- **Stippling**
  Paint is applied in small, even strokes so that tonal and color gradations can be created in a delicately broken surface. Although laborious, this technique offers the possibility of close and positive control of tone and color and the creation of rich surfaces. Stippling is ideal for fast-drying mediums such as tempera or acrylic.
- **Impasto**
  Paint is applied in heavy, opaque layers, which often involves painting wet-into-wet. This is can be a risky and very physical technique, allowing for heavy surfaces and expressive use of the brush.
- **Scumbling**
  Paint is built with an array of open marks pulled over the surface in a loose and uneven way to create a soft, broken and active surface. This is often used as a layering technique that allows for the color of one surface to be visible through the one above.
- **Knocking Down**
  A line or edge of wet paint is partially obscured and softened by pulling the end of a brush through it in a crisscross fashion.
- **Dragging**
  A brushstroke pulls one color into another, dragging both along the surface to create a kind of active blend.
- **Dry Brush**
  Only a very small amount of paint is taken up. The end of the brush is then dragged along the surface so that the paint is only picked up by its texture, creating a semitransparent layer.
- **Flooding**
  This is usually a watercolor technique where the artist uses a mop brush to apply a large amount of watery paint that floods into an area.

See also: *Underpainting* on page 202

1 Duccio (1255–1319)
Madonna, c. 1280, Tempera on wood, 36 × 23 in (91.4 × 58.4 cm)

A delicate elongated stippling of the paint is used to build subtle tonal transitions across the flesh.

2 Gustave Caillebotte (1848–94)
Paris: A Rainy Day (Detail), 1877, Oil on canvas, 83½ × 108¾ in (212.2 × 276.2 cm)

Scumbling is used to achieve broken layers of paint.

3 Gustave Courbet (1819–77)
Source of a Mountain Stream, 1876, Oil on canvas, 17⅞ × 23¼ in (45.4 × 59.1 cm)

A heavy impasto is applied over thinner layers of paint.

4 *Dragging*. Yellow is pulled across a layer of wet blue paint with a stiff bristle brush, creating a lively green.

5 Knocking down a line

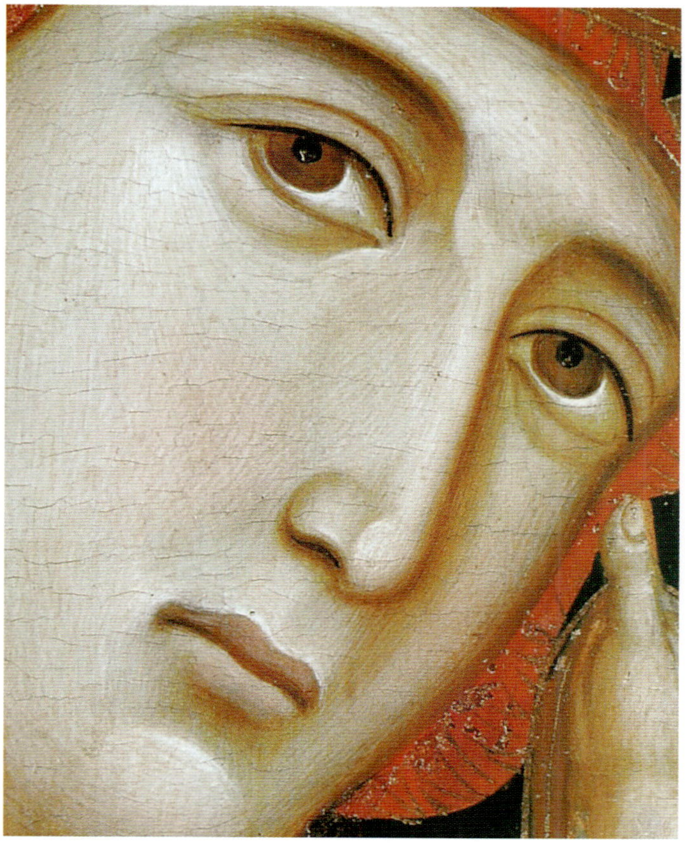

1

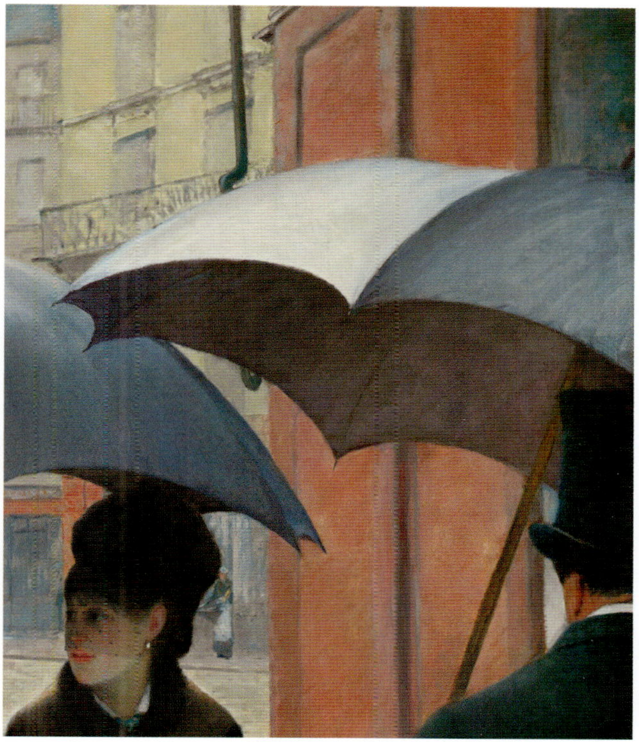

2

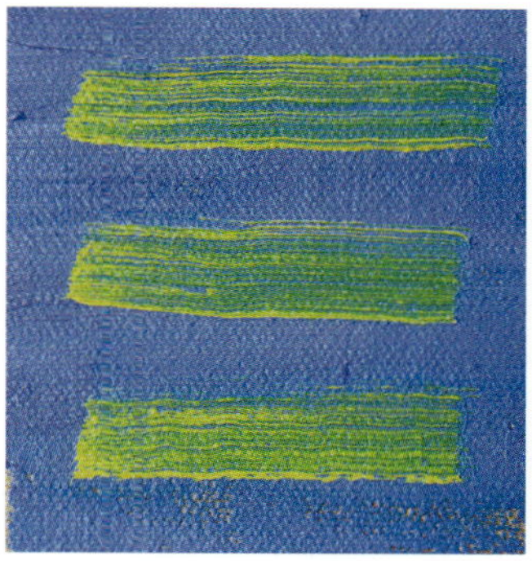

4

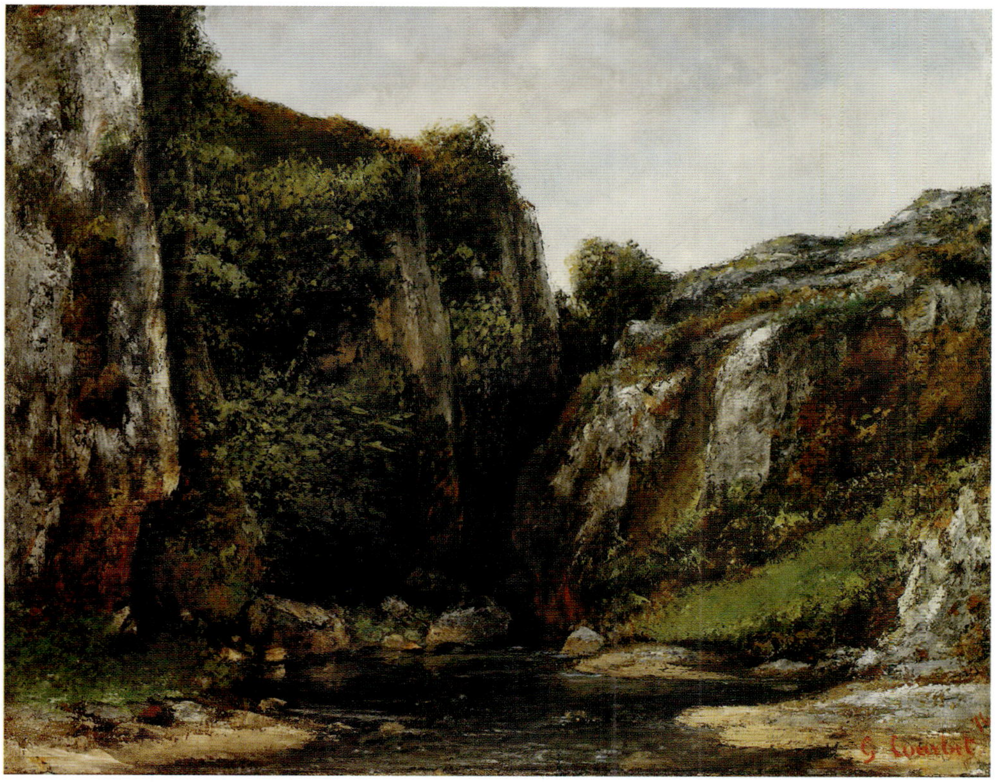

3

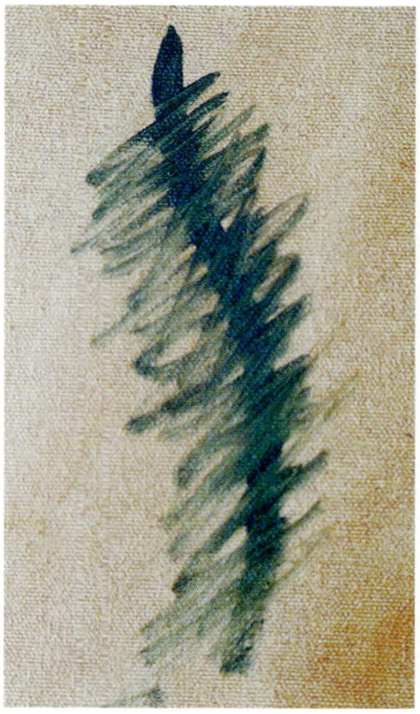

5

12 CHANCE

SURRENDERING CONTROL

Artists are usually interested in control, the skilled and thoughtful manipulation of a medium. But the actions of chance have always played some role in art making, and in the last one hundred years some artists have embraced uncertainties for a variety of purposes.

APPROACHES

- **Useful accident**
  The handling of any physical medium incorporates a certain element of chance. The painter can never be quite sure about how a particular wet brushstroke will look, and the sculptor can never guarantee exactly what is going to happen with the next strike of his or her chisel. In a sense the artist is always a little bit in the hands of chance and will negotiate many small "accidents" during the creation of a work. For instance, in a very brushy style of painting, the ongoing creation of accidents followed by a decision about whether to keep, modify, or erase them can be a deliberate strategy.
- **Generation of subject matter**
  Some modern artists have embraced a more direct role of chance, incorporating random occurrences as features of their works. Marcel Duchamp (1887–1968), for example, invented arbitrary rules for determining how parts of his *The Large Glass* would look based on the chance formations of a falling piece of string.
- **Access to the unconscious**
  Some artists, particularly the Surrealists, expressed an almost mystical belief in the actions of chance, suggesting that incorporating chance events puts the work in touch with the unconscious mind. This idea was influenced by Sigmund Freud's view that accidents precipitated by individuals are not accidents at all but rather expressions of unconscious desires.
- **Conceptual**
  Some artists contend that art does not have to be made by the artist but can be, instead, something whose fabrication the artist simply mediates. This is part of a broader strain of modernism that dissents from the Romantic claim that art is, or should be, a projection of the personality and identity of the artist. Using chance to make the work removes the personality of the artist from the equation altogether.

See also: *Process as Meaning* on page 138

1 Hans Arp (1886–1966)
Squares and Rectangles Arranged according to the Laws of Chance, 1917, Torn and pasted paper, 19 1/8 × 13 5/8 in (48.5 × 34.6 cm)

The Dadaist artist Hans Arp tore up pieces of paper and let them fall onto the floor to create chance compositions.

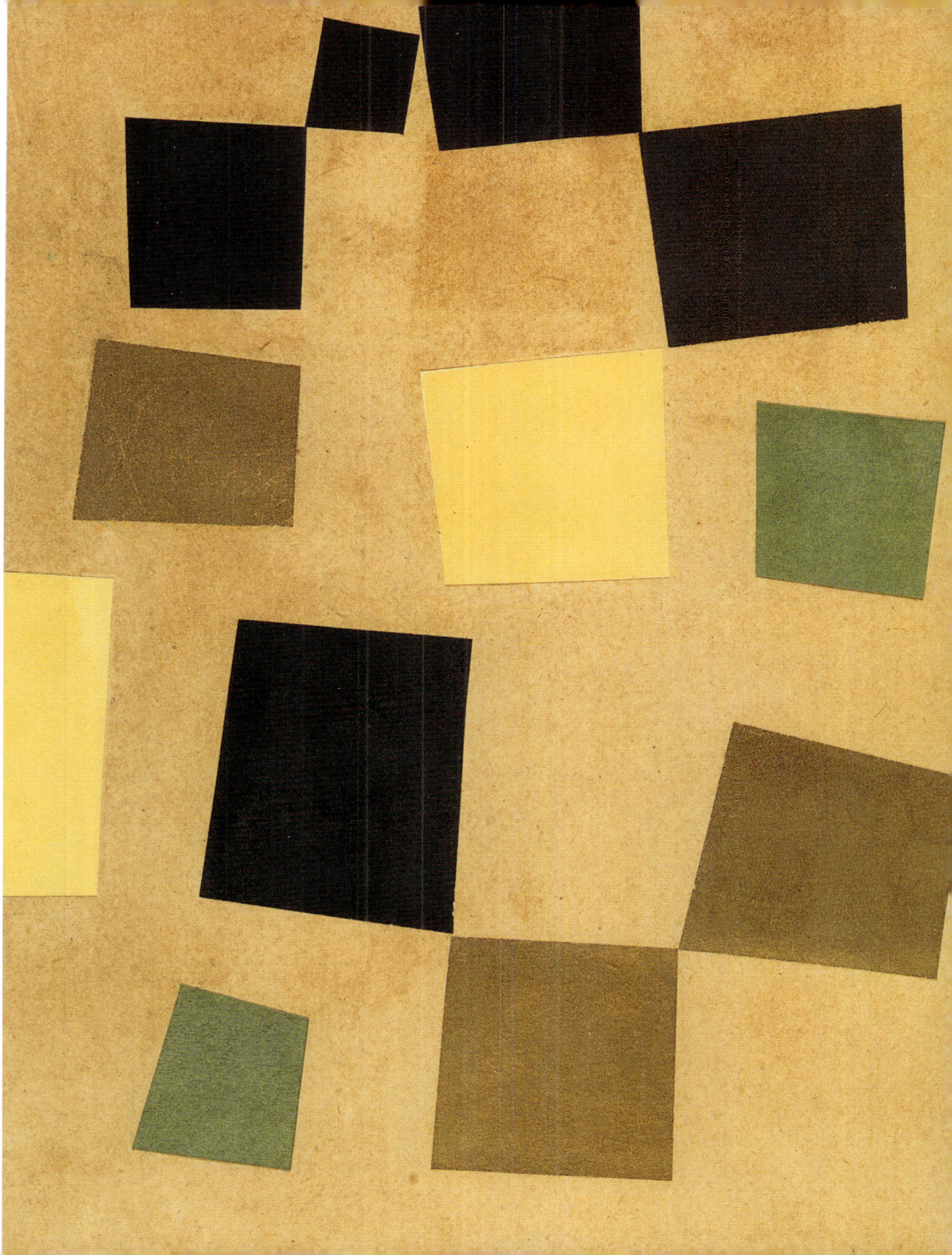

1

13 CLASSICISM AND RENAISSANCE

THE TENETS OF THE GRECO-ROMAN WORLD RECUR THROUGHOUT THE CENTURIES

Classicism is a recurring tendency in art defined by an adherence to the qualities of ancient Greek and Roman art, including clarity, orderliness, restraint, harmony, and a certain cannon of proportions. Although classicism emerged at various times during the Middle Ages, the Renaissance brought about its most impressive flowering. The rediscovery of artifacts and texts from the ancient world led Italian artists to embrace classical ideals both visually and intellectually. An interest in mathematics, proportions, and clarity of form were combined with ideas about naturalism in representation and humanism in terms of philosophy. In addition, ancient techniques, particularly bronze casting, were rediscovered.

Classicism continued into the seventeenth century in a more rigorous fashion when painters, such as Nicolas Poussin (1594–1665), used carefully structured geometric compositions, orderly intervals, stately rhythms, and rigidly edited content. Classicism reappeared toward the end of the eighteenth century in a guise that is generally referred to as Neoclassicism. Reacting to the organic and sometimes decorative painters of the late Baroque period, the French painter Jacques-Louis David (1748–1825) introduced a new severity based on classical structures and ideals. Revivals of classicism continued with the Pre-Raphaelites in the 1850s, and again in the modern era when art of the 1920s, particularly that of Picasso, introduced a classicizing strain into modernism.

CHARACTERISTICS

- **Proportions**
  Classicism tends to revisit proportions, such as the Golden Mean, as well as a rather stately sense of interval.
- **Clarity**
  Aristotle named clarity, or definiteness, as one of the components of beauty, and classical art epitomizes clarity and readability of form.
- **Restraint**
  Classic art prefers stateliness of movement and understatement of drama. Even in a sculpture of athletic movement, such as the Discobolus of the Greek sculptor Myron, the rhythm is restrained.
- **Harmony**
  Unity of structure was one of the ideals of classical art, and harmonious proportions, relationships, and color are prized.
- **Idealism**
  A strain of platonic idealism—the sense that ideal forms exist elsewhere of which forms in this world are an incomplete reflection—permeates classical art. The drive to simplification of form, particularly of the human body, may in part arise from this idea.

See also: *Beauty* on page 26; *Harmony* on page 84; *Proportion and Ratio* on page 140

1 ***Temple of Hephaestus***,
Athens, Greece
Photo: Guillaume Piolle

2 ***Reclining Dionysos***, from Parthenon east pediment, c. 447–433 BCE
Photo: Marie-Lan Nguyen

3 Jaques-Louis David (1748–1825)
Oath of the Horatii, 1786, Oil on canvas, 51¼ × 65⅝ in
(130.2 × 166.7 cm)

This Neoclassical masterpiece exhibits all the features of the style: clarity and simplicity of form, orderliness of composition, and somewhat static action.

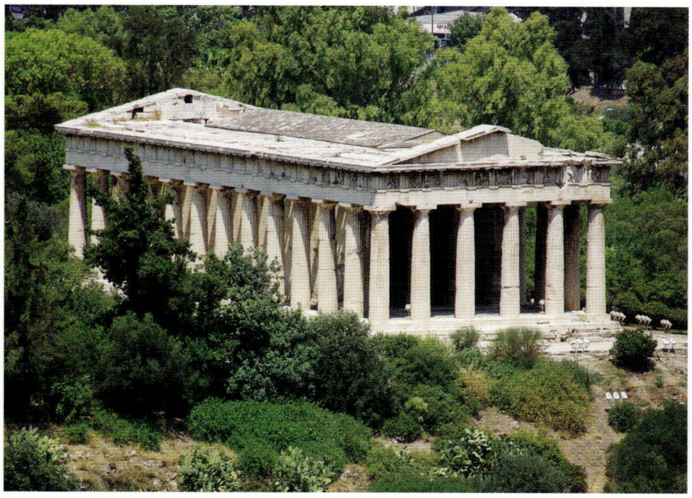

1

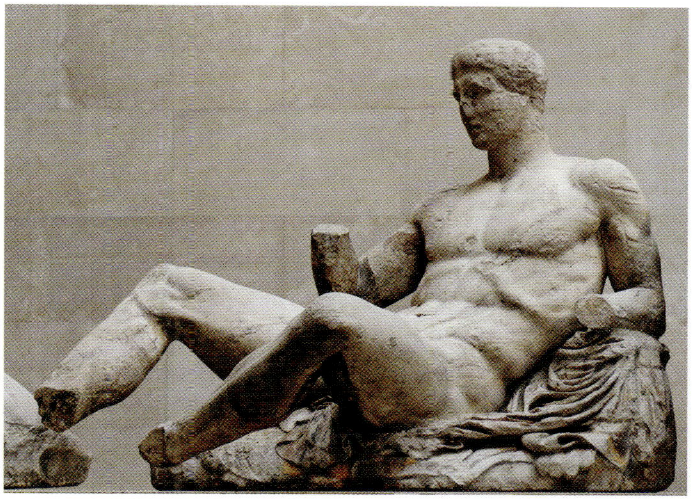

2

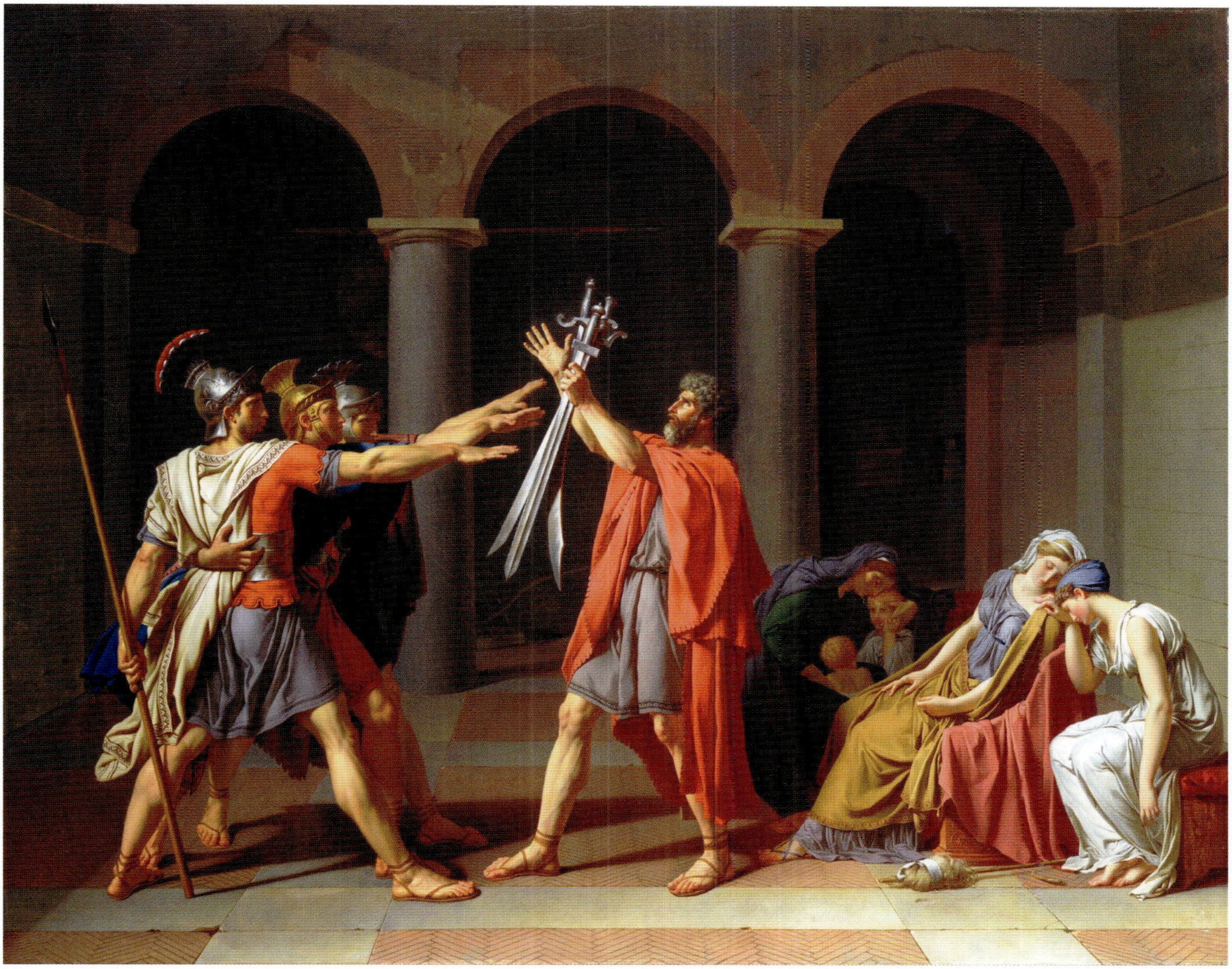

3

14 COLLAGE AND ASSEMBLAGE

BRINGING THE REAL WORLD INTO THE ARTWORK

The construction of pictures from disparate elements, often printed matter or photographs, is known as "collage." In sculpture the same approach is known as "assemblage," and differs only in that three-dimensional objects are collected and combined. In both cases, artists can select their source material to secure scale, color, texture, and content to their liking. Collaged items can also be combined with traditional art-making media.

STRATEGIES

- Images from disparate sources can be readily combined to create disjointed and challenging juxtapositions.
- Decorative formations can be made, in which elements are arranged into patterns.
- Photographs and photographic fragments can be combined to create an entirely new scene, an approach known as "photomontage."
- Collage elements can be selected for their adherence to a particular look or vision and then combined. In this case artists extend their vision through selection.
- Colored paper or prints can be collaged to form decorative or figurative compositions, an approach known as "découpage."
- The texture of paper and other materials can be important, for instance, in the combining of crepe paper, foil, tracing paper, and corrugated cardboard.
- Collaged elements may be combined with paint or other traditional media to make all manner of surfaces. Paint can be used to create visual unity, to adjust the color, to make a commentary about other parts of the collage, or simply to add excitement and intrigue. Sometimes a work that is essentially a painting or drawing is augmented by small amounts of collage.

HISTORY

Collage in some forms was used in ancient Chinese art, and arguably, to a certain extent in medieval art and Victorian interior design. However, it was not until the advent of modernism at the beginning of the twentieth century that collage came to the fore. Both Picasso and Georges Braque (1882–1963) included elements of newspaper text and other found objects in their Cubist works. The German artist Kurt Schwitters (1887–1948) turned it into a poetic form by placing found ephemera within elegantly designed compositions. Collage was a favorite of the Surrealists and played a major role in the art of the American Surrealist Joseph Cornell (1903–72).

See also: *Surrealism* on page 184

1 Georges Braque (1882–1963)
Man with Pipe, 1912, Charcoal and collage on paper, 24.5 x 19 in (62 x 48.6 cm)

2 Kathy Bruce
Specific Hungers, 2012, Collage on paper, 9 × 10 in (22.9 × 25.4 cm)

3 Reginald Case (1937–2009)
Dream, 2006, Assemblage, 17 × 25 × 4 in (43.2 × 63.5 × 10.2 cm)

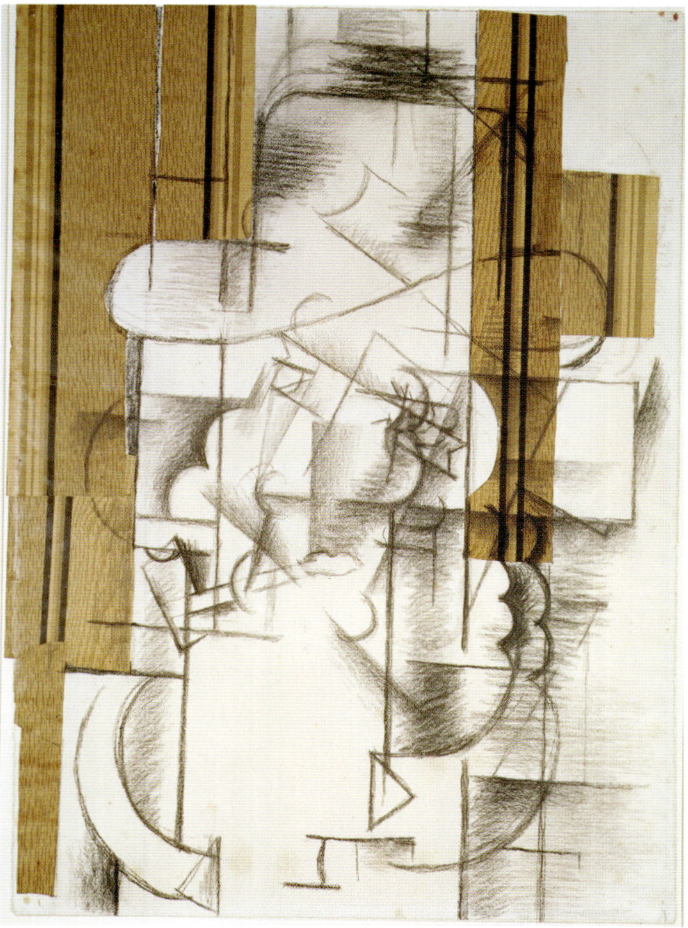

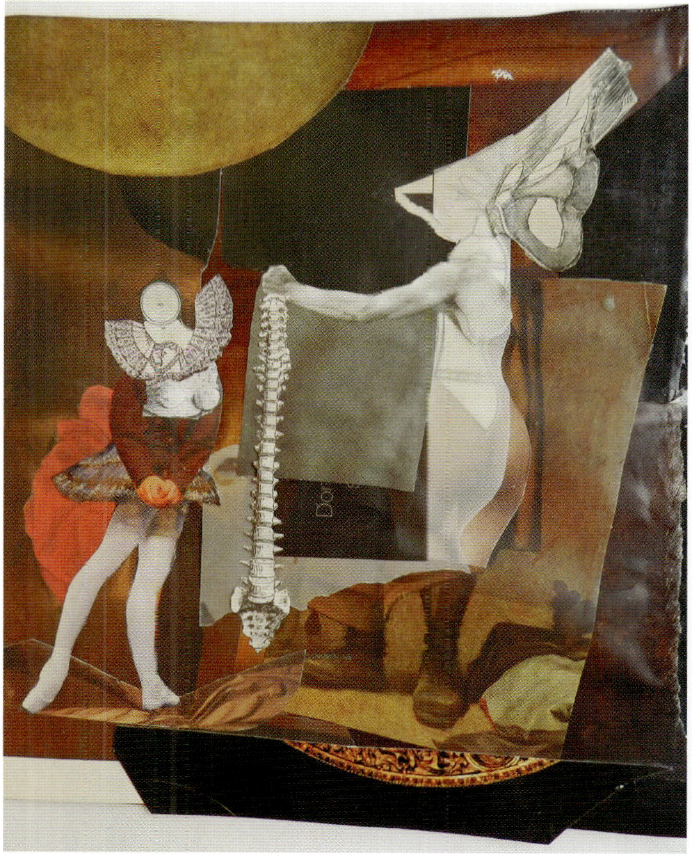

2

1

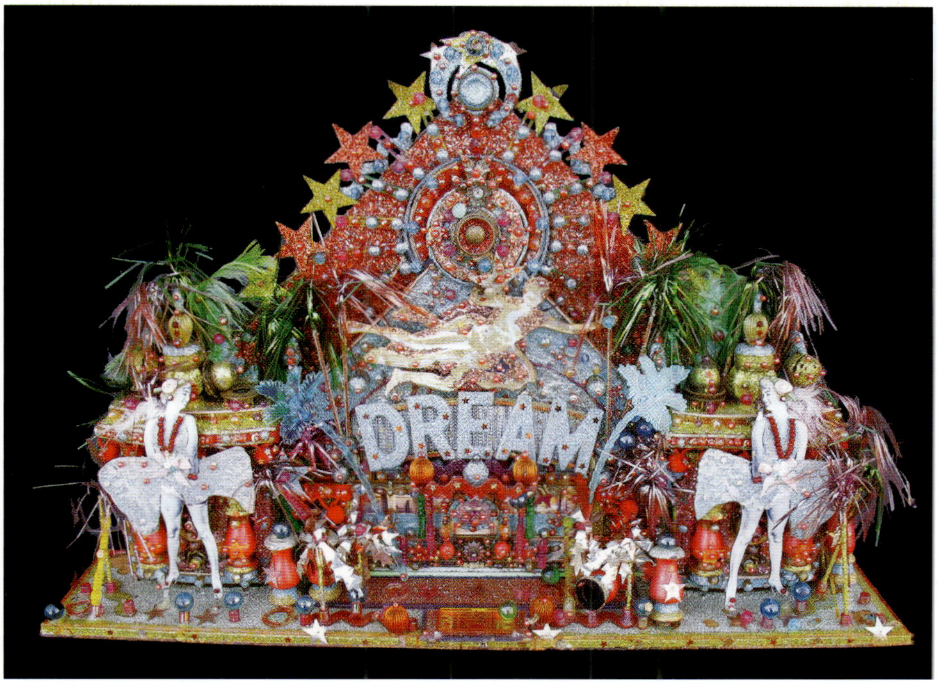

3

15 COLOR AS LIGHT

USING COLOR TO RECREATE THE SENSATION OF LIGHT

In the 1870s, a group of French painters that included Claude Monet (1840–1926) and Pierre Renoir (1841–1919) found a new way to recreate the sensation of light. They were dubbed "Impressionists." Up until then, almost all painters since the Renaissance had created light by describing tonal changes across forms and by building paintings along largely tonal lines. The Impressionists found that if they used small patches of brilliant color and built them into surfaces in which they alternated the color temperature, they could create a vivid sense of outdoor light. In looking at such paintings, the viewer's eye reconstitutes the color while retaining the lively action of the individual hues.

In the 1890s, another group of French painters, the Pointillists, built on the discoveries of Impressionism and applied a more systematic approach, creating light by building areas of color with tiny, uniform dots of paint.

While the development of this new approach grew from the interest in plein air ("open air") painting in the nineteenth century, it was also influenced by new scientific discoveries in optics, color, and perception. The work of physicist Hermann von Helmholz (1821–94) was particularly important and was popularized by the writings of Michel Eugène Chevreul (1786–1889). Chevreul published a color wheel showing opposing colors and intermediaries. He wrote considerably about color relationships and about the effects of juxtaposing brilliant small areas of color to create an impression of more complex color.

STRATEGIES

- Two colors placed close together will give an impression of a third color when seen from a distance.
- Every color in a visual field affects our perception of every other color in the field. Colors are experienced in relation to each other.
- The alternation of color temperature, warm and cool, contributes to the sensation of light.
- It is possible to exaggerate the saturation of color in a visual field in order to achieve a more powerful experience of light.

1 Michel Eugène Chevreul (1786–1889) ***Diagram of a color wheel***, 1855

2 Claude Monet (1840–1926) ***Woman with a Parasol—Madame Monet and Her Son***, 1875, Oil on canvas, 39 3/8 × 31 7/8 in (100 × 81 cm)

Monet presents a woman backlit by the sun so that her shadowed figure is vibrant with reflected light. To achieve this effect, he paints blues over soft warm browns throughout the figure's costume. The blues alternate between warmer violet blues and cooler turquoise blues. Under the forearm the color shifts to a yellow as the costume picks up light reflecting upwards from the grass. There is also a temperature alternation in the parasol, where the right hand side is a warm yellow green that becomes a cooler blue green in the middle before shifting to a warmer brown green on the left. The small broken marks throughout allow the color to remain active and clear.

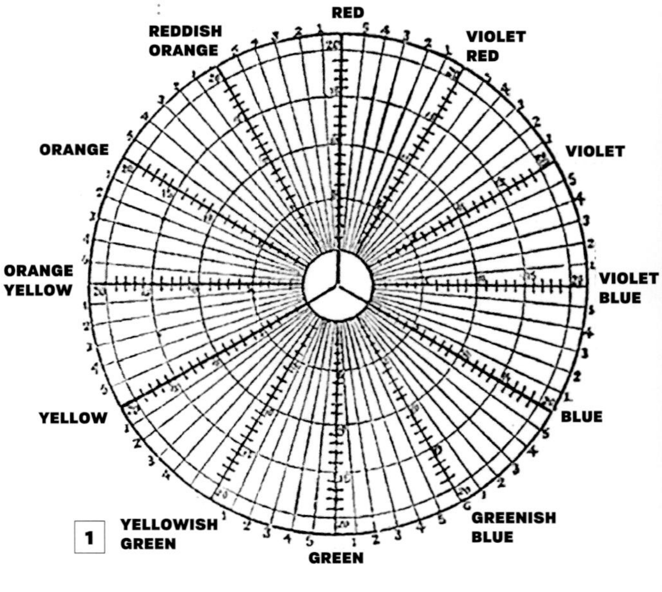

1

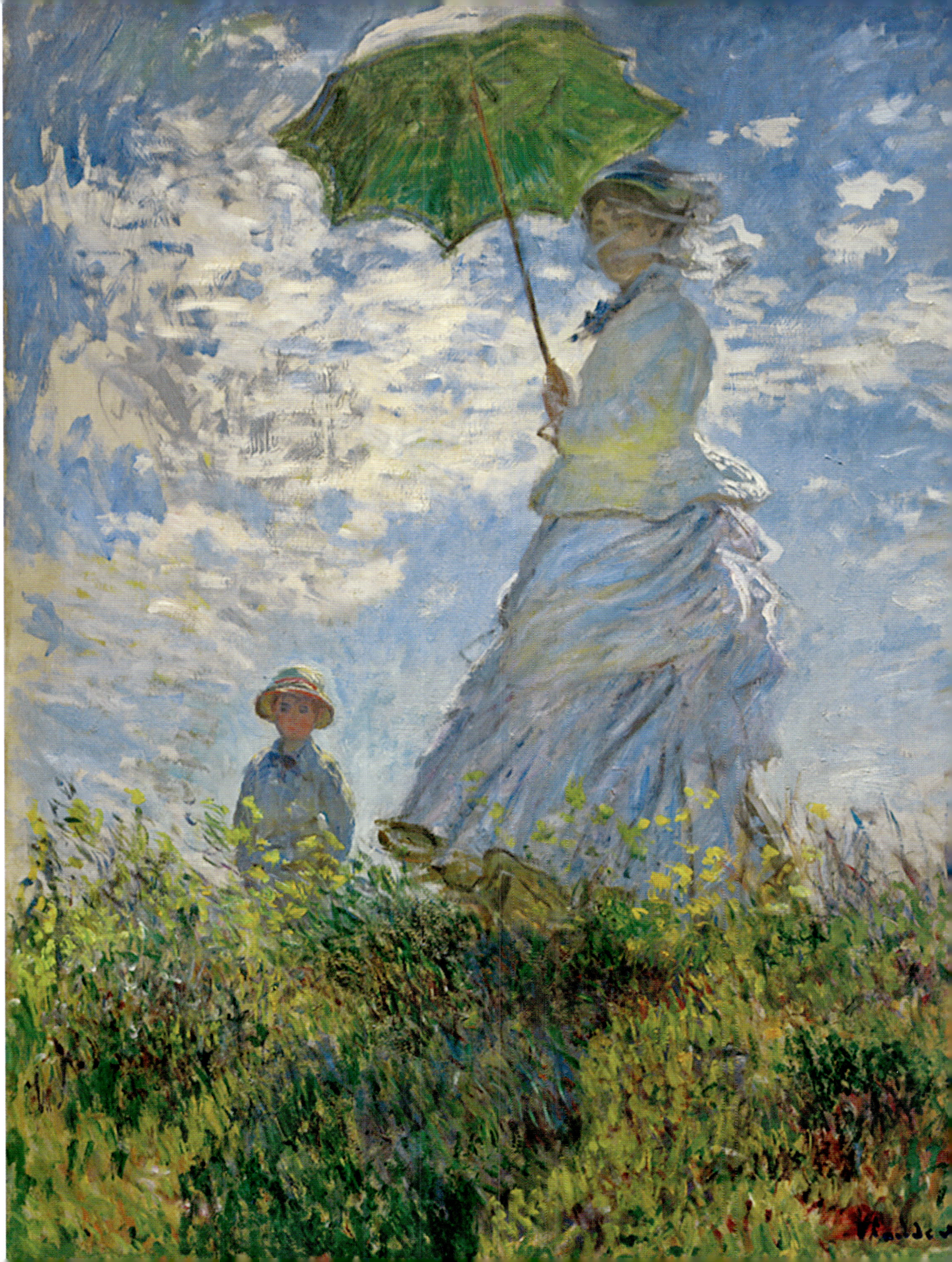

2

16 COLOR AS LIMIT

A LIMITED COLOR RANGE YIELDS EXPRESSIVE POSSIBILITIES

Limiting the color range within a painting can allow the creation of a work that has a distinctive identity, look, or atmosphere. By forcing a constrained range of color to create a fully rendered world, the painter can often create striking and sometimes highly emotive effects.

Limiting the color range within a work does not preclude representational or realist approaches. Creating an illusion requires that color relationships displayed in the world are transferred to the canvas. These relationships can be maintained even when the range of colors is restricted. Thus if we were to paint only with reds, we would be able to decide which was the yellowest red and even which was the greenest red. We could then construct an image that intimated the entire color world. But the result would be curious and perhaps evocative.

Many artists have limited their palettes in order to achieve a certain look and feel in the final image. Rembrandt painted with a palette limited to browns and blacks with an earthy yellow. This guaranteed warm harmony in the work and a kind of earthy stability that reinforced the sense of solidity and thoughtfulness in his painting. Similarly, the English artist Gwen John (1876–1939) worked with a palette of ochres and siennas, with just the occasional use of blue. The resultant generally warm harmonies give a sense of quiet and reflective calm to the work.

Perhaps the most extreme example of a limited palette is that of the Swedish painter Anders Zorn (1860–1920), who used only four colors: cadmium red medium, yellow ochre, ivory black, and white. Nonetheless, he succeeded in creating a very full impression of the world, while sustaining a somewhat cool and clear feel to the light.

See also: *Color as Light* on page 38; *Color Theory* on page 42; *Restraint* on page 156

1 John A. Parks (1952–)
Self Portrait, 2013, Oil on Linen,
18 × 14 in (45.7 × 35.6 cm)

Computer adjusted color limits show some of the expressive possibilities inherent in limiting color within an image.

2 **The Zorn Palette**

The entire palette is mixed from three colors and white. (Chart by Michael Lynn Adams)

3 Anders Zorn (1860–1920)
Omnibus, 1891–2, Oil on canvas,
39 1/8 × 26 in (99.5 × 66 cm)

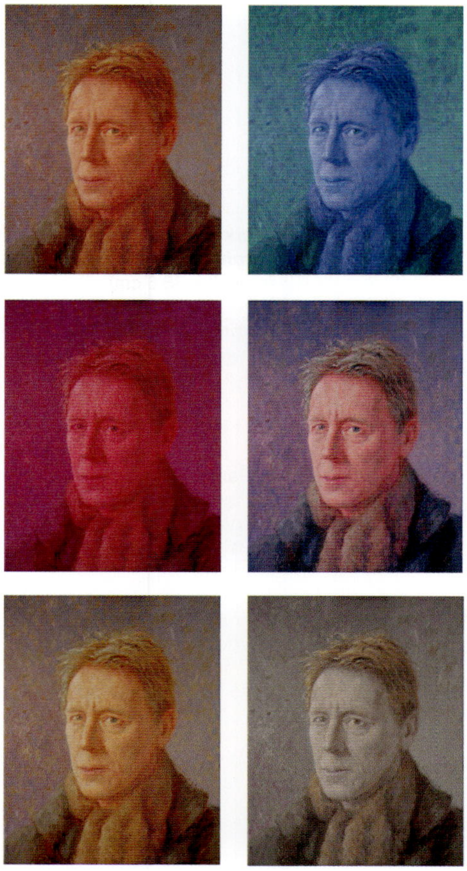

1

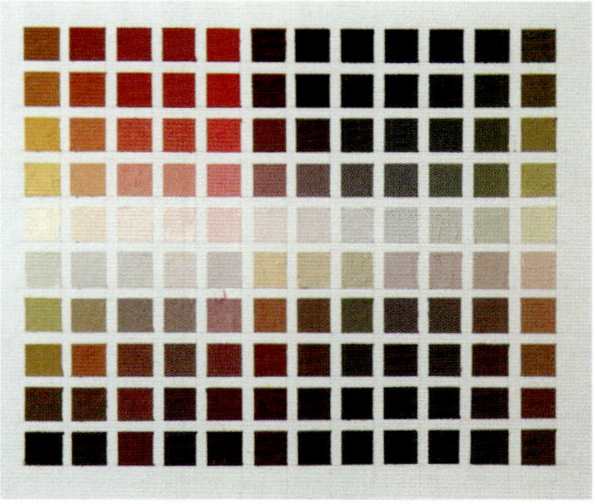

2

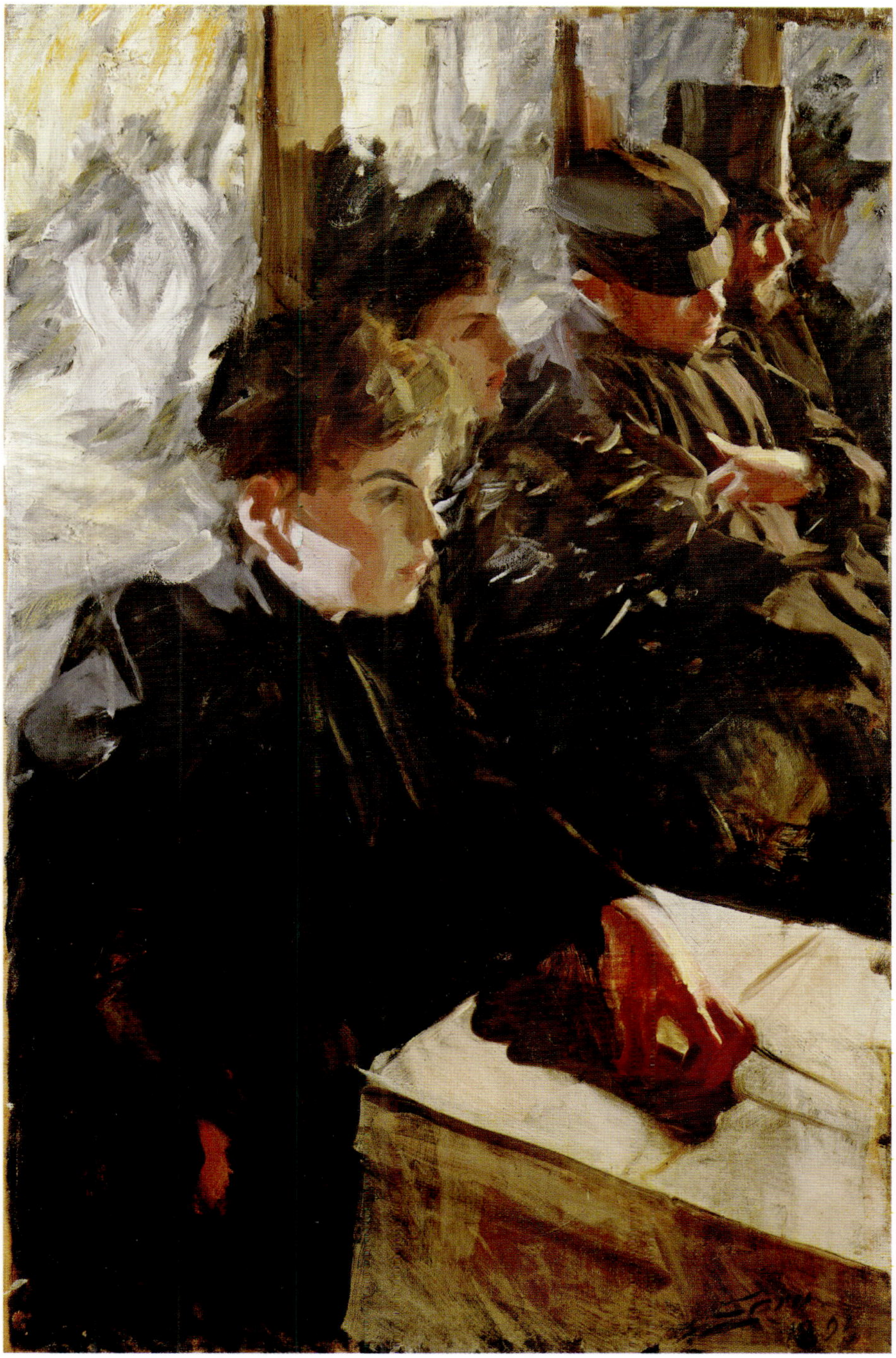

3

17 COLOR THEORY

UNDERSTANDING THE EXPERIENCE OF COLOR

From the Renaissance onward, artists and scientists sought a conceptual framework for understanding color perception. Both Alberti and Leonardo da Vinci wrote on the subject, but it wasn't until Sir Isaac Newton's *Opticks* was published in 1704 that the scientific world joined the search in earnest.

Arriving at a useful model of color relationships was made more difficult because reflective color (subtractive color), the kind experienced looking at a painting, combines in a very different way from that of pure colored light (additive color). Red, green, and blue pigments mix together to make a dark gray; conversely, red, green, and blue light wavelengths combine together to make white light. This is because pigments, when they reflect light, absorb one or more of the color wavelengths. A red pigment, for instance, absorbs all the wavelengths except red, which it reflects back. If the primary-colored pigments are mixed together, they absorb every color and leave only gray.

In the nineteenth century, useful color models began to emerge, and a standard color wheel was implemented in which primary colors stand opposite each other and are known as "complementaries." The relatively crude understanding of these relationships, projected in *The Laws of Simultaneous Contrast* by Eugene Chevreul in 1839, was superseded at the close of the century by the sophisticated Munsell Color System.

Albert Henry Munsell (1858–1918) was an American scientist who used experiments with human subjects to make a model of how color is perceived. He identified three properties of color:

- **Lightness**
  How light or dark a color is.
- **Chroma**
  The amount of color, or degree of saturation.
- **Hue**
  The position on the color wheel.

In order to model color relationships, Munsell proposed a sphere in which the hues of the color wheel form the equator. Lightness is represented by the north and south poles, with white at the top and black at the bottom. Chroma is at its maximum at the equator and progressively lessens toward the center of the sphere. By dividing the sphere into sections and employing a labeling system, Munsell's model allowed for the precise specification and recognition of colors. This had many industrial uses in cases where color consistency was required or specification of colors had to be communicated from place to place.

The development of color theory also played a central role in the invention of color printing. The most effective triad of color in inks is cyan, magenta, and yellow. In printing, these are joined by a black to make the CMYK process colors.

1 Subtractive color with cyan, magenta, and yellow inks. The center should technically be black but imperfections in ink formulations require that a black is also used in color printing.

2 A section of the Munsell color model

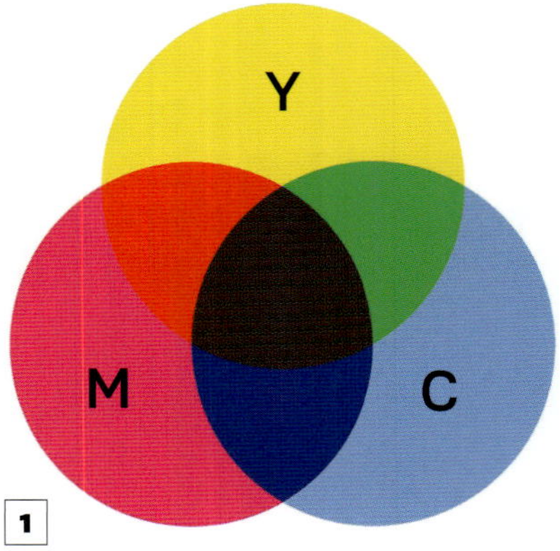

1

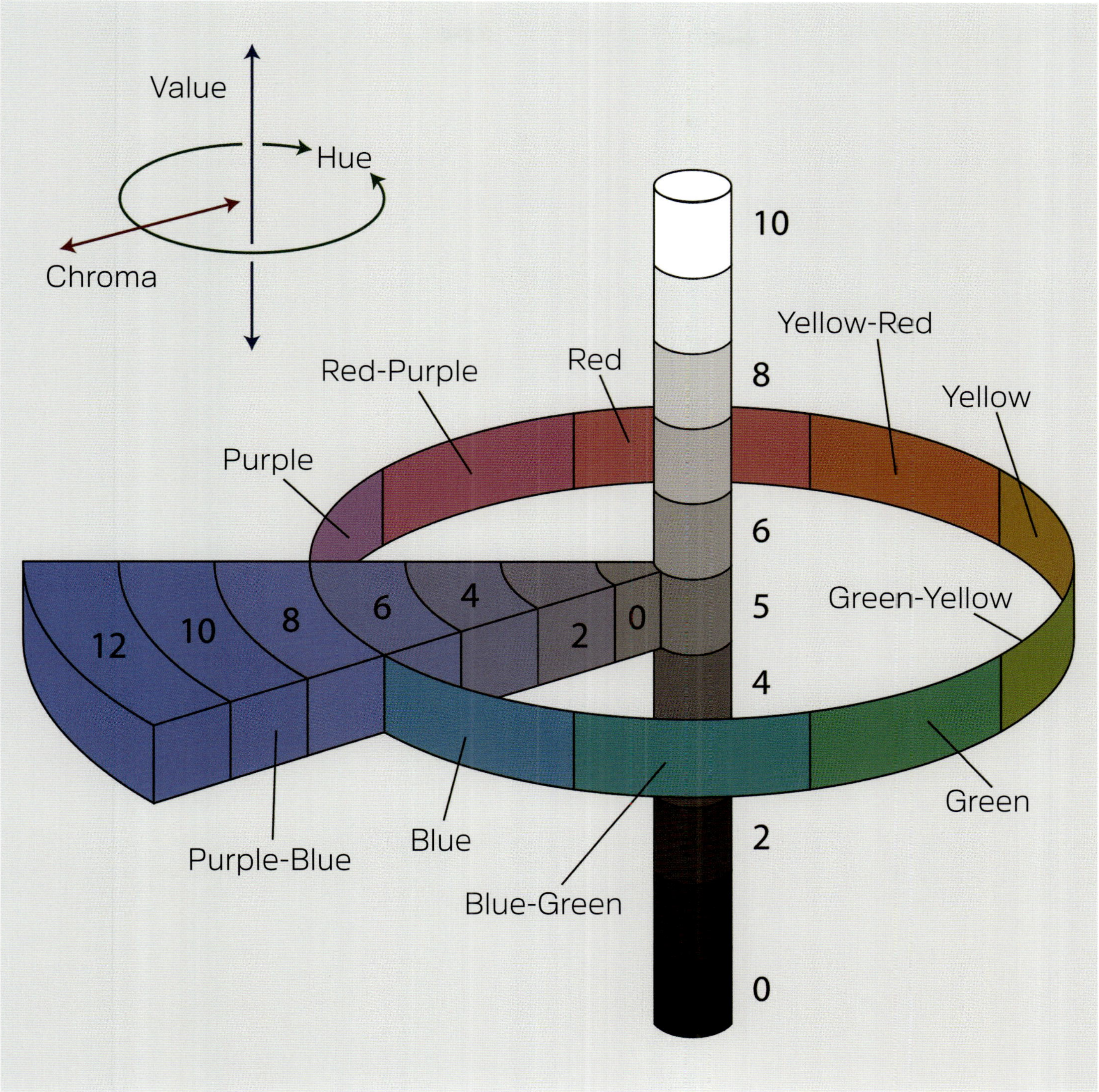
Value
Hue
Chroma
10
8
6
5
4
2
0
Yellow-Red
Red
Red-Purple
Yellow
Purple
Green-Yellow
12
10
8
6
4
2
0
Green
Purple-Blue
Blue
Blue-Green

2

18 COMPOSITION

THE ARTWORK AS AN ARRANGEMENT OF ELEMENTS

A work of art can be considered as a group of distinct elements that may be arranged by the artist in a fashion that furthers his or her artistic intentions. While compositional strategies are limitless in number and dependent on the intentions of the artist, there are a number of basic approaches that yield predictable results.

COMPOSITION BY GEOMETRY

In this approach, the artist applies a stable geometric pattern to the work and then places the principal elements to align with it. While almost any geometric pattern will achieve stability, some tend to make for more interesting or more pleasing compositions.

- **The Golden Mean**
  This is a ratio of 1:1.618. Division of a work by this ratio tends to convey a sense of harmony. (See *Proportion and Ratio* on page 140.)
- **The Rule of Thirds**
  Dividing the canvas into three equal lengths both horizontally and vertically allows for the placement of elements off center. This will avoid placements that bisect the image.
- **Dominant triangle**
  This is a simple idea in which the main elements of the composition form a triangle.
- **Grid**
  A grid of any proportion can help to stabilize a large composition.
- **Spiral**
  Arranging elements around a spiral is an excellent way of securing controlled movement in a composition.

DYNAMIC COMPOSITION

Elements within a composition can possess many qualities that affect how they function, especially when the artist wishes to achieve a sense of balance or dynamic stasis.

- **Weight**
  A dark element with a strident outline may feel "heavier" than a lightly tinted element with an amorphous outline.
- **Direction**
  Some elements will be perceived as moving in a particular direction because of their outline and placement within the composition. A simple example is an elongated triangle that will feel as though it is moving toward its apex.
- **Dominant identity**
  Some elements will command greater attention and weight simply because of their literal identity. A human figure, for instance, will seize the viewer's attention and therefore obtain, almost automatically, a powerful role in the composition.

1 Théodore Géricault (1791–1824)
The Charging Chasseur, 1812,
Oil on canvas, 137 × 105 in
(348 × 266.7cm)

Dynamic composition. *The artist places his central image diagonally on the canvas and creates powerful curving movements going upwards from bottom left toward top right. These are opposed by the backwards and downwards glance of the rider, an example of dominant identity where the viewer assigns great importance to the actions of a human being.*

2 Édouard Manet (1832–83)
Olympia, 1863, Oil on canvas,
51⅛ x 74⅞ in (130 x 190 cm)

Geometric. *Manet organizes his composition as a powerful two-dimensional design of interlocking dark and light shapes. The viewer's eye is drawn swiftly to the hard and somewhat indifferent gaze of the subject, whose face is starkly silhouetted against the dark wallpaper behind her.*

3 Raphael (1483–1520)
Saint Catherine of Alexandria,
1508, Oil on poplar wood,
28 × 20⅝ in (71 × 53 cm)

4 Katsushika Hokusai (1760–1849)
Yoshitsune Falls, 1833, Ink and color on paper, Woodblock print,
13⅝ × 9½ in (34.6 × 24.2 cm)

Spiral composition. *Two artists from very different traditions and eras both base their compositions on a spiral. In the Hokusai, the eye moves downwards with the flowing water to find the human action just a little below the midpoint of the print—two men are washing a horse. In the Raphael, the eye moves upwards through the figure and follows the saint's gaze to the golden light emanating from the heavens.*

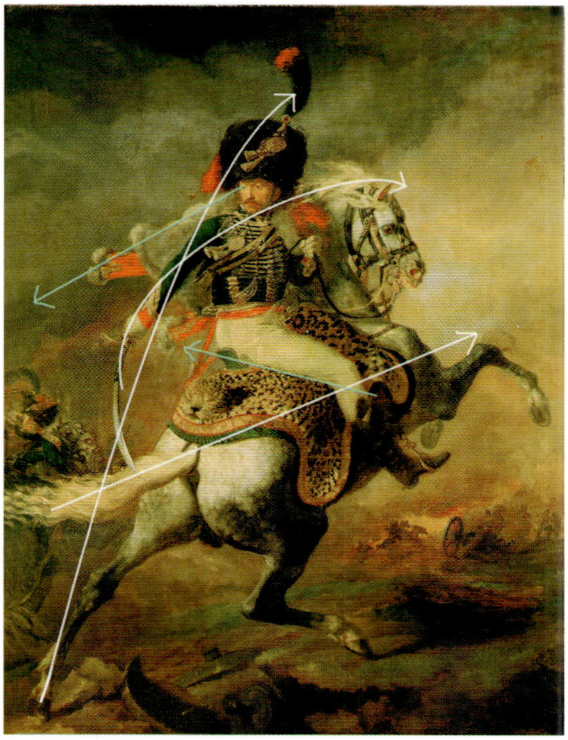

1

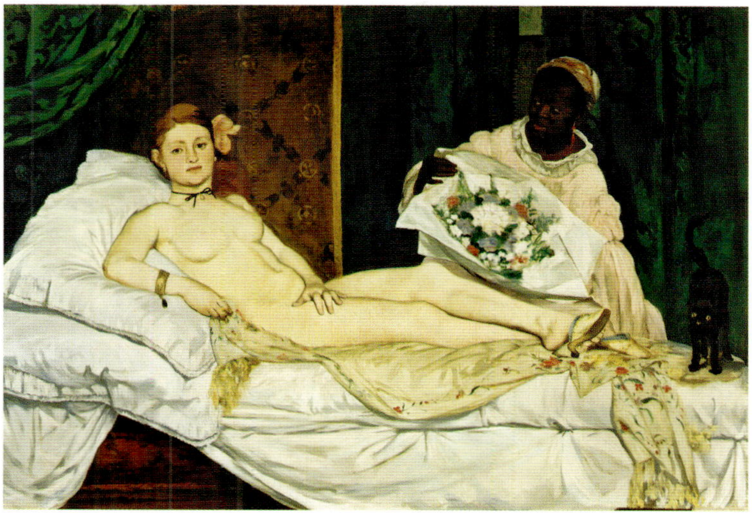

2

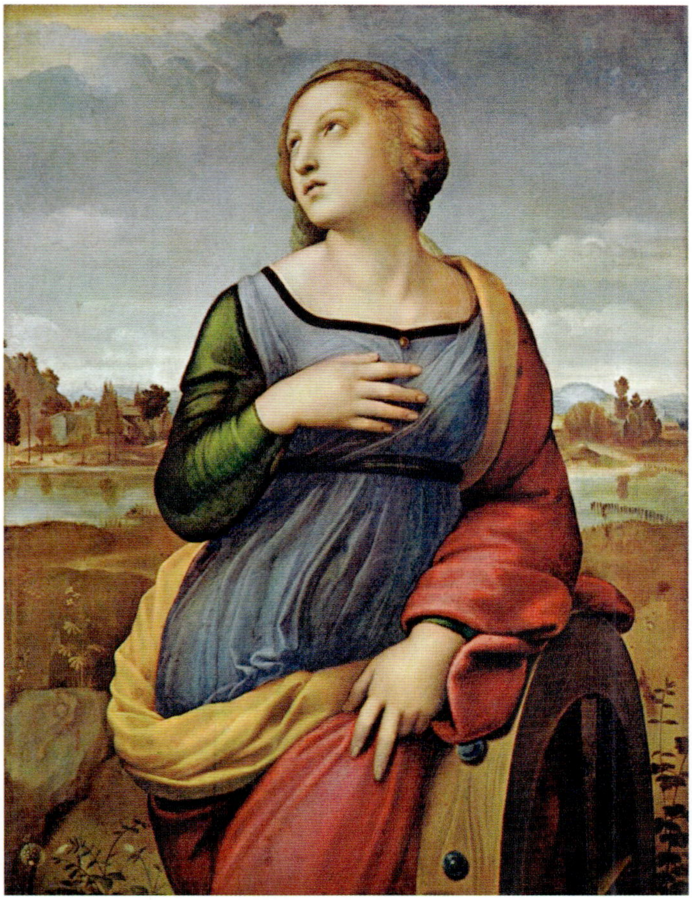

3

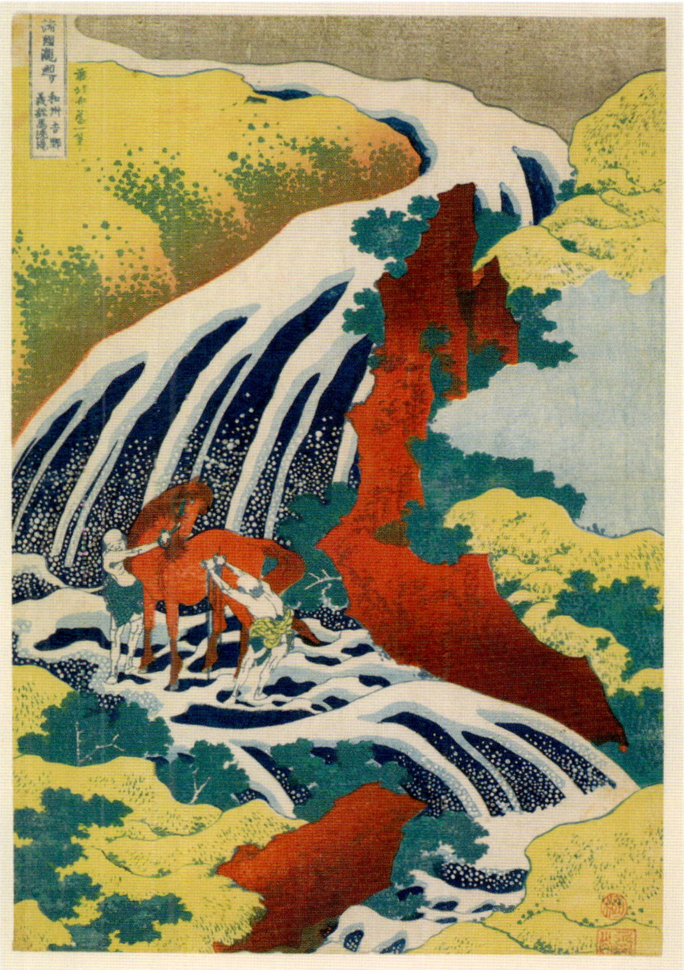

4

19 CONCEPTUAL ART

IDEAS AS ART

An artwork can be simply an idea or something generated totally by an idea, an approach known as conceptual art. Although examples of such artworks go back at least to the readymades of Marcel Duchamp in the early twentieth century, conceptual art emerged as an identifiable movement only in the 1960s. In *Art Forum*, in 1967, American artist Sol Lewitt wrote, "In conceptual art, the idea or concept is the most important aspect of the work. When an artist uses a conceptual form of art, it means that all of the planning and decisions are made beforehand and the execution is a perfunctory affair. The idea becomes a machine that makes the art."

STRATEGIES

- **Imaginary works**
  The artist supplies a description of something that would be impossible or very difficult to fabricate. The audience engages the work through imaginative contemplation.
- **Philosophical examination**
  The artist gives up the task of making objects in favor of a philosophical examination of the nature of art and art practice. This approach is favored by the English group Art and Language. They published magazines and articles from the late 1960s onward in which they applied the methods of linguistic philosophy to pursue a semantic investigation of art.
- **Instruction list**
  The artist invents the artwork as a concept and provides a list of instructions whereby anyone can fabricate it. In this approach, the art object is demystified; it is no longer imbued with the aura of uniqueness that is traditionally associated with a work of art. For instance, Sol Lewitt (1928–2007) made many wall drawings that exist as lists of instructions. They continue to be executed after the artist's death.
- **Designation**
  The artist designates an object or occurrence in the world as an artwork. For example, in 1960, Dutch artist Stanley Broun declared that all the shoe stores in Amsterdam constituted his art object.
- **Document**
  An event, object, or activity is documented, and the documentation is then exhibited as evidence of an artwork that can be contemplated but which may no longer exist.
- **Political/social statement**
  The artist employs the forum of the art exhibit in order to focus attention on a political or social issue. In 1971, artist Hans Haacke presented *Real Time Social System*, an investigation into the real estate holdings and commercial practices of a wealthy New York family, as an exhibit at the Guggenheim Museum. The museum abruptly cancelled the exhibition.

1 Art & Language
No Secret Painting XI, 2007,
Painting and text: Part 1 (painting) 2 × 2 1/16 in (5.1 × 5.2 cm); Part 2 (text) 3½ × 2 5/8 in (9 × 6.7 cm) © the artist; Courtesy, Lisson Gallery, London

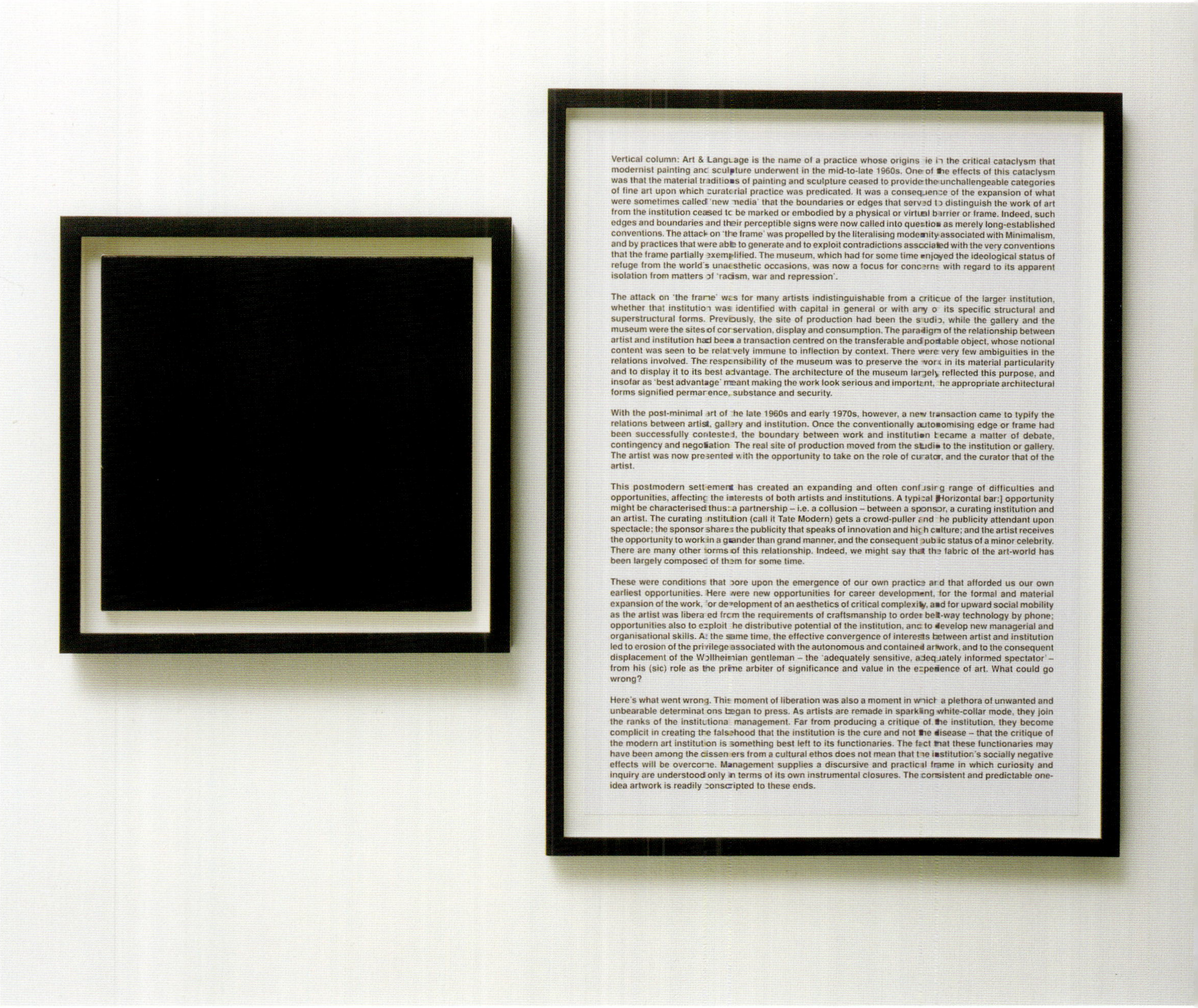
Vertical column: Art & Language is the name of a practice whose origins lie in the critical cataclysm that modernist painting and sculpture underwent in the mid-to-late 1960s. One of the effects of this cataclysm was that the material traditions of painting and sculpture ceased to provide the unchallengeable categories of fine art upon which curatorial practice was predicated. It was a consequence of the expansion of what were sometimes called 'new media' that the boundaries or edges that served to distinguish the work of art from the institution ceased to be marked or embodied by a physical or virtual barrier or frame. Indeed, such edges and boundaries and their perceptible signs were now called into question as merely long-established conventions. The attack on 'the frame' was propelled by the literalising modernity associated with Minimalism, and by practices that were able to generate and to exploit contradictions associated with the very conventions that the frame partially exemplified. The museum, which had for some time enjoyed the ideological status of refuge from the world's unaesthetic occasions, was now a focus for concerns with regard to its apparent isolation from matters of 'racism, war and repression'.
The attack on 'the frame' was for many artists indistinguishable from a critique of the larger institution, whether that institution was identified with capital in general or with any of its specific structural and superstructural forms. Previously, the site of production had been the studio, while the gallery and the museum were the sites of conservation, display and consumption. The paradigm of the relationship between artist and institution had been a transaction centred on the transferable and portable object, whose notional content was seen to be relatively immune to inflection by context. There were very few ambiguities in the relations involved. The responsibility of the museum was to preserve the work in its material particularity and to display it to its best advantage. The architecture of the museum largely reflected this purpose, and insofar as 'best advantage' meant making the work look serious and important, the appropriate architectural forms signified permanence, substance and security.
With the post-minimal art of the late 1960s and early 1970s, however, a new transaction came to typify the relations between artist, gallery and institution. Once the conventionally autonomising edge or frame had been successfully contested, the boundary between work and institution became a matter of debate, contingency and negotiation. The real site of production moved from the studio to the institution or gallery. The artist was now presented with the opportunity to take on the role of curator, and the curator that of the artist.
This postmodern settlement has created an expanding and often confusing range of difficulties and opportunities, affecting the interests of both artists and institutions. A typical [Horizontal bar:] opportunity might be characterised thus: a partnership – i.e. a collusion – between a sponsor, a curating institution and an artist. The curating institution (call it Tate Modern) gets a crowd-puller and the publicity attendant upon spectacle; the sponsor shares the publicity that speaks of innovation and high culture; and the artist receives the opportunity to work in a grander than grand manner, and the consequent public status of a minor celebrity. There are many other forms of this relationship. Indeed, we might say that the fabric of the art-world has been largely composed of them for some time.
These were conditions that bore upon the emergence of our own practice and that afforded us our own earliest opportunities. Here were new opportunities for career development, for the formal and material expansion of the work, for development of an aesthetics of critical complexity, and for upward social mobility as the artist was liberated from the requirements of craftsmanship to order belt-way technology by phone; opportunities also to exploit the distributive potential of the institution, and to develop new managerial and organisational skills. At the same time, the effective convergence of interests between artist and institution led to erosion of the privilege associated with the autonomous and contained artwork, and to the consequent displacement of the Wollheimian gentleman – the 'adequately sensitive, adequately informed spectator' – from his (sic) role as the prime arbiter of significance and value in the experience of art. What could go wrong?
Here's what went wrong. This moment of liberation was also a moment in which a plethora of unwanted and unbearable determinations began to press. As artists are remade in sparkling white-collar mode, they join the ranks of the institutional management. Far from producing a critique of the institution, they become complicit in creating the falsehood that the institution is the cure and not the disease – that the critique of the modern art institution is something best left to its functionaries. The fact that these functionaries may have been among the dissenters from a cultural ethos does not mean that the institution's socially negative effects will be overcome. Management supplies a discursive and practical frame in which curiosity and inquiry are understood only in terms of its own instrumental closures. The consistent and predictable one-idea artwork is readily conscripted to these ends.

1

20 CONSISTENCY OF VISUAL LANGUAGE

COHERENCE REQUIRES UNITY OF EXPRESSION

Consistency of language throughout a work of art is nearly always necessary if it is to be coherent. For example, it will be hard to make a representational painting read well if half of it is in black and white and the other half in color. Tonal and color structure must be consistent to sustain an illusion. The same principle applies to handling. It is nearly impossible, for example, to develop a unified painting in which part of the picture is executed in heavy brushstrokes and the rest of it is painted in very small and delicate brushstrokes. Similarly, it is hard to combine flawless rendering with other parts of a painting executed in a broken impressionistic style. This leads us to consider the idea that we generally require some form of unity to be present throughout a work of art, a principle that goes back to Aristotle's *Poetics*. More recently, the writer Somerset Maugham observed, "The essence of the beautiful is unity in variety."

In the modern world, an artist will sometimes break with the idea of consistency of language for effect. For example, Francis Picabia (1879–1953) often combined a tonal image with a linear drawing to create a kind of two-tier presentation in his works. The English artist Patrick Caulfield (1936–2005) sometimes inserted a passage of painting in a photorealist style into works that were otherwise executed in a simplified cartoon style. In these cases it is the concept of the piece that becomes the unifying element, the audacity and surprise of the discontinuity.

1 Francis Picabia (1879–1953)
Idyll, 1927, Oil on canvas,
[dimensions unknown]

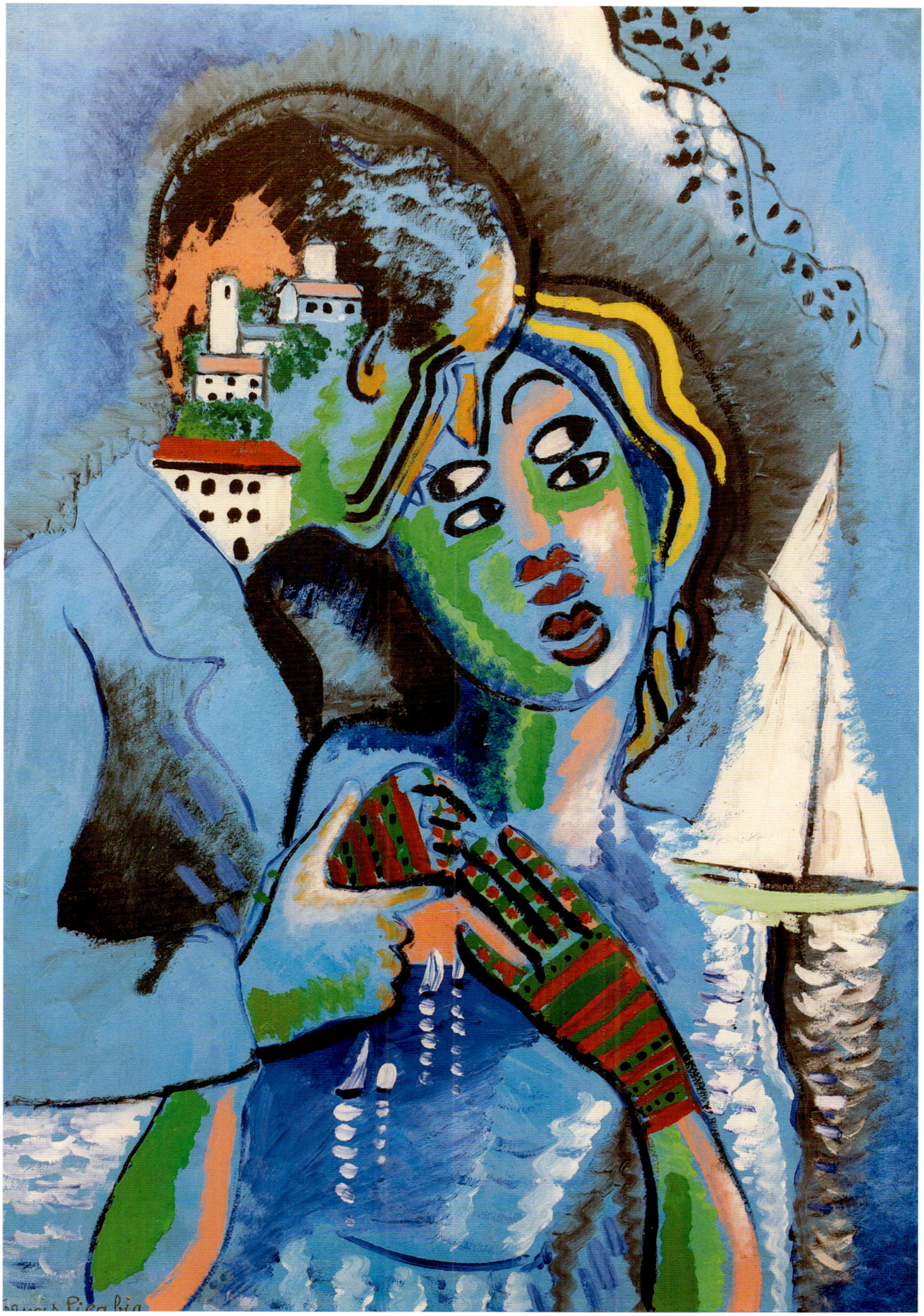

1

21 CRAFT

SKILL, EXPERTISE, AND WORKMANSHIP

Craft is the physical skill and expertise developed to perform a particular task. From the ancient world onward, the production of artworks was inseparable from the mastery of crafts, including carving, painting, weaving, and metalworking. In both Asia and Europe, crafts were passed through a system of apprenticeship, and in Medieval Europe, this system was formalized into guilds, associations of craftsmen that regulated their own trades. Even though academies of art began to appear in the late sixteenth century, the apprenticeship system, with its emphasis on craftsmanship, survived and flourished almost until modern times.

From the Romantic era onward, there was a growing recognition that art and craft were not exactly synonymous. In England, Joseph Mallord William Turner's decision to drop the traditional buildup of brown underpainting in favor of open and direct techniques dispensed with the laborious task of crafting carefully rendered forms. The matter came to a head when the American painter James Whistler (1834–1903) began to paint very loose and sketchy pictures in the 1870s. He was criticized by the critic John Ruskin (1819–1900) who accused him of "flinging a pot of paint in the public's face." Whistler sued, and the public was treated to a formal trial on the relationship of craft to art. Whistler prevailed, albeit with negligible damages.

Ruskin was a great champion of the desirability of craft and craftsmanship, which he closely related to his ideas about ideal societies in which such activity would play an integral role. Inspired by this philosophy, the Arts and Crafts movement was formed, centered on the enormous talents of William Morris (1834-96). He founded a company in London in 1861 that promoted simple, mostly flat design and such ideas as "truth to materials." He and his followers revived traditional crafts and looked to indigenous English folk art, medieval design, and vernacular architecture for inspiration. This philosophy spawned movements in both Europe and the United States, including the Wiener Werkstätte in Austria, a collective that sought to integrate craft, art, and design.

With the advent of modernism, craft has become increasingly divorced from the fine arts. Dadaist and Expressionist artists often used deliberately crude techniques. Most art movements have adopted crafting that is simply sufficient to the task at hand. With Conceptual Art and its promotion of the primacy of ideas over objects, the importance of craftsmanship disappears altogether. Postmodern artists, such as Jeff Koons (1955–) and Damien Hirst (1965–), often have their artworks made by somebody else.

See also: *Sufficiency of Means* on page 182

1 William Morris (1834–96)
The Golden Legend, 1892,
Woodcut title, 11 15/16 × 8 9/16 in
(30.3 × 21.7 cm)

2 Edward Burne-Jones (1833–98) and
William Morris (1834–96)
David's Charge to Solomon, 1882,
Stained-glass, about 80 × 80 in
(200 × 200 cm)

The Arts and Crafts movement inspired the painter Burne-Jones to engage in traditional crafts such as stained glass.

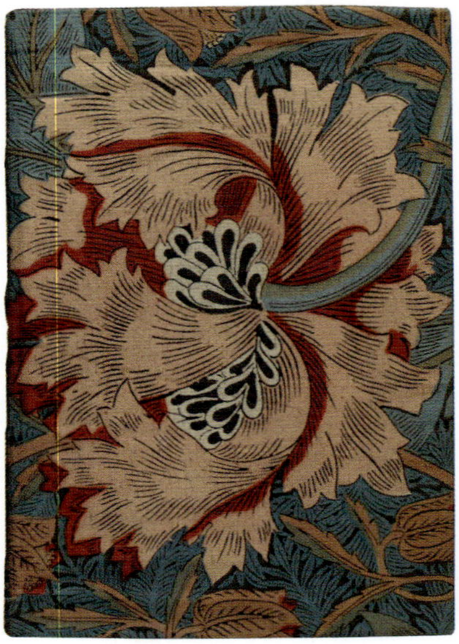

1

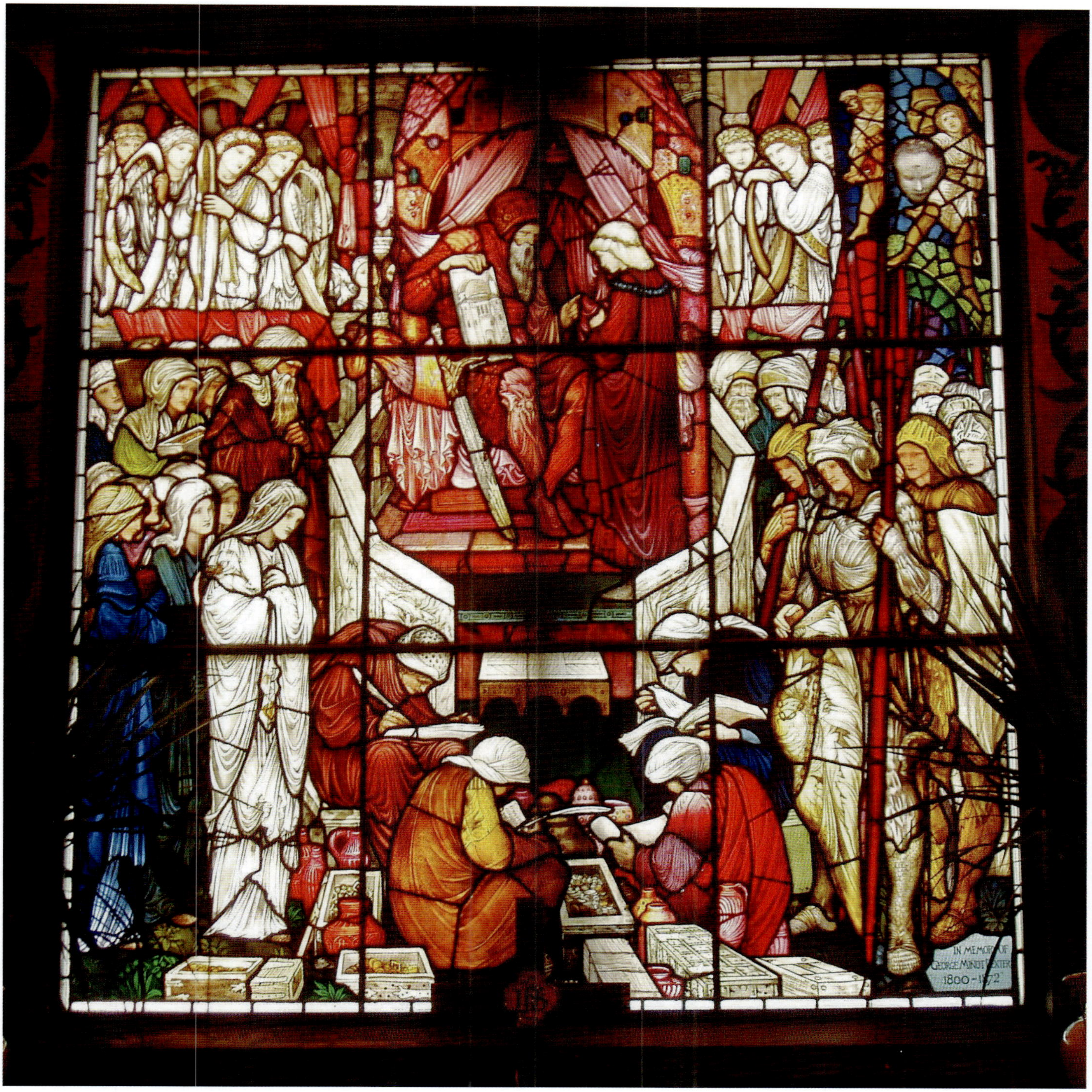

2

22 CREATIVITY

ANALYZING THE PROCESS OF MAKING SOMETHING NEW

Creativity, the generation of new ideas, insights, and previously unimagined images and artifacts, is usually thought of as central to the making of art. It is a surprisingly recent idea. Greek philosophy regarded the visual arts as largely imitative, while inspiration for poetry was provided by the Muses or the Gods. It wasn't until the Renaissance that creation began to be seen as a characteristic of human beings, and not until the beginning of the Romantic era that any serious thinking was applied to the function of the imagination. Any useful consideration of the creative process did not emerge until the end of the nineteenth century, and the first good attempt at analyzing it only appeared in 1926, when Graham Wallas (1858–1932) published *The Art of Thought*. He proposed the following model:

Preparation
An initial assessment of a problem

Incubation
A waiting period while the mind absorbs the task

Intimation
A sense that there is a solution

Illumination
A creative insight occurs

Verification
Examination of the solution's success

Since Wallas, several more models for the creative process have been proposed:

- **Divergent thinking**
  J. P. Guilford (1897–1987) advanced a distinction between convergent and divergent thinking. Convergent thinking is a process that focuses on a particular problem and seeks to arrive at one correct solution. Divergent thinking attempts to look at a problem from a variety of points of view and seeks multiple answers. Such thinking is inherently more creative.
- **Bisociation**
  This model was proposed by Arthur Koestler (1905–83) to describe a process by which conceptual frameworks from two different matrices of thought are combined. Common examples of this phenomenon occur with analogies, metaphors, comparisons, and jokes.
- **Honing theory**
  First proposed by psychologist Liane Gabora, this theory regards creativity as a product of a "self-mending, self-organizing" process, whereby humans continually adjust their worldview, or gestalt, to accord with new facts or experiences. "Creative individuals wrestle with issues or ideas that are, for them, ill-defined, or in a state of potentiality, which become well-defined in the process of considering them from different perspectives, or contexts."*

Most accounts of creativity report on the role of time away from considering a problem. As Einstein once observed, "Creativity is the residue of time wasted."

*Gabora, L. (2011) "Problem Solving as the Recognition and Actualization of Potentiality," *Report from Dagstuhl Seminar 11351*, page 104.

1 Paul Klee (1879–1940)
Cat and Bird, 1928, Oil and ink on gessoed canvas, mounted on wood, 15 × 21 in (38.1 × 53.3 cm)

2 Paul Klee (1879–1940)
Lamb, 1920, Oil and pen and ink on cardboard, 16 × 12 3/8 in (40.7 × 31.5 cm)

Klee combined the visual language of various early twentieth century art movements, including Expressionism, Surrealism, and Cubism, in a highly personal manner. He produced modest-sized paintings in vast quantities, following an intuitive path of freely associated imagery, rich color, and varied handling. A fountain of creativity, he left behind more than nine thousand works of art.

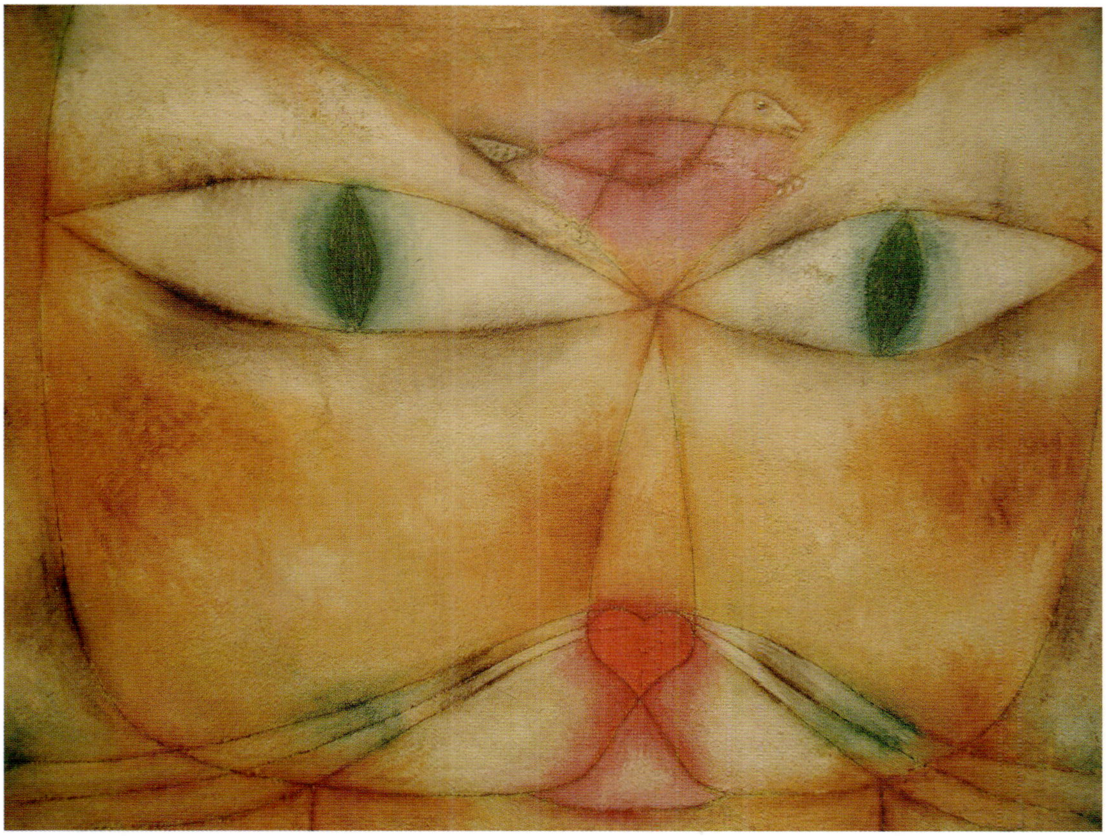
1

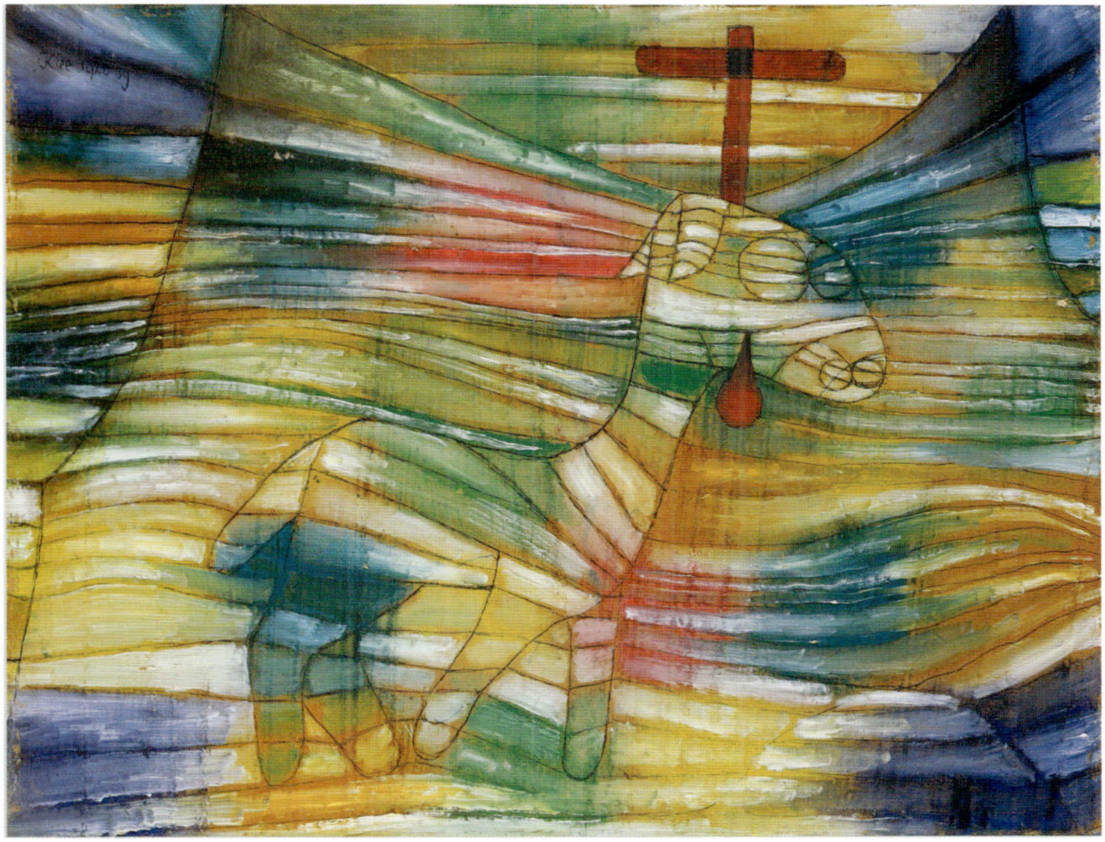
2

23 CROSS-CULTURAL FERTILIZATION

CULTURES INSPIRE EACH OTHER WHEN THEY MEET

One of the continual driving forces in the ongoing evolution of art is the energy that occurs when the works of one culture become available to another. For instance, the Romans were heavily influenced by Greek sculpture. In the colonial era, imported artworks from China and India seized the attention of European artists. Rococo artists, such as François Boucher (1703–70), made designs based on Chinese textiles and paintings during the resulting chinoiserie craze of the eighteenth century. Similarly, in the 1850s, when Japan was opened to European traders, the following influx of Japanese prints and artifacts fueled a revolution in design and painting. Vincent Van Gogh was directly influenced by Japanese prints, of which he had a large collection. At the close of the nineteenth century, an expanded flow of artifacts from Africa and the Pacific influenced Picasso and many other artists, inspiring a taste for simplified, or even brutal, forms and a new sense of the dramatic in painting and sculpture. Paul Gauguin (1848–1903) even went to live in Polynesia, absorbing native forms and imagery into his work. In the twentieth century, the German Expressionists were intrigued by tribal forms. Emil Nolde (1867-1956) took a long trip to the Pacific and made many paintings based on imagery he had collected there.

The cross-cultural flow is rarely one-way. Japanese printmaking was heavily influenced by European art in the second half of the nineteenth century. European conventions, such as perspective, tonal rendering, and classical organization were introduced, creating a new hybrid form of art. Similarly, Indian miniature painting absorbed European approaches and devices as Indian artists became aware of European art during the British rule.

With the advent of the Internet and the global availability of information, it is unclear how much culture will remain local at all. Hybridization of forms and ideas can now happen in a much shorter time frame, and the dialogue between nations and cultures now occurs at a rate never before possible.

1 François Boucher (1703–70)
The Chinese Garden (Detail), 1742, Oil on canvas, $15^{15}/_{16} \times 18^{7}/_{8}$ in (40.5 × 48 cm)

2 M. V. Dhurandhar (1867–1944)
Untitled, 1941, Watercolor on paper, $19^{3}/_{16} \times 12\frac{1}{2}$ in (48.8 × 31.8 cm)

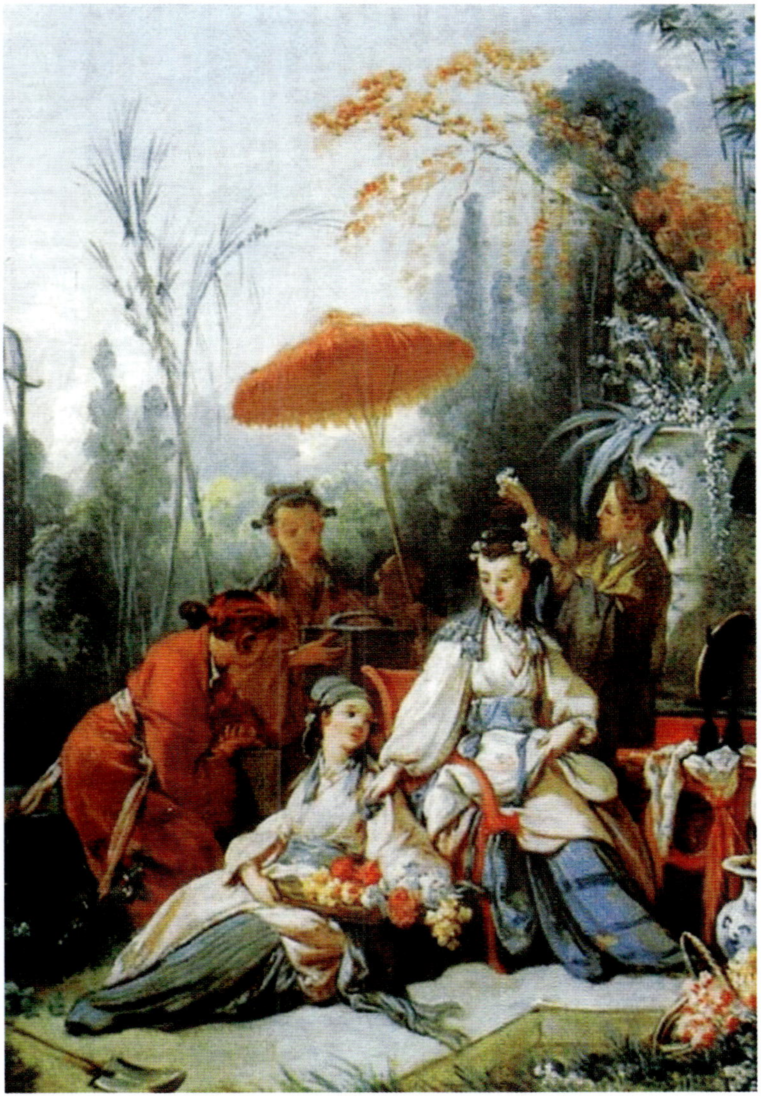

1

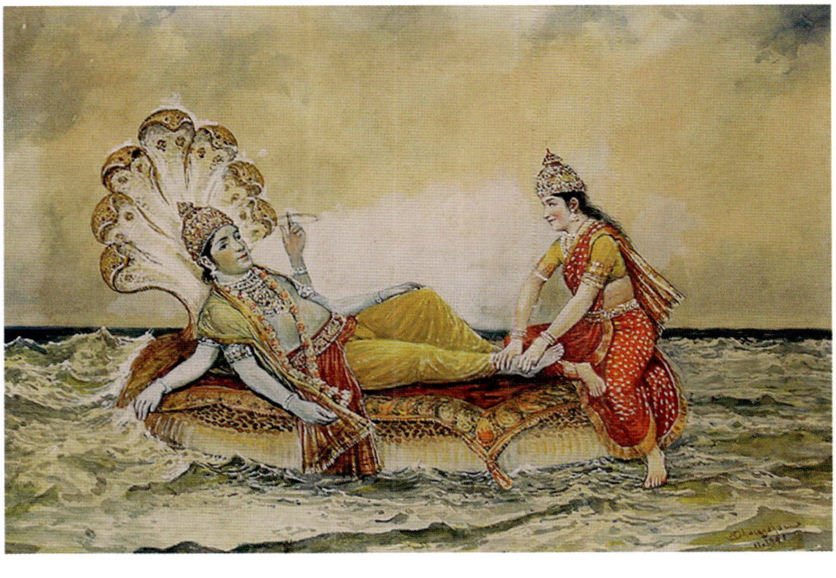

2

24 CUBISM

THE LANGUAGE OF MULTIPLE VIEWPOINTS

Cubism was a movement that emerged in Paris around 1907 and profoundly altered the way artists thought about the nature of painting and its ability to represent the world. Inspired in part by the paintings of Paul Cézanne (1839–1906), whose work incorporated shifting points of view, the Cubists constructed images that combined multiple viewpoints in a shallow picture space. By abandoning traditional perspectival space and continuous description of form, they asserted a new autonomy for painting, freeing it from the task of conventional representation. In sculpture, the recombination of fractured forms introduced similar possibilities in three dimensions.

Pablo Picasso (1881–1973) is generally credited with the first Cubist painting, *Les Demoiselles d'Avignon*. Other prominent Cubists include Georges Braques (1882–1963), Juan Gris (1887–1927), and Albert Gleizes (1881–1953).

COMPONENTS

- **Simplification**
  Subjects are generally reduced to simpler versions built from straight lines, cubes, circles, or cones.
- **Fracturing**
  Simplified outlines of the subject are broken up so that only partial views of each element are visible.
- **Shallow planes**
  Elements formed of fractured outlines of the subject are presented as the edges of planes. These are rendered simply using a tonal shift across them. The effect is to suggest a shallow space both in front of and behind the picture plane.
- **Recombination**
  Elements are recombined so that multiple viewpoints are melded together to form a single image in which the viewer can move smoothly from one outline to the next. Cubist painters tried a number of different approaches to this, including the suggestion of translucency of the elements.
- **Composition and design**
  The foregoing processes still left the Cubists with traditional challenges in terms of composition and design. It might be argued that the aesthetic attraction of painters such as Picasso, Braque, and Gris, was their innate taste and almost classical sense of interval and proportion.
- **Color restriction**
  Early Cubist painting tended to use restricted palettes to create a more unified surface. Later on, some of the Cubist painters, particularly Robert Delauney (1885–1941), experimented with richer color.
- **Time**
  The ability to show multiple viewpoints also allowed for viewpoints from different times. The time-lapse photography of Eadweard Muybridge (1830–1904) had already inspired a number of painters, and Cubism now provided a way to deploy its discoveries. Marcel Duchamp's *Nude Descending the Staircase* (see page 119) is a prime example. The Italian Futurists, much influenced by Cubism, made broad use of this approach.
- **Surface**
  The relative flatness of Cubist painting allowed for the inclusion of collaged elements and textured paint surfaces.

1 Pablo Picasso (1881–1973)
Les Demoiselles d'Avignon, 1907, Oil on canvas, 96 × 92 in (243.9 × 233.7cm)

2 Diego Rivera (1886–1957)
Still Life, 1915, Oil on canvas, 31¼ × 25⅛ in (79.4 × 64.1 cm)

3 Juan Gris (1887–1927)
Portrait of Pablo Picasso, 1912, Oil on canvas, 36¾ × 29¼ (93.3 × 74.4 cm)

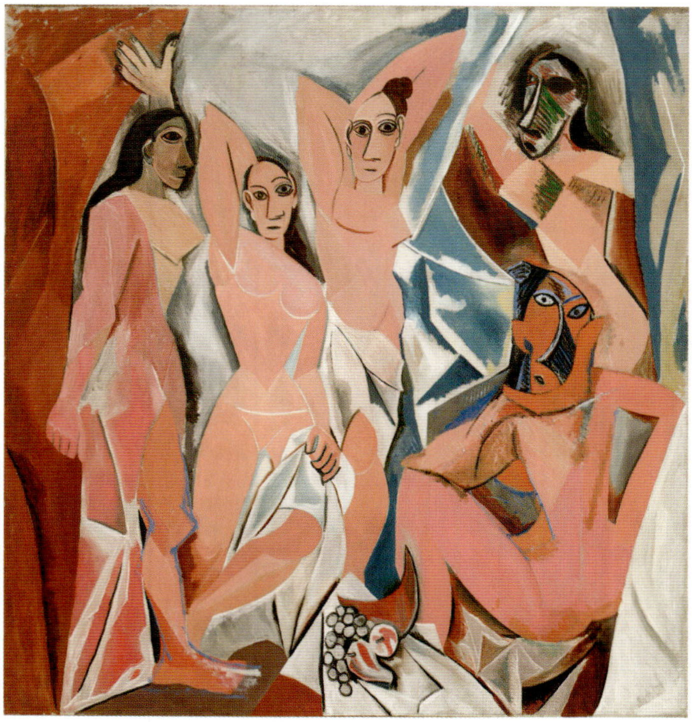

1

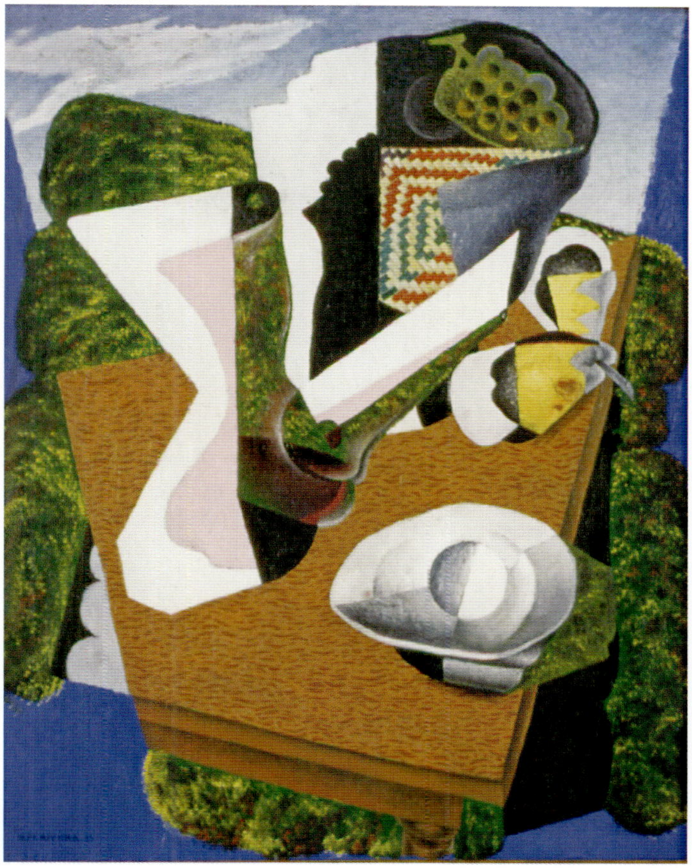

2

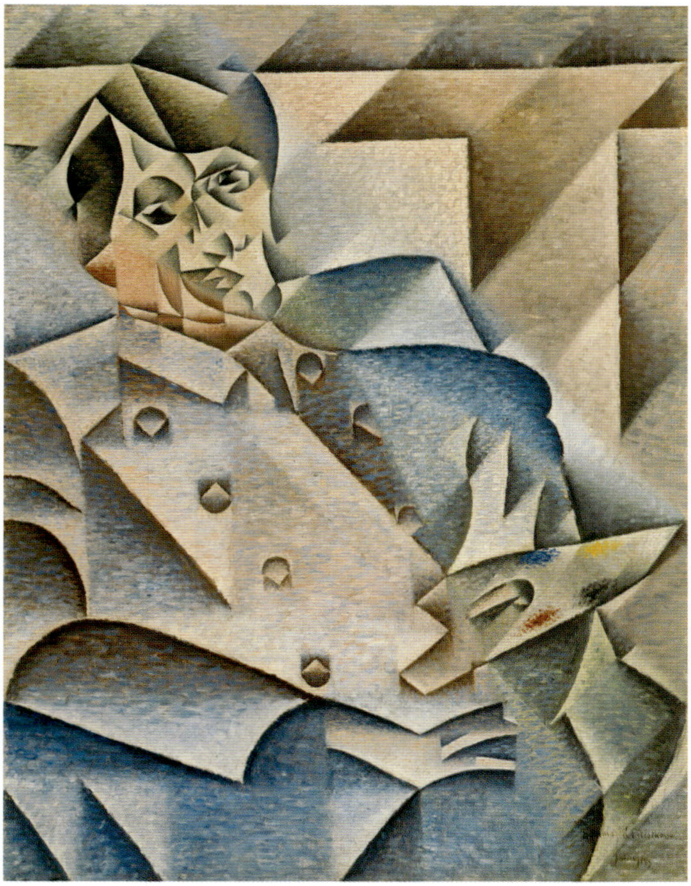

3

25 DADA

NONSENSE, NON-ART, AND CREATIVE MAYHEM LEAD TO NEW VITALITY IN ART

In 1916, a group of artists working in Zurich, Switzerland, named themselves by the nonsense word "Dada." Meeting in and around the Café Voltaire, they promoted an art of rejection and extreme behavior, using poetry, theater, painting, and sculpture to mount an attack on what they saw as the entrenched bourgeois values that had driven Europe into World War I. Led by the poet Tristan Tzara (1896–1963), along with artists Hugo Ball (1886–1927), Hannah Höch (1889–1978), Francis Picabia (1879–1953), and others, the movement embraced the irrational and nonsensical in an exuberant and highly experimental fashion. Performances included simultaneous poetry (two poems being read at the same time), cacophonous music, and nonsensical plays. German artist Hans Richter (1886–1976) observed that Dada was not art but "anti-art."

Paradoxically, this attack on art created a liberated artistic environment in which new forms emerged that would have far-reaching effects on later twentieth-century art. Performance art, photomontage, multimedia events, readymades, and assemblage all had their start with Dada. The movement promoted itself over the next few years with publications and manifestos that allowed it to spread throughout Europe and into the United States. In Berlin, in 1920, the First International Dadaist Fair opened, an exhibition of more than 200 works by artists including Francis Picabia, Otto Dix, Max Ernst, and others. In New York, Marcel Duchamp's seminal work *Fountain* (see page 147) was a direct product of Dadaist influence.

STRATEGIES

- **Irrationality**
  Poetry, performances, and artworks that deliberately undermine common sense challenged the rational underpinnings of bourgeois culture.
- **Spontaneity**
  Artworks and events embraced spontaneous behavior and extemporaneous outpourings.
- **Novelty**
  New experimental forms, such as readymades, photomontage, and multimedia, emerged from a willingness to accept anything as art.
- **Humor**
  Dadaist poetry and commentary adopted humor and a sense of the absurd to ridicule and undermine prevailing cultural values.
- **Politics**
  Dadaists vehemently opposed the political structures in France and Germany that had brought about the war. They supported communist ideals for ending private property and transferring power to the masses.

1 Hugo Ball performing at the Café Votaire

2 Hannah Höch (1889–1978)
Cut with the Dada Kitchen Knife through the Last Weimar Beer-Belly Cultural Epoch in Germany, 1919, Collage on paper, 56 11/16 × 35 7/16 in (144 × 90 cm)

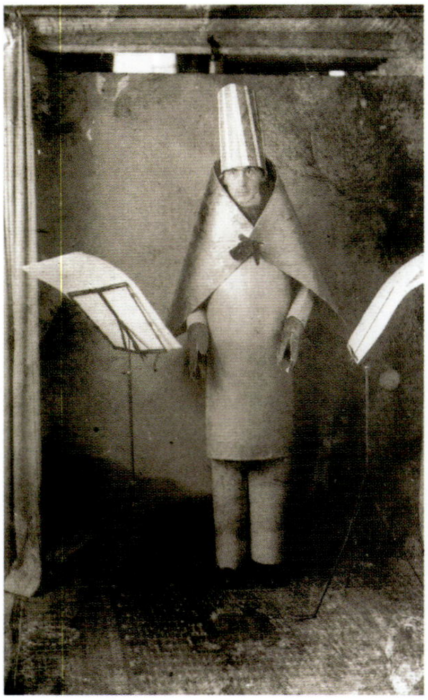

1

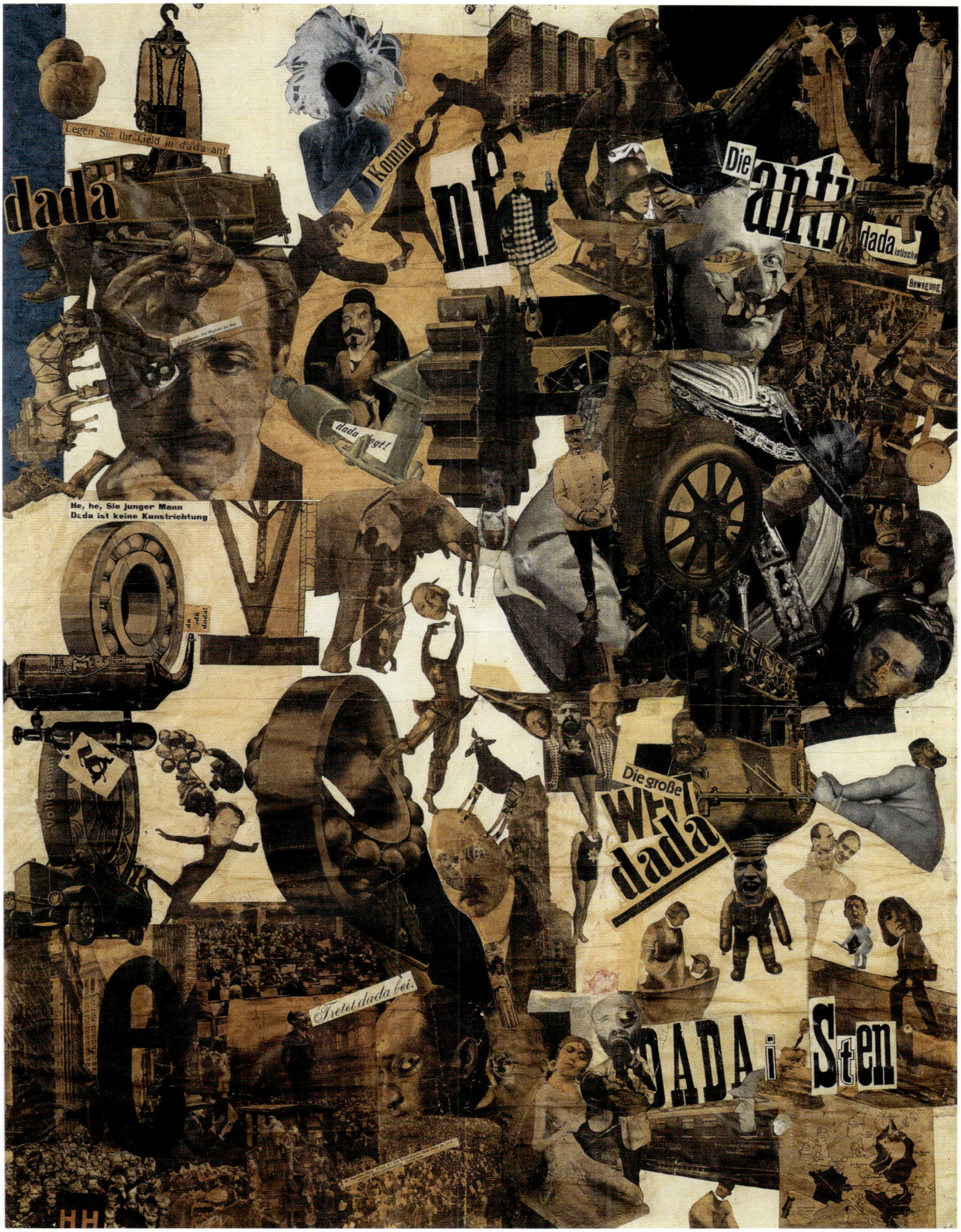
Legen Sie Ihr Geld in dada an!
dada
Komm
Die anti
dada istische
Bewegung
He, he, Sie junger Mann
Dada ist keine Kunstrichtung
Die große
dada
Tretet dada bei.
DADA i Sten
HH

2

26 DECORATION

THE PLEASURES OF ADORNMENT

Art that is intended to simply please the eye, to adorn a surface, or to act as ornamentation is generally referred to as "decorative." Much, but not all, decorative art deploys pattern, a repeated motif that forms a geometric regularity. Pattern making and its use to adorn surfaces appears in much tribal art and forms one of the most basic behaviors in art making. Moreover, some patterns and habits of decoration are identified with particular groups of people and specific periods in their history. Decorative elements, such as the Greek key pattern and the French fleur-de-lis, have become emblematic of entire cultures.

The arts of some cultures have been dominated by the decorative instinct. Celtic and a considerable amount of medieval art are overwhelmingly decorative, while Islamic religious art is almost entirely decorative. In the Western tradition, decorative art extends not merely to architectural and textile surfaces, but also to body art, religious artifacts, fashion design, and landscape design. In most of these arts, decorative elements are often integrated into structural design and form an active component of the look and feel of the artifact.

BASIC PATTERN TYPES

- **Grid**
  A motif is repeated tile fashion in horizontal, vertical, or diagonal rows.
- **Repeat**
  A more complex motif is designed so that it can repeat, with one side of the motif fitting into the other side of its next appearance.
- **Stripes**
  Parallel lines are repeated, usually in various colors.
- **Meander**
  A single line runs continuously and repeats the same motif. The Greek key pattern is the most famous example.
- **Other regularities**
  Nature provides examples of patterns formed from spirals, fractals, and other regularities or near-regularities, such as the cracking induced by shrinkage in mudflats or the undulations of sand dunes.

1 Sidney Parkinson (1745–71)
Tatoo, Maori, published 1784, probably sketched in 1769, Engraving, 13³⁄₁₆ × 10¼ in (33.5 × 26 cm)

The artist drew this image during Captain Cook's first exploration of New Zealand.

2 William Morris (1834–96)
Design for Tulip and Willow, 1873, Watercolor on paper

A repeat motif

3 **Friday Mosque**, Herat, Afghanistan

4 **Linsdisfarne Gospels**, Saint Matthew, 8th century, Ink, pigments, and gold on vellum

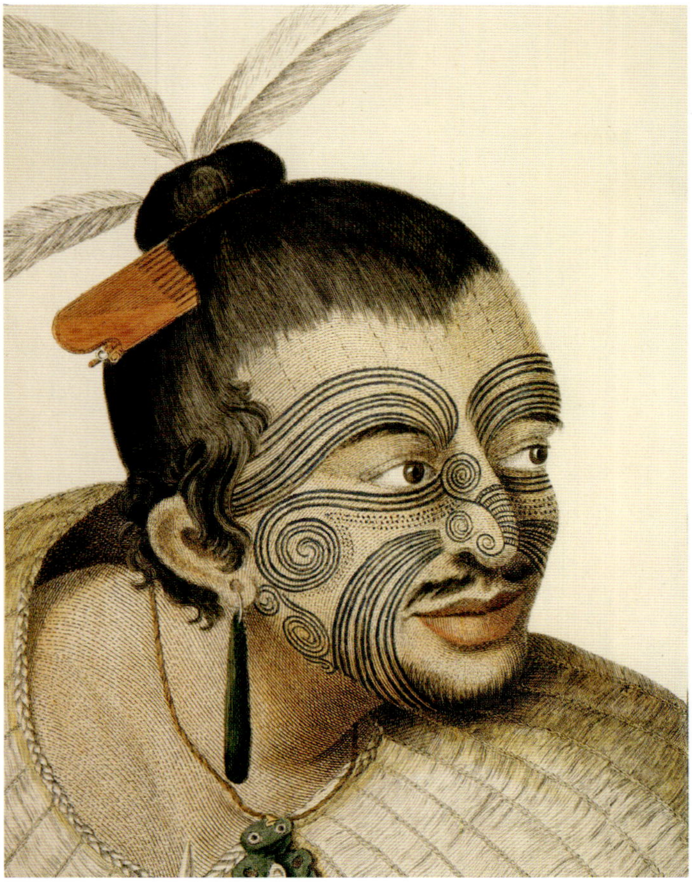

1

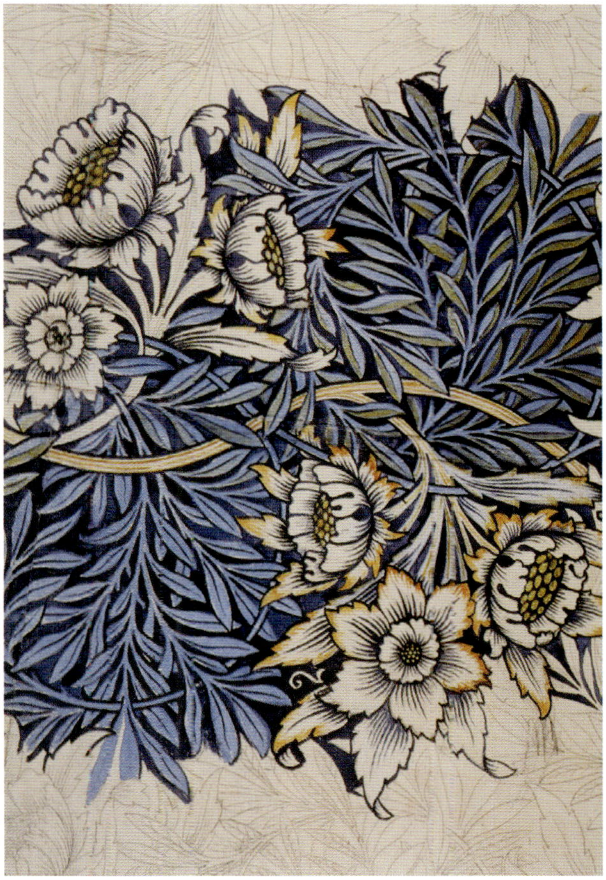

2

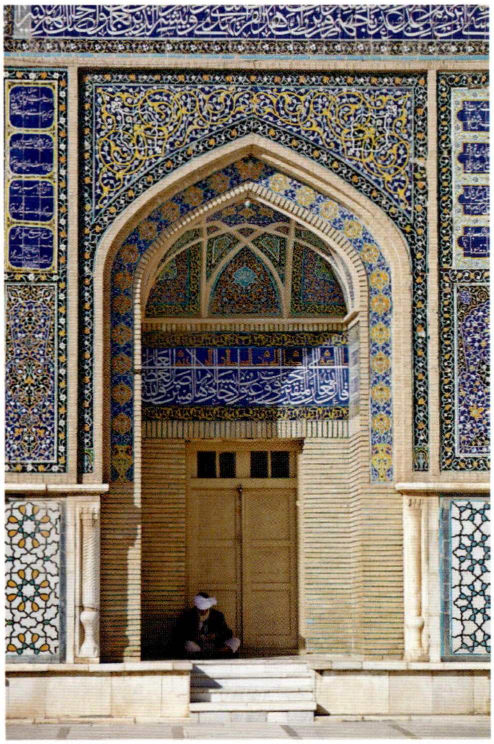

3

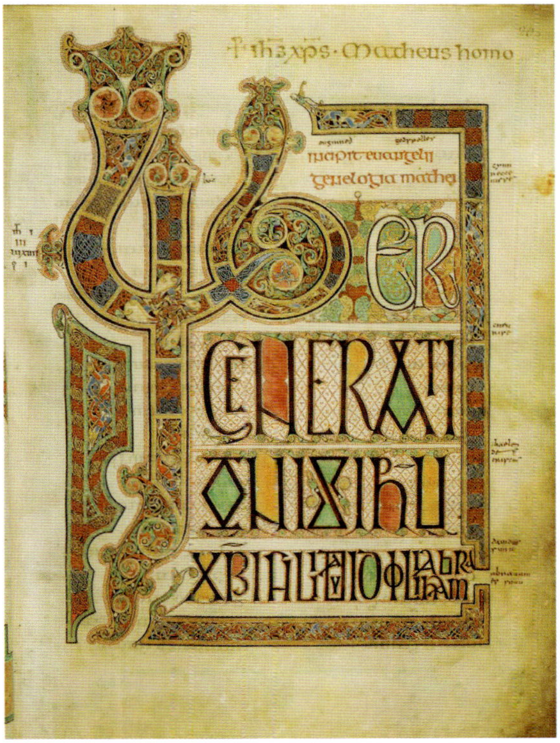

4

27 DISTORTION

BENDING, TWISTING, STRETCHING, AND PULLING

Distorting a form, a figure, or a face is one of the most dramatic and powerful statements an artist can make. Many approaches are possible.

- **Facial distortion**
  In much tribal art, images of the human head are subject to gross distortions. Eyes are often fantastically large, while teeth or noses may be prominent or nonexistent. The effect can be deeply disturbing, even frightening. Modern Western caricaturists routinely distort the head, exaggerating features of public figures as a form of humor.
- **Figural distortion**
  Byzantine artists routinely elongated figures, particularly on the walls of churches, to create a sense of presence. The Cretan artist El Greco (1541–1614), borrowed from this tradition and brought the power of elongated forms into Spanish painting with highly expressive effect. The German Expressionist painters of the twentieth century often brutally distorted figures for dramatic effect. The French painter Balthus (1908–2001) experimented with full-length portraits in which hands and feet were impossibly tiny and foreheads flat. More whimsical artists, such as Britain's Stanley Spencer (1891–1959), also distorted figures, often conveying a kind of awkward and simple charm.
- **Spatial distortion**
  Perspectival space can be distorted or skewed by adjusting the geometry. This can create surprising or alarming shifts in space. Edvard Munch (1863–1944) sometimes used this strategy to create a sense of alienation and unease. Similar results, in a harder style, were achieved by the American Surrealist artist George Tooker (1920–2011).
- **Distortion as style**
  Some artists adopt a distorted notion of form and space as an individual style. The Columbian artist Fernando Botero (1932–) paints all the figures in his paintings as though they were enormously fat. He has made a whole career out of playing endless games with this one idea.

1 **Fang mask**, Gabon, Wood, 26 in (66 cm) high

2 Edvard Munch (1863–1944) ***Self-Portrait with a Bottle of Wine***, 1906, Oil on canvas, $43^{5}/_{16} \times 47^{1}/_{4}$ in (110 × 120 cm)

The artist distorts the perspective so that it closes in on the sitter and is somewhat unstable on the right.

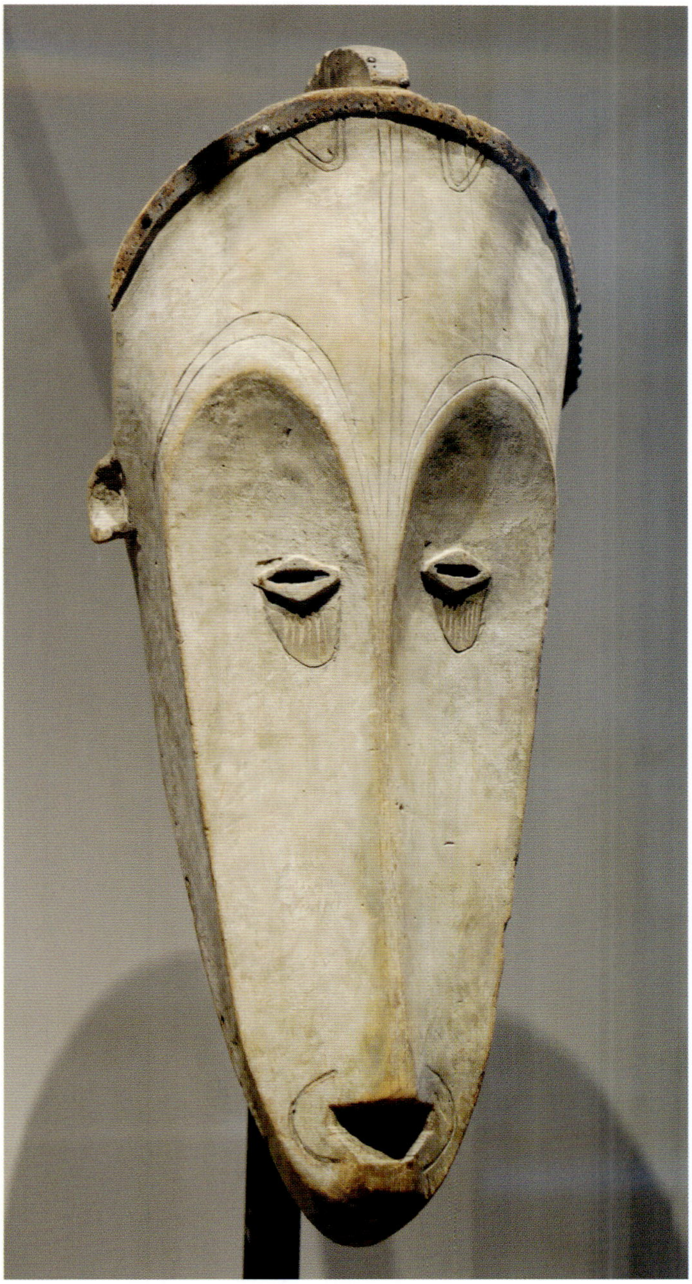

1

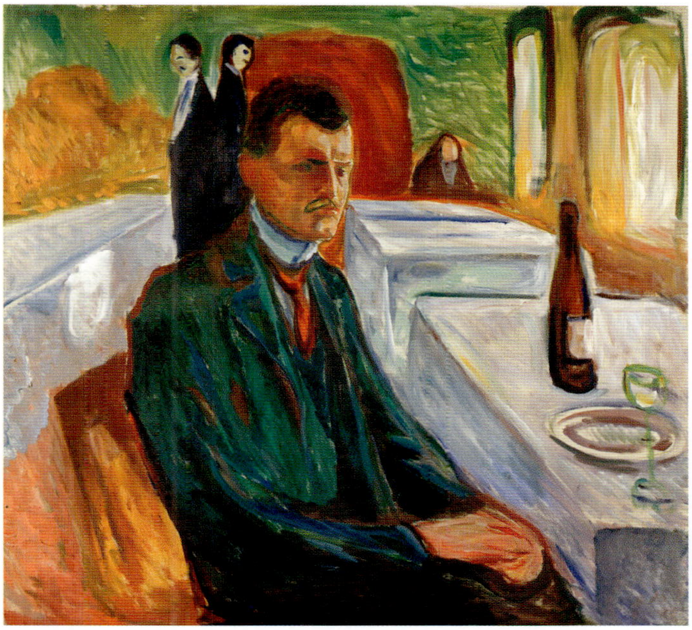

2

28 DISTRIBUTION

ARRANGEMENT ACROSS A SURFACE

The way in which elements are distributed across a surface is an important consideration in composition, particularly in abstract painting. This is especially true when the elements are small relative to the area of the canvas. Elements can be clustered or scattered, concentrated or dispersed. The viewer's eye tends to rush toward concentrations and moves more slowly in sparse areas. This makes a wide range of dynamics possible in which the eye is pulled or pushed in various directions.

Composition by distribution can be combined with other ideas. Elements can be set up in shapes or laid out in lines to suggest movement or convey meaning. Further reinforcement of these ideas can be achieved with the nature of the elements themselves. A narrow, pointed shape, for instance, will tend to create a greater sense of movement and direction than a soft, amorphous shape.

Careful control of distribution can confer extra properties on the elements in the work. They can be made to appear "sticky"—to have the tendency to stick together—or they can be made to feel airy and free floating.

The idea of distribution can also be important in organizing the color in a painting. The placement and grouping of related colors within a composition can greatly affect their appearance and function.

See also: *Composition* on page 44

1 Anonymous artist, ***Kata-gami***, umbrellas, water and pine needle clusters, late nineteenth century, stencil, mulberry paper, lacquer made from persimmon juice, silk thread, 321 mm, 12.64 × 16.73 in (32.1 × 42.5 cm)

2 Claude Monet (1840–1926) ***Waterlilies***, 1920–26, Oil on canvas, 86 3/16 × 237 in (219 × 602 cm)

In this mural, Monet orchestrates the natural distribution of water lilies into clusters, pulling the viewer's eye along the surface of the picture. The simple use of perspective allows the artist to achieve an intimation of depth even as the painting itself remains essentially flat.

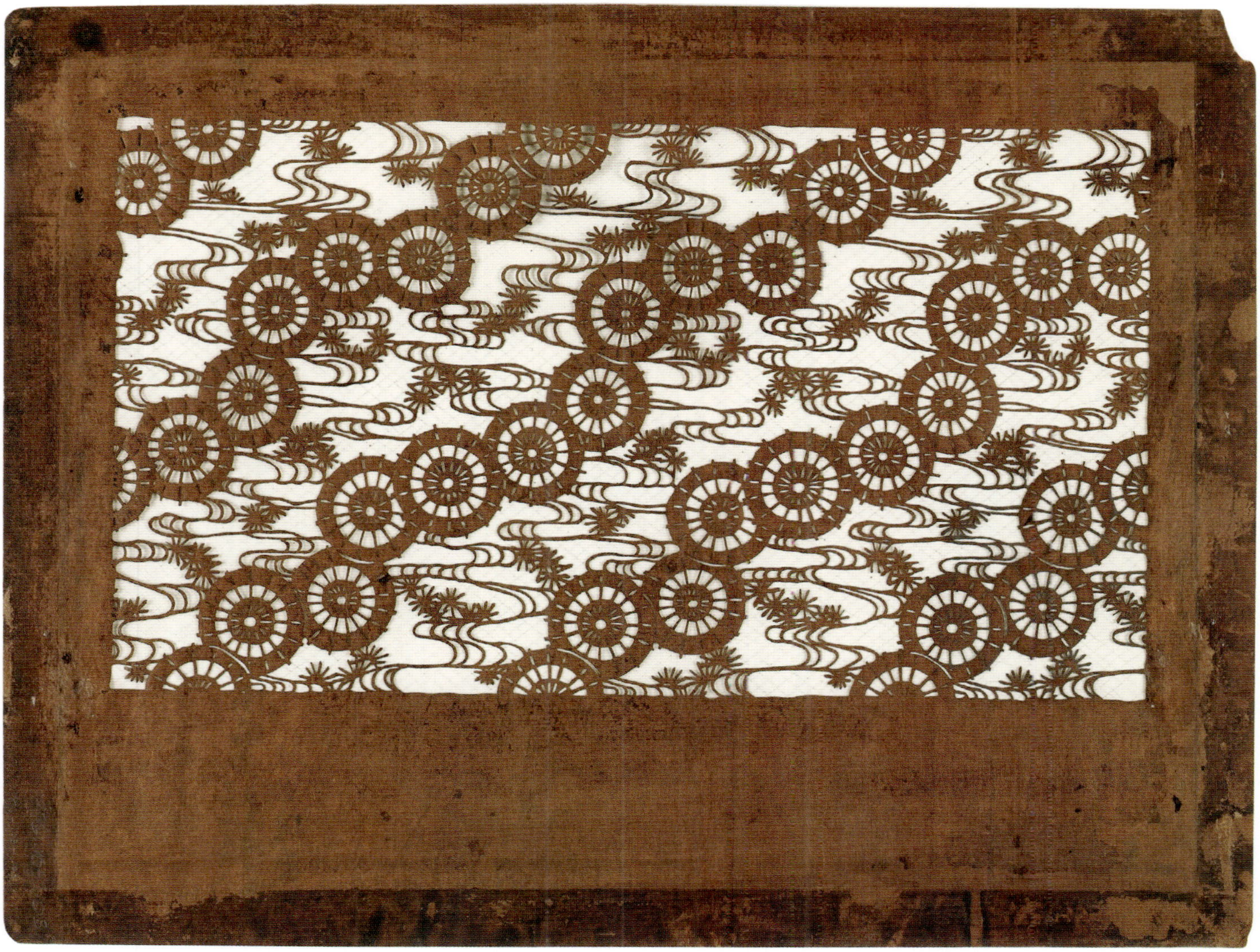

1

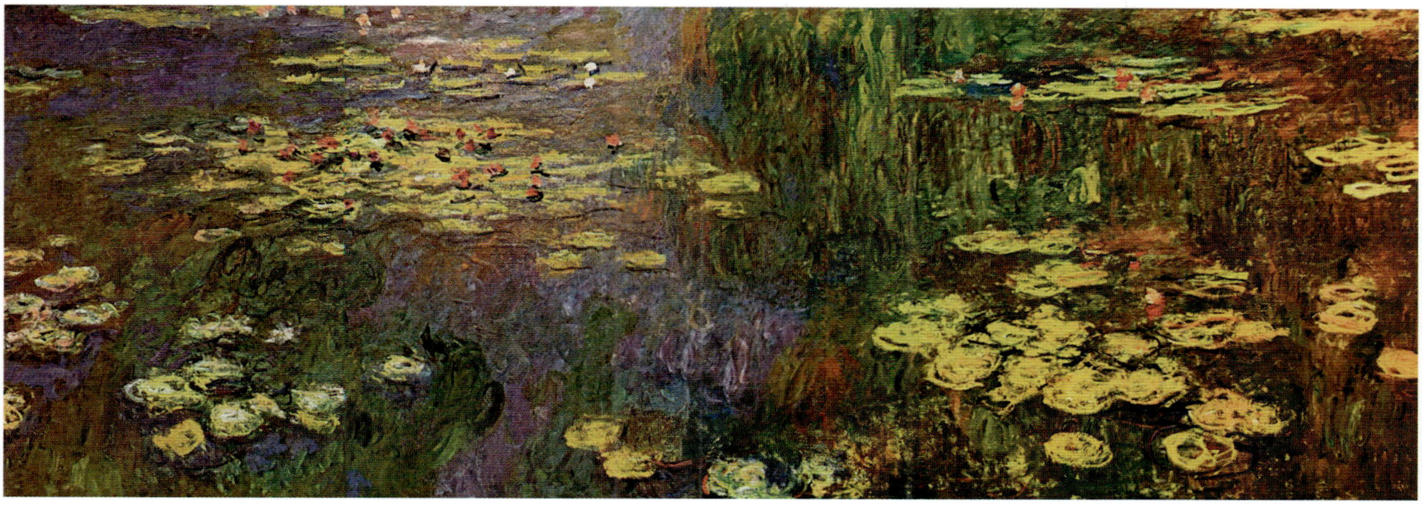

2

29 DRAWING LANGUAGE

THE SYNTAX OF DESCRIPTION

In the Western tradition, drawing is a complex array of approaches to description and notation. The choice of a particular technique or strategy depends on the artist's intention for the work.

STRATEGIES

- **Simple outline**
  A line is drawn around the shape of an object. It can be modulated in thickness, continuity, and strength of movement (see *Linear Basics* on page 104).
- **Contour**
  Lines are drawn along the contours of a form, describing the interior in more or less the same way that a contour map operates. This allows the artist to make a precise description of form, an approach often favored by sculptors.
- **Hatching**
  Multiple lines are drawn closely together in parallel to create areas of tone. The lightness or darkness of the tone depends on the concentration of hatched lines. This technique is often used in etching and pen and ink. The lines can also be built in crisscross fashion, a technique called cross-hatching.
- **Contour hatching**
  This is a combination of contour drawing and hatching in which contour lines are placed only in the shadows and built running across each other in crisscross fashion. This allows for both the accurate description of volume and the creation of a strong tonal illusion. It was a technique much favored by Renaissance draftsmen and became the basic vocabulary of engraving.
- **Tone**
  Tone is built into the shadows to create an illusion of light. This can be achieved in many materials, including charcoal, conté crayon, pencil, and wash (see *Tone as Structure* on page 194).
- **Line and tone**
  Simple linear description can be combined with areas of tone to create a hybrid form of great flexibility. The most popular way of doing this is by combining pen lines with monochrome watercolor wash.
- **Colored pencil**
  Modern colored pencil technology allows for the addition of color to any of the approaches listed above. Hatching or crosshatching with a variety of hues allows the artist to build rich and subtle areas of color.
- **Pastel**
  Pastel techniques can combine the strengths of drawing and painting. Pastels create a much denser surface than colored pencils and can be built in successive layers to achieve a richness rivaling that of paint (see the Degas pastel on page 19).

1 Albrecht Dürer (1471–1528)
Female Nude Praying,
1497-1500, Pen and brown ink on laid paper, 8 7/16 × 5 3/8 in (21.5 × 13.7 cm)

The artist combines outline with contour hatching that builds into a loose tonal rendering. The varied weight of the line contributes to the sense of space and movement.

2 Albrecht Dürer (1471–1528)
Two Studies of an Elderly Man's Head, 17th century, After Sir Peter Paul Rubens, Pen and brown ink with brown wash on laid paper,
7 5/8 × 5 11/16 in (19.4 × 14.5 cm)

The form is laid out with a pen line and the tonal areas are then established with a wash. In some sections, both contour hatching and wash are used in combination.

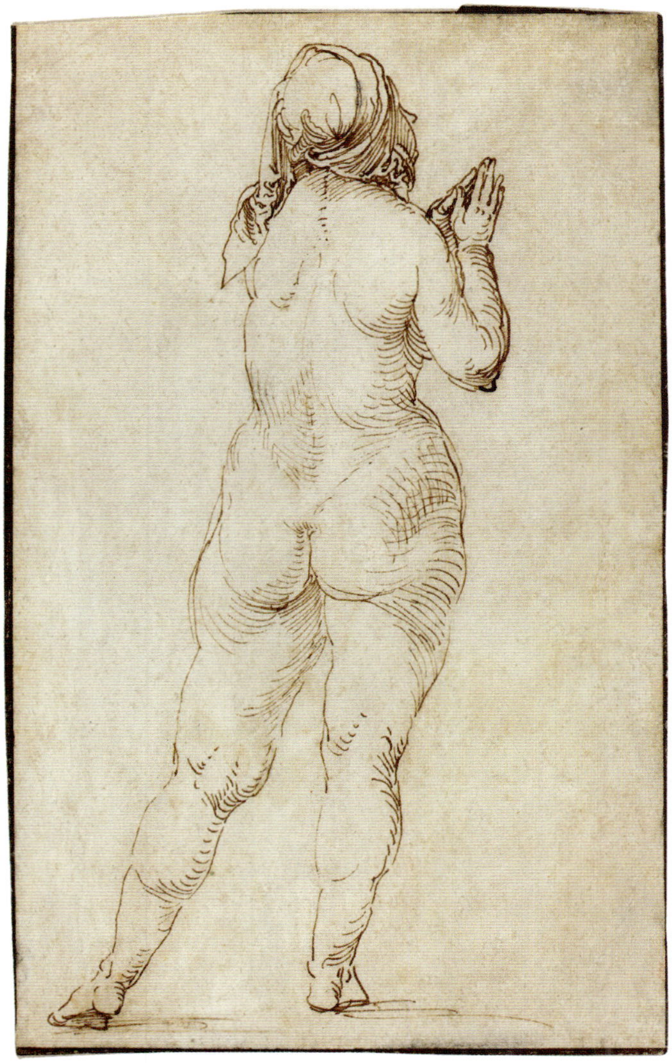

1

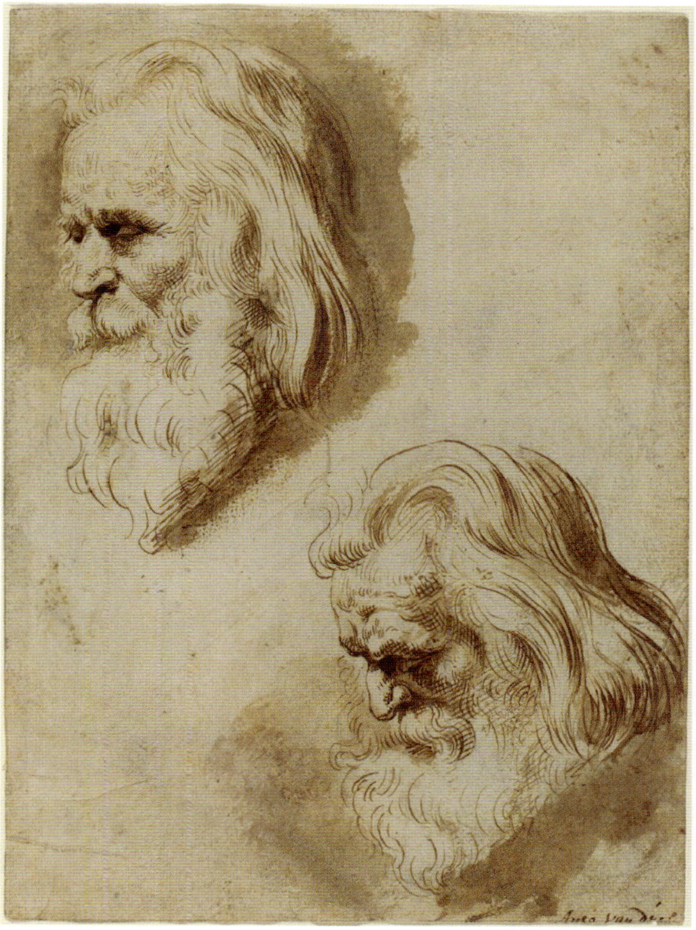

2

30 THE EMOTIVE OBJECT

THE ARTWORK ELICITS AN EMOTIONAL RESPONSE

The work of art can itself become an emotive force. When the artist seeks to create a powerful emotional reaction in the viewer, the enterprise is referred to as "expressionist." A variety of approaches and techniques can be used and combined to achieve this.

- **Exaggeration or distortion of the form of the subject**
  The artist might elongate, twist, compress, stretch, or otherwise distort the subject, creating an uneasy relationship to a normal realist representation.
- **Use of disturbing subject matter**
  The artist might depict subjects that incorporate emotionally charged themes, such as violence, alienation, and sexuality.
- **Use of heavy and very physical line**
  A heavy, wide line can carry a sense of weightiness and even brutality.
- **Severe angular shifts**
  The creation of acute angular relationships between elements in a painting or sculpture tends to bring about a dynamic sense of unease.
- **Use of strong and non-natural color**
  This can cause a visceral response in the viewer.
- **Heavy and stressed surfaces**
  The surface of the painting or sculpture can be made to feel stressed through heavy impasto, energetic brushing, or the addition of other materials into the paint.

HISTORY

Modern expressionism begins with Vincent Van Gogh and was taken up by the Norwegian artist Edvard Munch. A broader Expressionist movement began in Germany early in the twentieth century. Its principal exponents were Ernst Ludwig Kirchner (1880–1938), Erich Heckel (1883–1970), and Max Beckmann (1884–1950). In France, the work of Georges Rouault (1871–1958) and Chaim Soutine (1893–1943) also followed expressionist lines. In the 1980s, a Neo-Expressionist movement emerged, again primarily in Germany, championed by artists such as Anselm Kiefer (1945–) and Georg Baselitz (1938–).

See also: *Touch Communicates* on page 196; *Texture* on page 190; *Linear Basics* on page 104

1 Ernst Ludwig Kirchner (1880–1938)
Qualen der Liebe, 1915, Color woodcut from two blocks on wove paper, 13 1/16 × 8 9/16 in (33.2 × 21.7 cm)

Kirchner uses distorted form, unnatural color, and a dynamic angular composition to create a work that projects a powerful and disturbing energy.

2 Edvard Munch (1863–1944)
The Scream, 1893, Oil, Tempera and Pastel on Cardboard, 36 × 28 7/8 in (91.4cm × 73.3cm)

Munch uses a heavy and brutally insistent line in combination with distorted form and unnatural color to create one of the most famously disturbing images of the modern era. The deliberate flattening of the image allows the artist to connect the line running through the right side of the figure with the lines running into the landscape, thereby combining the two elements in an unnerving fashion.

2 Vincent Van Gogh (1853–90)
Wheatfield with Cypresses, 1889, Oil on canvas, 29 × 36¾ in (73 × 93.4cm)

The artist uses heavy line, abrupt angular changes, and exaggerated color to create a sense of energetic movement and unease.

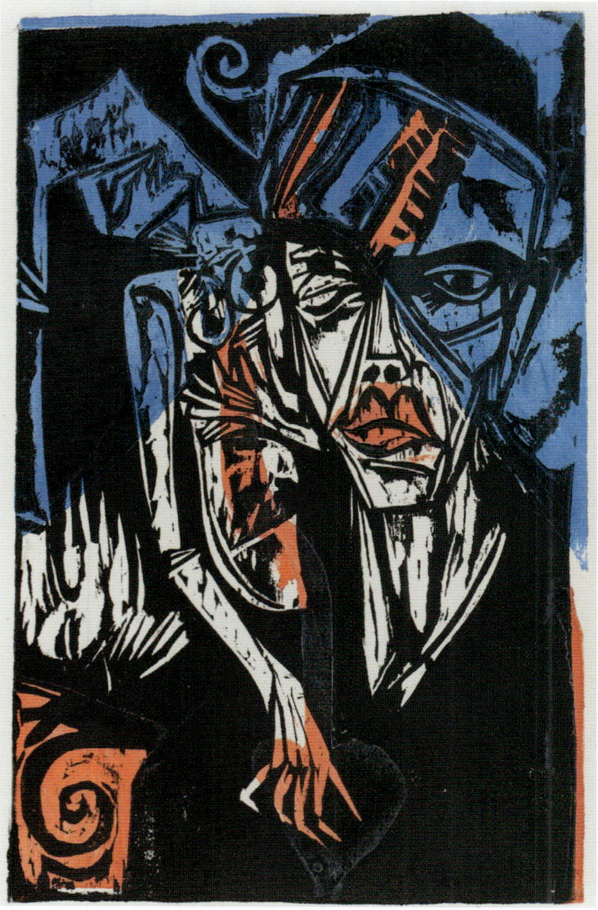

1

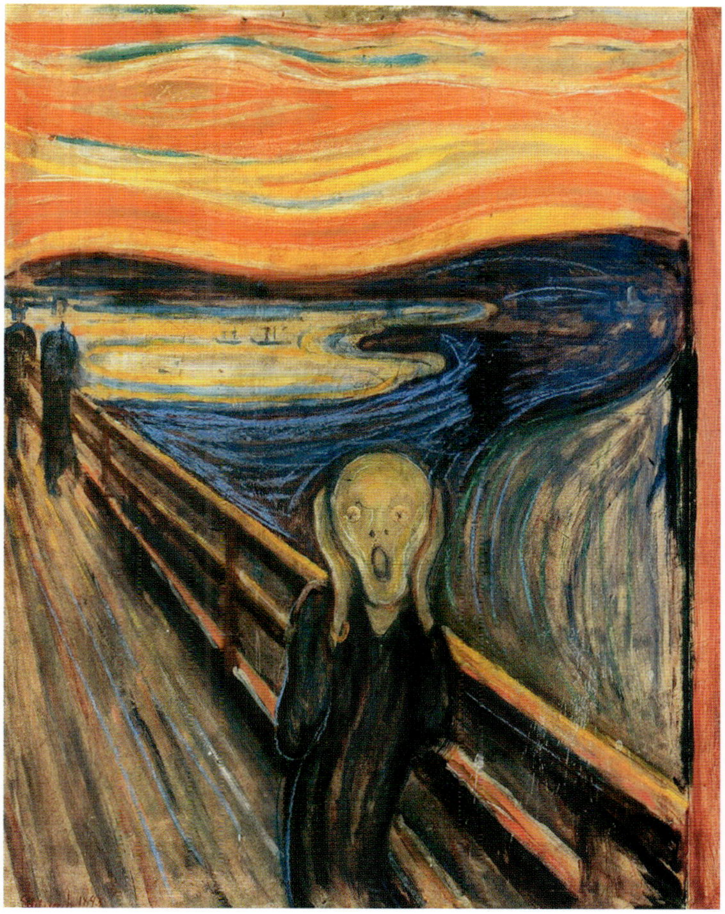

2

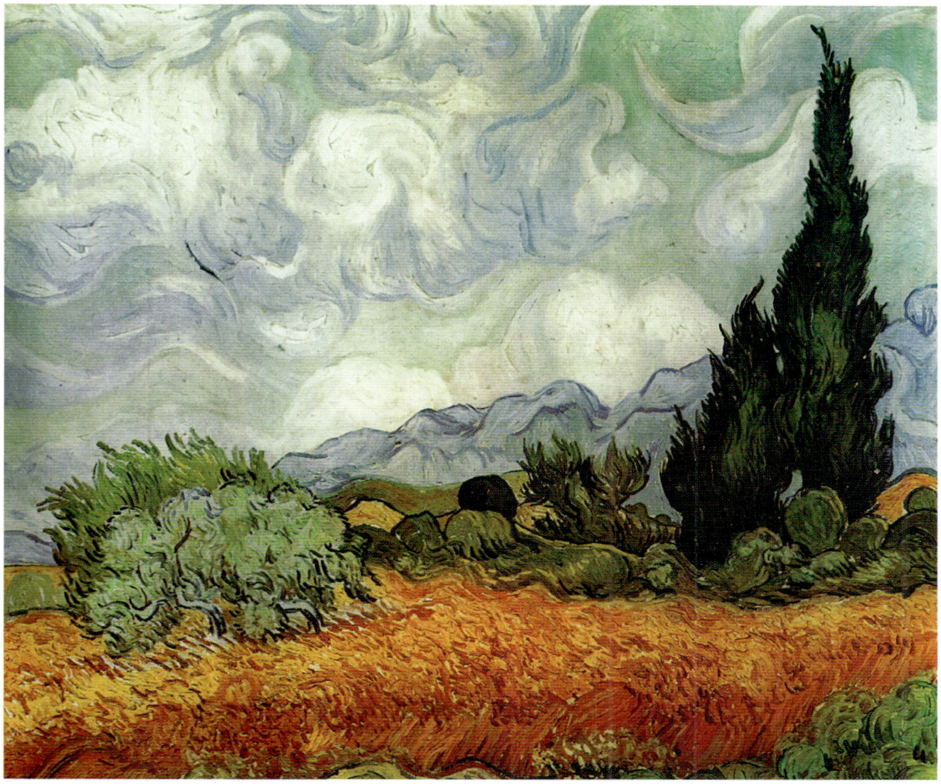

3

31 EROTIC ART

THE AESTHETICS AND POLITICS OF DESIRE

An image can be sexually interesting in its own right, and erotic artworks appear in more or less all cultures, both ancient and modern. Excavations at Pompeii, for instance, have unearthed troves of sexually explicit frescos.

In post-Roman Western art there is a history of unease with erotic imagery, attributable perhaps to the way in which Christian religious practice sought to control and contain sexual behavior. Erotic works appear in medieval art only in discreet places, hidden under choir seats or relegated to obscure corners of illuminated manuscripts. In the Renaissance, artists made sexually explicit images, but they were generally displayed only in private. Eroticism was acceptable in publicly displayed imagery that related to the classical past, and a certain canon of scenes illustrating the sexual behavior of classical deities came into being. Many artists painted Jupiter and Io, Leda and the Swan, or simply displayed a comely nude Venus. The arrival of printmaking threatened to open new markets for erotica. Giulio Romano (1499–1546) was quite safe in making a series of erotic drawings for a private client, but when Marcantonio Raimondi (1480–1534) made engravings of them under the title *I Modi*, the pope ordered the works confiscated and Raimondi jailed.

Limiting erotic imagery to the context of classical subjects, at least in publicly acceptable art, continued until the nineteenth century. With the advent of modernism this understanding dissolved. The writings of Freud and his followers at the end of the nineteenth century brought a new focus on sexuality and called into question norms of social and sexual behavior. In Paris, Manet painted *Le Dejéuner sur l'Herbe*, deliberately removing a classical nude from its "safe" setting by surrounding her with men in modern dress (see page 145). A few years later in Vienna, Gustav Klimt (1862–1918) and then Egon Schiele (1890–1918) began to make images that were newly raw and explicit.

Although there are many examples of erotic imagery in twentieth-century American art, it didn't become mainstream until pinup photographs and provocative movie stills found their way into pop art in the 1960s. In the 1970s and '80s, the advent of the gay rights movement freed photographer Robert Mapplethorpe (1946–1989) to make powerful homoerotic photographs. Today the art world, and the wider culture, is more tolerant than ever of sexual content. Contemporary painters such as John Currin (1962–) and Lisa Yuskavage (1962–) have enjoyed enormous success with paintings that explore erotic fantasies in graphic detail.

1 Egon Schiele (1890–1918)
Young Woman Resting on Both Elbows, 1917, Black chalk and gouache on paper, $17^{7}/_{16} \times 11^{5}/_{16}$ in (44.3 × 28.7 cm)

2 Betty Tompkins (1945–)
Kiss Painting #4, 2012, Oil on canvas, 60 × 72 in (152.4 × 182.9 cm)
Courtesy of Gallerie Radolphe Jansen, Brussels

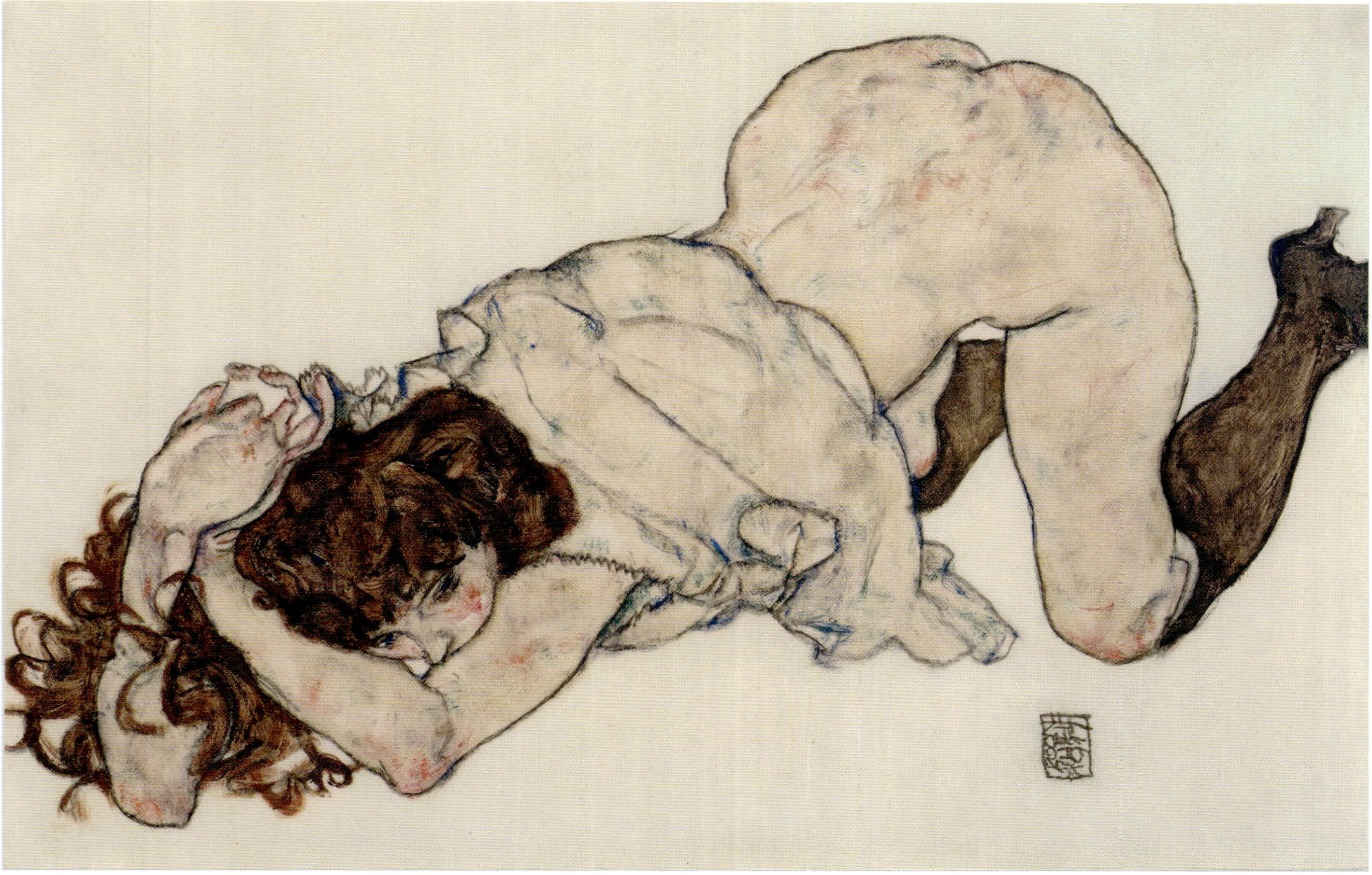

1

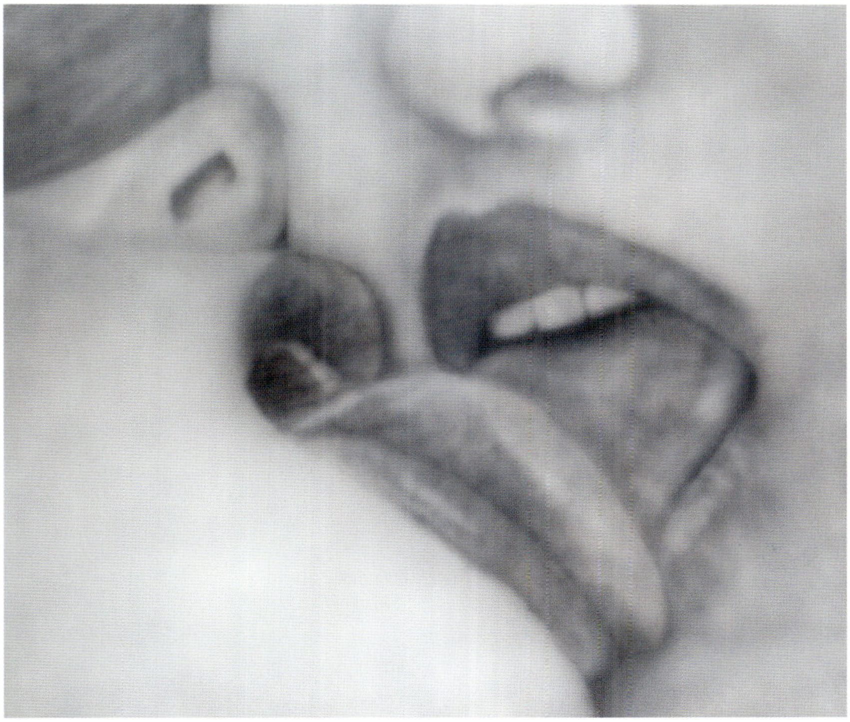

2

32 EXPRESSION IN THE ABSTRACT

TRANSMITTING FEELING THROUGH NON-OBJECTIVE IMAGERY

Art can elicit a powerful emotional response from the viewer by using abstract rather than figurative means. Abstract Expressionism, a 1950s American-based art movement, was the first to explore the possibilities of this approach. Its principal exponents were Willem De Kooning (1904–97), Jackson Pollock (1912–56), and Robert Motherwell (1915–91). These painters stripped down and fragmented figurative elements, remaking them as dynamic visual features composed of paint marks, drips, splashes, and heavily built surfaces. This new vocabulary was deployed in large-scale canvases creating a flattened pictorial space and bringing about a whole new form of painting.

STRATEGIES

- **Mark making through gesture**
  Large, energetic, and dynamic brush marks can record and even dramatize the physical gestures used to make them. This can have an immediate visceral effect on the viewer.
- **Scale**
  The sheer size and scope of an abstract painting can have an overwhelming physical and psychological impact.
- **Texture**
  Heavy impasto paint or addition of textural materials to the paint increases the physical presence and insistence of a painting.
- **Color and tone**
  Very high tonal contrast can be used for dramatic effect. Color palettes can be manipulated to achieve disturbing, mysterious, disquieting, or uncomfortable effects.
- **Surface tension**
  Expressive elements can be composed across a surface so that the entire painting feels taut and present.
- **Suggestion**
  While keeping a painting abstract, it is possible to deploy elements that suggest or hint at representational counterparts.

See also: *The Emotive Object* on page 68; *Texture* on page 190

1 Willem de Kooning (1904–97) ***Rosy-Fingered Dawn at Louse Point***, 1963, Oil on canvas, 80 × 70 in (203.5 × 177.8 cm)

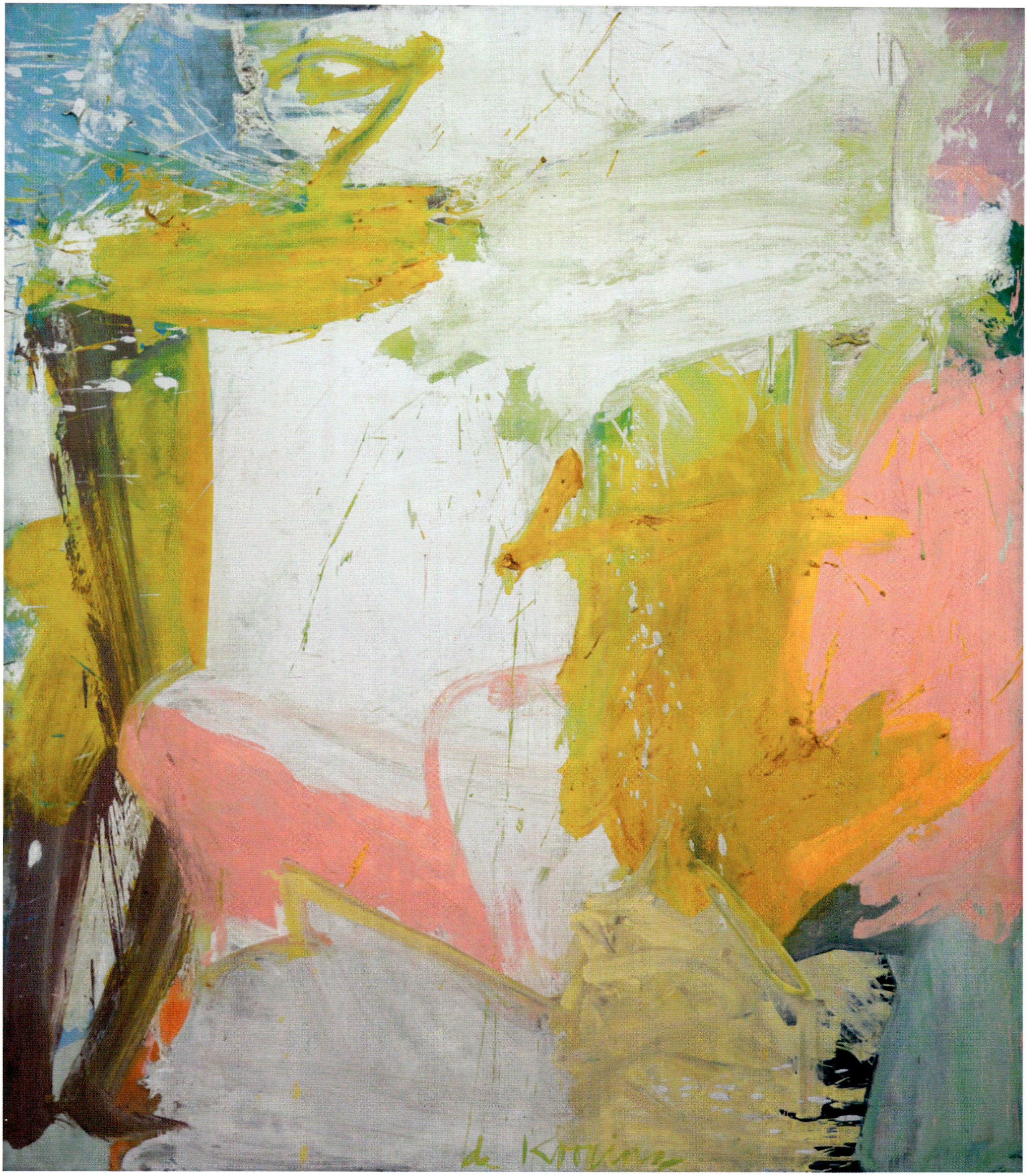

1

33 FANTASY AND VISIONARY ART

INVENTING NEW WORLDS

In fantasy art, the artist renders a credible and coherent image of a world that does not, and in many cases cannot, exist. There has always been some element of fantasy at play in Western painting, particularly in religious and allegorical painting. However, fantasy as a genre first gained real currency with the advent of the Romantic movement toward the end of the eighteenth century, when a new interest in the powers of the imagination and the autonomy of the artist as creator came to the fore. Goya (1746–1828) made many fantastic works in which he explored sometimes alarming and highly personal imagery. In the same period, the Swiss artist Henry Fuseli (1741–1825) and the English artist William Blake (1757–1827) also pursued fantastic imagery. Fantasy again enjoyed currency toward the end of the nineteenth century when Symbolist artists like Gustave Moreau (1826–98) and later James Ensor (1860–1949) used avant-garde painting styles to conjure highly personal and sometimes disturbing images.

In the twentieth century, the Surrealist movement embraced fantasy techniques to explore images that were connected with the workings of the unconscious mind. Other artists deployed fantasy from time to time, perhaps most notably Marc Chagall (1887–1985), who combined a kind of lyrical open cubist style with fantastic elements. Since World War II, fantasy art has largely remained in the realm of illustration, where highly rendered imagery is at a premium for certain genres of popular literature, science fiction, science fantasy, comic books, and animated films.

Visionary art is a subgenre of fantasy art in which the artist creates images that purport to show religious revelation or apocalyptic scenarios that may have a religious dimension. The work of William Blake, with its highly personal and idiosyncratic religious imagery, fits into this category.

APPROACHES

- **Anthropomorphism**
  Animals and objects take on human characteristics.
- **Otherworldly settings**
  Fantasy worlds often feature heightened color, unnatural lighting, and flora and fauna unknown on earth.
- **Improbable or impossible happenings**
  Gravity may be suspended, humans and objects may behave or respond in unnatural or unexpected ways.
- **Recombination**
  Features or denizens of the natural world may be recombined. Fairies, for instance, are miniature humans with wings. Centaurs are a combination of men and horses.
- **Theatrical illumination**
  Visionary art, in particular, often makes use of strikingly powerful light sources, generally emanating from above.

1 William Blake (1757–1827)
The Great Red Dragon and the Woman Dressed with the Sun, 1805–10, Watercolor on paper, 15¾ × 12 13/16 in (40 × 32.5 cm)

2 Gustave Moreau (1826–98)
Oedipus and the Sphinx, 1864, Oil on canvas, 81¼ x 41¼ in (206.4 × 104.8 cm)

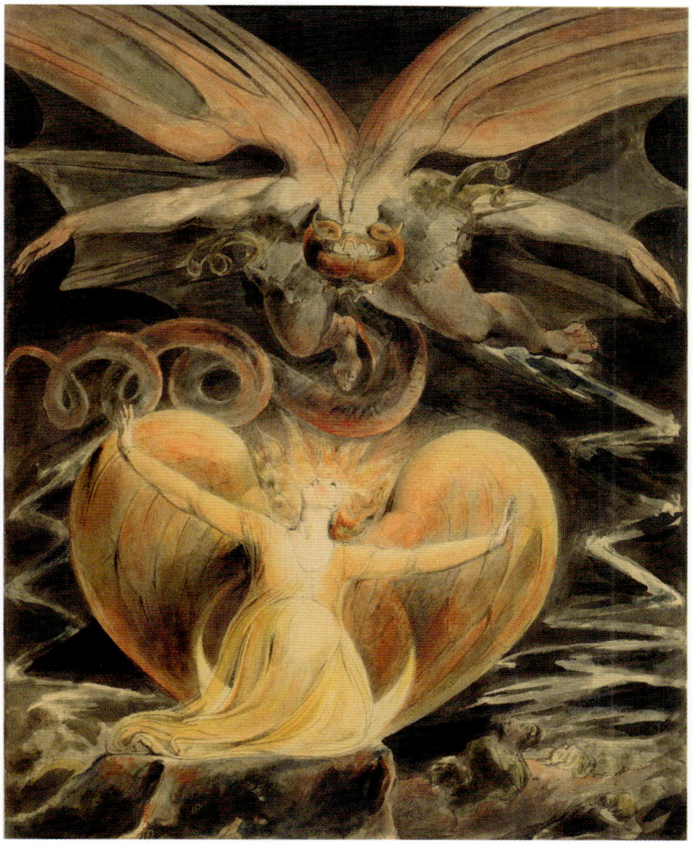

1

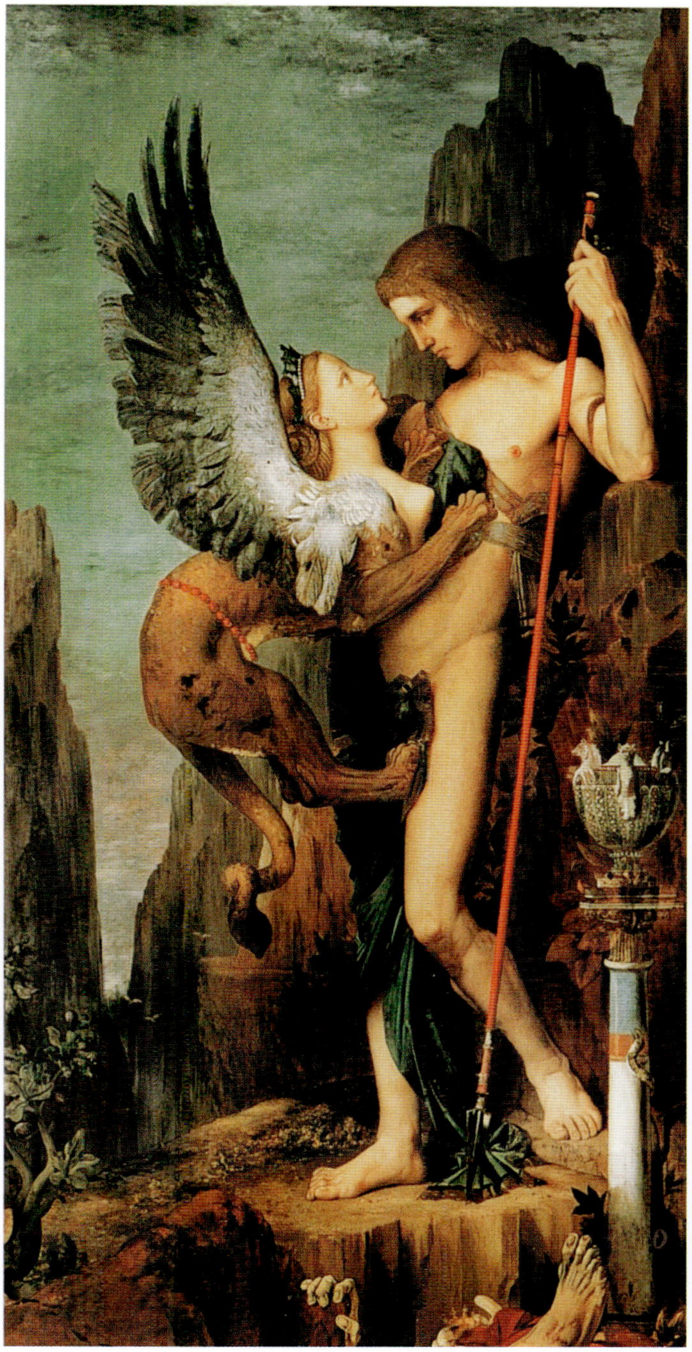

2

34 FINISH

POLISHING TO PERFECTION

"Finish" in art refers to the final polishing-up of a work, especially when it implies the last manipulation to secure a seamless illusion in representational painting. A painting by Jean Auguste Domnique Ingres (1780–1867), with its flawlessly executed rendering and fine glazing, would be considered to have "finish." This kind of crafting and its ambition to obtain a dazzling illusion honed to perfection was seen as a highly desirable component of Neoclassical and academic painting in the nineteenth century. Conversely, painters of the Romantic persuasion preferred more open and direct painting styles that did not embrace a sense of finish and could be left in a somewhat raw state.

Whether finish is desirable in a contemporary work depends in large part on the intention of the artist and the thrust of the piece. A photorealist painting will demand a high finish, while an expressionist work will usually find it unnecessary and counterproductive. In general, modernism avoided highly finished painting, associating it with the academies and outmoded styles of painting that sought to produce high quality history paintings and fine portraiture in previous centuries. For the most part, the moderns adopted a sense of adequacy in craftsmanship (see *Sufficiency of Means* on page 182). However, some postmodern painters have revisited finish for effect. The erotic works of John Currin (1962–) use a high finish in a way that brings to mind fashion photography and certain kinds of pornography. The German artist Gerhard Richter (1932–) has explored a kind of dead commercial finish in some of his representational paintings.

TECHNIQUES

Techniques used are different for painting and sculpture.

- **Painting**
  Layers of glaze or thin paint are built up and blended with a fan brush to achieve almost photographic smoothness. The finished work may then be varnished, sometimes with several coats, to give a completely smooth surface.
- **Sculpture**
  Depending on the material, sculpture can be polished and coated in a wide variety of ways to create a smooth and seamless finish.

1 Lawrence Alma-Tadema (1836–1912)
Unconscious Rivals, 1893, Oil on canvas, 17¾ × 24⅝ in (45.1 × 62.6 cm)

Typical of late Victorian English painting, this work combines a high finish with a strong literal narrative.

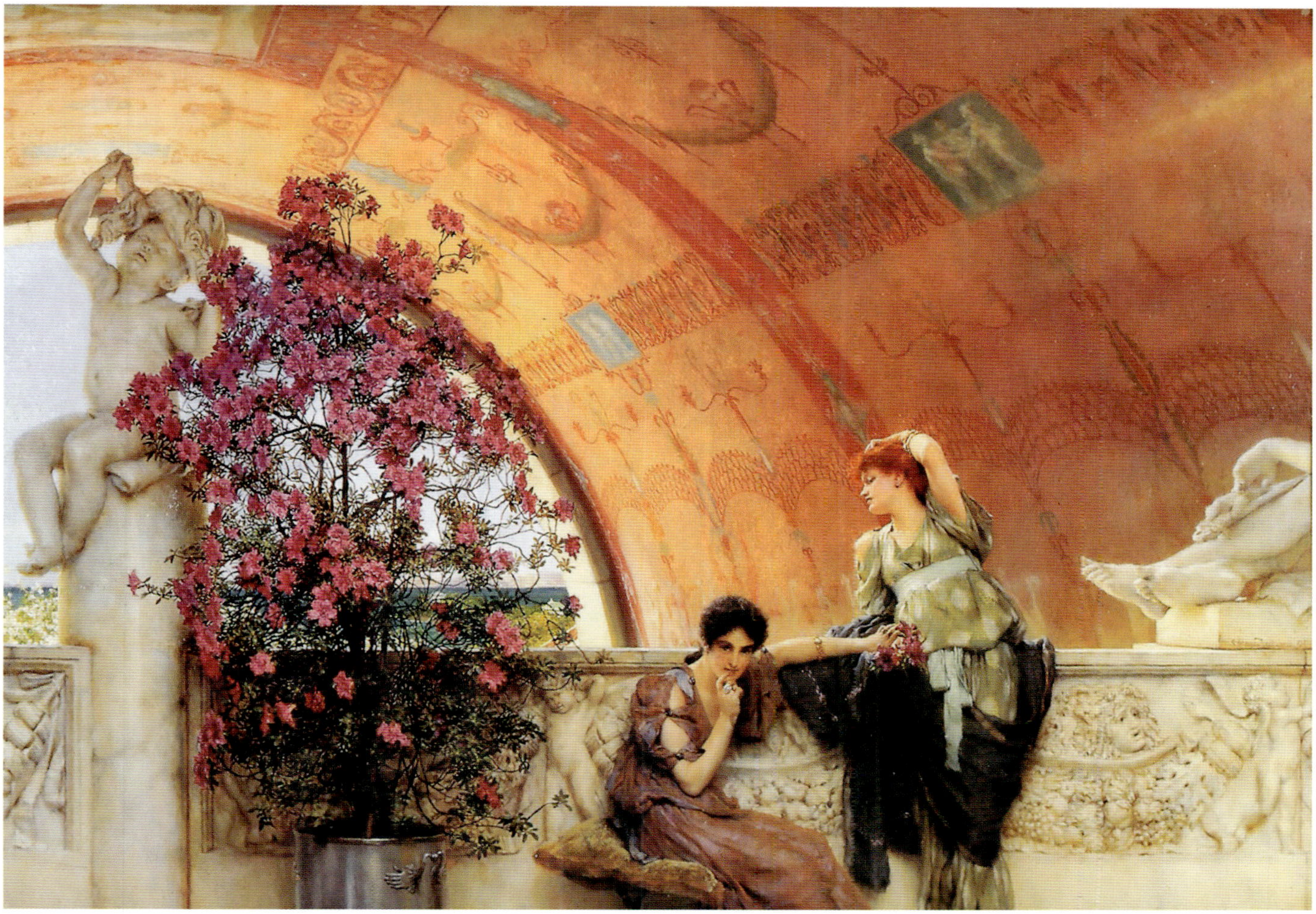

1

35 FORMAL INNOVATION

GROUND-BREAKING ARTWORKS CAN CHANGE THE WHOLE GAME

From time to time, an artwork is produced that radically changes the formal means by which art may be made. Such changes usually signal not only a change in style and technical possibilities, but also broader cultural shifts. For example, development of fully rendered perspectival space in fifteenth-century Italy was not only an extraordinary formal innovation, it also heralded a broader intellectual and scientific movement, evidenced by humanistic ideals, new discoveries in mathematics, and a fresh spirit of intellectual enquiry.

Not all formal innovations are quite so radical, but they are always important. Caravaggio's development of a highly theatrical presentation of human drama, clothed in a newly pungent sense of realism, was both shocking and persuasive to his audience at the end of the sixteenth century. Similarly, the Romantics Joseph Mallord William Turner (1789–1862), John Constable (1776–1837), Francesço Goya (1748–1828), and Èugene Delacroix (1798–1863) introduced innovations in which spontaneity, open brushing, and highly flexible compositions replaced more stable and calculated approaches to painting, reflecting a sea change in sensibility across an entire culture.

The next great formal innovation was Impressionism in the 1870s, one of the most profound shifts in representational language, in which artists discovered a whole new way to recreate a sense of light in painting. Again this came at a time of enormous social, political, intellectual, and cultural upheaval. New discoveries in science and optics combined with a new sense of the nature of art and the role of the artist to bring this about.

From the late nineteenth century onward, the pace of formal innovation accelerated as social and political change also began to move at a faster pace. Postimpressionism, Symbolism, Fauvism, Cubism, Futurism, Orphism, Dadaism, Surrealism, and Expressionism each presented new formal innovations all within a space of fifty years or so. The second half of the twentieth century was no less prolific. The advent of Abstract Expressionist painting constituted another quite radical innovation in the way that painting can function and be appreciated. Similarly, Minimalism and Conceptualism also mark entirely new beginnings for art making, offering new visual languages, means of presentation, and aesthetics.

It is worth noting that formal innovation is nearly always associated with art of the highest quality. On the other hand, formal innovation is not a prerequisite for good art and is still a comparatively rare phenomenon.

1 Pietro Perugino (1446–1523)
The Gift of the Keys to Saint Peter, 1481-2, Fresco, 11 × 18 ft (3.4 × 5.5 m), Sistine Chapel

The mastery of perspective was one of the great formal innovations in Western art.

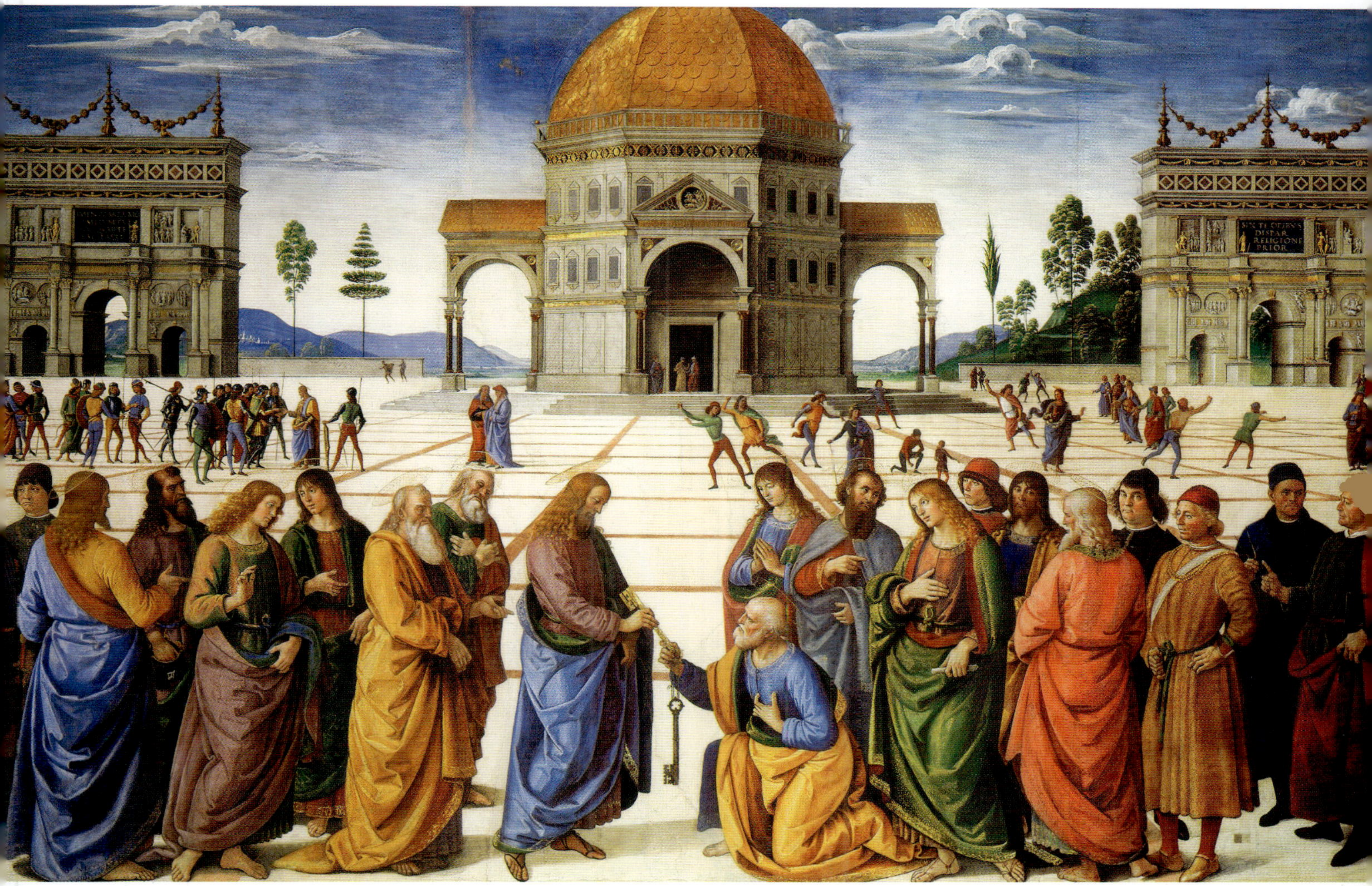

1

36 FORM RENDERED

DESCRIBING THREE-DIMENSIONAL FORM IN TWO DIMENSIONS

Rendering three-dimensional forms on a two-dimensional surface is one of the central recurring tasks of representational painting. While both ancient and medieval painters made some headway with rendering, it wasn't until the Renaissance that artists finally discovered how to make a completely comprehensive and consistent description of form in space. An early example is *The Marriage of the Arnolfini* by Jan Van Eyck (1390–1441), painted in 1432. The artist has succeeded in meshing extremely credible drawing with meticulous tracking of the tonal and color changes across all the various forms in the painting. In Italy, artists made a similar journey from an essentially linear art to a fully rendered version of three-dimensional form. The High Renaissance found Michelangelo, Raphael, and Leonardo da Vinci all demonstrating mastery of rendering.

In practice, successful rendering of form relies on three interlocking tasks. First, the drawing or outline must be accurate. Second, the tonal change across the form as the light strikes it must be recorded accurately. Third, the color change across the form must be tracked with some precision.

One of the features of rendering that presents the most difficulty is the change of color with the play of light across the form. When a form is illuminated, the viewer perceives the color to be different at each point on the object. Usually it is not sufficient when rendering a form to simply adjust the tone of the local color. It is rather necessary to secure a sense of the changes of the optical or perceived color.

See also: *Underpainting* on page 202

TECHNIQUES

- **Monochrome underpainting**
  Painting an image in a monochrome, usually a muted warm color, allows for adjustment of drawing and tone before the business of color is addressed. The color is applied on top in glazes or with stippling so that a sense of the underpainting is transmitted from beneath. This usually results in a more powerful sense of form.
- **Grayscale and palette control**
  Academic painters often found it advantageous to lay out a grayscale on the palette and then mix color in strings or runs, using the grayscale to accurately measure the tonal position of the color.
- **Finish**
  Rendering smooth forms, such as flesh or fabric, can require soft gradations that involve blending painted surfaces. Traditionally, artists use a fan brush to achieve this, dragging the very top of the paint surface in multiple directions with a light touch.

1 Jean Auguste Domnique Ingres (1780–1867)
The Grand Odalisque, 1814,
Oil on canvas, 35$^{13}/_{16}$ × 63¾ in (91 × 162 cm)

2 Ingres left unfinished this second version of ***The Grand Odalisque***, revealing his underpainting technique. Color would have been added in glazes on top of this monochrome rendering.

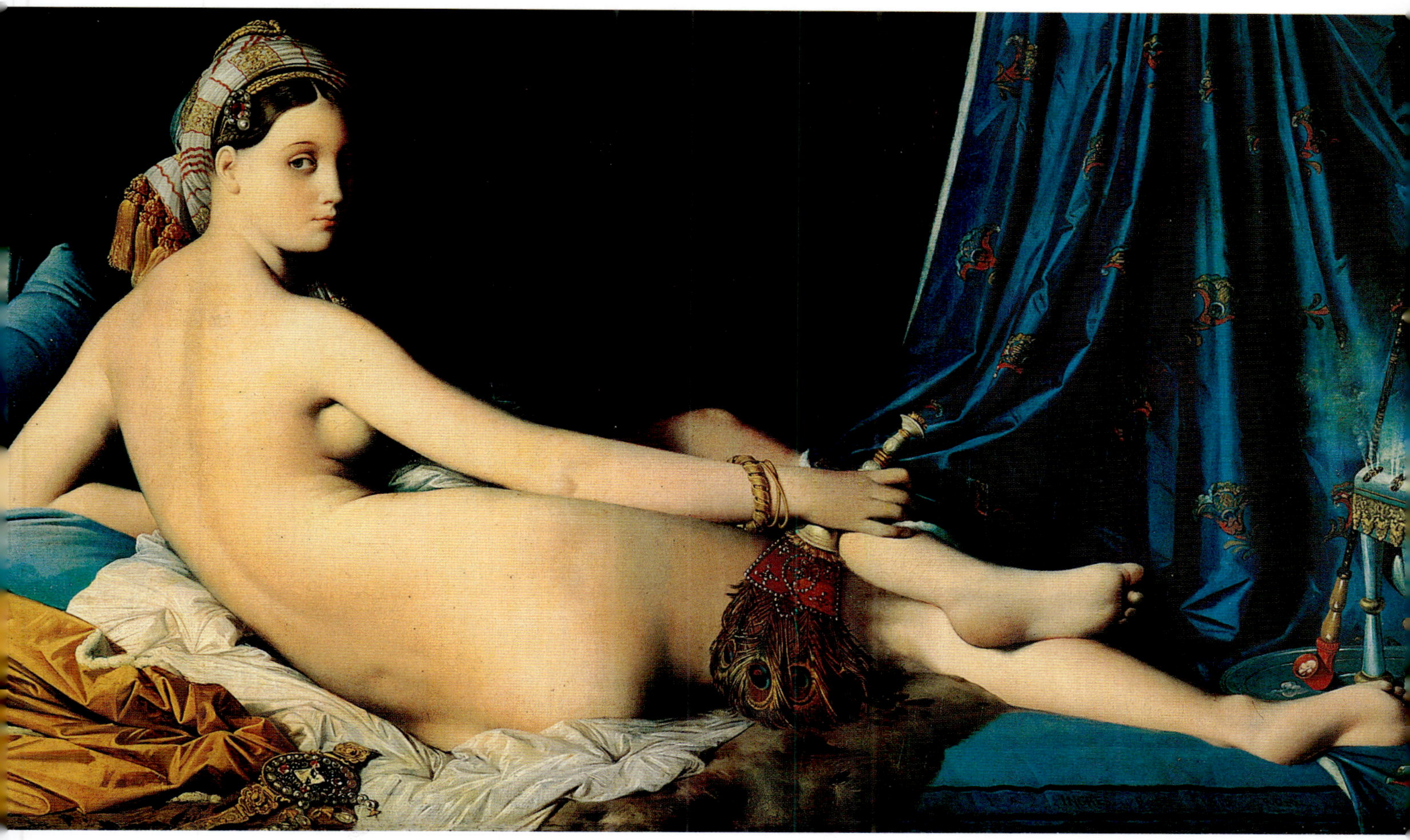

1

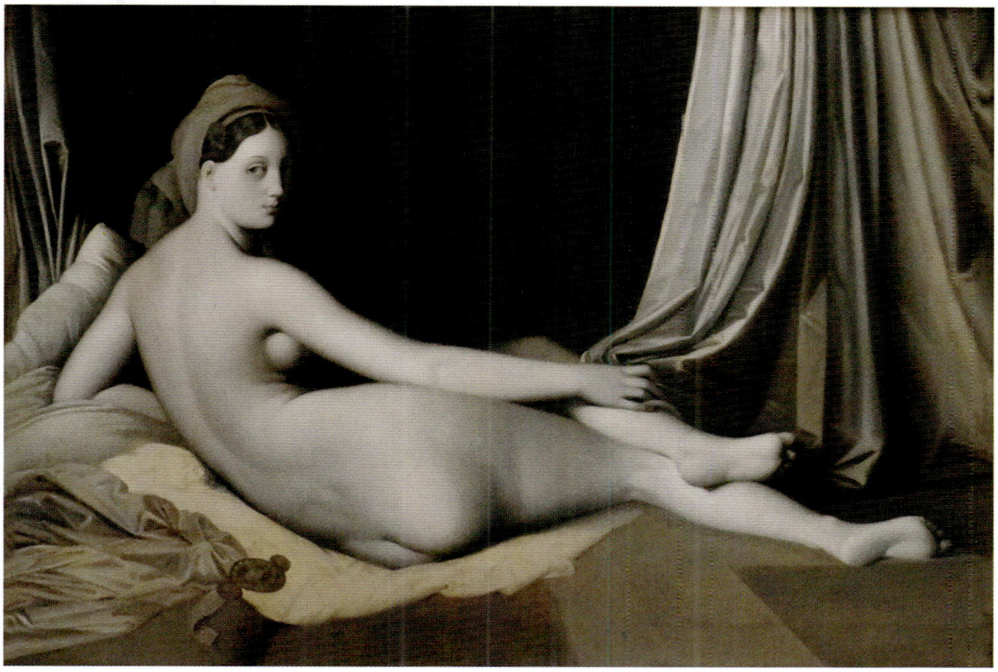

2

37 GENDER

AN ESSENTIAL BIOLOGICAL DISTINCTION AFFECTS WHO PARTICIPATES IN ART AND HOW

Since the inception of the feminist movement in the 1960s, there has been much discussion about the nature of art made by women and the level of participation of women in art. The basic questions are as follows:

- Is there a difference between the art made by men and women?
- Given that women have been historically underrepresented in the arts, does this show that a male-dominated culture has consistently discounted the qualities or concerns of women's art? Or does it mean that in their traditional (and biological) roles as mothers, women have not had the time, freedom, and professional access to gain the skills and experience needed to achieve excellence?
- What steps can be taken to increase the representation of women in the arts?

The answer to the first question has been studied in some depth in large-scale studies of children's drawings. These provide overwhelming evidence that boys and girls consistently display marked differences in drawing and that these are almost entirely content based. Boys tend to draw more active, violent, and machine images, often embracing war. Girls tend to draw more passive activities and choose more natural subjects, such as flowers and landscapes.

While such findings are not disputed, many feminists contend that gender roles are assigned by societal pressure. This view is somewhat undermined by evidence that unsupervised children self-organize into gender groups and that the establishment of gender identity is an important part of socialization. How far childhood differences in art making extend into adulthood is open to question. Certainly the difference is far less marked, if it exists at all. In those few cases where women have achieved major recognition, their art compares in quality and style to the best of their male contemporaries. In her seminal 1971 essay, "Why Are There No Great Women Artists?" Linda Nochlin argues that over the centuries women have not been admitted to the apprenticeships and schooling required to achieve the highest standards of art.

How then to bring more women into the art world? That challenge was taken up by Judy Chicago (1939–), the most prominent feminist artist of the 1970s. While teaching a women-only class at Fresno State College, she opened private studio space for her students and encouraged close cooperation and networking to develop and promote their art. Similarly, many organizations sprang up during the 1970s to promote women's art. Since then, new generations of female artists have embraced careers in art, but lists of top-selling artists continue to be dominated by men.

1 Claudia DeMonte (1947–)
Abundance: Shoes, 2011, Cast bronze, 8.5 × 6 in (21.6 × 15.2 cm)

Demonte addresses issues of female fetish in a playful but direct manner.

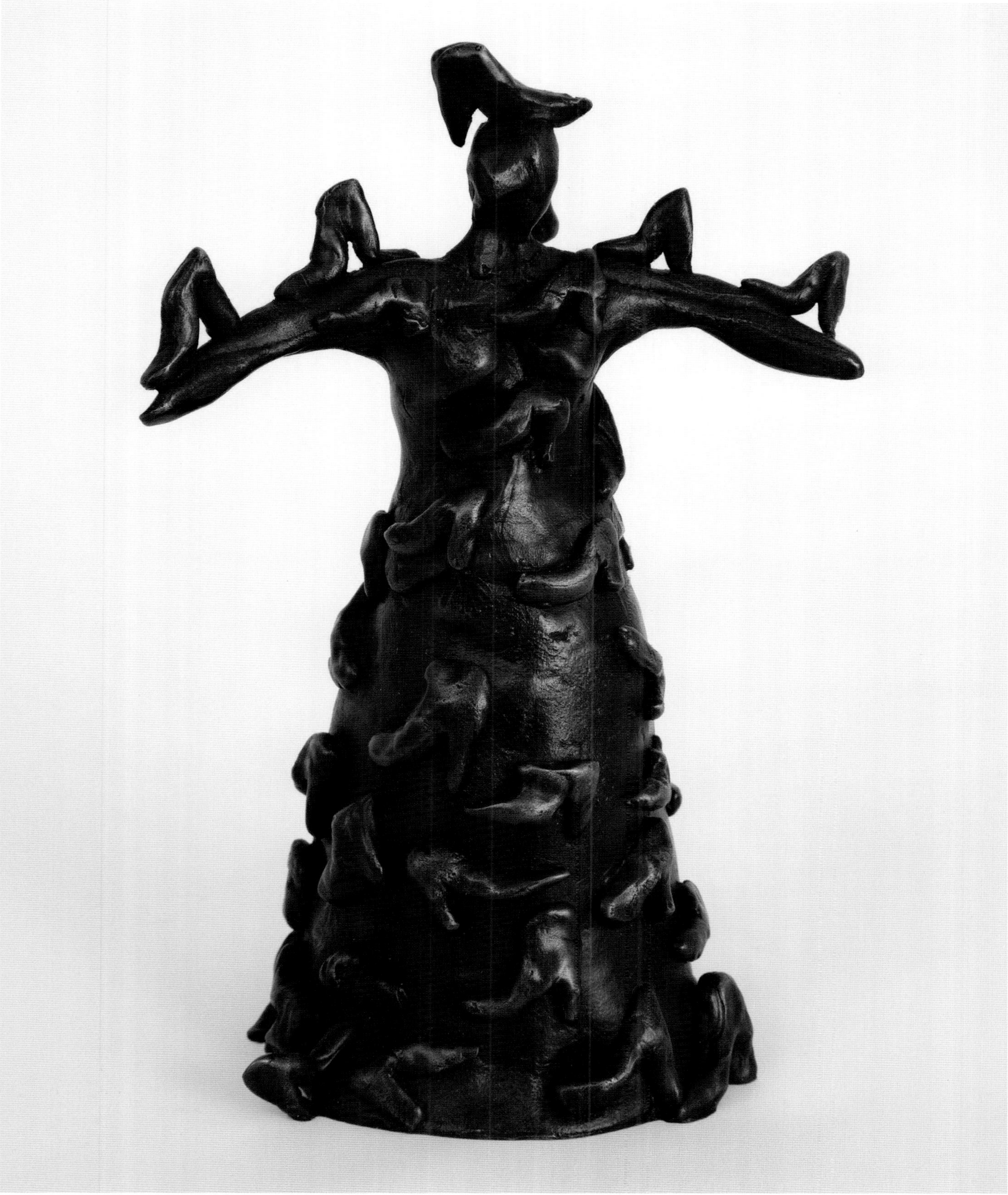

1

38 HARMONY

ELEMENTS WORKING TOGETHER FOR THE GOOD OF THE WHOLE

Harmony is achieved in a work of art when all its parts are integrated into a whole in which the relationships between the elements are mutually beneficial and aesthetically pleasing. In music, harmony is a result of certain mathematical relationships between notes. Mathematical relationships can also play a role in visual harmony where variations in shapes, areas, and angles have some sort of mathematical consistency. Similarly, colors that stand in an orderly relationship to each other within a color solid will tend to feel more harmonious than those in a disorderly relationship. However, perception of color can be influenced by a great many factors, including context, personal association, minute variations in color purity, saturation, and hue, all of which make a scientific recipe for harmony all but impossible. In the last resort, harmony is an aesthetic response, a judgment of feeling as much as an objective measure.

The obverse of harmony is discordancy, which results when relationships are disordered, chaotic, or stridently opposed. Discordancy is sometimes exploited by visual artists for effect. Henri Matisse (1869–1954) deployed discordant color in many of his paintings during the Fauvist era.

STRATEGIES

- **Shapes**
  Groupings of shapes that have similar characteristics will tend to form harmonious compositions.
- **Proportions**
  Elements that differ in scale by ratios that are consistent will tend to confer harmony. Similarly, intervals within a composition that stand in simple and consistent proportions to each other will also confer a sense of clarity and harmony.
- **Color**
  There are many theories of harmonious color, most of which involve the application of simple geometries to a color wheel or color solid. The most simple of these is the use of complementary colors, which will give a dynamic balance to a composition. A slightly less active harmony is achieved with a so-called "split complementary" where, say, a red is replaced by a red-violet and a red-orange and placed within a composition opposed to a green. Applying other geometric shapes to a color wheel, such as rectangles or triangles, also yield simple harmonies. For a quieter effect, artists can choose analogous harmonies, arrangements of colors that are very close together on the color wheel.
- **Association**
  Harmony by association is most often achieved with color where a palette that is associated with, say, autumn conveys a sense of order because the viewer makes the same association and accepts the combination as natural.

1 Georges Seurat (1859–91)
The Seine at the Grande Jatte, 1888, Oil on canvas, $25\frac{9}{16} \times 32\frac{5}{16}$ in (65 x 82 cm)

An example of triadic harmony where greens are balanced by blues and a beige (yellow-orange). The sense of harmony is enhanced by the inclusion of warm and cool versions of each hue.

2 Robert Delaunay (1885–1941)
Nude Woman Reading, 1920, Oil on canvas, $36\frac{13}{16} \times 32\frac{3}{16}$ in (93.5 x 81.7 cm)

Soft interlocking shapes form a harmonious grouping. The color forms a simple harmony in which the major pairs of complimentaries—blue/orange, yellow/violet, and red/green—are balanced.

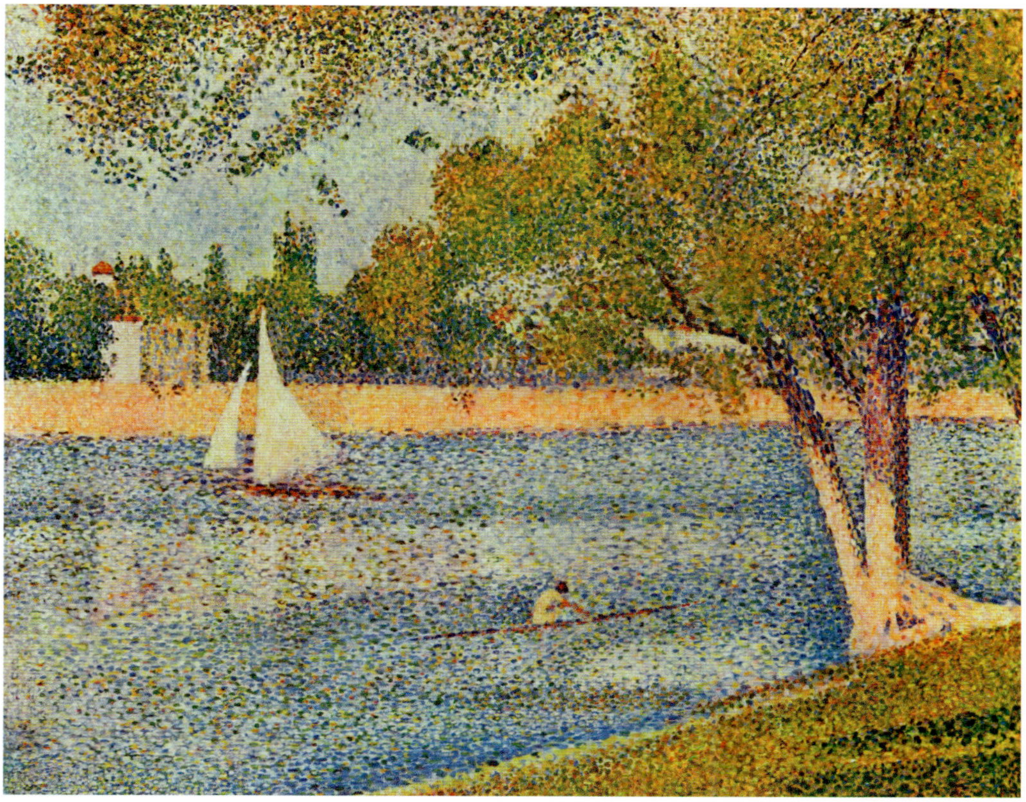

1

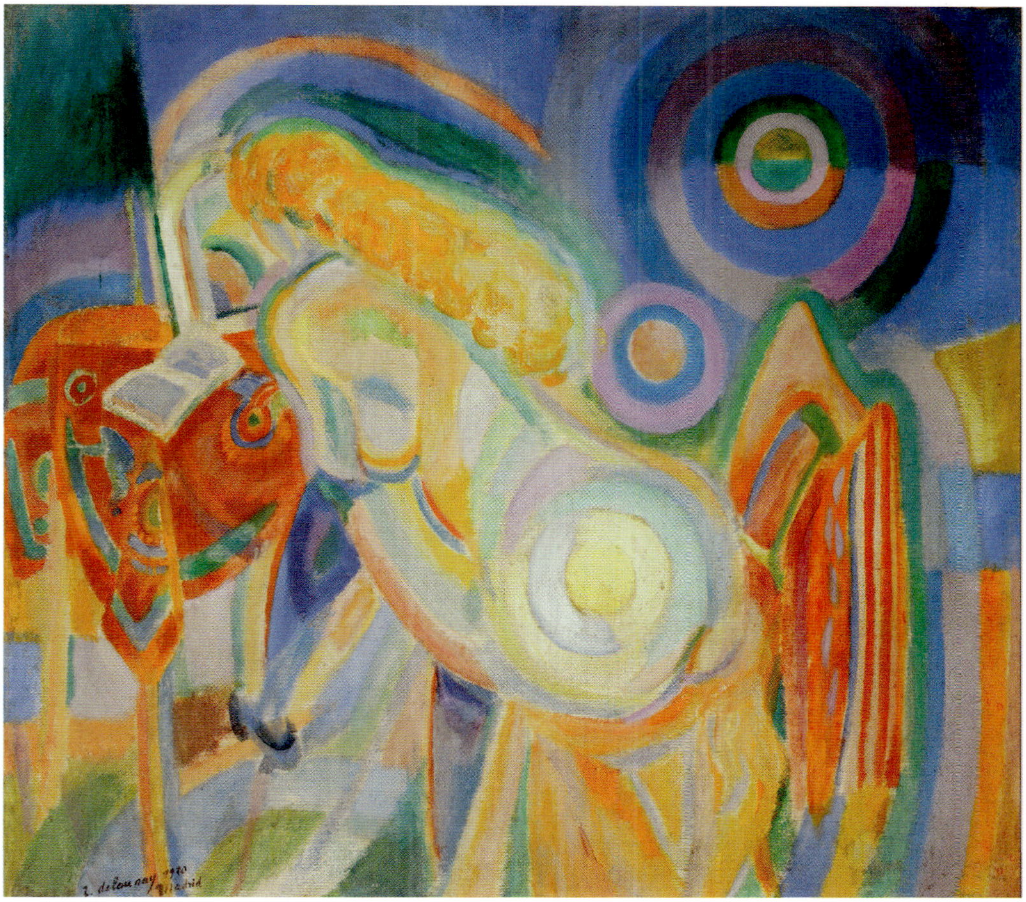

2

39 HIERARCHICAL PROPORTION

THE IMPORTANCE OF RELATIVE SIZE

Hierarchical proportion is a convention in representational art in which figures are scaled relative to their importance or social status. Thus, in Egyptian art, pharaohs are generally shown as larger figures than their surrounding attendants. This convention extended for millennia across much of the world's art, including Mayan, Persian, Indian, Carolingian, and Gothic art. Even in the Sienese painting of Duccio (1255–1319), the central religious figures in compositions are painted on a larger scale than the lower status attendants. This convention meshed well with other narrative advantages of a flat or shallow picture space. Objects need not be made larger or smaller depending on their distance from the viewer. And they can be stacked up to be seen in full, rather than being obliged to stand behind other elements.

When perspective arrived in the first part of the fifteenth century, the determination of scale was fixed by the geometry of the piece and new means had to be found to differentiate the status of figures in a composition. Artists quickly developed a vocabulary of placement, lighting, gesture, and clothing to indicate the relative importance of their subjects.

With the advent of modernism and a new interest in flat pictorial space, only a few artists have chosen to revisit the idea of hierarchical proportion. These include Marc Chagall (1887–1985), in whose works relative proportion and even the forces of gravity are often sacrificed to poetic license. It also appears in the work of the Columbian artist Fernando Botero (1932–), where it is sometimes used rhetorically to poke fun at the status of the ruling elite.

1 Mayan carving from Cancun showing the ruler Tajal Chan Ahk

2 Duccio (1255–1319)
Maestà, c. 1308-11, Tempera and gold on panel, 84 × 157 in (213 × 400 cm)

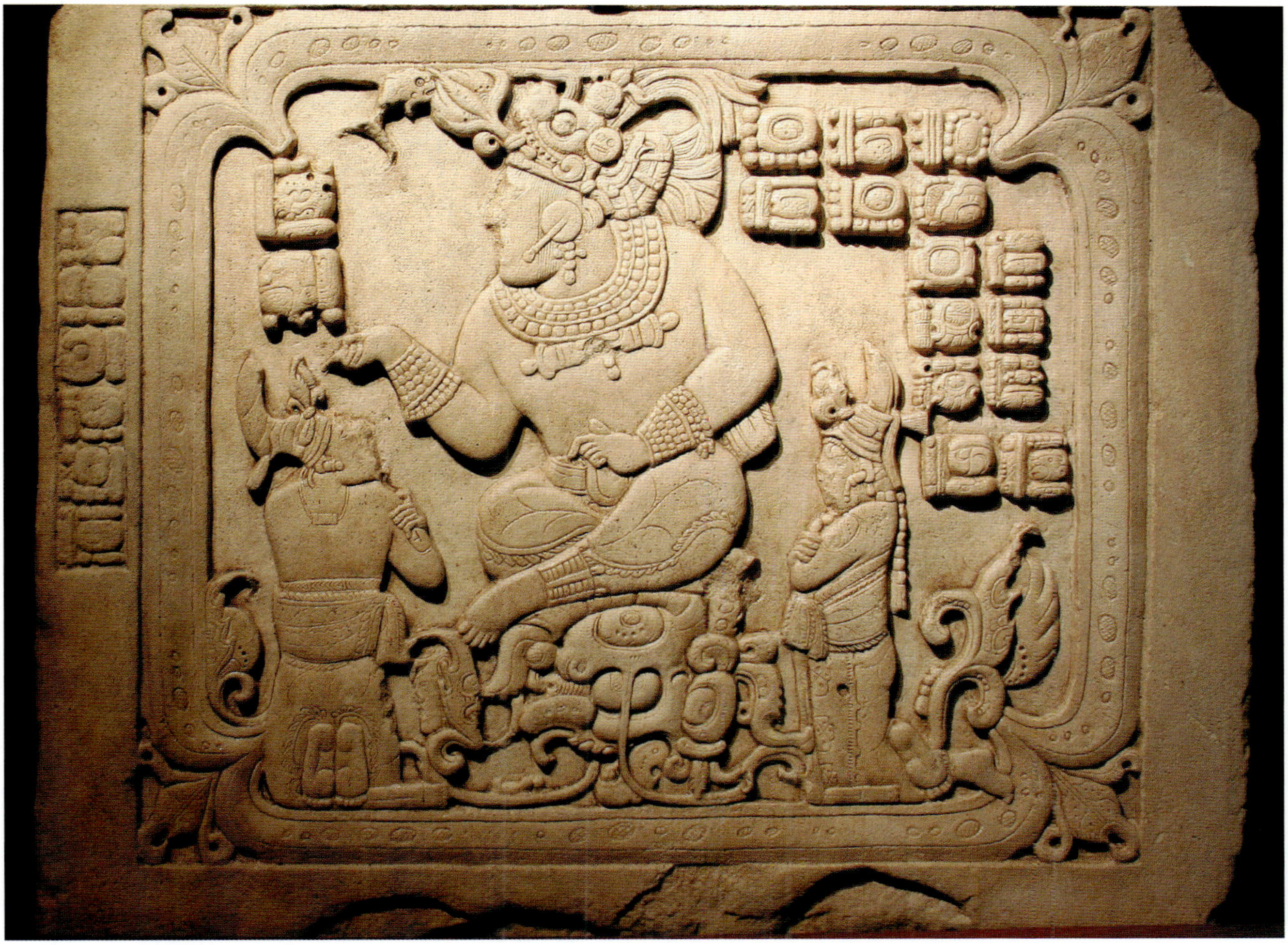

1

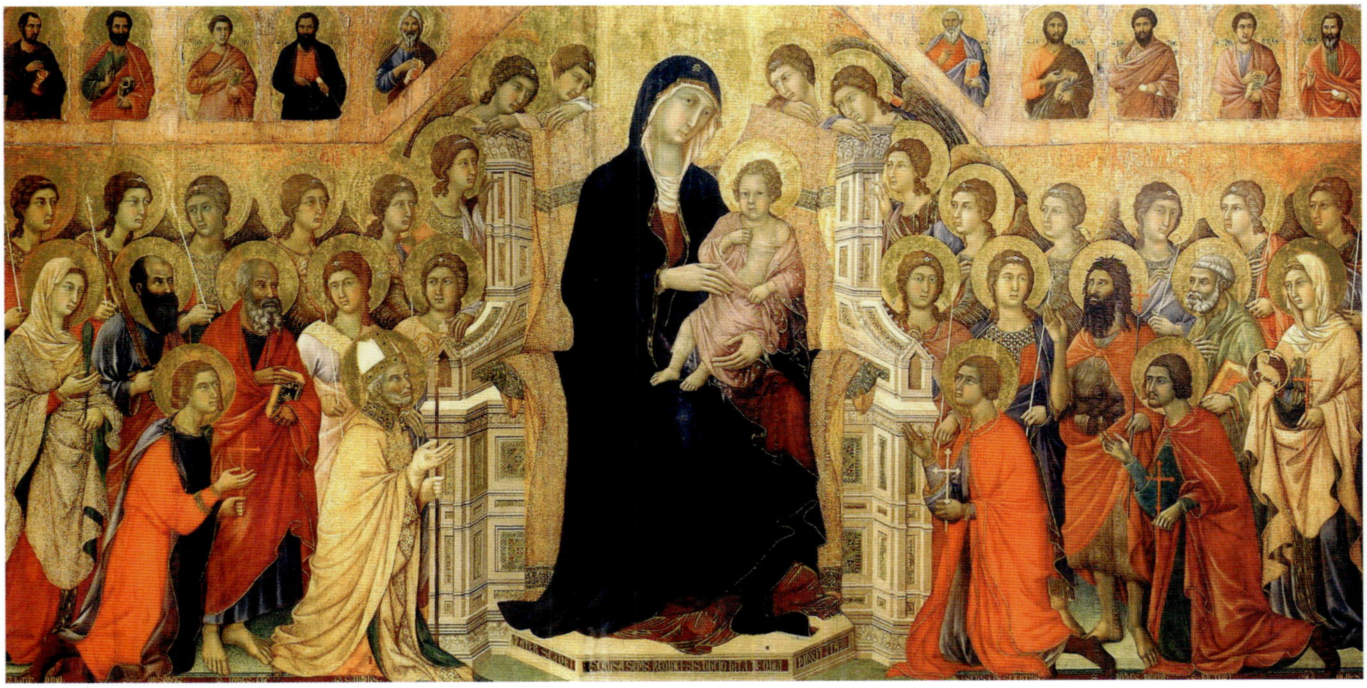

2

40 IMAGINATION

A FACULTY THAT INVENTS AND ORGANIZES

Imagination is a faculty that allows us to generate mental pictures, ideas, and sensations that do not exist in the world and in some cases cannot exist. These abilities are unique to human beings and no doubt emerged from evolutionary pressures allowing us to predict outcomes of all manner of events, both social and mechanical, and to project desirable strategies for survival.

Today we tend to link imaginative and creative powers and to value them as the engine that underpins much artistic endeavor. This was not always so. Prior to the late seventeenth century, the word was generally paired with "fancy" and thought of as a somewhat mechanical faculty capable of recombining information already experienced. It was also associated with memory and its ability to revive past impressions in the mind. A product of fancy might occur with, say, the combination of a man and a horse, creating a centaur. These kinds of inventions, often referred to as "grotesques," were seen as entertaining but not central to art making.

From the Renaissance onward, most thinkers regarded the rational mind as the most noble and desirable part of human thought, even when it came to the production of artworks. This changed with the advent of the Romantic movement and in particular with the writings of the English poet Samuel Taylor Coleridge (1772–1834). In his *Biographia Literararia* of 1817, Coleridge makes a powerful case for the imagination, observing that it not only invents but also combines elements in a way that is coherent and compelling. In other words, he gives to the imagination the creative powers needed to produce works of art. "It dissolves, diffuses, dissipates, in order to recreate; or where this process is rendered impossible, yet still at all events it struggles to idealise and unify. It is essentially vital, even as all objects (as objects) are essentially fixed and dead."

Coleridge felt that this molding and unifying power of the imagination was so important that he coined a new word for it: "esemplastic." This was radical because it presented the idea, central to the Romantic movement, that art is not generated from nature or artistic precedent, nor was it merely reflective of ideal Platonic realms, but rather comes directly from an individual human being.

See also: *Fantasy and Visionary Art* on page 74; *Creativity* on page 52; *Romanticism* on page 160

1 Samuel Palmer (1805–81)
Harvesters by Firelight, 1830, Pen and black ink with watercolor and gouache on wove paper,
11 5/16 × 14 7/16 in (28.7 × 36.7 cm)

2 Joseph Mallord William Turner (1789–1862)
The Evening of the Deluge,
c. 1843, Oil on canvas,
29 15/16 × 29 15/16 in (76 × 76 cm)

Both these nineteenth-century artists presented imaginative transformations of landscape in which elements were simplified and then subsumed into an organic and spirited vision.

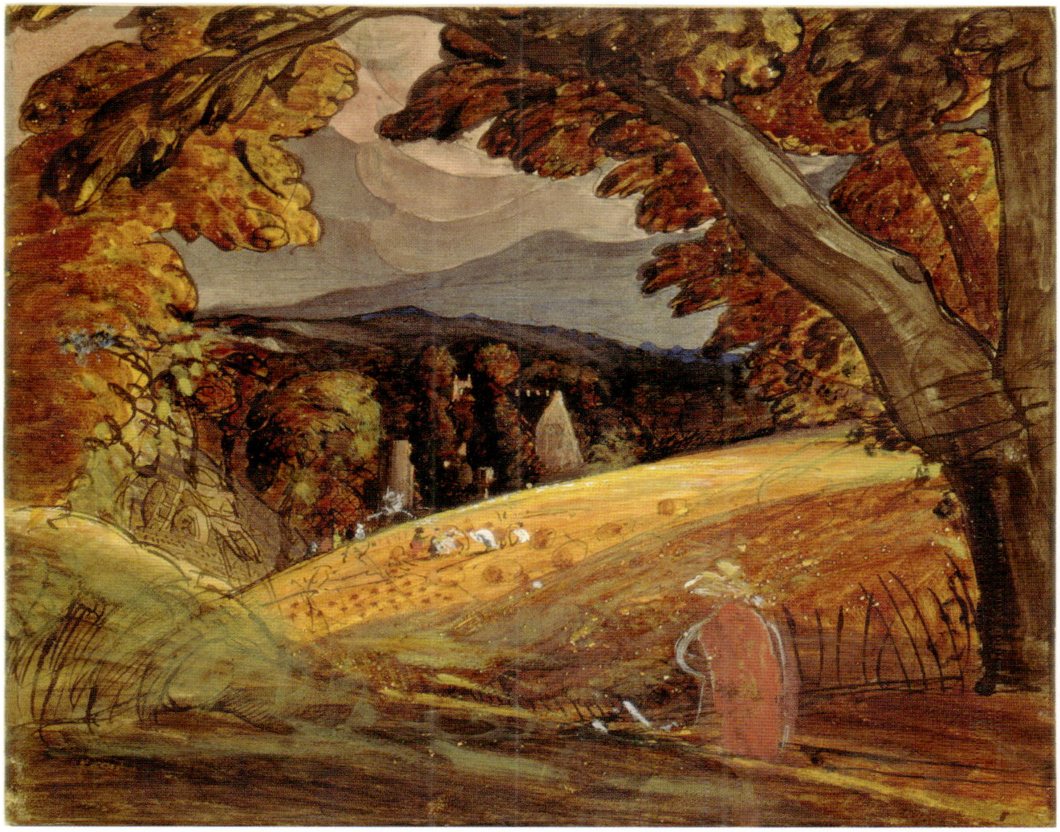

1

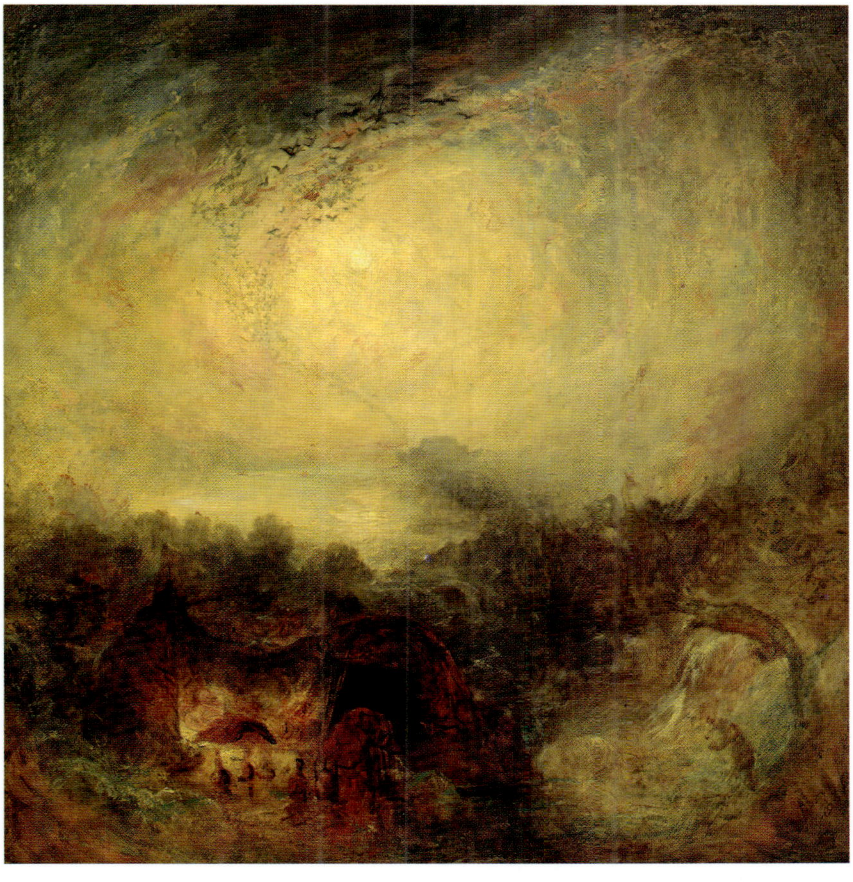

2

41 INSTALLATION

SCULPTURE BECOMES ENVIRONMENT

Installation art is a genre in which the artist creates a complete or partial environment. As such, it moves away from the traditional concept of sculpture as an object to be contemplated by a viewer; the sculpture now surrounds and involves the viewer completely.

With its interest in the transformation of the appearance and feel of interior spaces, installation art rubs shoulders with the disciplines of architecture, interior design, and theater. Many installations share certain features with fairground entertainment and other popular forms of diversion.

OPTIONS

- **Transformation**
  An interior essentially becomes something else: An art gallery becomes a bar or a living room, or an empty room becomes a garden.
- **Color Enclosure**
  A space is transformed by color.
- **Lighting**
  A space is redefined by light or its absence.
- **Sound**
  Sound ambience can create a powerful sense of place, create a particular mood, or bring other associations to mind.
- **Video**
  Installations involving video screens continue to proliferate as the technology improves. Projected images can provide an almost unlimited array of experience and reference.
- **Interactive**
  The audience is invited to participate. This might involve providing structures to climb on, or slides, swings, and other obstacles to be negotiated. Computer consoles can also offer the opportunity to interact in different ways. Motion detectors and other electronic devices can allow the audience to affect the artwork in prescribed ways.
- **Space**
  Elements are deployed to make palpable or to define a space. One artist has filled rooms with balloons, obliging the viewer to press through the space. String and other lightweight elements can be used to make palpable the physical space of an interior.

See also: *Land Art* on page 100; *Video* on page 204; *Interactive Art* on page 94

1 **Judy Pfaff installation at the Rose Gallery**, Brandeis University, 1995, String, tree trunk, tree roots, rope

Although the term "installation art" did not appear as a description until the late 1960s, the genre goes back at least to Dadaism and the early work of Marcel Duchamp (1887–1968) and Kurt Schwitters (1887–1948). In 1937, for instance, Duchamp designed an exhibition of Surrealist art by hanging twelve hundred sacks of coal from the ceiling of the elegant Galerie des Beaux Arts. The paintings were attached to a series of discarded revolving doors. On the opening night the lights were turned off and visitors were handed flashlights to find their way through the exhibit.

See also: *Conceptual Art* on page 46

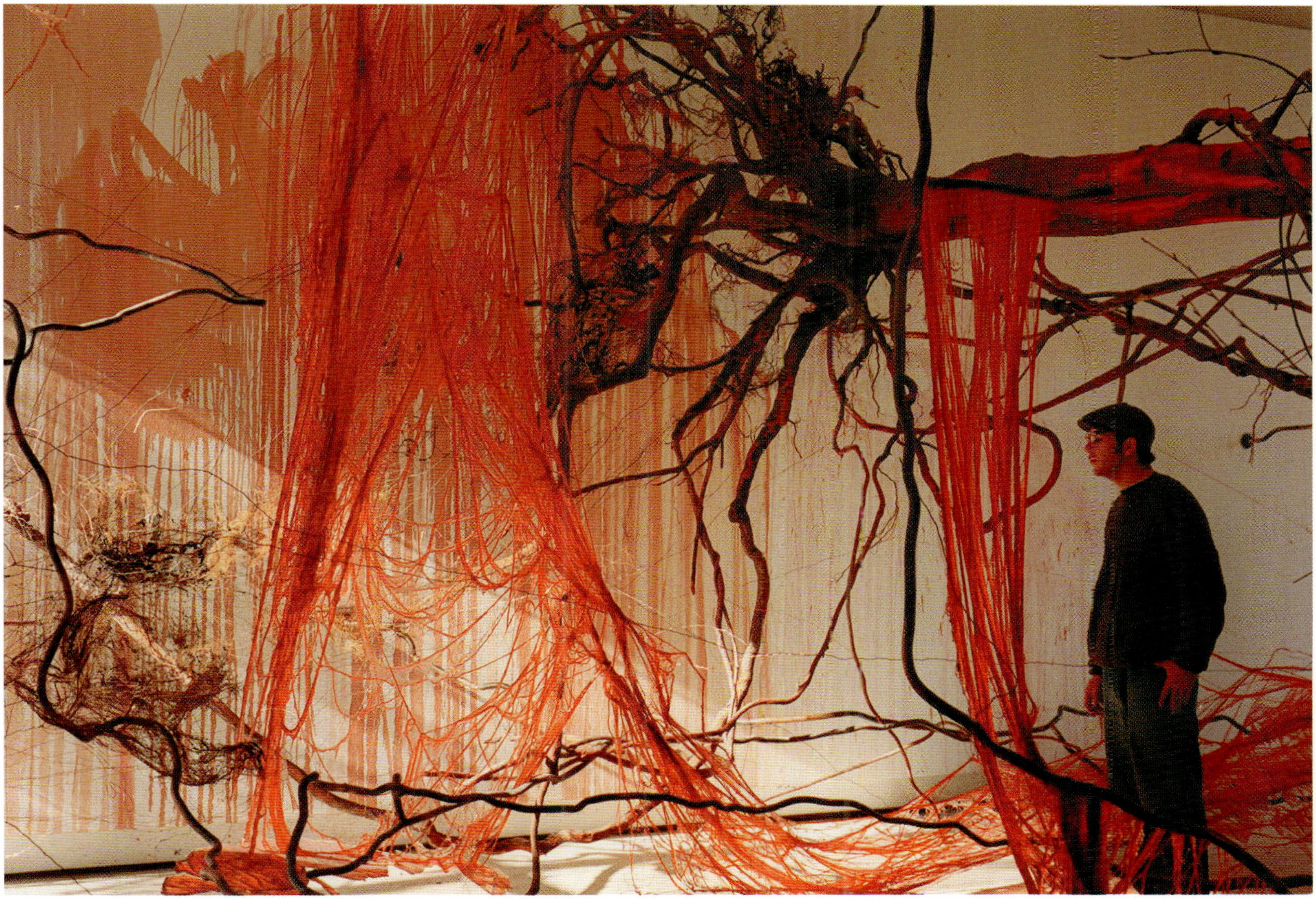

1

42 INTENTIONALITY

THE ARTIST PLANS AN OUTCOME AND PROCEEDS ACCORDINGLY

Intentionality is the idea that works of art are an expression of an intention on the part of artists to achieve specific results. For instance, artists may be seeking to create works that impart a sense of mystery, present an entirely satisfying experience of color harmony, or deliver a highly resolved experience of a set of forms. Whatever their intentions, artists will employ the formal means at their disposal in order to achieve them. Choices about composition, color organization, simplification, visual language, and other tools will be aligned in service of the overall intention. Central to this idea is the notion that art can be used to communicate and persuade and that formal means can be marshaled and content edited to achieve this.

The antithesis to this point of view is one that holds that artists undergo a process of discovery or exploration in making a work of art and that the resulting artwork emerges with its own authority. In a more extreme case, we might argue that some artists undertake an activity by which something is completed that they didn't necessarily intend to be a work of art but which is, nonetheless, regarded by others as a work of art.

Many artists report a sense of distancing from the creative process. The poet T. S. Elliot (1888–1965) said he felt that he was merely present at the creation of a poem. The Swiss French painter and sculptor Alberto Giacometti (1901–66) maintained that the works he created were merely the by-products of an unsuccessful attempt to achieve something else—namely a resolved and coherent vision of the space around him. This point of view acknowledges that artistic insights are rarely linear developments of straightforward ideas and that the creative act is more usually governed by intuitive processes. For this reason, many artists adopt procedures that allow for serendipitous events in the hopes of avoiding the lure of straightforward, intentional achievements.

1 Peter Paul Rubens (1577–1640)
Descent from the Cross, 1611–14, Oil on panel, 165 5/8 × 126 in (420.6 × 320 cm)

The intentions of the artist are fairly clear in this large-scale Baroque work. The central panel of an altarpiece, the painting is designed to elicit a strong emotional response and close association with the subject on the part of the viewer. As part of the campaign of the Counter-Reformation, the picture seeks to use theatrical effect and luxurious presentation to retain allegiance to the Roman Catholic faith. To realize his intentions, the artist uses a powerful composition with a descending arc that reinforces the downward carriage of the body of the dead Christ. High contrast lighting creates drama. He has deployed acidic color to emphasize the lifelessness of the corpse. Meanwhile, the facial expressions and postures of the figures are carefully observed in order to convey the emotional nature of the scene.

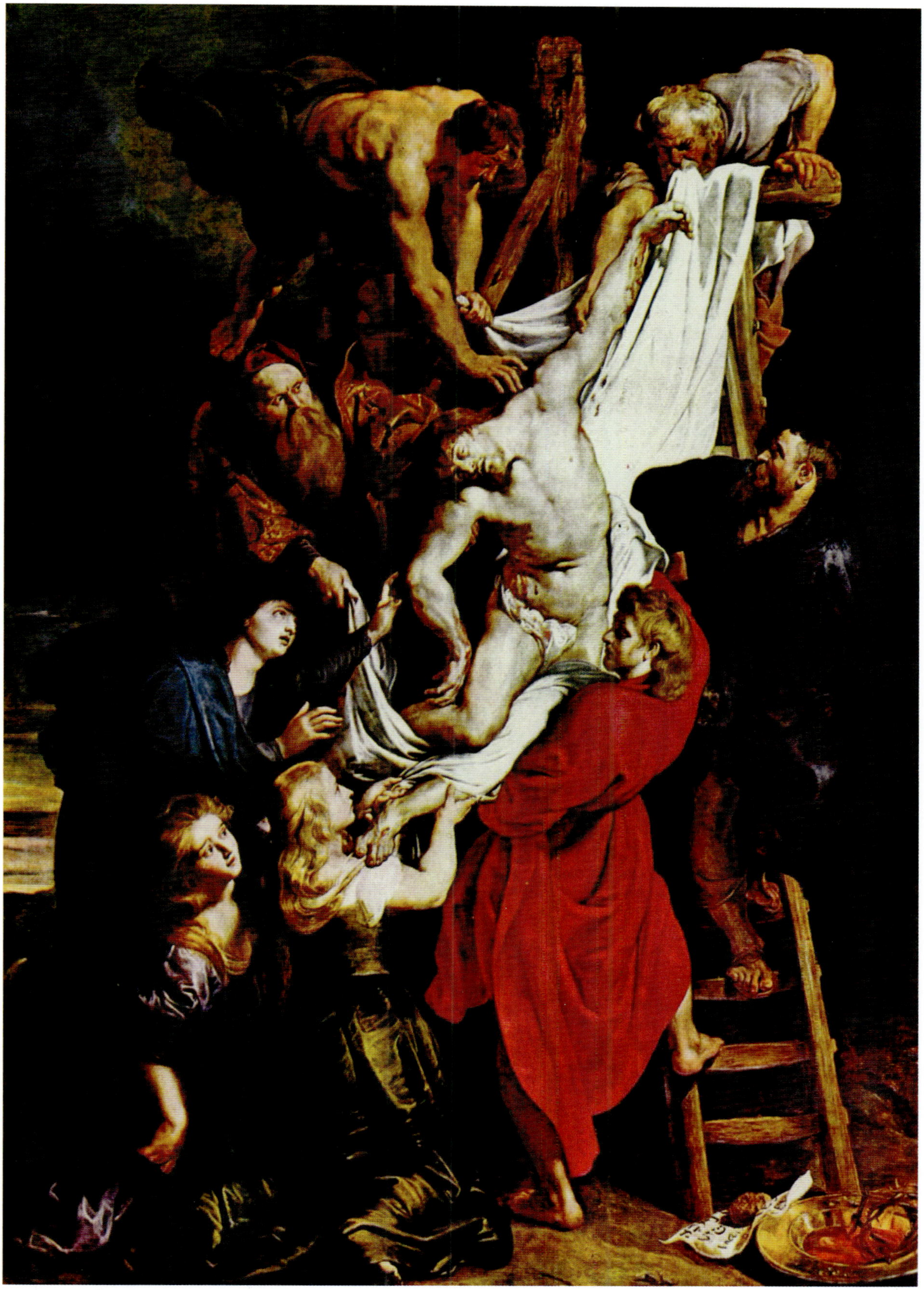

1

43 INTERACTIVE ART

THE AUDIENCE PARTICIPATES WITH THE ARTIST IN CREATING THE ARTWORK

Interactive art is a contemporary genre in which the audience is invited to participate in an artwork, effecting change in its appearance, outcome, and meaning. By giving the audience this authority, the work departs radically from a long tradition of authorial control. New technologies, such as electronic sensors, video, computer networking, and a variety of display and input techniques, offer a vast range of possibilities. At the same time, some of the most successful interactive artworks have used very simple technical means.

METHODS

- **Static input**
  The audience is invited to make suggestions or provide guidance for the future progress of an artwork under construction. The artist follows this guidance as he or she continues to make the work.
- **Physical interaction**
  The audience is invited to touch, move, and manipulate a physical object or objects. For example, in *Half the Air in a Given Space*, by Martin Creed (1968–), a gallery space is filled with thousands of balloons of the same color. The audience is obliged to push through them to negotiate the space. Many artists have also constructed environments that make use of traditional playground experiences, such as slides, swings, and distorting mirrors to engage the audience in an immersive experience.
- **Co-building**
  The audience is invited to contribute to the construction of an artwork. This could be as simple as taking up a brush and paint to work on a canvas, or as complex as making web-based changes to a graphic or multimedia work.
- **Sensor responsive**
  The movements or physical attributes of the audience are picked up by sensors and the data used to affect the appearance or behavior of an artwork. A particular movement by an audience member, for instance, might change the content and movement of a video display. Or the proximity of an audience member may cause a sculpture to move or otherwise respond.
- **Performance interaction**
  Audiences are often invited to interact with, or become part of, performance art pieces. This can be as simple as the traditional theater's invitation for an audience member to step up on the stage or it might involve the actions and behavior of the entire audience.

The above strategies are often combined. For example, physical interaction can readily be meshed with sensor technologies.

See also: *Performance Art* on page 126; *Video* on page 204

1 Birthe Blauth
The Gift, 2011, Video projection and computer operated sensors

A viewer sits at a table and reaches out to take a gift from a figure on a projected video. A movement sensor shifts the video frame so that the figure releases the gift.

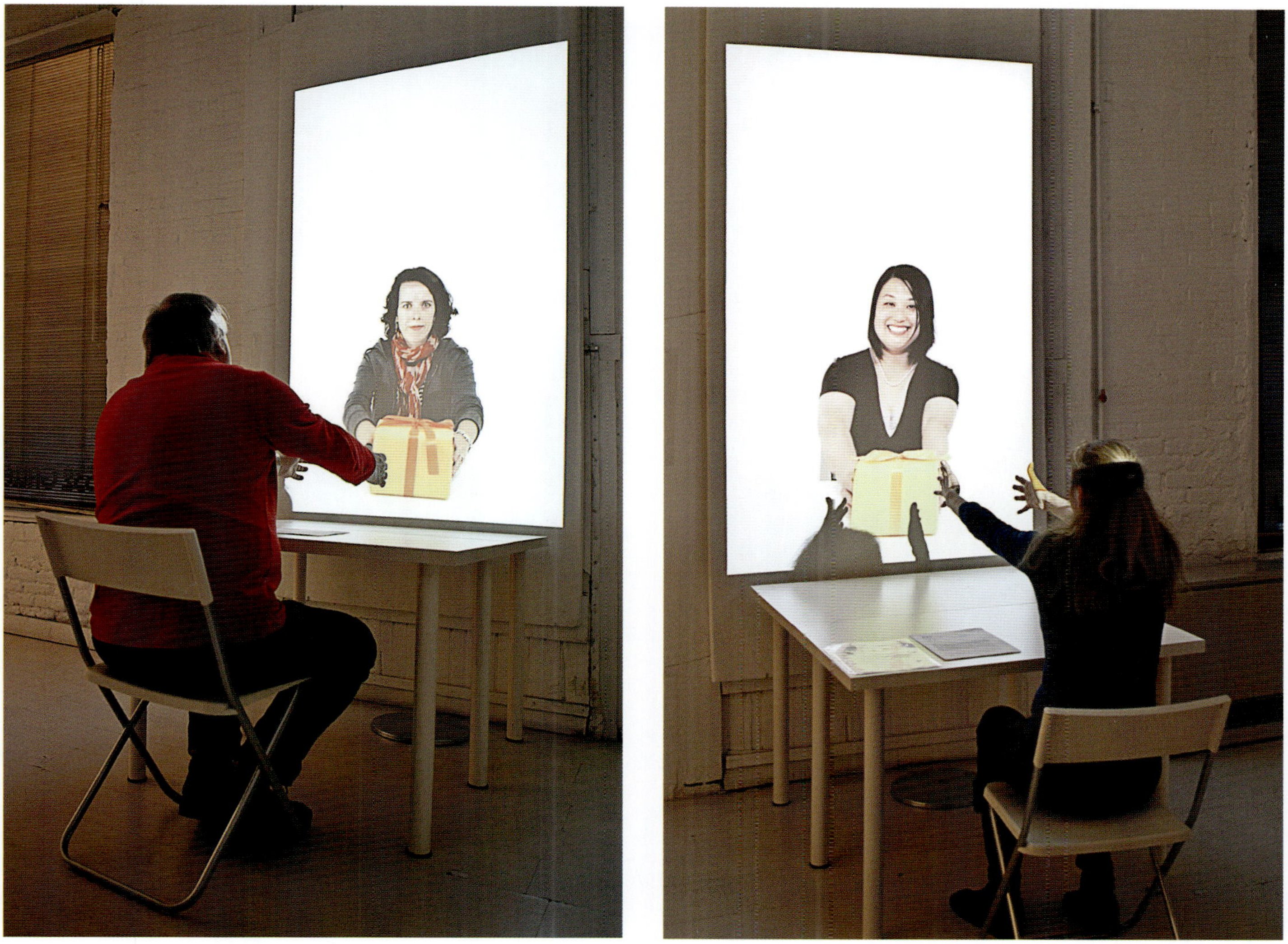

1

44 JUXTAPOSITION

THE DYNAMICS OF BRINGING DISPARATE ELEMENTS TOGETHER

Juxtaposition is a procedure in which one element is placed next to another in such a way that a new dynamic takes place. This is particularly effective where the literal meaning of an element combines with that of another to make a new meaning. Juxtaposition can also be a purely optical or abstract strategy in which shapes, colors, or textures are placed next to each other to create new relationships.

IN ACTION

- **Subversion**
  An image of a train is quite commonplace, but if it is juxtaposed with an image of, say, a jellyfish, the viewer will experience a sense of surprise and perhaps unease as he or she attempts to make sense of the combined image. The expected norms of the viewer's world are upended. The possibilities of subverting meaning through juxtaposition were pursued strongly by the Surrealists, a twentieth-century movement that sought to expose and explore the workings of the unconscious mind through art. André Breton (1896–1966), the founder of the movement, quoted the nineteenth-century poet the Comte de Lautréamont when he described a startling juxtaposition "as beautiful as the encounter of an umbrella and a sewing machine on a dissecting table."
- **Dramatic effect**
  Many classical and religious paintings rely on creating drama through juxtaposition. There are many depictions (e.g., Caravaggio, Guido Reni, Carlo Dolci) of the severed head of John the Baptist held by a delicate and very feminine Salome. The juxtaposition of gruesome violence with female beauty becomes a potent source of frisson and interest.
- **Poetic**
  The Surrealist discovery of the power of nonsensical juxtapositions quickly gave rise to the understanding that juxtapositions can be used to convey quite nuanced meanings. The American artist Joseph Cornell (1903–72), for instance, used very carefully selected images which, when juxtaposed to each other, created a sense of wistful and poetic charm.
- **Polemic**
  A specific political or sociological point can be made by juxtaposing one image with another. In his Vietnam era painting *F-111* (see page 133), James Rosenquist (1933–) juxtaposed images of American consumerism with a depiction of a fighter bomber, deliberately inviting the viewer to consider the connection between the two.
- **Positive association**
  A technique often used in advertising. For instance, the image of a healthy, young athlete will be paired with an image of a beer bottle. The viewer is invited to associate the positive qualities of the healthy athletic life with beer drinking.

See also: *Surrealism* on page 184

1 René Magritte (1898–1967)
Son of Man, 1964, Oil on canvas, 45⅝ x 35 in (116 x 89 cm)

1

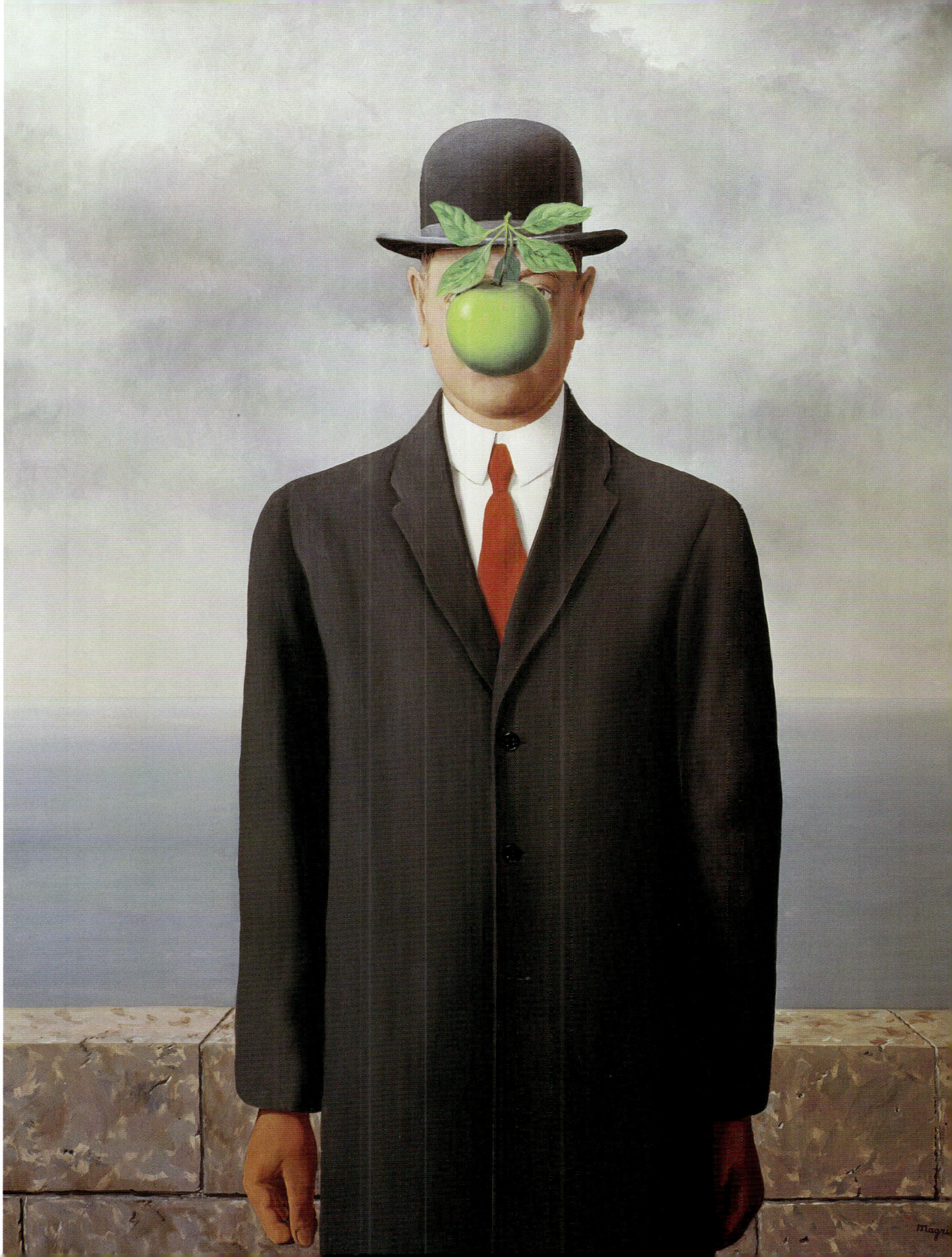

45 KINETIC ART

MOVEMENT IN REAL TIME OFFERS NEW OPTIONS FOR EXPRESSION

Kinetic art is a term that describes artworks that actually move. Fine artists became interested in movement toward the end of the nineteenth century when photography began to reveal the secret appearance of objects in motion. It wasn't until the twentieth century, however, that artists began to make works that incorporated real motion. The Russian artist Naum Gabo (1890–1977) is generally thought to have made the first kinetic sculpture, *Standing Wave*, in 1920. This consists of a single piece of metal placed vertically and made to oscillate by a mechanism in its base. The resulting waveform encloses a three-dimensional space.

Other artists soon took up the task, including fellow Russians Alexander Rodchenko (1891–1956) and Vladimir Tatlin (1885–1953). It fell to an American artist, Alexander Calder (1898–1976), to develop the idea into a fully fledged art form when he invented the mobile. His mobiles come in two forms: object mobiles and suspended mobiles. An object mobile is usually based on the floor and consists of a central form from which mobile forms are projected. A suspended mobile hangs from the ceiling or a projection from the wall. Elements are hung from cross beams that are carefully balanced so that they move gently with surrounding air currents. Calder's output of such works was enormous, and his approach varied from highly geometric pieces to forthright representational works (see page 24).

Later twentieth-century artists experimented with a wide variety of approaches to kinetic art. The Swiss artist Jean Tinguely (1925–91) became famous for a number of sculptures that were designed to self-destruct. Made from an improbable conglomeration of disused machine parts and discarded materials, these sculptures had deliberately short lives, suggesting a radical and nihilistic view about the role of art and indeed the nature of life. Gentle movement of sculptural elements has been incorporated into the work of George Rickey (1907–2002), Jesús Soto (1923–2005), and many others. It is fair to say that some degree of actual movement is now an acceptable part of the vocabulary of sculpture. Continued improvement in technical options, including robotic devices, servo-motors, computerized feedback, electronic sensors, and lightweight materials, offer ever wider scope to kinetic artists.

See also: *Movement* on page 118

1 David Beck (1954–)
Trigger Fish, 2002, Boxwood, mother of pearl, brass, 8 × 3¼ × 3¼ in (20.3 × 8.3 × 8.3 cm)

The American artist David Beck makes small-scale sculptures whose elaborate mechanics hark back to the clockwork curiosities of the eighteenth and nineteenth centuries. Meanwhile, the bizarre, idiosyncratic, and sometimes disturbing quality of the subject matter marks them as thoroughly modern.

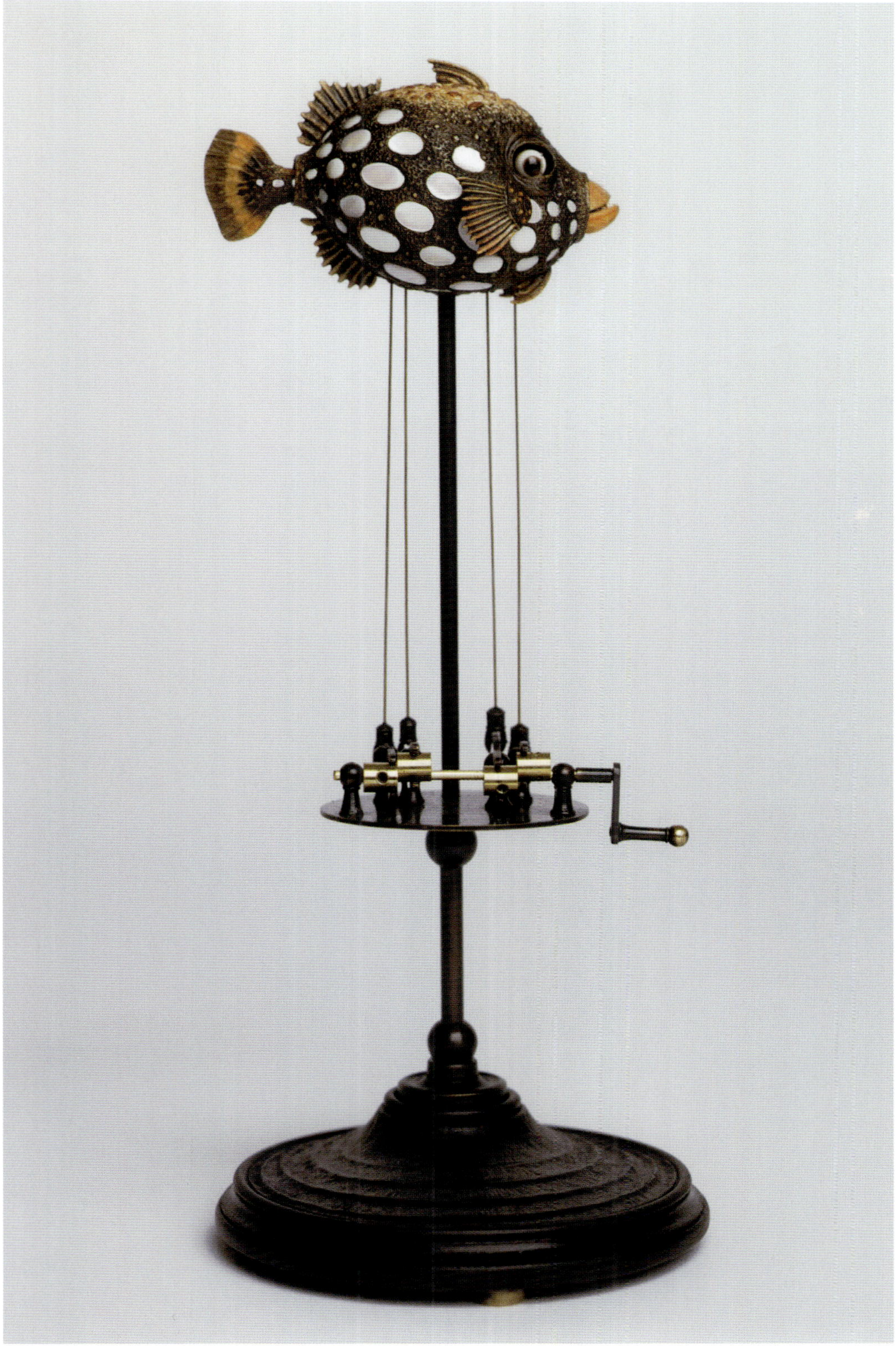

1

46 LAND ART

TRANSFORMING THE GREAT OUTDOORS

Site-specific outdoor art is generally known as land art. Although humans have made outdoor constructions since prehistoric times, often for religious purposes, the practice of making pure art in this way dates from the late 1960s. One of the first practitioners was Michael Heizer (1944–), a California artist who began to make simple ephemeral works in the desert, often consisting of groups of geometric trenches dug into the desert floor. These would be photographed and the resulting documentation displayed in a gallery or museum. Heizer was quickly joined in this kind of enterprise by Walter de Maria (1935–2013), Robert Smithson (1938–73), and a host of lesser lights. It soon became clear that gestures made out in the landscape could occupy an interesting niche between the then-active movements of Minimalism and Conceptual Art. Minimalism had opened the way for extremely stripped-down artworks, and Conceptualism had pioneered the taste for art as documentation of an artwork that wasn't present or, in some cases, didn't exist at all.

By the early 1970s, a decided taste for gigantism emerged. Robert Smithson's *Spiral Jetty* involved moving around nearly 5,000 tons (4,536 metric tons) of dirt along the shores of the Great Salt Lake. In 1969–70 Heizer created *Double Negative*, a piece consisting of two trenches cut into the eastern edge of Mormon Mesa in Utah whose total length is 1,500 feet (457 m), each trench being some 50 feet (15.3 m) wide by 30 feet (9 m) deep. More than 250,000 tons of rock were removed to achieve this, and the piece is quite visible from outer space. Walter de Maria created *Lightning Field* in 1977, a 1 mile (0.6 km) by 1 kilometer (5/8 mile) grid consisting of 400 steel rods that attract spectacular effects during thunderstorms.

Meanwhile, land artists elsewhere, particularly in Britain, adopted an approach that displayed more sensitivity to nature and place. English artist Richard Long (1945–) based most of his projects on the idea of taking certain kinds of walks. Artworks made during these outings are ephemeral, site-specific constructions usually involving lines of stones or circles made from materials lying about. Later artists such as Alastair Noble (1953–) have continued to make works that are ephemeral and reflective of the landscape in which they are placed.

See also: *Minimalism* on page 112; *Conceptual Art* on page 46

1 Alastair Noble (1953–)
Mapping Arcadia. Cazenovia and the Topography of Place, 2009, Flags, string

A contour map of the Stone Quarry Art Park in Cazenovia, New York, is reproduced on the ground mapped out in red flags. The artist uses the topography of the place as the subject matter of the piece, reflecting the landscape back on itself.

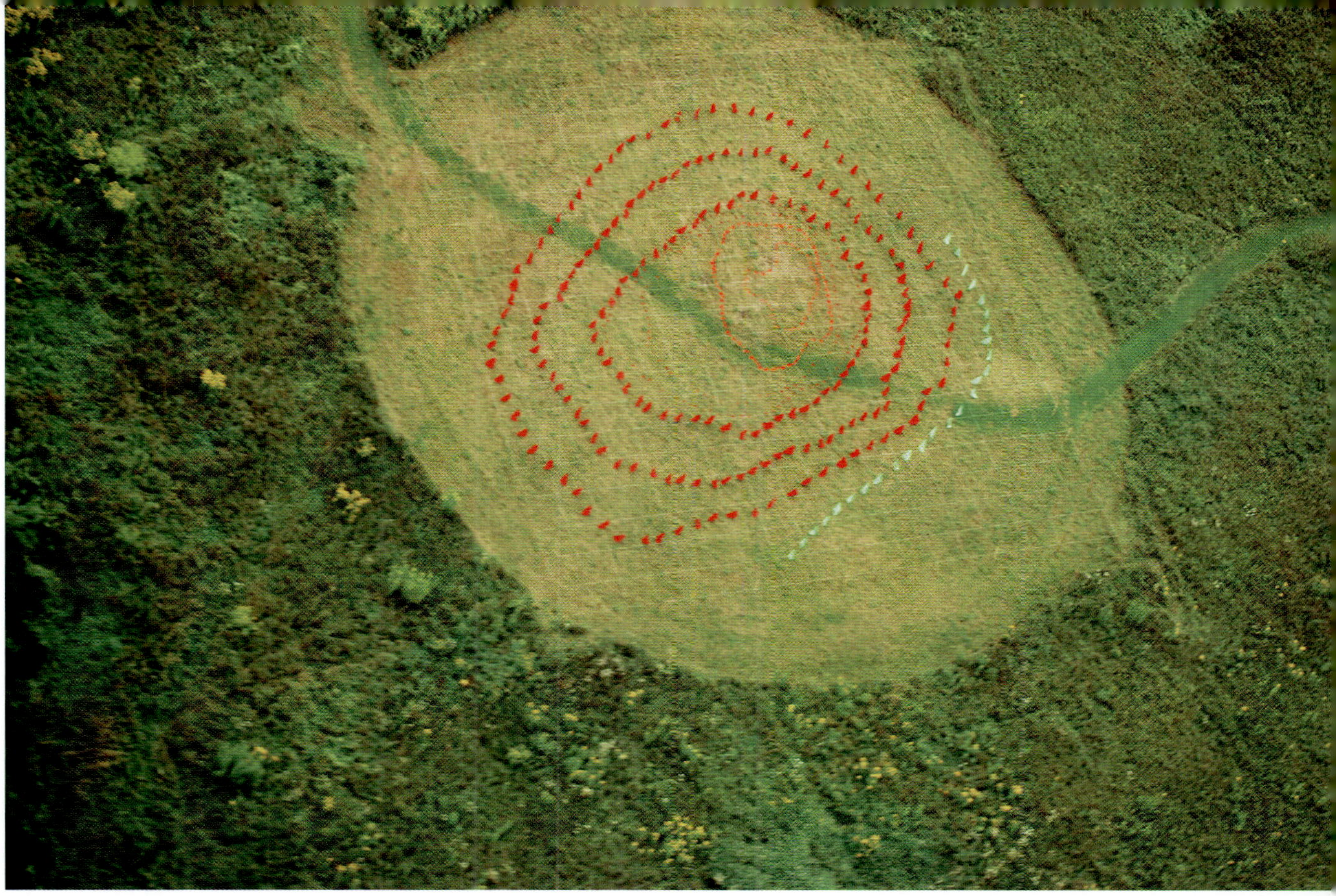

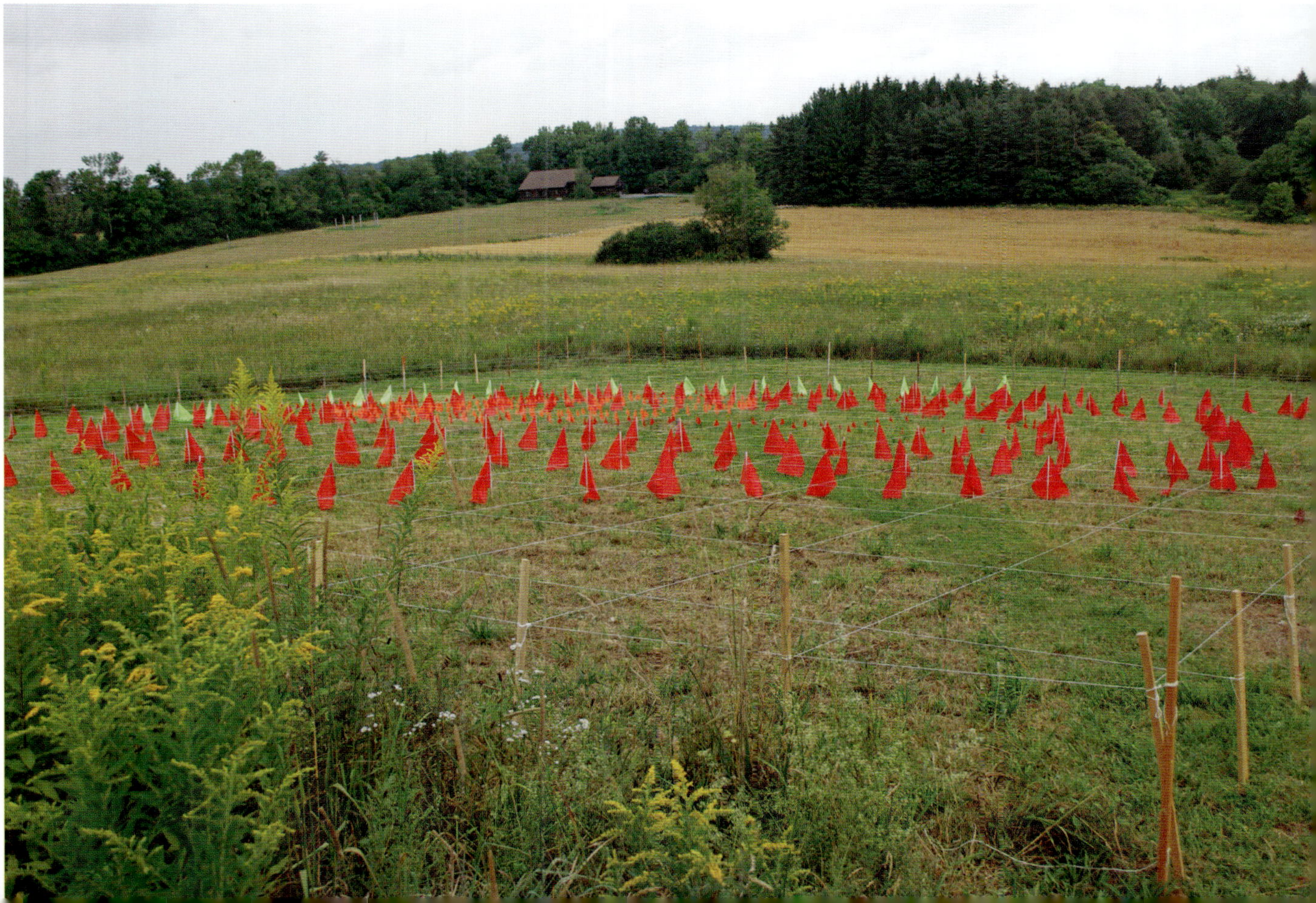

1

47 LAYERS

SHALLOW SPACE, VEILS, AND OVERLAPS

With the development of abstract art in the twentieth century, it became clear that one of the principle features of an abstract painting vocabulary would be layering. Successive applications of paint can be construed by the viewer as elements lying within a shallow depth close to the picture plane. By manipulating the transparency of the paint, the color, and the way that elements overlap each other, painters are able to control the sense of space and the dynamics of the painting across the surface. Cubist art, which generally sought to manipulate the shallow "picture space" of a painting by using selectively drawn edges of elements, also used layering to augment the space. Later artists relied on layering alone. The spatial effects arising from layering paint were particularly important for the American Abstract Expressionists. Painters such as Jackson Pollock (1912–56), Willem De Kooning (1904–97), Adolph Gottlieb (1903–74), and others built paintings by layering paint marks to create highly charged spatial relationships.

STRATEGIES

- **Transparency**
  Layers of semitransparent paint built on top of one another will tend to create an automatic sense of depth.
- **Color**
  By manipulating the color in successive layers of transparent paint, the artist can create rich translucencies that can take on a remarkable feeling of depth.
- **Overlapping**
  Elements painted in opaque paint can be overlapped in layers to create a wide range of effects.
- **Mixed media**
  Paint can be combined with collaged elements to create a physical layering.

See also: *Brush Techniques* on page 30

1 Joan Thorne
Yangon, 2013, Oil on canvas,
60 × 69 in (152.4 × 175.3 cm)

Layers in both transparent and opaque paint create a sense of shifting depth. The artist is able to confer different senses of movement for each layer, setting up a lively pictorial experience for the viewer.

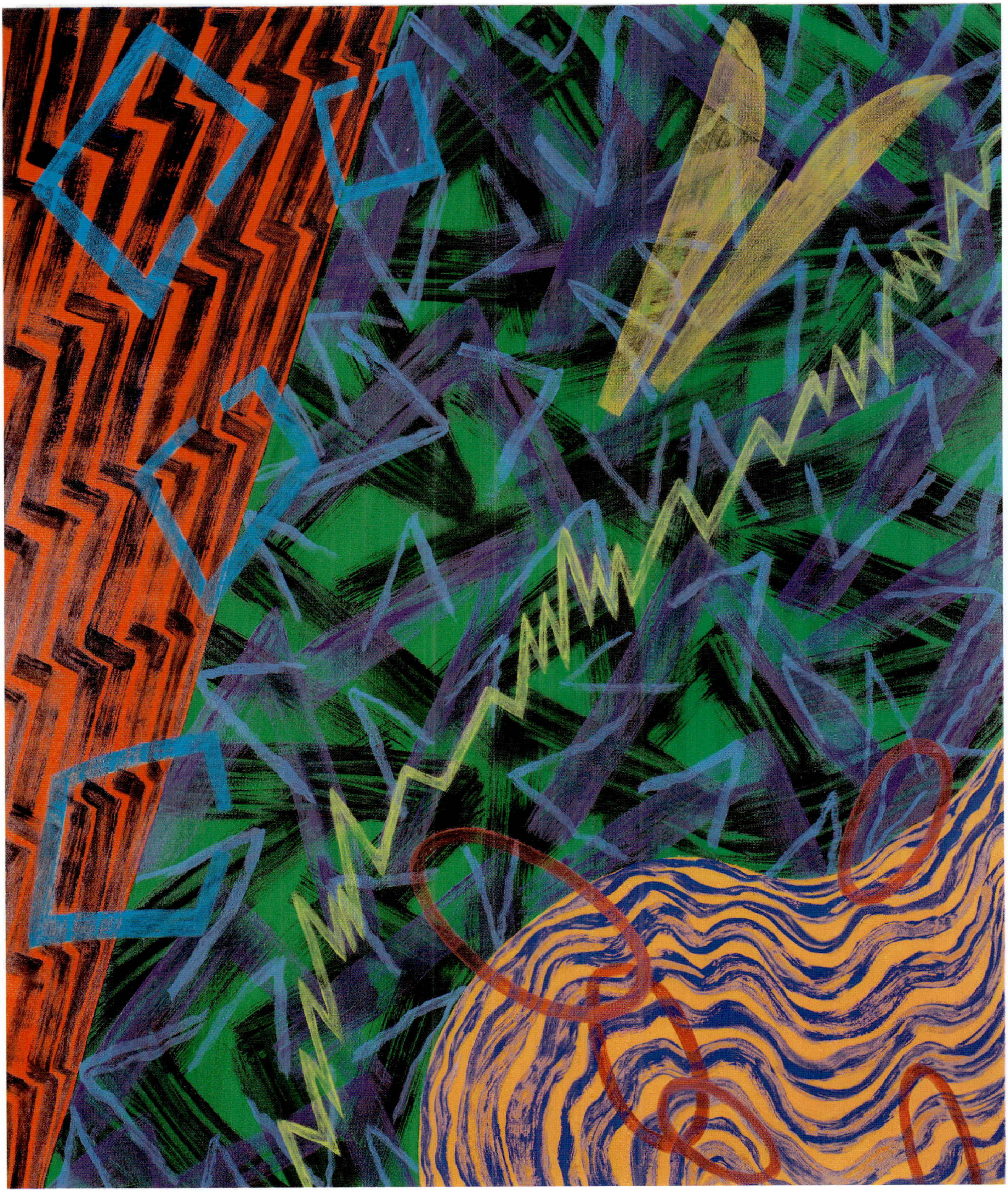

1

48 LINEAR BASICS

LINE IS THE MOST BASIC AND MOST VERSATILE VISUAL ELEMENT

Line is a primal and fundamental component of visual thought. Some of the earliest known works of art are line drawings of seals on a cave wall in Nerja, Spain, that are approximately 42,000 years old. The construction of a line requires the most simple of mechanical means: a point is moved across a surface leaving behind a long, narrow mark. Almost all tribal cultures make images with lines, sometimes incised into a surface and sometimes drawn onto surfaces with a variety of implements and mediums. It appears, therefore, that the formation of representational shapes using combinations of lines is a very basic human behavior.

In more complex cultures, line has achieved enormous descriptive and expressive power. In Western art, various qualities of line are admired, including clarity, precision, stylishness, fluidity, flexibility, and strength. Matisse, one of the great masters of line, observed, "Drawing is like making an expressive gesture with the advantage of permanence."

In practice, line can be used in a great variety of ways:

- To create simple divisions.
- To construct shapes and designs.
- To make letterforms, signs, and symbols.
- To render or suggest form by using varying weight in the line.
- To create dynamic movement by using the "pull" of the line. The viewer apprehends the way the line was made and interprets the speed of travel.
- To create a powerful sense of expression by exaggerating the weight and movement of the line.
- To suggest three-dimensional space.
- To create a patina or texture.
- To transmit the touch or "hand" of the artist.
- To describe form by delineating contours.
- To build into tone through hatching.
- To be used in combination with tone or color, offering limitless possibilities.

1 Sir Anthony van Dyck (1599–1641)
Two Seated Male Figures,
Pen and black ink on buff laid paper,
3 15/16 × 3 1/16 in (10 × 7.7 cm)

Van Dyke uses a pen line to suggest the pose of two figures in preparation for a composition. Here line is used as shorthand for more elaborate rendering to come later. There is considerable pleasure in the free movement and energy of the line.

2 Vincent van Gogh (1853–1890)
Ploughman in the Fields near Arles, 1888, Reed pen and brown ink over graphite on wove paper, 9 15/16 × 13 7/16 in (25.3 × 34.1 cm)

Here Van Gogh uses line in multiple ways. It creates movement, particularly in the trees where the "pull" of the line carries the eye upwards along twisting paths. Line is also used here to suggest three-dimensional space, building textures by massing lines of various qualities.

3 **Laxe dos carballos petroglyph**,
in Campo Lameiro, Galicia,
4th–2nd millennium BCE

Drawings made by incising designs into rock faces (petroglyphs) are one of the earliest uses of line.

4 Eugène Delacroix (1798–1863)
Charioteers, Pen and black ink with black wash on wove paper,
16 3/16 × 14 9/16 in (17.3 × 37 cm)

One of the great romantic artists, Delacroix uses an energetic line and a fast open technique to infuse his composition with dynamism and movement.

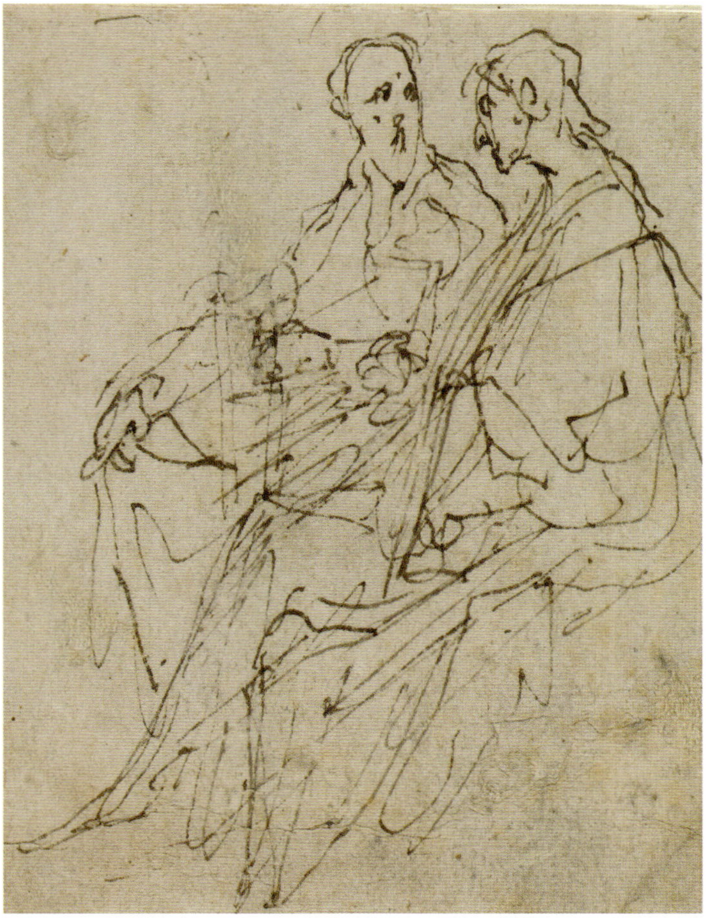

1

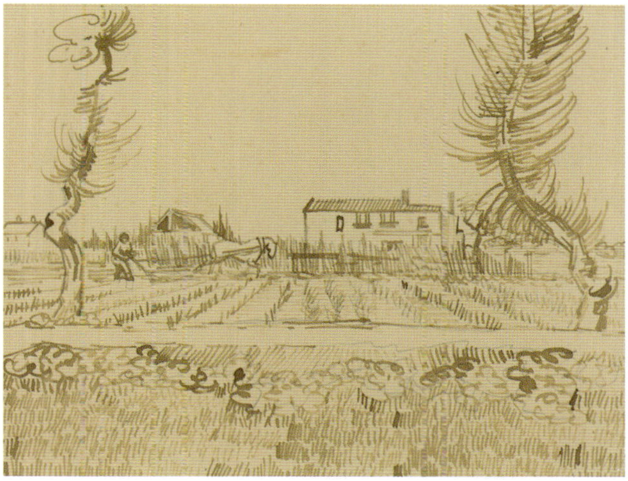

2

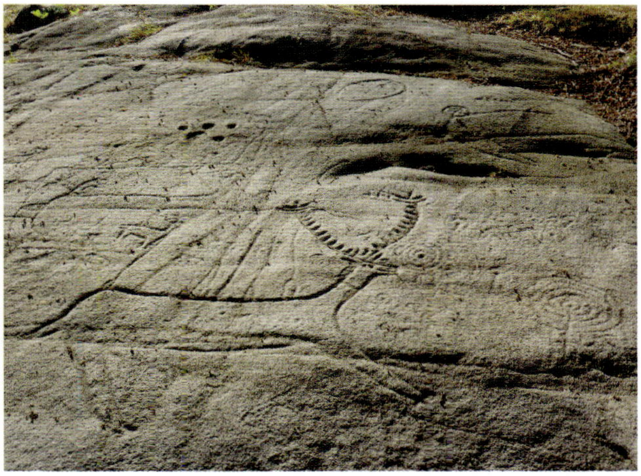

3

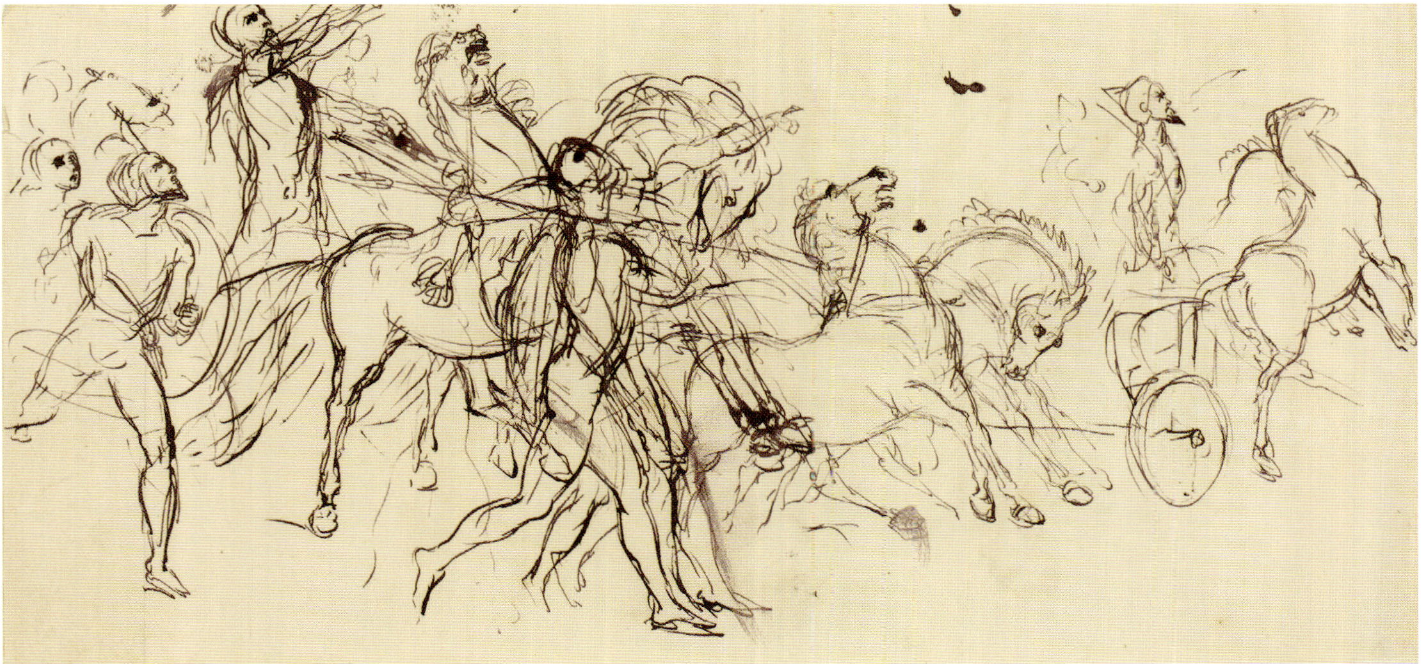

4

49 MANNERISM

TRADING BEAUTY AND REPOSE FOR EXCITEMENT AND MOVEMENT

Mannerism is a style that emerged immediately after the High Renaissance in Italy and lasted from about 1520 to 1580. It might best be thought of as both a reaction to, and an extension of, the perfection and repose of the High Renaissance style exemplified by Raphael, Leonardo, and Michelangelo. In the work of those masters, clarity of form, classical repose, and a balance of naturalism and idealism had reached a pitch that was hard to improve. With Raphael's death in 1520, a younger generation of artists began to make works that dramatized aspects of classicism in ways that were sometimes surprising and disturbing. Compositions became more disorganized, oppositions of forms and colors more strident, and certain exaggerations, such as the elongation of forms, came to the fore. The overall effect, in paintings by artists such as Jacopo Pontormo (1494–1557) and Giulio Romano (1499–1546), is somewhat enervated, frenetic, and uncomfortable. The style was developed into something more ornate and more literary as the century developed, with painters taking on more complex iconography to appeal to their educated clientele.

COMPONENTS

- **Distortion**
  Forms are often elongated.
- **Contorted poses**
  Figures are sometimes posed in ways that would be all but impossible for a human body to assume.
- **Rendering**
  The rendering of forms is usually very careful even when the forms themselves are distorted. The later Mannerism of Bronzino (1503–72) displays unparalleled artistry and sensitivity in the rendering.
- **Coolness**
  Particularly in portraits, Mannerist paintings present people as distant and aloof.
- **Compositions**
  Mannerist paintings often present disjointed compositions in which the narrative is sometimes difficult to ascertain at first sight.
- **Space**
  Unlike the smooth, continuous space of High Renaissance painting, Mannerist painting often presents flattened or discontinuous space.
- **Quoting**
  Mannerist painters were fond of quoting other artists. Their work often derived more inspiration from previous art than it did from nature.

Mannerism is perhaps the best example of what might be termed "The Iron Law of Styles." Any style, even one as sublime as the High Renaissance, will eventually be replaced by another. Mannerism itself was superseded in the 1580s by a new realist style championed by Caravaggio (1571–1610). Each generation finds a way to make art that speaks to its own sense of the world.

1 Jacopo Pontormo (1494–1557)
Joseph in Egypt, 1518, Oil on canvas,
17 5/16 × 19 5/16 in (44 × 49 cm)

Pontormo's composition breaks away from the repose of High Renaissance models by introducing frenetic movement and sweeping lines. Figures are elongated unnaturally and postures are somewhat forced.

2 Angelo Bronzino (1503–72)
Allegory of the Triumph of Venus,
1540–45, Oil on panel,
57½ × 45 5/8 in (146 × 116 cm)

Distortion of some of the figures is combined with highly finished modeling and unnatural gestures to give a curiously artificial quality to the image.

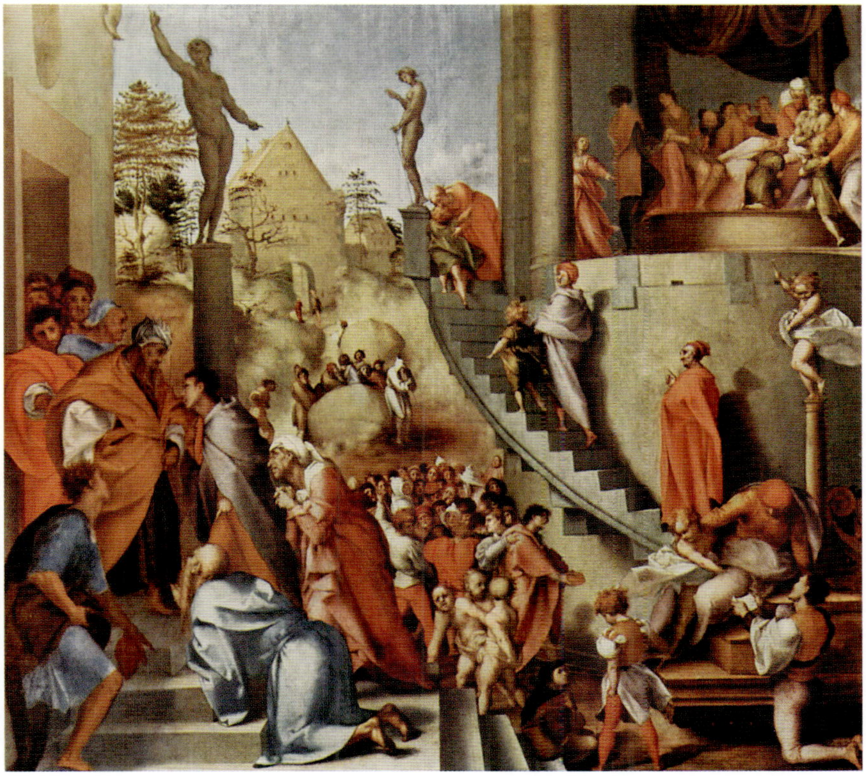

1

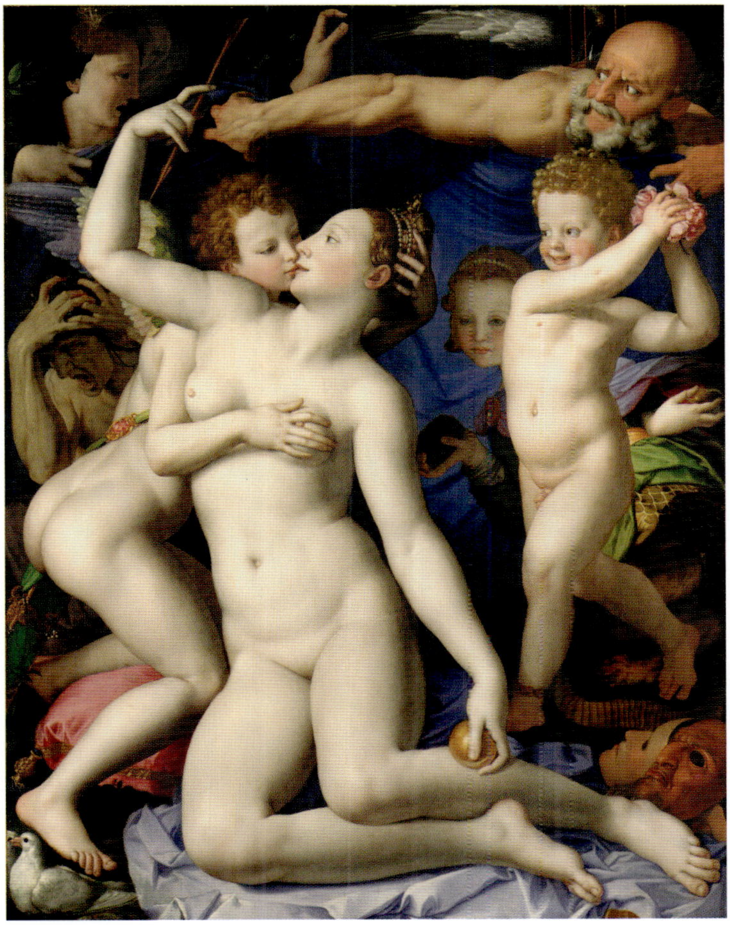

2

50 MASS

SOLIDITY, WEIGHT, AND VOLUME

In art, the term "mass" is used to describe a perceived quality of solidity and weight combined with a sense of volume. One of the enormous sculpted stone heads of Easter Island would certainly be said to have mass. In sculpture, mass is quite physical and is usually more spectacular with an increase in scale. This quality can be an important feature of the expressive power of an artwork. Auguste Rodin's (1840–1917) sculpture of Balzac for example, depends on the concentrated mass in the upper half of the body combined with the upwards lift of the overlarge head. We get an impression of weightiness increasing as we move up the body, so that at last the great forehead and its piercing intelligence take center stage.

Mass can also play an important role in pictorial compositions. In Diego Vélasquez's (1599–1660) *Water Seller of Seville*, the mass of the glass goblet as it changes hands becomes the focal point of the painting. Meanwhile, the greater mass of the stone jars is mirrored by the massive solidity of the water seller himself.

In painting, a sense of mass can be communicated by a number of devices:

- A low viewpoint will tend to increase the sense of scale and weight of a subject.
- Powerful contrast and the use of "key" lights can enhance a sense of volume and weight.
- Some colors inherently contribute to a sense of mass: browns, blacks, deep reds. Other colors tend to diminish a sense of mass: pinks and yellows.

In abstract painting, elements can be endowed with a sense of mass through the layering of paint and the choice of shape and color. Robert Motherwell's (1915–91) *Spanish Elegy* series, for example, uses heavy black paint built into foreboding shapes to create a series of apparently massive elements suspended uneasily across the canvas.

1 **Moai at Rano Raraku**, Easter Island, Stone

2 Diego Vélazquez (1599–1660) ***Water Seller of Seville***, 1618, Oil on canvas, 41 × 31 in (105 × 78.7 cm)

3 Auguste Rodin (1840–1917) ***Monument to Balzac***, 1891–97, Bronze, 9 ft 3 in × 4 ft × 3 ft 5 in (2.82 × 1.22 × 1.04 m)

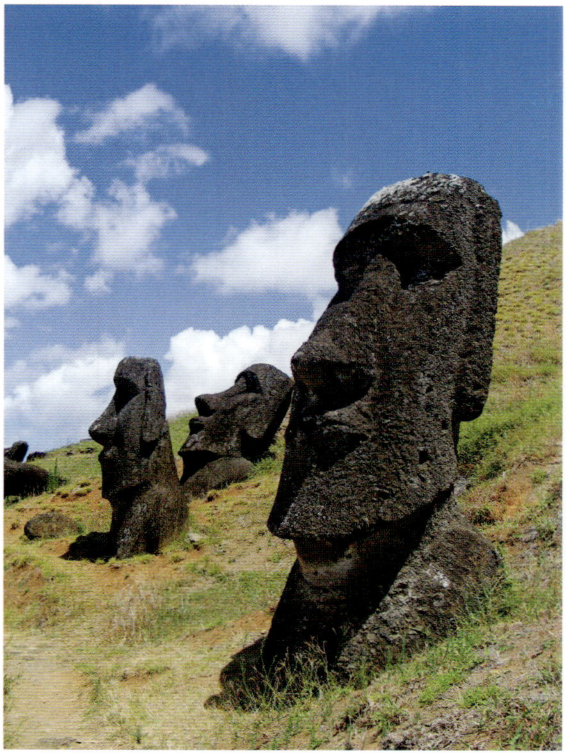

1

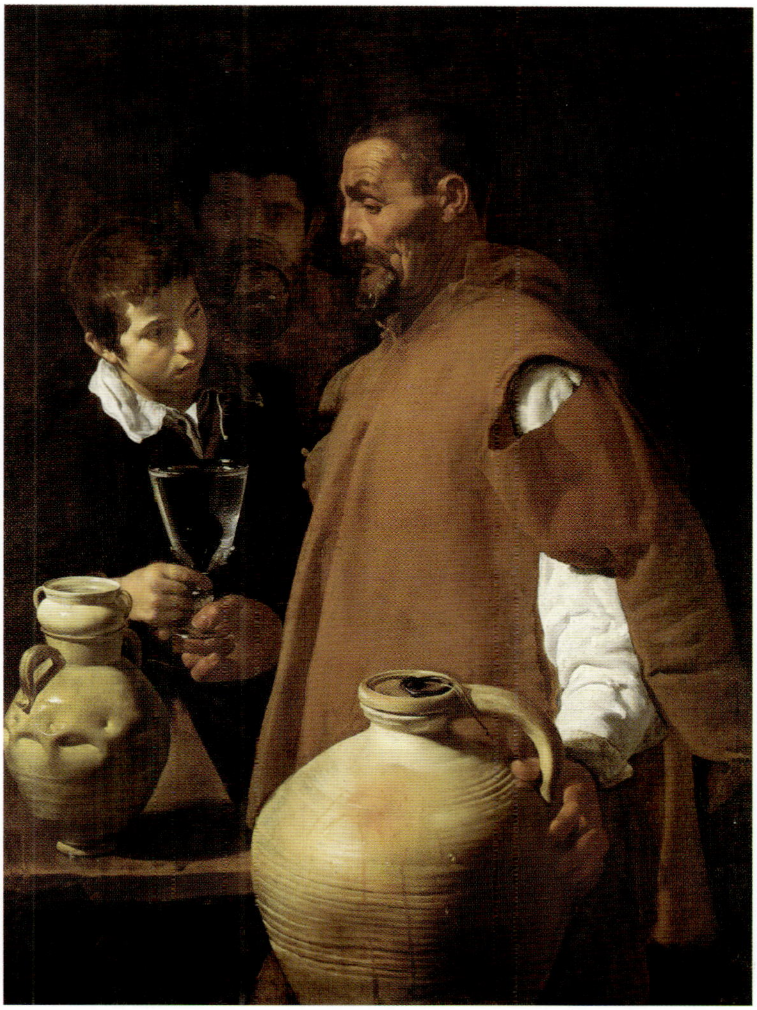

2

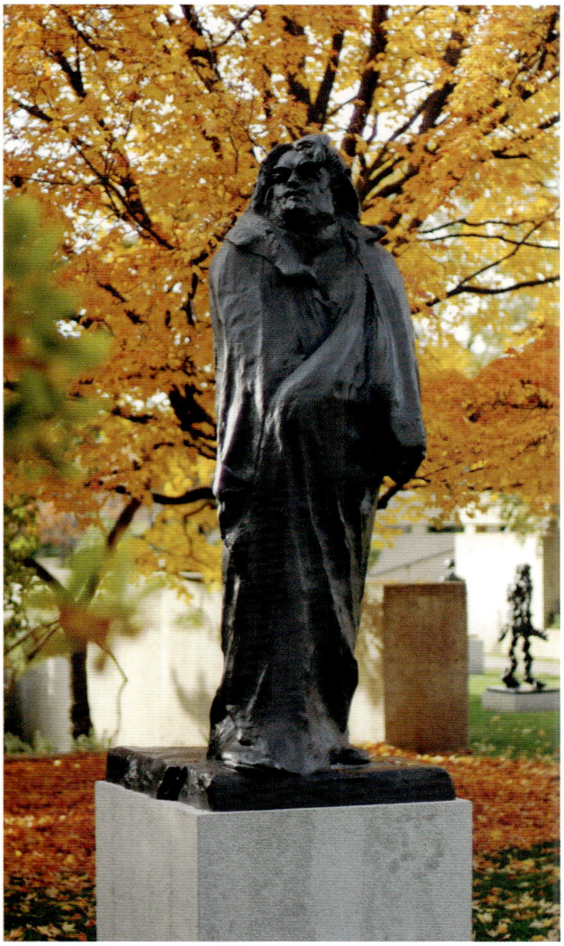

3

51 MATERIALS AS ART

ART CAN BE GENERATED THROUGH ENGAGEMENT WITH A PARTICULAR MATERIAL

In the late twentieth century, a number of artists began to make work whose central feature was the behavior of the medium in which they worked. Thus the New York painter Morris Louis (1912–62) made pictures in which he poured thin layers of paint onto large swaths of unprimed canvas. The resulting pictures are fundamentally demonstrations of how paint behaves under these circumstances, staining and spreading to create soft-edged veils. This approach was expanded upon by the painter Paul Jenkins (1923–2012), who devised an array of mechanical means to pour and mix paint onto a surface, revealing sometimes surprising properties of the material.

A more aggressive approach was taken by Lawrence Poons (1937–) in the 1970s when he began to pour large quantities of very thick paint onto canvases. The paint was allowed to move freely as successive colors were combined, building to three-dimensional surfaces.

In a rather different vein, the gargantuan steel sculptures of Richard Serra (1939–) are dependent on the physical properties of enormous steel plates. They rely in large part simply on the behavior and appearance of medium.

The rather prosaic substance of concrete is central to many of the sculptures of Rachel Whiteread (1963–), in which its capacity to pour, fill, and set hard is used to render palpable interior volumes that are usually filled with air. A more challenging example is the work of Dan Flavin (1933–96), who made many artworks using commercial fluorescent light fixtures. The resulting pieces incorporate both the fixtures and the light envelopes they engender.

In the work of all these artists there runs the idea that the artwork gains authority by promoting, exploring, and dramatizing the characteristic behavior and appearance of a medium.

1 Liza Lou (1969–)
Kitchen, 1991–96, Glass beads

In this life-size kitchen, all the surfaces are created with beadwork, an example of a look and enterprise driven by a medium, in this case that of traditional beading techniques. The artist has continued to use beadwork for her sculpture even as it has become more abstract and minimal.

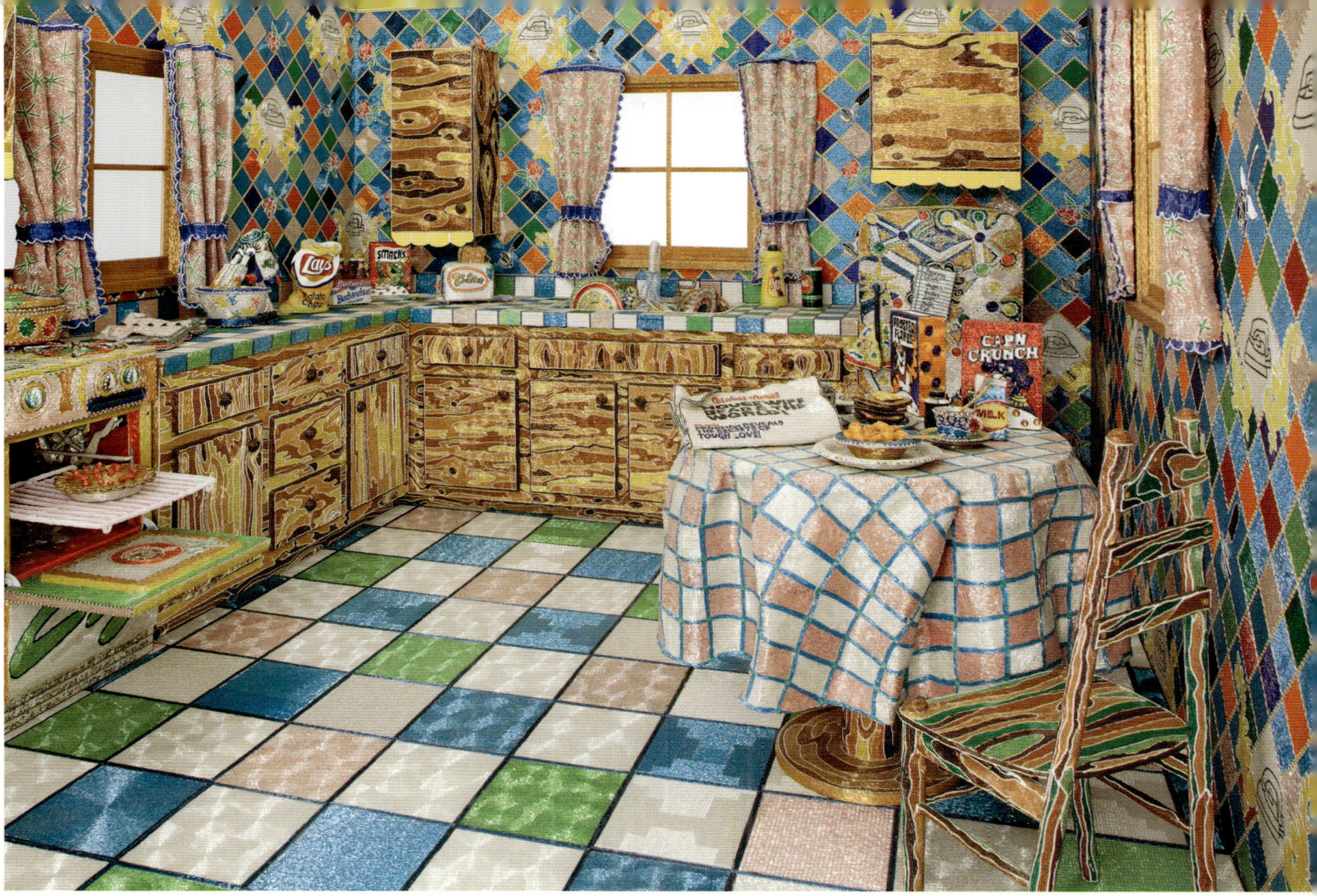

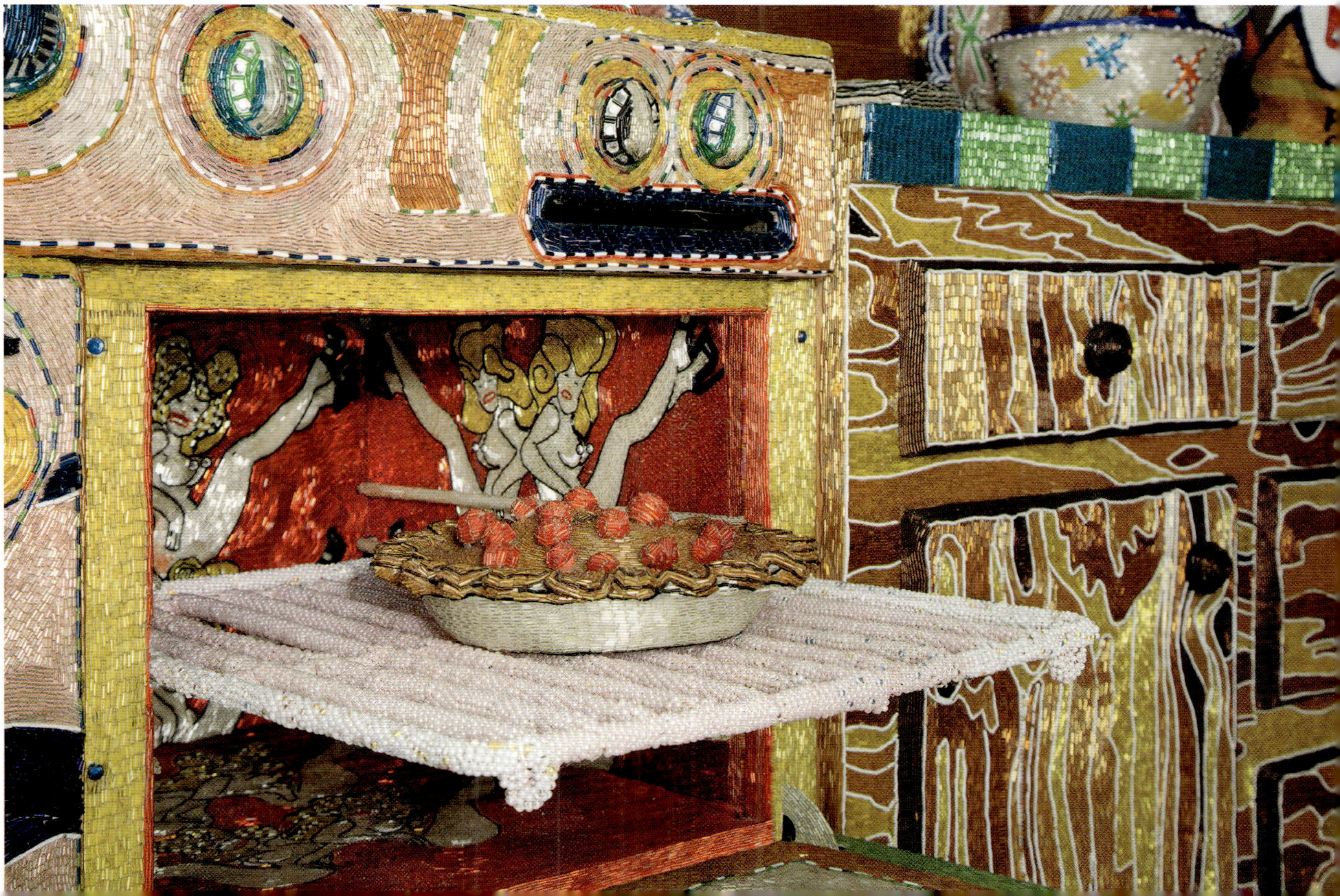

1

52 MINIMALISM

ART STRIPPED BARE

Minimalism is a broad art movement that emerged at the end of the 1950s, in part as a reaction to the foregoing style of Abstract Expressionism. It is characterized by artworks that seek to strip away the traditional endeavors of art such as personal expression, narrative content, aesthetic engagement, compositional hierarchies, or symbolic meaning. Instead, Minimalist artists asserted the primacy of the object itself and the importance of the experience of the object for the viewer unmediated by the artist. Amongst the most important practitioners of Minimalism are Donald Judd (1928–94), Frank Stella (1936–), Carl Andre (1935–), Sol LeWitt (1928–2007), and Robert Morris (1931–).

STRATEGIES

- **Use of simple geometric shapes or forms**
  Frank Stella's early paintings, for instance, consist of parallel stripes with narrow, bare strips between them painted on thick, shaped canvases that reflect the formation of the stripes. Sol LeWitt made sculptures that consisted entirely of open cubes made from wood strips and painted white. "The most interesting characteristic of the cube," he wrote, "is that it is relatively uninteresting."
- **Use of primary colors**
  Any emotive or referential qualities of color are neutralized by using simple, pure hues.
- **Use of industrial or non-art materials**
  By deploying media not usually associated with art, such as concrete or aluminum, artworks can avoid provoking traditional responses. Carl Andre, for example, used metal squares placed on the floor.
- **Repetition of elements**
  By repeating simple elements in rows or grids, the artwork avoids any suggestion of hierarchy, compositional balance, or meaning. The parts of an artwork, said Donald Judd, should be "just one thing after another."
- **Use of techniques that do not display the touch or hand of the individual artist**
  Impersonality is an important component of Minimalism. Flat painting techniques together with mechanically ruled edges and lines avoid recording the artist's brushstroke and touch. Similarly, in sculpture, industrial techniques of fabrication remove the possibility of a physical trace of the artist.

In practice, it turned out to be very difficult to remove all aesthetic and expressive qualities from artworks even when they consisted of little more than geometric shapes or forms. The cool, clean products of Minimalism and the equally cool gallery and museum spaces in which they were displayed quickly developed into a new "look" or style.

1 Donald Judd (1928–94)
Untitled, 1991, Stainless steel with red Plexiglas

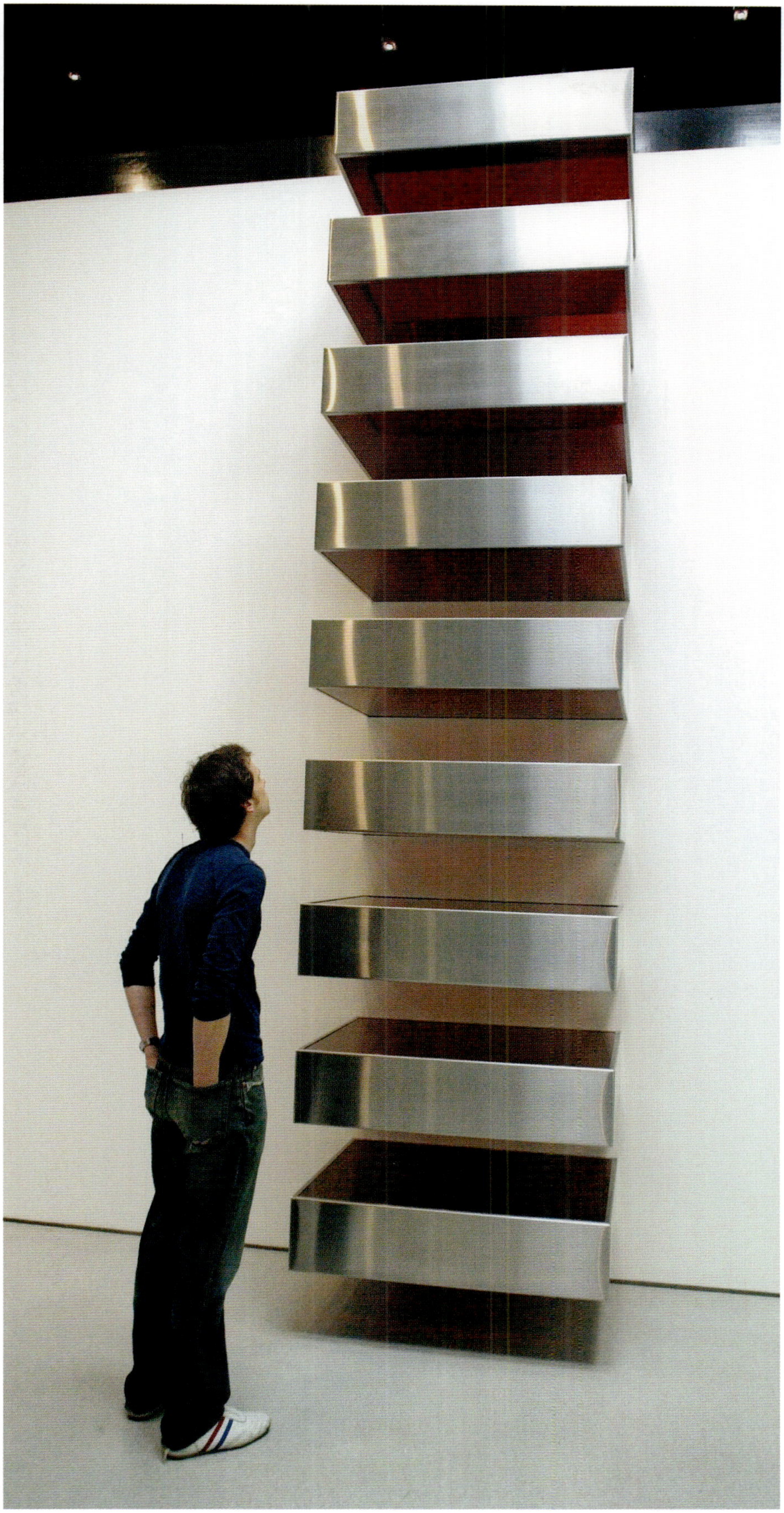

1

53 MIXED MEDIA AND MULTIMEDIA

COMBINING MATERIALS AND MEDIUMS FOR STRIKING EFFECTS

One of the features of modern Western art is its embrace of combinations of media. Traditionally, artists have worked in one medium at a time, but in the mid-nineteenth century, a new taste for experimentation began. Edgar Degas (1834–1917), for example, combined monoprints with pastel to create a hybrid form. The twentieth century saw a broadening of this approach. Pablo Picasso (1881–1973) and Georges Braque (1882–1963) combined collage and painting while Paul Klee (1879–1940) often combined pen and ink, watercolor, collage, and oil in the same work. Later in the century, several Pop artists, including Robert Rauschenberg (1925–2008) and Andy Warhol (1928–87), combined silkscreen images with acrylic paint.

This approach of combining various more or less traditional media in the same work is known as "mixed media." It requires some technical care to avoid using materials that will not do well together over time. For instance, applying acrylic paint over dry oil paint will eventually result in the cracking of the acrylic. The temptation to use ephemeral collage materials, say, printed matter on low quality paper, can result in discoloration over time and perhaps the eventual disintegration of the work.

The term "multimedia" is more contemporary and refers to artworks that combine quite disparate disciplines. A piece might combine handwritten text with video, stereo sound, and various sculptural elements. Like other experimental forms, such as installation art and performance art, multimedia is extremely open. It may or may not be interactive. It may be linear, running uninterruptedly for a set time, or it may be static or sporadic.

One of multimedia's more spectacular practitioners in recent years is the English artist and filmmaker Peter Greenaway (1942–). At the 2009 Venice Biennale, he staged a work using a life-size reproduction of *The Wedding at Cana*, a large painting by Paolo Veronese (1528–88). The event took place at the convent of San Giorgio Maggiore, where the painting was first installed in 1562. (It was removed by Napoleon and now hangs in the Louvre.) A fifty-minute presentation involved projecting digital imagery onto the reproduction and surrounding walls, including diagrams that revealed compositional structures and other geometries. Close-ups of the various figures were also projected while a soundtrack played imaginary conversations of the more than a hundred wedding guests figured in the painting.

1 Edgar Degas (1834–1917)
Little Dancer Aged Fourteen, 1878–81, Yellow wax, hair, ribbon, linen bodice, satin shoes, muslin tutu, wood base, 38 15/16 × 13 11/16 × 13 7/8 in (98.9 × 34.7 × 35.2 cm)

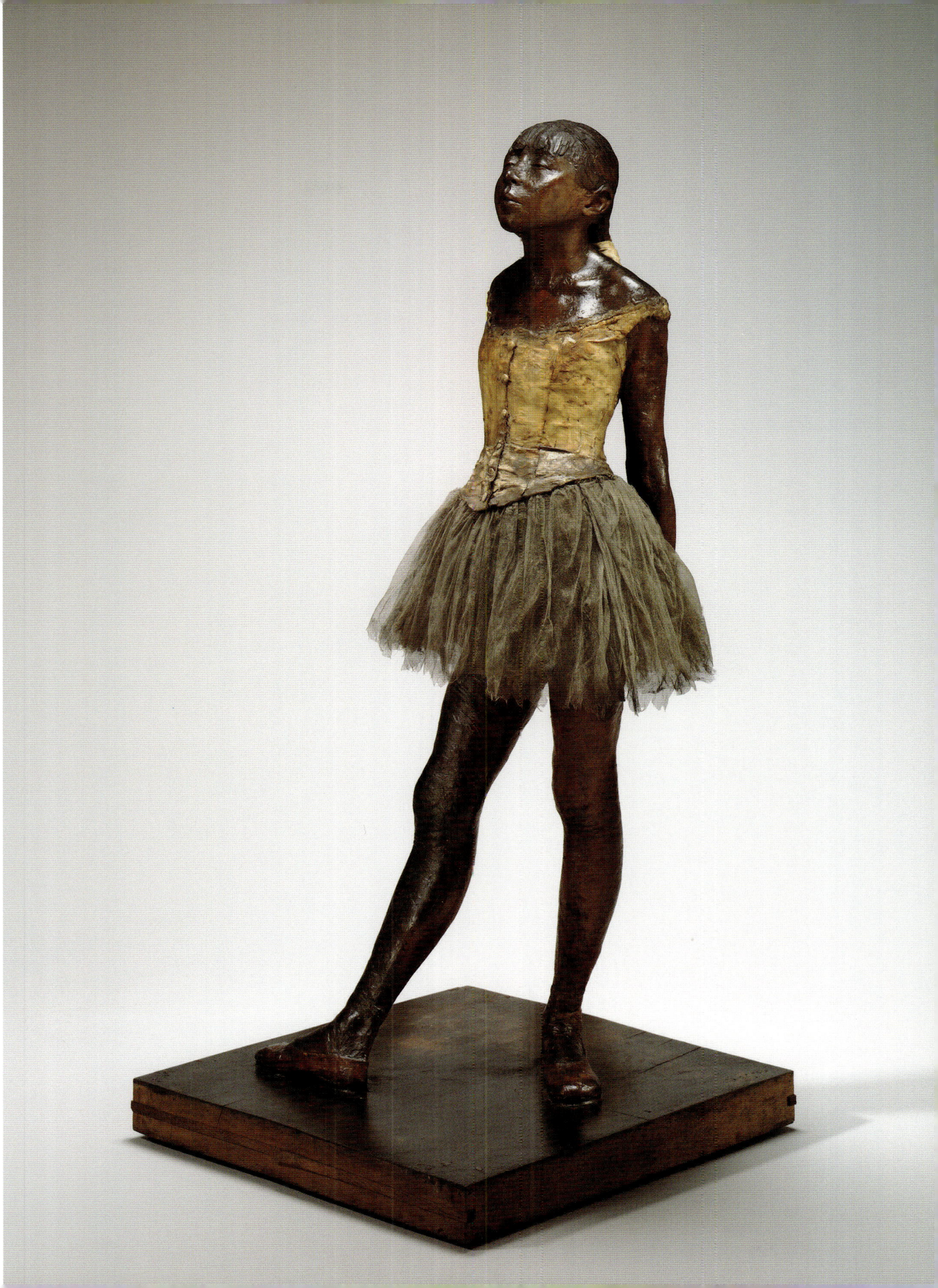

1

54 MOTIF

A RECURRING IDEA

A motif is an element in a composition or design that can be used repeatedly for decorative, structural, or iconographic purposes. A motif can be representational or abstract, and it can be endowed with symbolic meaning. Motifs can be repeated in multiple artworks and often recur throughout the life's work of an individual artist.

APPROACHES

- **Decorative**
  The motif as an individual element is repeated within a strict geometry to form a decorative whole. This is most usually the case in textile or wallpaper design.
- **Structural**
  A motif is repeated within a composition to create or reinforce a stable structure. The Russian artist Wassily Kandinsky (1866–1944) used a variety of abstract motifs, triangles, points, lines, and circles to construct numerous compositions. A somewhat different approach was pursued by Claude Monet (1840–1926) when he did paintings in series. He used repeated motifs to provide a stable structure within which he could explore the changing effects of light on an individual subject. Thus one series features a group of haystacks, another features a particular view of Rouen Cathedral, and yet another, a line of poplar trees.
- **Symbolic**
  A motif is given symbolic significance and then deployed as part of a composition to carry a precise meaning. For example, in Christian art, a lamb generally signifies Christ. Symbolic motifs may also be more personal and harder to interpret. The German artist Max Beckmann (1884–1950) used a recurring set of motifs throughout his life, including horns, masked faces, and crowns. Their exact meaning is not clear.
- **Narrative**
  A motif is given a particular meaning within a narrative context and then reused to carry the narrative forward. This is usually used in works that show multiple scenes within a single setting.

1 Wassily Kandinsky (1866–1944)
Points, 1920, Oil on canvas,
43 7/16 × 36 1/8 in (110.3 × 91.8 cm)

2 Claude Monet (1840–1926)
Waterloo Bridge, London, at Dusk,
1904, Oil on canvas,
25 7/8 × 40 in (65.7 × 101.6 cm)

3 Claude Monet (1840–1926)
Waterloo Bridge, London, at Sunset, 1904, Oil on canvas,
25 13/16 × 36½ in (65.6 × 92.7 cm)

Monet paints the same scene under different light conditions. The subject matter becomes a motif.

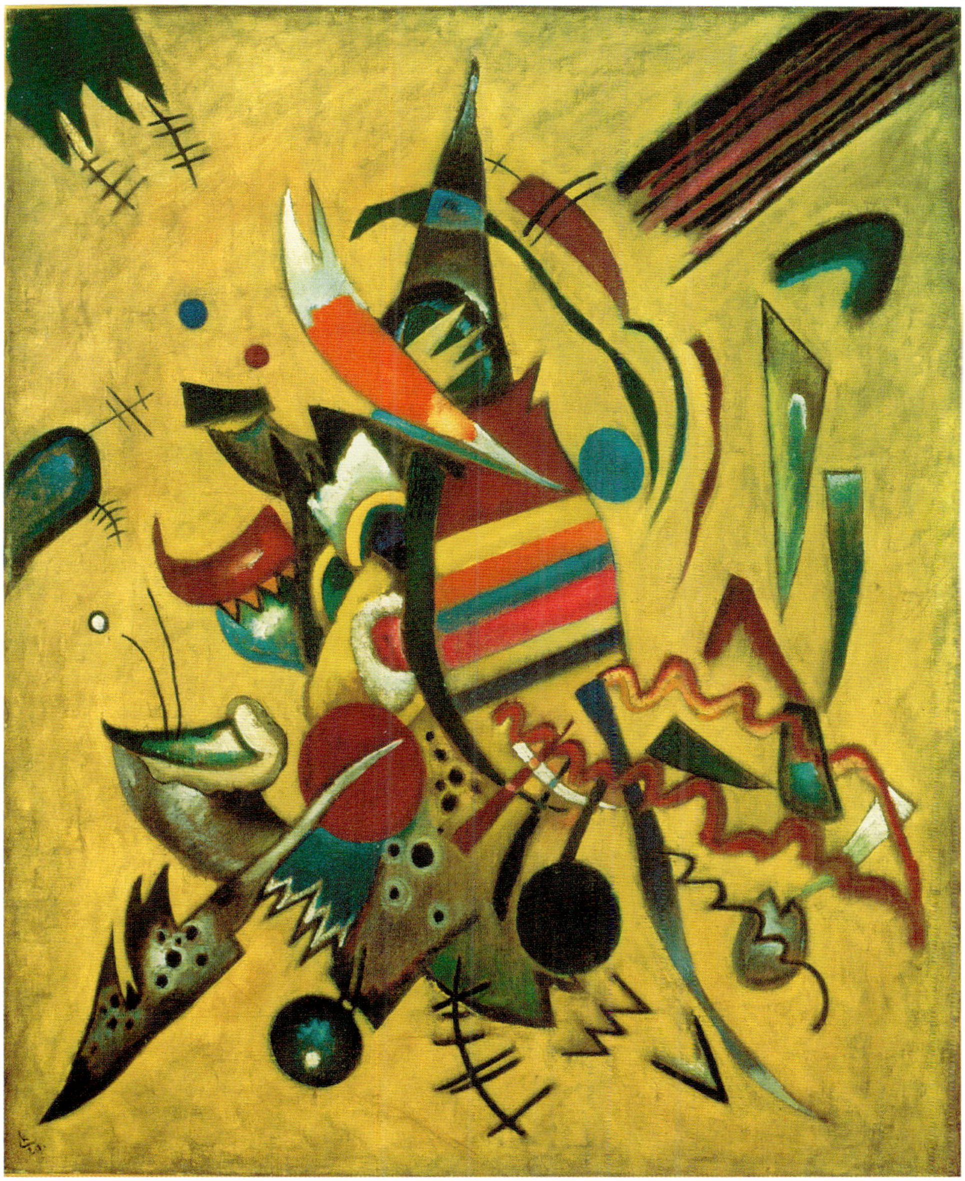

1

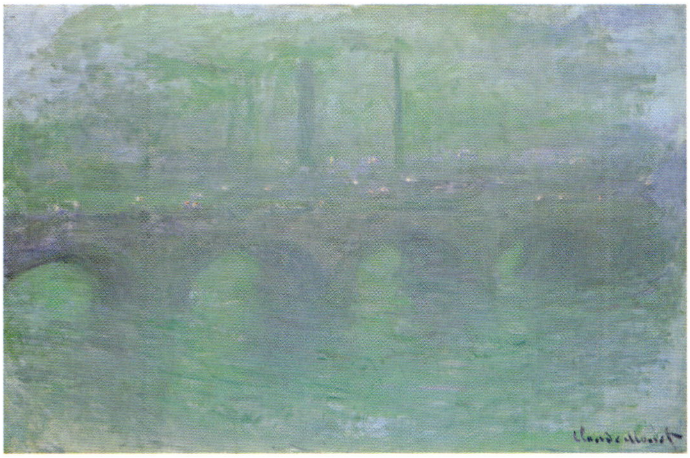

2

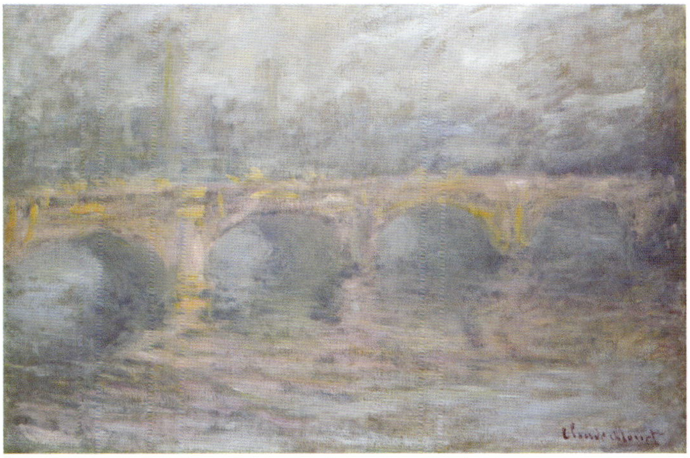

3

55 MOVEMENT

THE REWARDS OF DESCRIBING MOVEMENT WITH A STATIC MEDIUM

Although inherently static, painting and sculpture do sometimes try to convey a sense of movement. In classical and Baroque painting, figures were often depicted in motion, and the sense of motion was often increased by the use of devices such as flowing lines running through the composition as well as the literal depiction of moving forms. In the early twentieth century, the Italian Futurists Filippo Marinetti (1876–1944), Gino Severini (1883–1966), Umberto Boccioni (1882–1916), and Giacomo Balla (1871–1958) used stop-motion images to convey the dynamics of motion, which were much influenced by the photographs of Eadweard Muybridge (1830–1904). Muybridge pioneered stop-motion photographic techniques and made an exhaustive exploration of both human and animal movement. The Futurists were also influenced by the chronophotography of Etienne-Jules Marey (1830–1904). Marey's technique involved a camera that took twelve exposures in one second, which were then printed together on a single plate.

The advent of the motion picture largely shifted movement into the realm of another art form. Even so, many modern artists have mimicked the effects of photographic blur and stop-motion. Other photographic effects such as cropping, as well as new information from photography about how various creatures and objects actually appear when in motion, has added considerably to the vocabulary of movement.

OPTIONS

- Dynamic movements within the composition
- The depiction of forms or figures that are clearly in motion
- Overlayed or sequential stop-action images
- The rendering of photographic effects associated with motion, such as edge blur, dragged forms, and cropping

(For artworks that incorporate real movement, see *Kinetic Art* on page 98.)

1 Eadweard Muybridge (1830–1904)
Boys Playing Leapfrog, 1883–86, Collotype, 6^3/$_8$ × 17¼ in (16.2 × 43.8 cm)

Muybridge's photographs revolutionized the way people thought about movement. His influence was felt by the Cubists and Futurists, as well as by Marcel Duchamp and later artists, such as the British Expressionist Francis Bacon (1909–92).

2 Joseph Mallord William Turner (1775–1851)
Calais Pier, 1803, Oil on canvas, 67¾ × 94½ in (172 × 240 cm)

Turner brilliantly captures the violent movement of wind and waves by running powerful swirling lines through the composition.

3 Umberto Boccioni (1882–1916)
Elasticity, 1912, Oil on canvas, 39^3/$_8$ × 39^3/$_8$ in (100 × 100 cm)

The Italian Futurist Boccioni attempts to describe the movements of people and vehicles in the city with multiple brushstrokes that emulate the effect of stop-motion photography.

4 Marcel Duchamp (1887–1968)
Nude Descending a Staircase. No. 2, 1912, Oil on canvas, 57^7/$_8$ × 35^1/$_8$ in (147 × 89.2 cm)

Exhibited at the Armory Show in New York in 1913, the painting caused a sensation. Using devices familiar to Cubist and Futurist art, the painting tracks the motion of a naked model moving down a staircase. The simplified forms reduce the human figure to a machinelike entity.

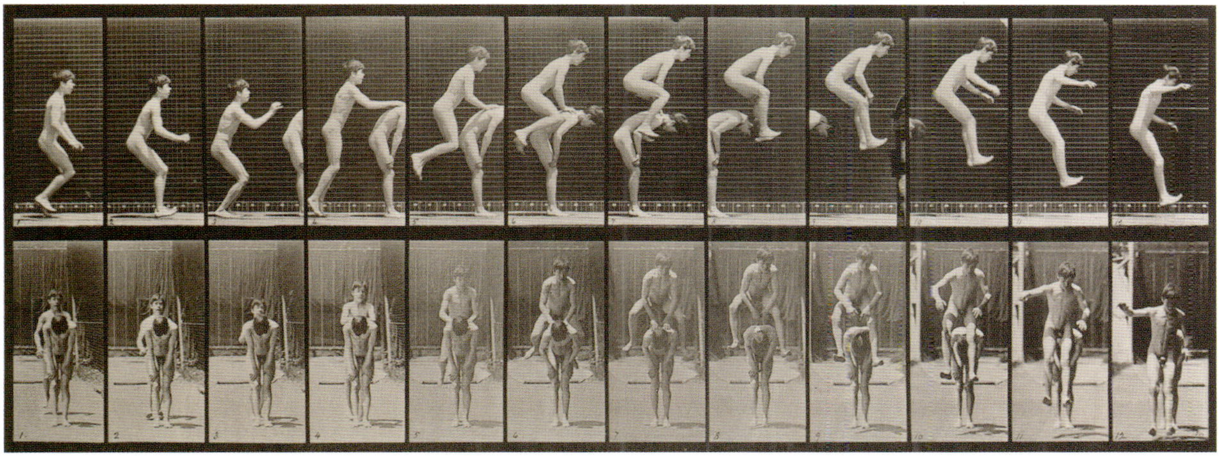

1

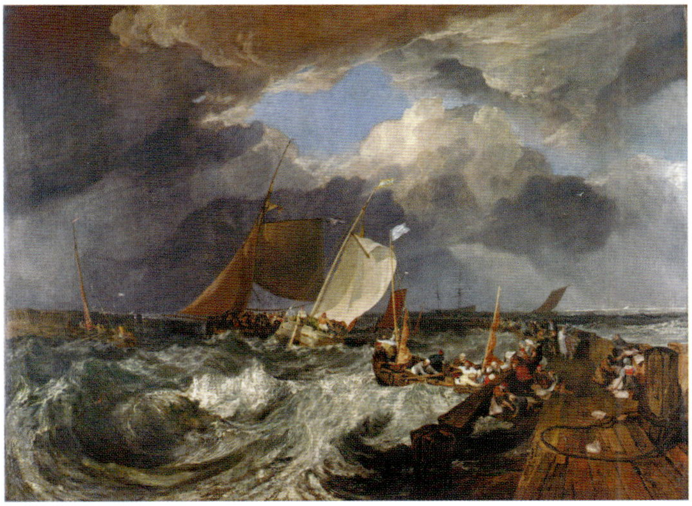

2

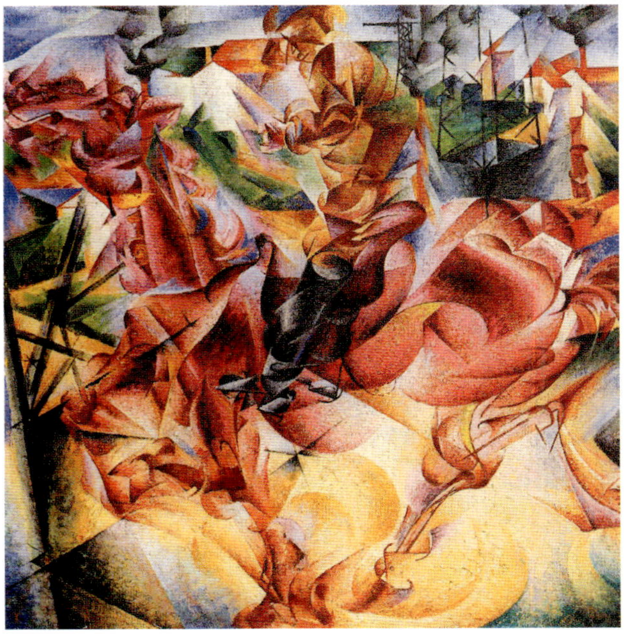

3

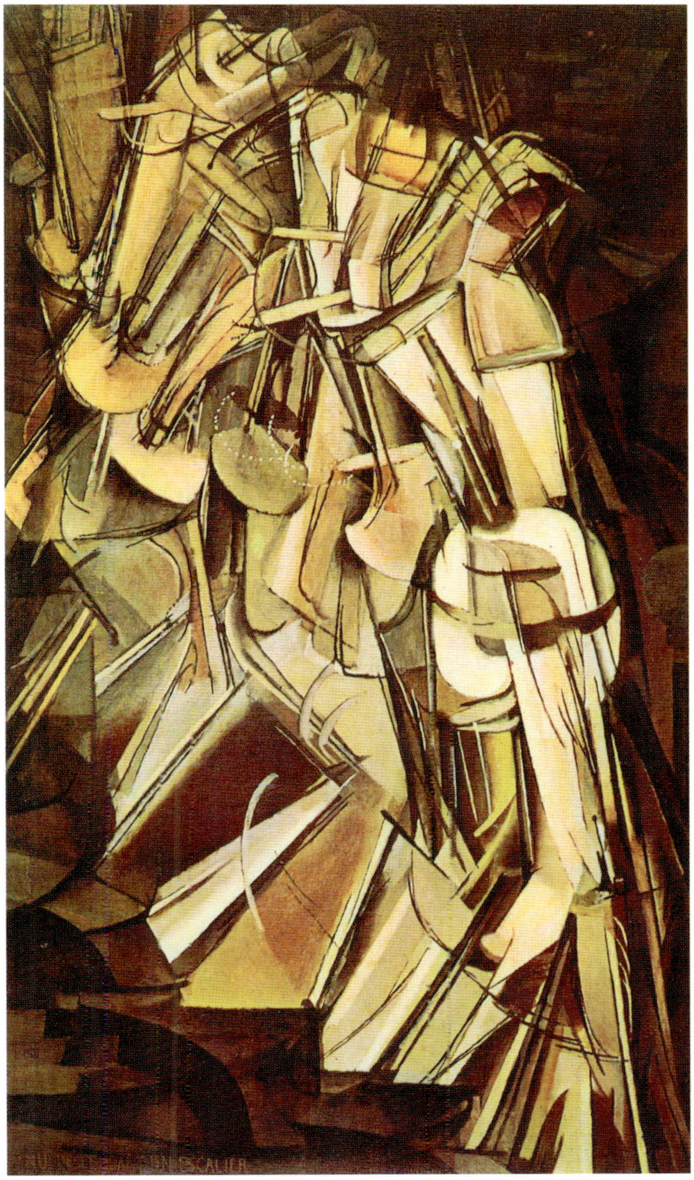

4

56 NARRATIVE

VISUAL STORY TELLING

Narrative or storytelling can be highly effective in painting and sculpture. Because the image is static, however, narrative strategies are very different from those of film or literature. Stories unfold over time so painting and sculpture are obliged to find ways of suggesting the passage of time and the continuity of action. The main techniques are as follows:

- **Single scene**
  One moment in the narrative is depicted. The selection is usually a pivotal moment in a story. Most narrative art follows this pattern, from Greek amphorae to Renaissance religious paintings.
- **Continuous scene**
  A narrative continues through various events within a single frame. Ancient examples include the metope on the Parthenon, Trajan's Column, and the Bayeux Tapestry.
- **Multi-scene**
  Multiple events within a narrative are depicted in a single scene, with characters making repeated appearances. While this can sometimes tax the viewer who is trying to discern the sequence, it has the advantage of simultaneity. Various components of a story can be experienced at the same time.
- **Panoramic**
  Multiple events take place within a single scene. However, they do not show repeated views of the same characters but rather events within a broader unfolding drama. This was a technique more often used in ancient art to depict the progress of a war or ongoing doings of various gods.
- **Progression in location**
  Multiple events take place within a single scene at a specific location. The idea is to show a sequence of actions in time at a particular place.
- **Sequential framing**
  Each event is placed within its own frame and the frames are arranged in sequence. This is the technique of comic books, manga, and graphic novels. Many variations are possible, including variety of shape, orientation, and size of frames; images that break out of frames; addition of speech balloons, verbal sound cues, and accompanying narrative or descriptive text.

1 William Hogarth (1697–1764)
A Rake's Progress, 1732–35,
Oil on canvas, 24⅝ × 29½ in
(62.6 x 74.9 cm)

One of a series of eight paintings showing the dissolution of a spendthrift young gentleman who squanders his inheritance on prostitutes, alcohol, and gambling.

2 Apollodorus of Damascus
Battle against the Dacians. Retreat by the Dacians into the Mountains,
Trajan's Column, 113 CE, Bas relief,
Height of base: 5 ft 7 in (1.7 m);
Height of shaft: 88 ft 3 in (26.9 m);
Diameter of shaft: 12 ft (3.7 m)

A series of historical events are shown in sequence in a spiral ascending the column.

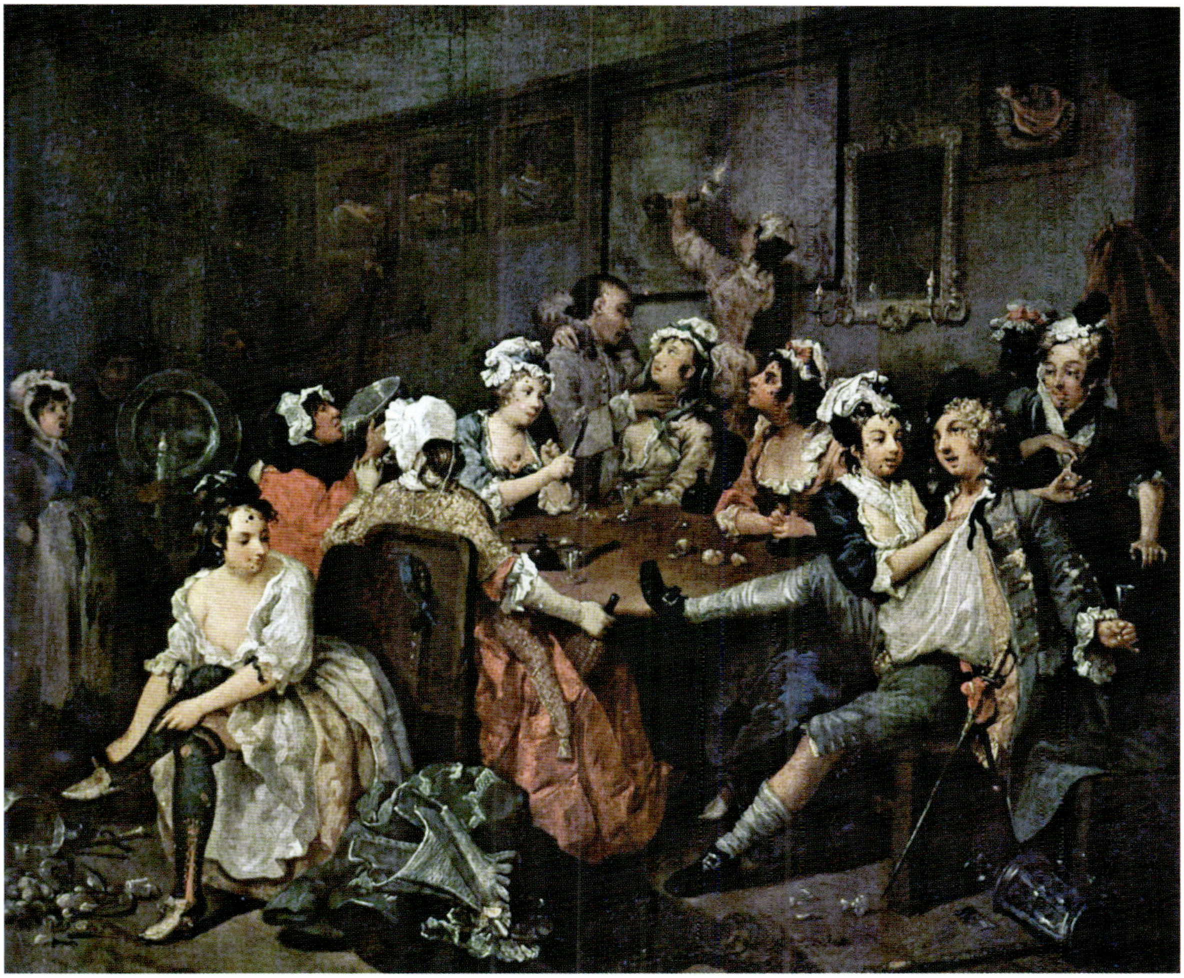

1

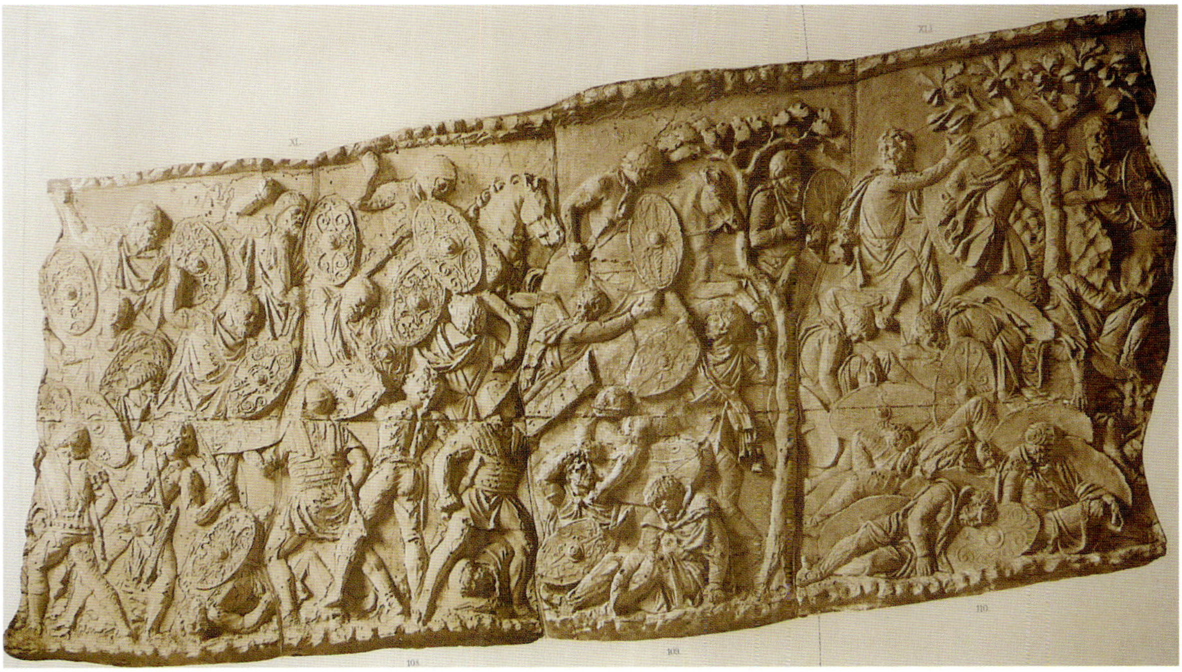

2

57 OP ART

PERCEPTUAL TRICKERY YIELDS VISUAL EXCITEMENT

"Op art" is a contraction of the term "optical art," and applies to art that creates a perceptual illusion or visual disturbance on the surface of the canvas. This is usually achieved by deploying various kinds of geometry in which the viewer's eye is confused when figure/ground relationships compete, or when improbable perspectival distortions are displayed. Thus in Brigitte Riley's painting *Zephyr* of 1976, closely packed wavy lines cover the canvas creating a shimmer in the viewer's eye that conveys both a sense of movement and an illusion of rippling space on the surface of the canvas.

Interest in optical effects goes back at least to the 1920s, when Marcel Duchamp (1887–1968) experimented with rotating discs painted with spirals to create powerful illusions. In the 1930s, Victor Vasarely (1906–97) produced works that created a sense of spatial distortion on the surface of the canvas using black and white geometric formations. In the United States, the postwar paintings of Joseph Albers (1888–1976) with their concentration of perceptual relationships between color and geometry were particularly influential. The term "Op Art" was coined in *Time Magazine* in 1964, when a more powerful interest was emerging in such art. The Responsive Eye, an exhibition at the Museum of Modern Art in New York in 1965, brought together the major practitioners of the form, including Victor Vasarely, Bridget Riley (1931–), Jesús Soto (1923–2005), Yaacov Agam (1928–), Julio Le Parc (1928–) and François Morellet (1926–).

IN PRACTICE

- **Linear**
  Closely packed, nearly parallel lines, usually in black and white, are arranged in formations, waves, or zigzags to provoke a sense of movement and shimmer.
- **Perspectival**
  Lines or shapes are arranged so that they appear to shift in three-dimensional space close to the surface of the canvas.
- **Chromatic**
  Colored shapes or lines can be made to appear to shimmer or fluctuate, particularly when saturated color of similar tonality is juxtaposed.
- **Pattern sequencing**
  A motif is progressively altered as it is arranged in a pattern to bring about an illusion of movement and spatial position. This is a form particularly favored by the Argentinian artist Julio le Parc.
- **Moiré**
  A three-dimensional form is created in which densely packed grid formations are placed over one another creating a spatial illusion that shifts as the viewer moves in front of the work.

These strategies can be elaborated and combined with each other or with other elements to create endless possibilities.

See also: *Trompe l'Oeil* on page 200

1 Bridget Riley (1931–)
Zephyr, 1976, Acrylic on linen, 88 3/8 × 42¼ in (224.5 × 107.3 cm)

2 Vasarely paintings at auction

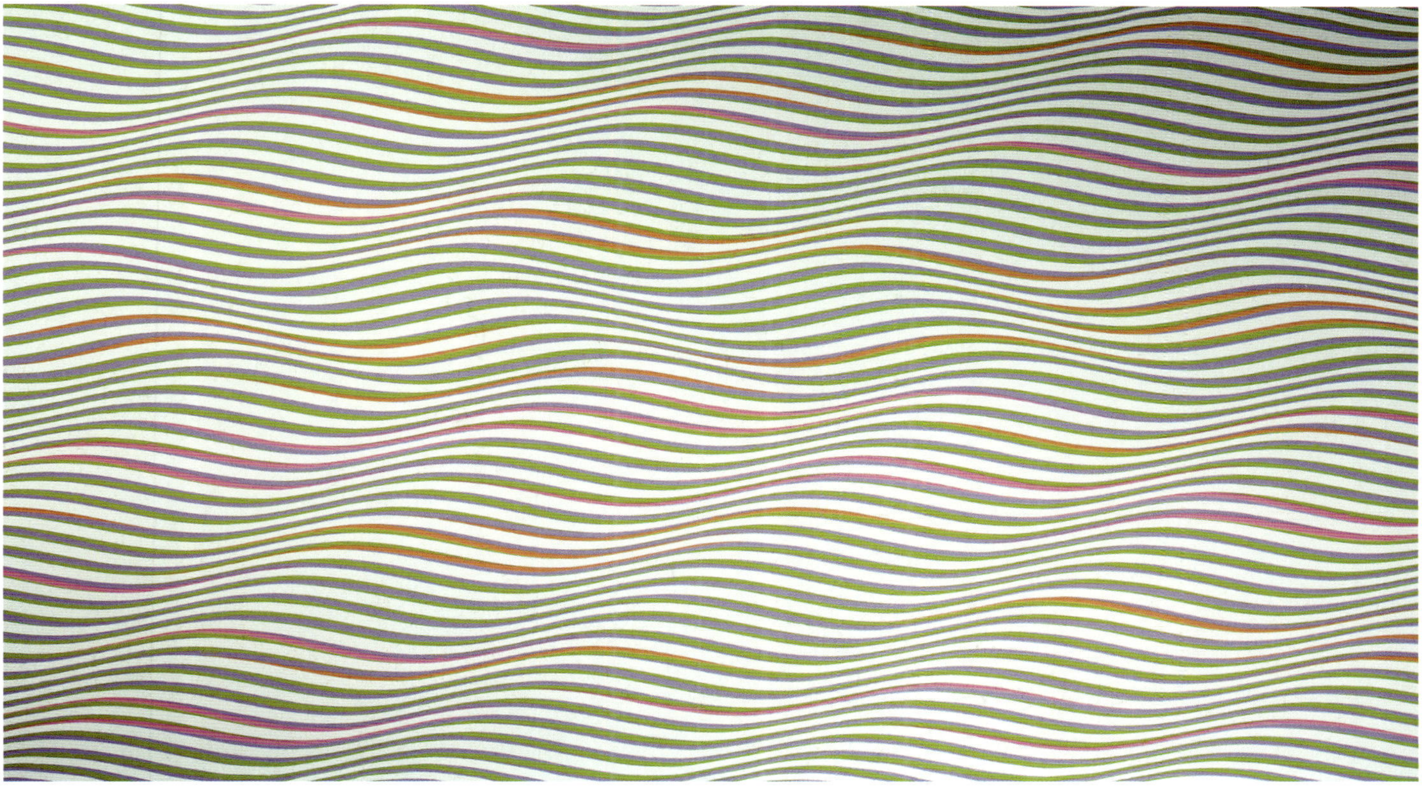

1

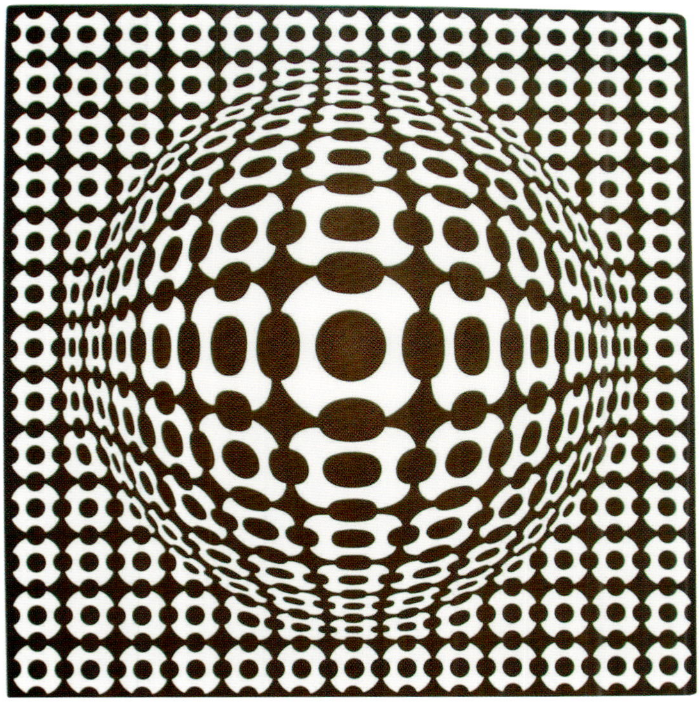

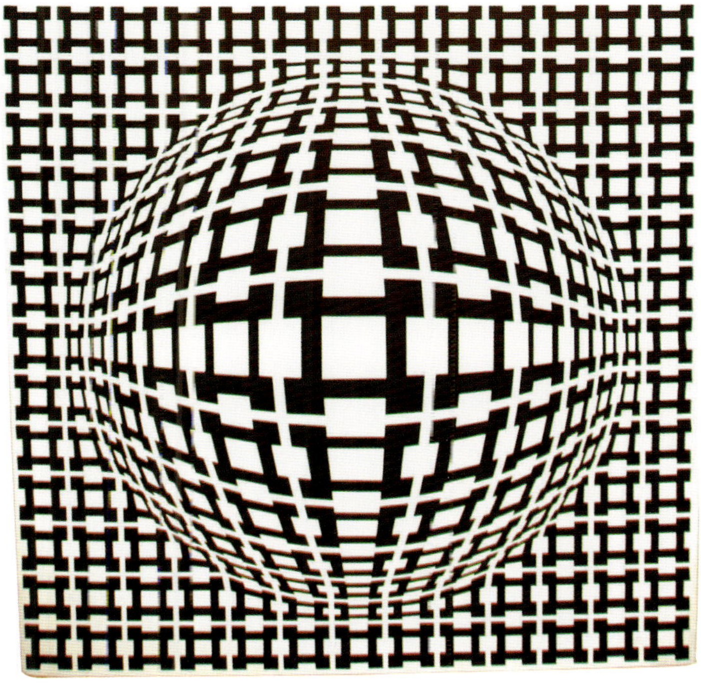

2

58 OVERLOAD

PACKING AN ARTWORK WITH INFORMATION

A work of art can sometimes be made more compelling and engaging by increasing the amount and density of information it displays. Overloading an image, creating a surfeit of incident and interest, can be a spectacular but also a somewhat primitive strategy. Some early northern European art delighted in a great wealth of visual information, packing each part of a composition with dazzling rendering and elaborately crafted detail. Such artworks often suffer from the negative feature of overload—the lack of clarity that results from the absence of a clear hierarchy of importance within the image.

A number of modern artists have deployed a sense of overload as a positive strategy. The very quality of surfeit and the almost unpleasant sense of claustrophobia that results from it take on an expressive roll in the work of artists such as Audrey Flack (1931–) or Donald Roller Wilson (1938–).

Overload is not limited to representational art and may be equally applied to abstract or decorative art.

1 Pieter Aertsen (1508–75)
Butcher's Stall with the Flight into Egypt, 1551, Oil on wood panel, 48½ × 59 in (123.2 × 149.9 cm)

The painting dazzles with a wealth of descriptive detail, but the key narrative, the flight of the Holy Family into Egypt, is all but obliterated by the visual pyrotechnics.

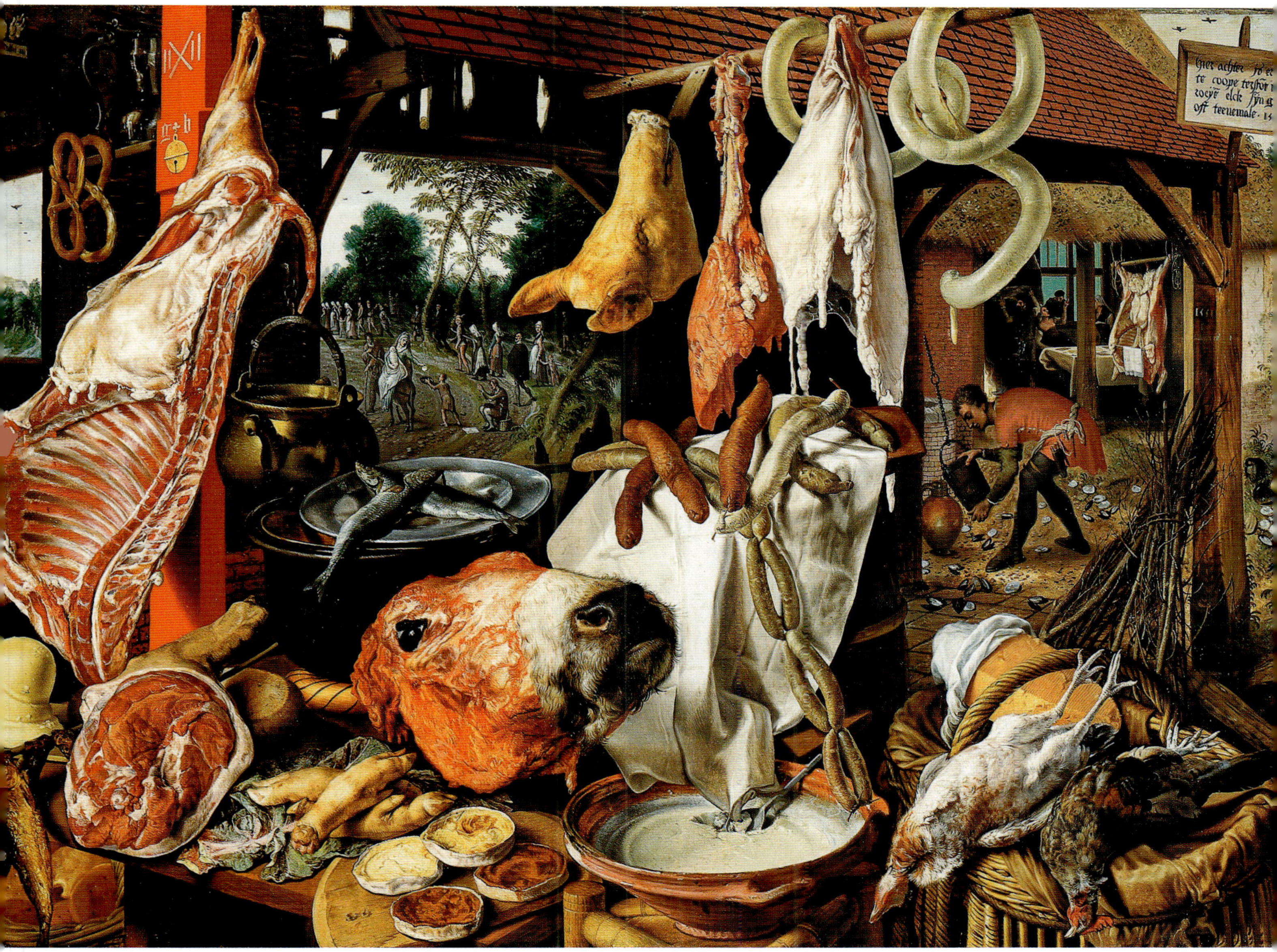

1

59 PERFORMANCE ART

THE ARTIST BECOMES THE ARTWORK

Performance art is a modern form in which the artist is the focus for a live interaction with an audience. The form is extremely open and may incorporate speech, singing, acting, dance, props, multimedia displays, other performers, music—in fact, almost anything the artist cares to dream up. Such events generally differ from theater in that they rarely seek to simply entertain, nor do they follow traditional conventions of stage narrative. On the other hand, there are times when performance art is indistinguishable from such mainstream forms as dance, stand-up comedy, poetry reading, mime, and circus.

Although the term "performance art" wasn't coined until the 1960s, the practice goes back to the Dada movement in Zurich, in 1916, when a group of young artists gave performances at the Café Voltaire often featuring simultaneous poetry, cacophonous music, and other kinds of provocative behavior. The idea that art was generated in real time, that it couldn't be bought and sold, and that it could address immediate ideas and issues, all came about at this time.

The 1960s found the form taken up by the Fluxus group, an association of international artists who arranged performances around the world, often involving the American composer John Cage (1912–92). Famous practitioners in recent years include Yoko Ono (1933–), Chris Burden (1946-), Eric Bagosian (1953–) and Marina Abramovic (1946–).

APPROACHES

- **Audience participation**
  Individuals or groups are invited to enter into the performance.
- **Body as medium**
  Artists use their own bodies as vehicles. For instance, in 1971 the artist Christ Burden had an assistant shoot him in the arm from a distance of about 16 feet (5 m) in front of a live audience.
- **Time extension**
  Some performance artists have put on pieces of enormous length, ignoring the customary time frame of traditional theater. At an exhibition at New York's Museum of Modern Art, Marina Abramovic staged a work called *The Artist is Present*, in which she sat for more than seven hundred hours in the lobby, inviting visitors to sit and face her.
- **Disorienting behavior**
  The artist behaves in ways that are hard or impossible to decipher.
- **Autobiography**
  The artist uses speech, movement, and perhaps multimedia to present an autobiography. The openness of form allows for any kind of innovation in storytelling, acting-out, and self-revelation.

See also: *Dada* on page 58

1 Krzysztof Zarebski (1939–)
BEBECHY, 2012, Performance/installation, Space Womb Gallery, New York (KESHER V Performance Art Event)
Photo: Zosia Zeleska-Bobrowski

2 Nadja Verena Marcin
Zero Gravity, Video-still of performance, Tampa, Florida, 2013
Photograph: Violetta D'Agata
Sponsored by WARP & Aurora Aerospace

The artist recites lines from Nietzsche while undergoing zero gravity in a diving aircraft.

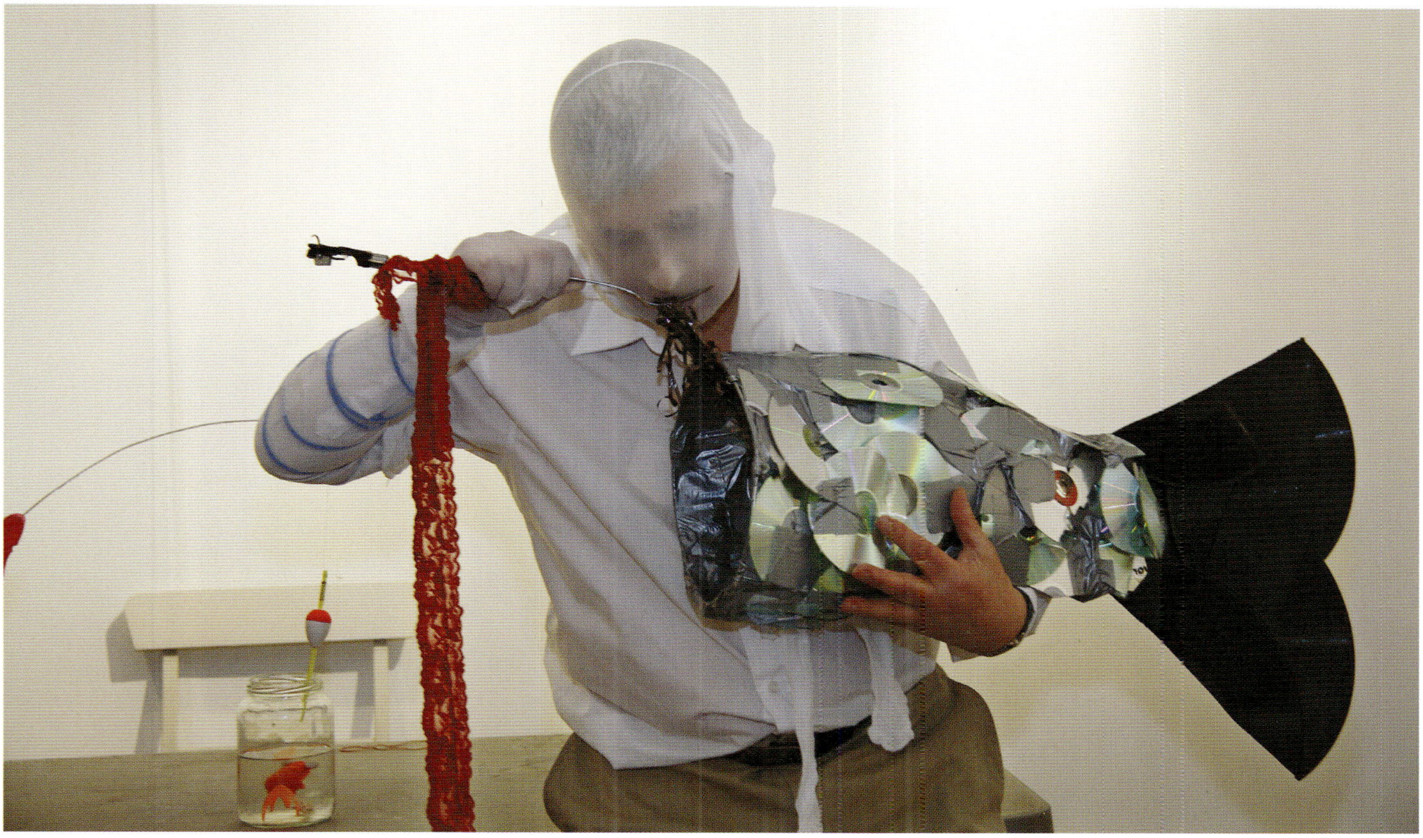

1

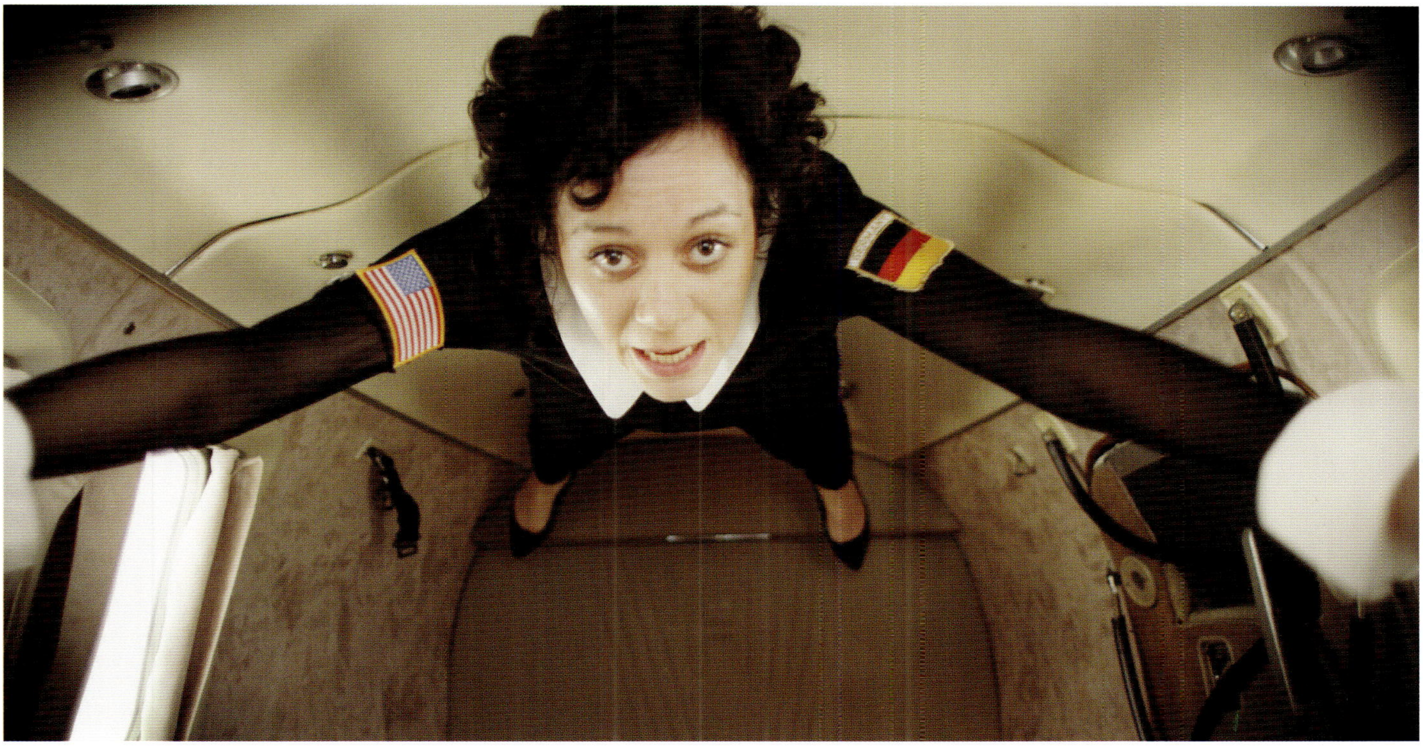

2

60 PERSPECTIVE

A SOPHISTICATED CONVENTION FOR DESCRIBING THREE-DIMENSIONAL SPACE

Perspective is the principal convention whereby a uniformly coherent three-dimensional space can be depicted on a flat surface. It is conceived as follows: The viewer looks at a scene from a fixed point. Between the viewer and the scene is a defined flat plane. This plane corresponds to the picture and is known as the "picture plane." Rays of light from the subject pass through this plane on their way to the viewer's eye. If their points of passage through the plane are recorded and reproduced, the resultant image is identical to the viewer's experience of the real scene.

A number of features immediately become evident from this approach:

- Objects that are more distant will appear to be smaller.
- Objects lying obliquely to the viewing angle will appear to be distorted because they will get smaller in the plane extending away from the viewer but remain stable in the plane standing at right angles to the viewer. Thus a circle will appear as an ellipse. This effect is known as "foreshortening."
- Parallel lines not lying in the same plane as the picture will appear to get closer together as they recede and eventually appear to join. The point at which they join is known as the "vanishing point."
- Parallel lines receding at ninety degrees horizontally to the viewer will appear to meet on the horizon line.
- Multiple vanishing points can be contained within the same work.
- When drawing simple cubic forms, it is possible from some viewpoints to achieve an image with a single vanishing point. More complex constructions might involve two vanishing points, while works that incorporate all three axes will have three vanishing points.

LIMITATIONS

Perspective does not accommodate the distortions of image that occur on the edge of a wide viewing angle. It is also limited to representing the world from a single fixed viewpoint.

1 Albrecht Dürer (1471–1528)
Perspective apparatus, 1525,
Woodblock print 3 × 8 7/16 in
(7.7 × 21.4 cm)

Dürer published a treatise on perspective in which he showed several kinds of apparatus for achieving a correct perspective drawing. Here the artist holds his eye at a fixed viewpoint defined by a pointed column. The picture plane is a wired grid beyond which lies the subject. The artist has drawn a grid on his paper in the same proportions as that of the picture plane. He then marks off key points of the subject on his paper as they appear to him viewed through the grid.

2 A viewer (v) observes three poles of identical height—(a), (b), and (c)—standing at different distances. As the light crosses the picture plane (p), the pole that is farthest away creates the shortest image.

3 Single-point perspective is demonstrated in the real world. Planes receding at right angles to the picture plane appear to meet at the horizon.

HISTORY

Perspective as a system was not known in ancient cultures, although both Greeks and Romans created some depth in their paintings by overlapping images. Medieval artists were aware that distant objects could be represented as smaller than closer objects, but they lacked an optical theory that could codify the phenomenon. The first person to fully comprehend perspective was the Renaissance architect Filippo Brunelleschi (1377–1446) in about 1413. According to artist and art historian Giorgio Vasari (1511–74), in his book *Lives of the Artists*, Brunelleschi first discovered vanishing points when he did a painting of buildings in Florence by working on top of a mirror. The entire theoretical basis of perspective was later published by Leon Battista Alberti (1404–72) in his *De Pictura* in 1436.

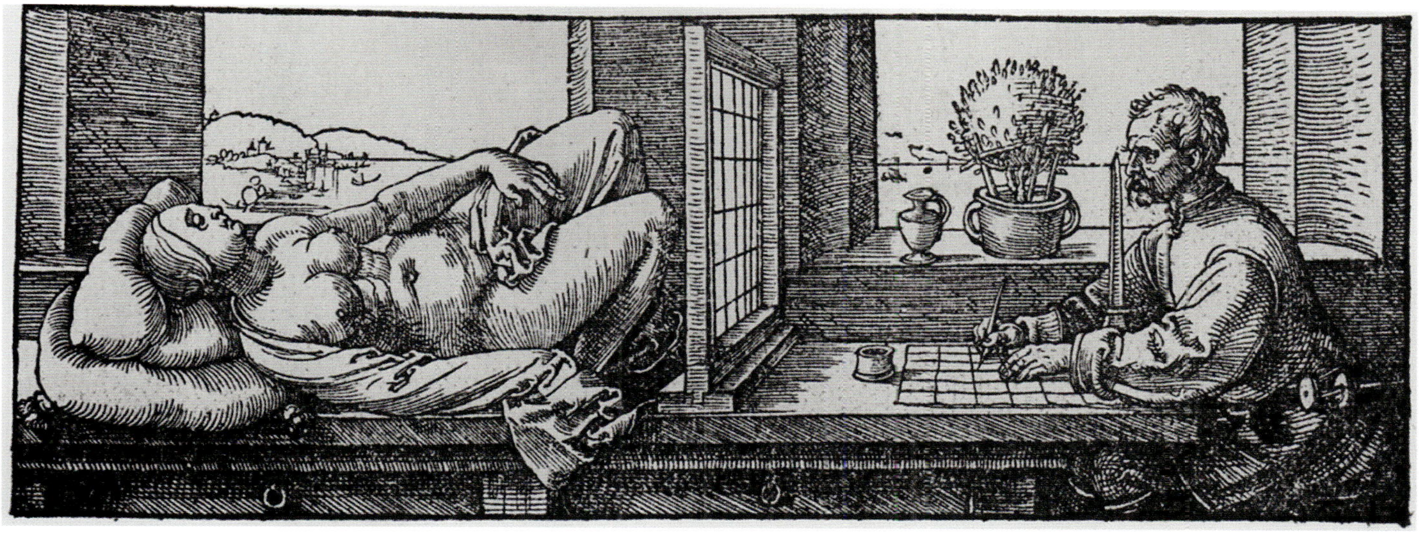

1

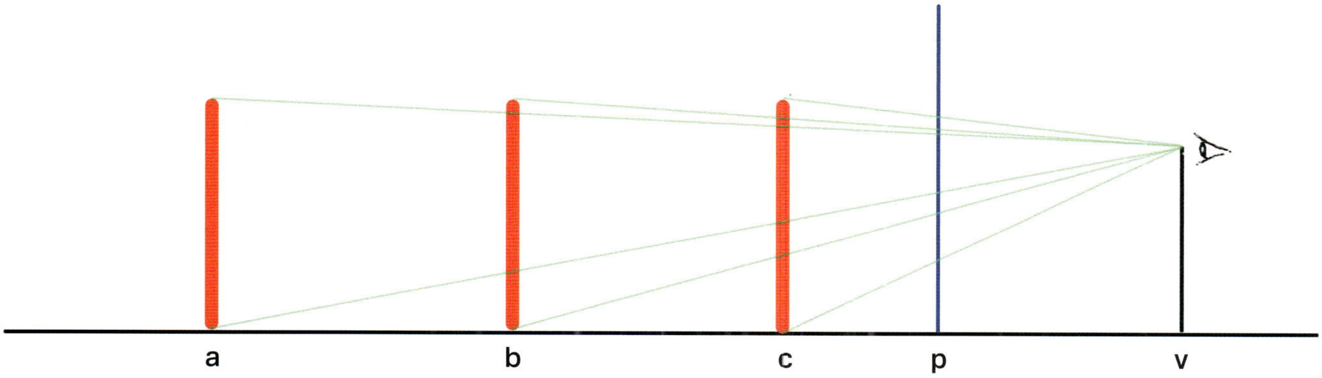

2

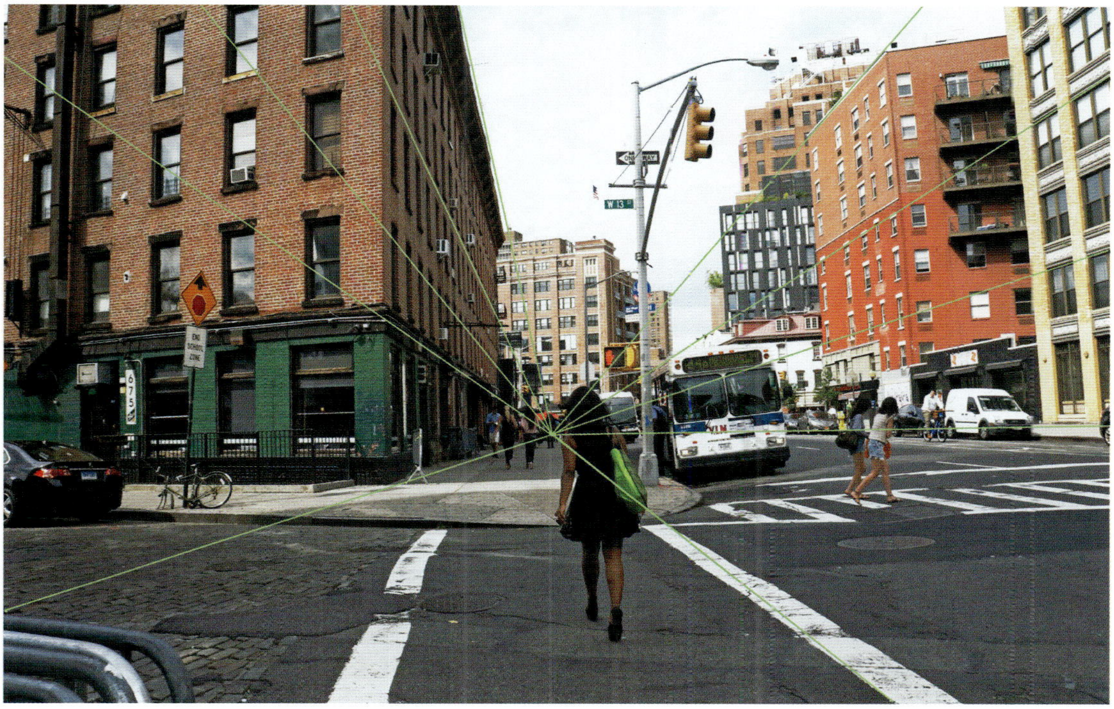

3

61 PLASTICITY

THE MEDIUM TAKES ON THE QUALITIES OF THE SUBJECT

Plasticity is the process by which a medium takes on the properties of the substance that it represents. The most common and effective examples of plasticity occur in painting when the artist manipulates the layering and fluid properties of the paint so that the paint film itself takes on a fleshlike appearance. This is very apparent in many Baroque-era paintings by artists such as Rembrandt, Velasquez, and Rubens. It has also been used to spectacular effect by a number of contemporary artists, including Lucian Freud (1922–2011) and Jenny Saville (1970–).

Plasticity is not limited to the rendering of flesh, and the history of painting is full of ravishing examples in which the physical handling of the paint takes on the qualities of such subjects as silk, satin, lacework, masonry, and foliage. John Constable (1776–1837) was able to lay on paint so that it feels like clumps of leaves, grass, or rocks. Many passages of painting by Velasquez use heavy brushing to remake buckles, embroidered clothing, elaborate hair styles and rich fabrics. Still life painters such as Jean-Baptiste-Siméon Chardin (1699–1779) and Luis Meléndez (1716–1780) built rich paint surfaces that in themselves provide equivalents for the variety of densities and textures within their subjects.

In sculpture, artists such as Antonio Canova (1757–1852) were able to manipulate the polished delicacy of marble to become an extraordinary equivalent for flesh. Sculpture also offers the artist the option of using multiple materials in a single work in order to render a more powerful sense of the varying natures of elements within the subject.

Plasticity is not the same property as direct mimicry or trompe l'oeil. It is possible, as in the case of waxworks, to build a sculpture that will more or less deceive the eye and be taken for the subject itself. But with plasticity, viewers are invited to enjoy the spectacle of transmutation taking place, to entertain the notion that what they are looking at is the subject as built in the medium.

See also: *Trompe l'Oeil* on page 200

1 Diego Velázquez (1599–1660)
Portrait of a Bufoon with a Dog, (Detail) c. 1650, Oil on canvas, 55 7/8 × 42 1/8 in (142 × 107 cm)

The artist uses lively layers of brushing to recreate the texture and density of the clothing with paint itself.

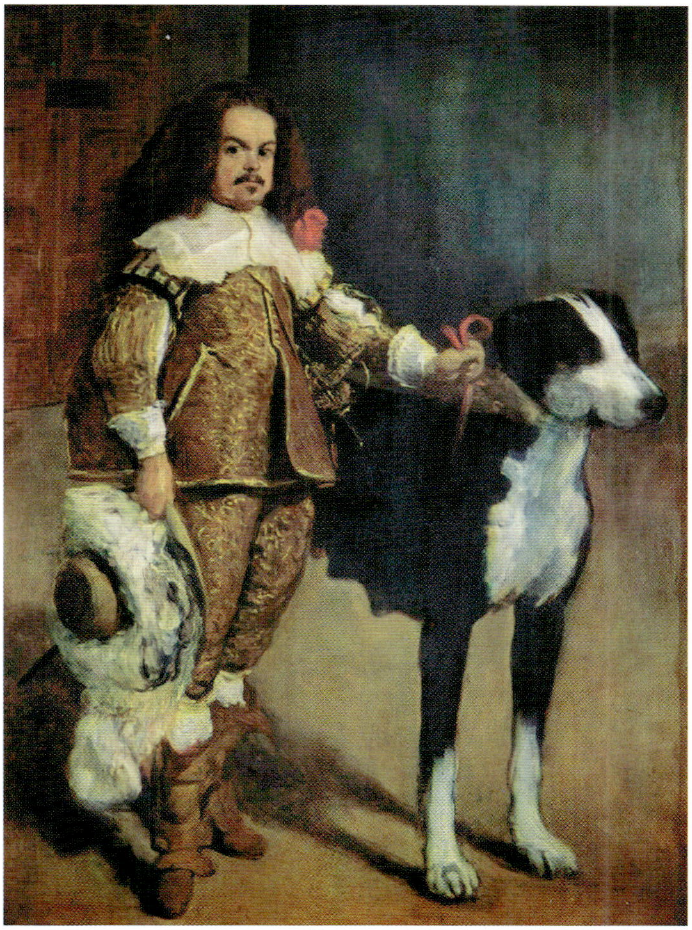

1

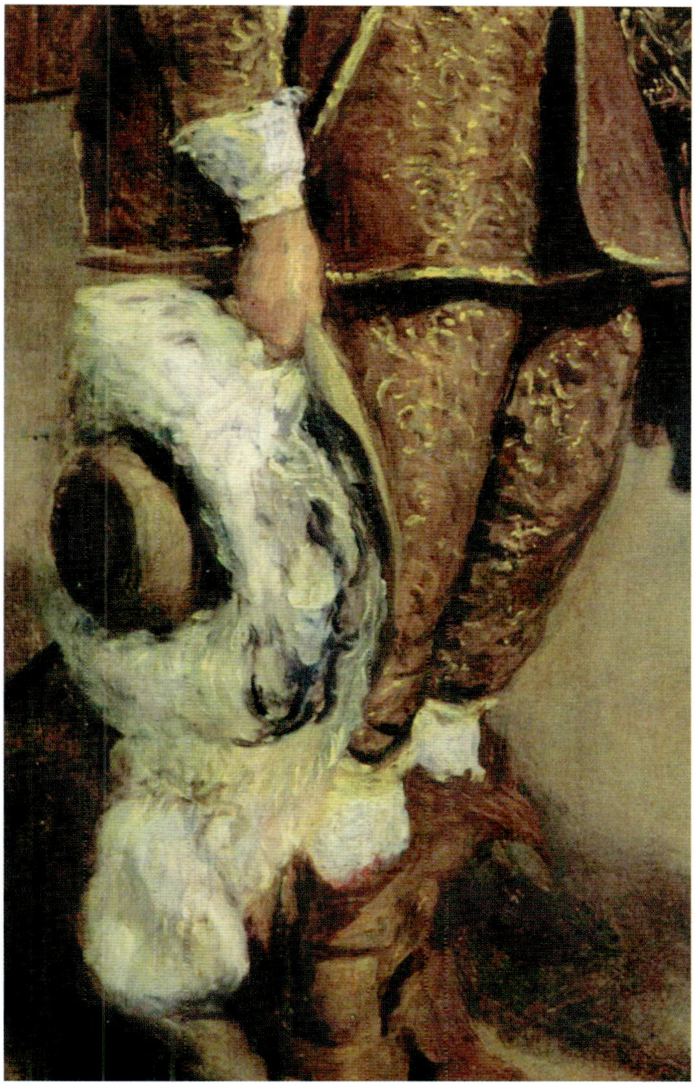

62 POLITICS AND POLEMICS

ART CAN SOMETIMES ADVOCATE, TAKE A POSITION, OR PERSUADE

From time to time, artworks have taken on a powerful voice in public debate. However, since political crises tend to be a product of a particular time and place, they rarely make lasting subject matter for painting or sculpture. Here are a number of potent polemical images that have stood the test of time.

The Disasters of War, 1810–20. Françesco Goya (1746–1828). A suite of etchings that makes a ferocious attack on the brutality and debasement that war inevitably generates. The images use a deadpan descriptive style and bitingly sarcastic titles to bring the events depicted uncomfortably close to the viewer.

The Raft of the Medusa, 1868–9. Théodore Géricault (1791–1824). The artist used all the new weapons of romantic painting to make a potent political image: energetic paint handling, enormous scale, active figures in unusual and somewhat contorted poses, along with dramatic elements such as corpses and wounded flesh.

Execution of the Emperor Maximilian, 1867–9. Édouard Manet (1832–83). Manet used flattened space and graphic strength to convey the machinelike brutality of the execution. Maximilian was placed on the Mexican throne by Napoleon III after French troops intervened in Mexican politics in the 1860s. Opposed by local forces, his regime eventually collapsed and he was caught and shot. The Mexican firing squad wears European-style uniforms, giving a deliberately generic quality to the action.

Guernica, 1939. Pablo Picasso (1881–1973). Picasso uses a highly personal vocabulary of images developed through his cubist adventures and subsequent involvement with more classical imagery. The elements stand in a shallow space arranged so that their powerful graphic shapes have maximum dramatic effect. The painting is an outraged response to the bombing of the town of Guernica in northern Spain by right-wing forces armed by Germany.

F-111, 1964. James Rosenquist (1933–). Executed in the style of billboard painting at the height of the Vietnam War, the 86-foot (26.2 m)-long picture depicts an *F-111* fighter-bomber juxtaposed with images of consumerism.

1 Françesco Goya (1746–1828)
Esto es peor, Plate 37, ***The Disasters of War*** series, 1810–20, Etching, 9¾ × 13⅜ in (24.8 × 34 cm)

The title means "This is worse." A mutilated corpse is left speared to a bush as a warning to others. Reprisals and killings of civilians were a feature of the Peninsular Wars.

2 Théodore Géricault (1791–1824)
The Raft of the Medusa, 1818–19, Oil on canvas, 16 ft 1 in × 23 ft 7 in (4.9 × 7.2 m)

The painting reflected public anger at the officers of a French naval ship who abandoned their cargo of passengers to a makeshift raft while seizing the lifeboats for themselves.

3 James Rosenquist (1933–)
F-111, 1964–5, Oil on canvas with aluminum, 23 sections, 10 × 86 ft (3 × 26.2 m)

The painting points out the complicity between middle-class consumerism and the U.S. war machine.

1

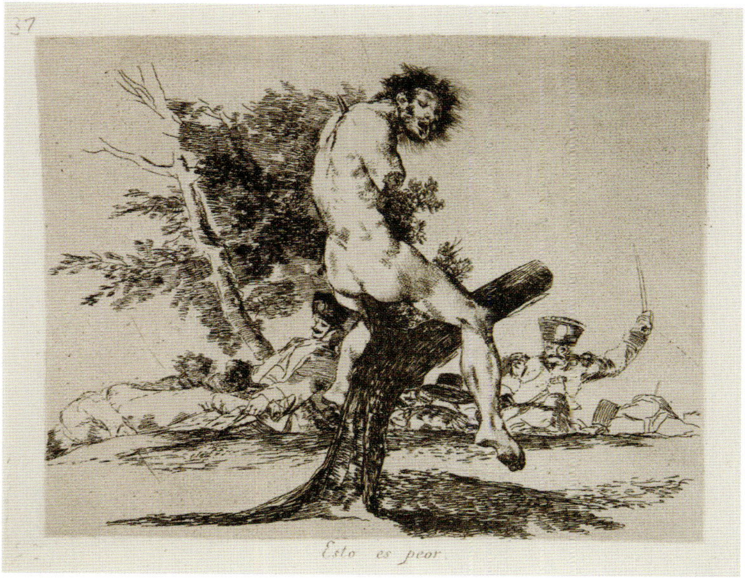

2

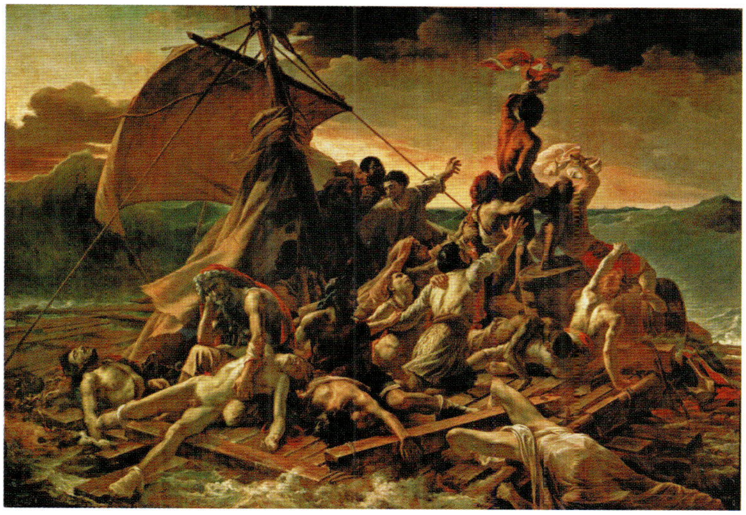

3

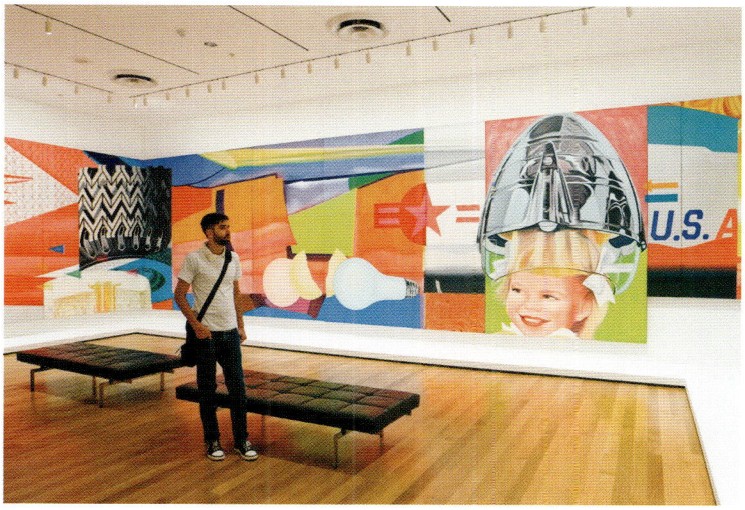

63 PREPARE AND DEVELOP

PLANNING PRACTICES AND TECHNIQUES

Many artists engage in planning and developmental stages for works of art. Although approaches to such planning can be infinitely various, a number of methods have proved fruitful and popular over the centuries. Ideas can be worked up in rough sketches, drawings, finished drawings, and even full-scale rough versions of the more finished work to come. In Italian Renaissance art, cartoons, or full-scale drawings, were used in preparation for frescos and other large-scale works such as tapestries or murals. The use of sketchbooks began almost as soon as paper became available, and they continue to be widely used by artists as a private space where ideas can be explored and problems solved. Sculptors often make preparatory models, called *maquettes*, for large sculptures.

Preparatory stages can also include presentation pieces for client approval prior to going on to the finished work. Small-scale renderings for approval of proposed projects were known as *modellos* in Italian art. The same term was used for architectural models of proposed buildings.

Some of the components of an artwork that can be resolved in a preparatory stage:

- **Conception**
  The artist will often toy with a basic idea for a work in sketch stage. Initial sketches can sometimes be thumbnails, tiny blocked outlines of an idea.
- **Placement**
  Sketches and drawings allow the artist to move elements around with ease. Artists may use tracing paper or visualization paper to manipulate multiple layers.
- **Tone**
  A tonal sketch allows the artist to think about the distribution of tone within the work.
- **Color**
  A color sketch can be made to explore color distribution, balance, and activity.
- **Engineering**
  Sculptors may use maquettes to determine balance, giving them a sense of how the work might be engineered successfully.
- **Scale and balance**
  Full-scale color sketches give a good sense of how a painting is going to feel and look. John Constable (1776–1837), for instance, did full-size oil sketches. With their loose handling and strong brushing, they are now sometimes more prized than his finished work.

Some of the most intriguing and interesting insights into the work of individual artists come from their sketchbooks and drawings. Prior to the modern era, such things were rarely exhibited; consequently, they often provide a window into the private realm of the artist.

1 Giovanni Battista Tiepolo (1690–1770)
Saint Clemens modello for an altarpiece, c. 1730–35, Oil on canvas, 27 3/16 × 21 5/8 in (69 × 55 cm)

2 Jean-Baptiste Carpeaux (1827–75)
Maquette for monument at Valenciennes, 1863–64, Plaster

3 John Constable (1776–1837)
Dedham Lock sketch, 1819, Oil on paper laid on canvas, 8¾ × 10¾ in (22.2 x 27.3 cm)

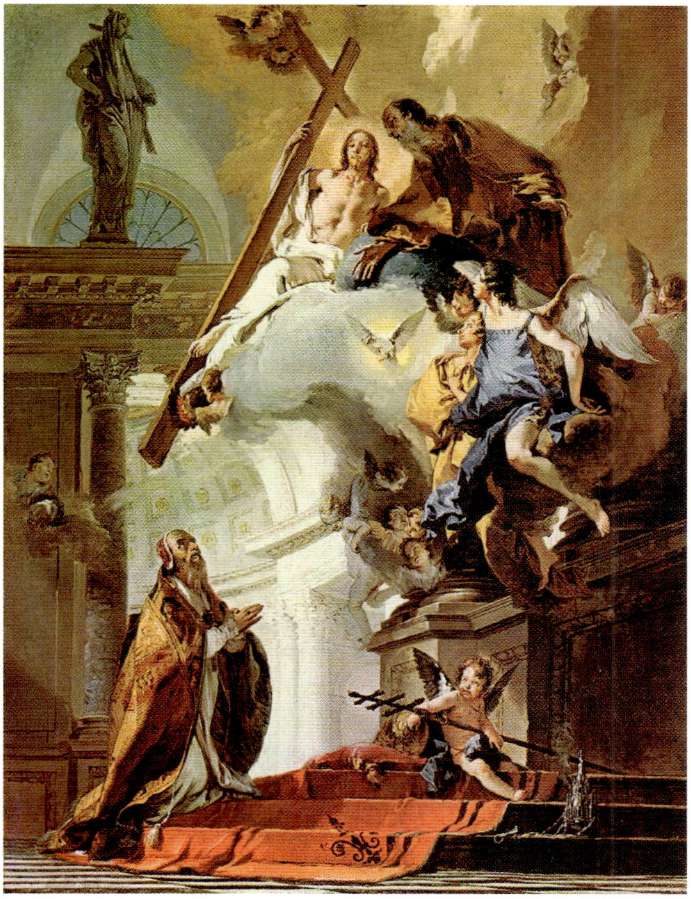

1

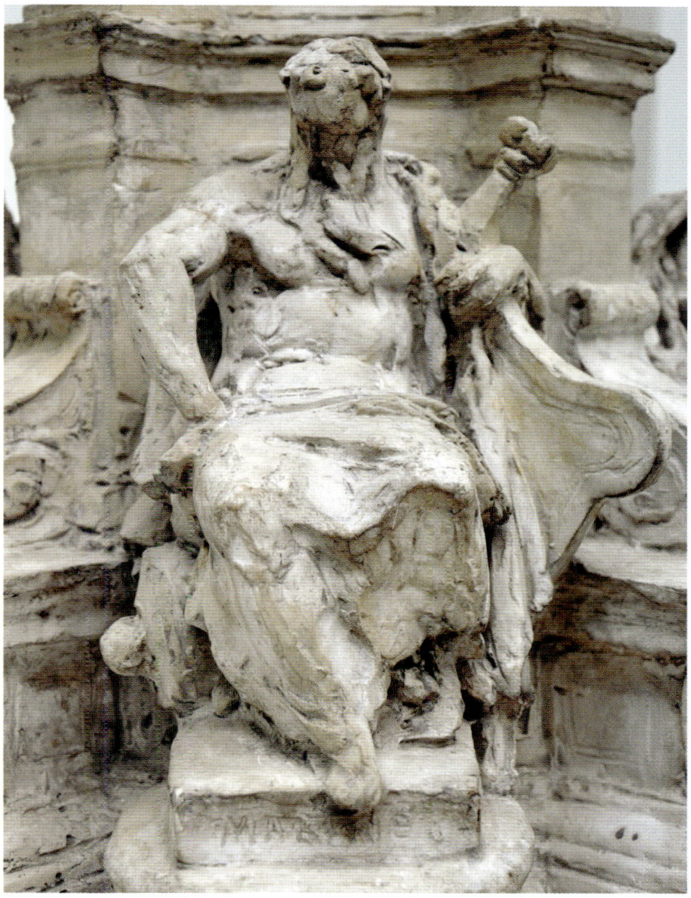

2

3

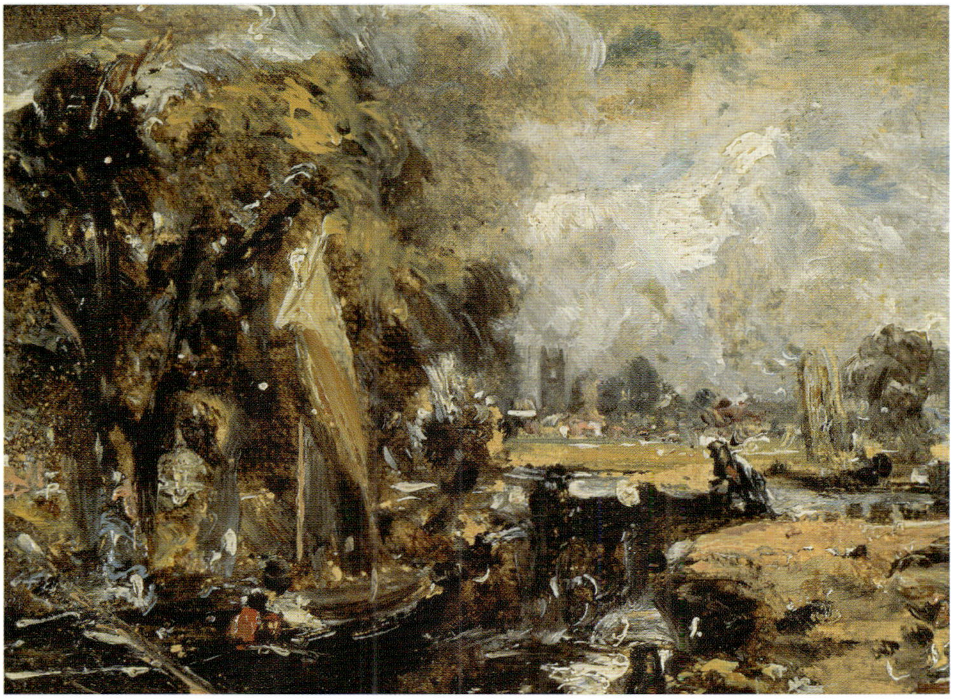

64 PRINTMAKING

REPRODUCTION BROADENS THE AUDIENCE FOR ART

Printmaking creates multiple impressions, allowing wider dissemination and lower cost. Since the mid-nineteenth century, artists have numbered and signed their prints, creating limited editions.

PRINCIPAL METHODS

- **Relief**
  The artist carves into a surface or "matrix," removing areas that are to remain white in the final image. The matrix is then inked and paper placed on top. This is pressed onto the surface either with a barren or by running it through a press. Woodblock and linocut are relief techniques.
- **Intaglio**
  The artist makes a cut into the surface of a metal plate.

  Engraving. The line is gouged using a very sharp engraving tool. The surface is inked and then wiped clean so that only the line retains the ink. It is then transferred onto paper in a press.

  Etching. The plate is covered with thin wax ground. The artist draws on the ground with a needle, removing the wax. The plate is then bathed in acid which bites into the surface where the wax has been removed. The plate is then inked and printed like an engraving.

  Drypoint. The artist uses a sharp tool to scratch the surface of the plate, raising a burr on the edge of the line. Inking and printing proceed as with engraving. This gives a rich, warm line but since the burr is fragile it will only yield a few good impressions.

  Mezzotint. The artist prepares the surface with a tool that makes thousands of tiny holes. These hold the ink to make a rich dark tone. The artist makes the image by burnishing into this prepared surface. The more he flattens it, the less ink it will hold and the lighter it will print.
- **Planographic**
  The surface of the matrix is changed by the action of chemicals to make parts of it resist inking. The main technique is lithography, which proceeds thus:

  1. Image is drawn with a greasy crayon onto a limestone or prepared aluminum matrix.
  2. Matrix is bathed in acid, fixing the grease to the surface.
  3. Matrix is covered with water, which is resisted by the areas where grease was applied.
  4. Ink is applied to the matrix and adheres only to the parts that were greasy

  Paper is pressed onto the surface in a press, transferring a replica of the initial drawing.
- **Stencil**
  Ink is pressed through a stencil to make a clearly outlined shape. In silkscreen printing, a fine mesh screen is used to allow ink to be smoothly pushed through with a squeegee.

1 Torii Kiyomasu (c. 1690–1720)
Kabuki actor Ichikawa Danjuro in the role of Takenuki Goro,
c. 1690–1710, Woodblock print on silk, 21½ × 12½ in (54.7 × 32 cm)

2 Lucas Cranach the Elder (1472–1553)
Venus and Cupid, 1506, Woodcut in red on laid paper, 11 5/16 × 7 13/16 in (28.7 × 19.8 cm)

3 Jacques Callot (1592–1635)
Franca Trippa and Fritellino,
c. 1622, Etching, 2 13/16 × 3 9/16 in (7.1 × 9.1 cm)

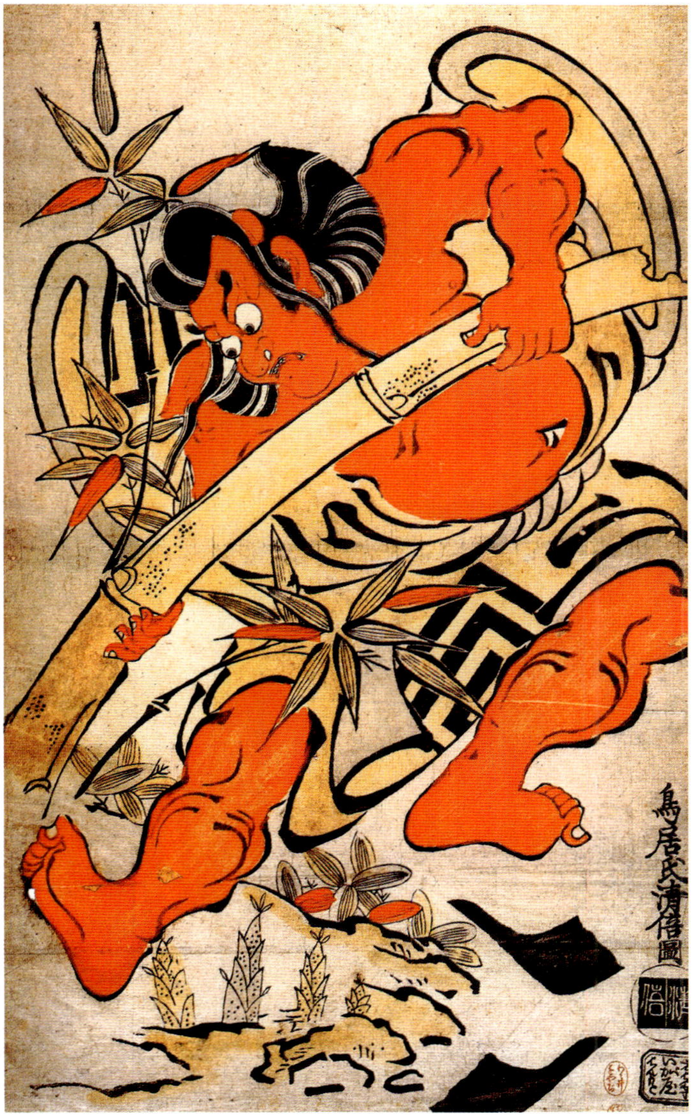

1

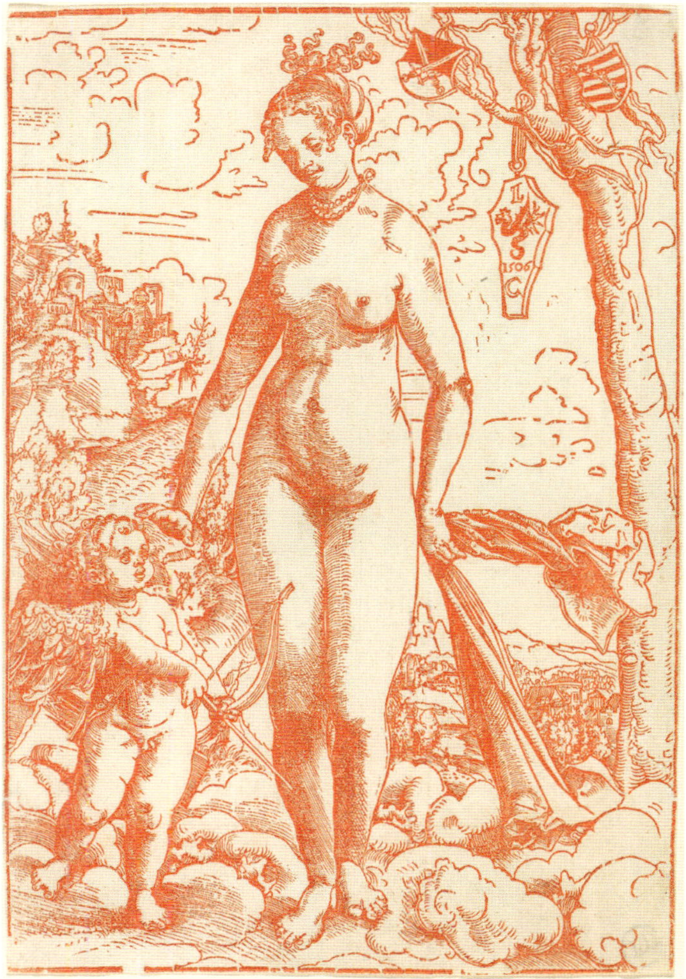

2

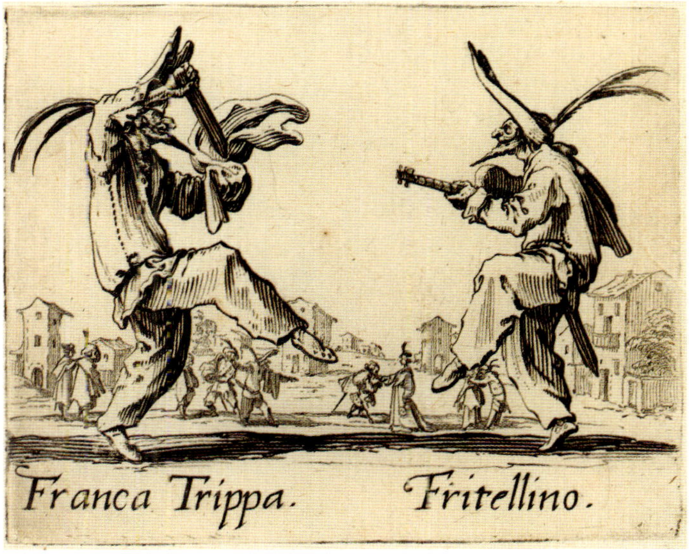

3

65 PROCESS AS MEANING

ART WORKS CAN BE ENGENDERED BY ENGAGING IN PRESCRIBED PHYSICAL PROCESSES

Instead of engaging in complex, intuitive decision making in producing a work of art, some contemporary artists have chosen to adopt an approach of simply carrying out a mechanical process. The American painter Jackson Pollock (1912–56) abandoned his early figurative work to make pictures by swinging paint across large canvases using brushes held well away from the surface to form long swirling arcs of splattered pigment. The resultant formations derive from the largely serendipitous distribution of the paint. Various sculptors quickly followed Pollock's example, most notably Robert Morris (1931–), who produced many works in which the end product is defined by the physical process it took to make it. Works in felt, for example, might be folded, cut, and moved in various defined ways until the work is deemed to be finished.

One compelling idea behind the notion of art as process is that artworks are the result of the movements of the human body, that they are necessarily defined by our physiology and our mechanical prowess. It invites us to make artworks that do not carry the traditional baggage of art, the requirements that it hold meaning, convey the intentions of the artist, and provide complex kinds of aesthetic pleasure. Writing about such works in 1952, the critic Howard Rosenberg observed, "What was to go on the canvas was not a picture but an event. The big moment came when it was decided to paint 'just to paint.' The gesture on the canvas was a gesture of liberation from value—political, aesthetic, moral."

The drawback of this idea is that it jettisons most of the notions of what many find interesting in art—the control of mediums and elements in ways that transform our experience of the world and provide various kinds of aesthetic pleasure.

1 Jackson Pollock (1912–56)
Autumn Rhythm Number 30, 1950,
Oil on canvas, 105 × 207 in
(266.7 × 525.8 cm)

2 Robert Morris (1931–)
Untitled, 1973, Brown felt

Several pieces of felt are draped in sequence over a pole. The form of the work is simply a result of carrying out this process.

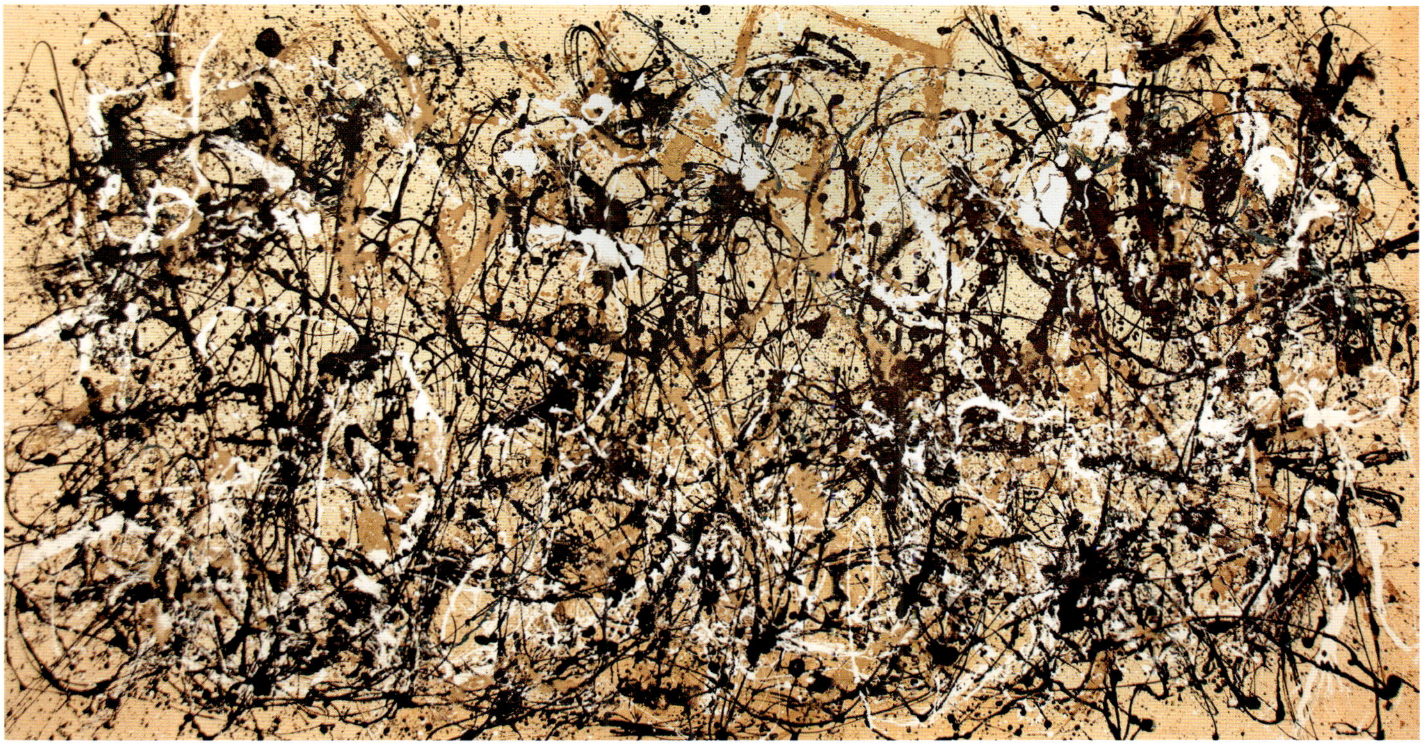

1

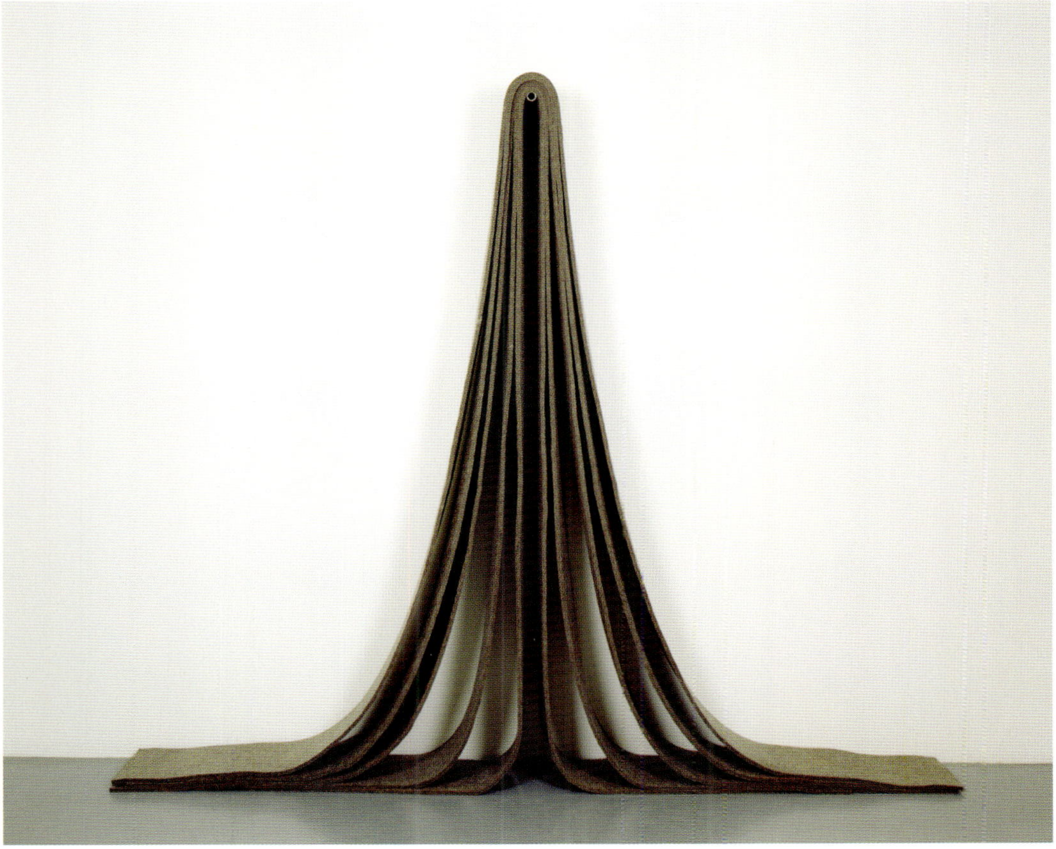

2

66 PROPORTION AND RATIO

MATHEMATICS MEETS AESTHETICS

Proportion and ratios are integral to the way in which elements relate to each other within an artwork and play a vital role in the success of representational constructs.

Proportion is the relationship in size between one element and another or between an element and the whole work. Proportions can be a key factor in conveying a sense of identity both to geometric shapes and to representational elements. The proportions of the human body, for instance, while somewhat variable, will have to fall within certain limits to be credible. The Roman architect Vitruvius (c. 80–15 BCE) suggested that a canon of beauty could be deduced from the proportions of the human body, an idea that a number of Renaissance artists took up (see *Beauty* on page 26).

Knowledge of proportions also helps artists to "scale up" a work, often from a sketch to a full-sized piece. The usual method is to draw a grid over the sketch and then draw a grid in the same proportions on the larger canvas. The drawing can then be easily transferred by eye.

RATIOS AND THE GOLDEN MEAN

A ratio is a mathematical expression of the relationship between one measurement and another. A ratio of two to one is expressed as 2:1 and means that one element is twice the size of the other. Since the Greek mathematician Euclid cited it, a ratio called "The Golden Mean" has fascinated artists and scientists alike. It is defined as the ratio between two elements in which the proportion of the larger of the two to the sum of the whole is the same as the proportion of the smaller to the larger. This turns out to be an irrational number, 1:1.6803...

For centuries, artists have felt that this ratio is inherently attractive and there are a number of artworks, particularly from the Renaissance, where it has certainly been used. The Italian writer Luca Pacioli (1445–1517) dubbed it the "Divine Proportion" in his 1507 book, *De Divina Proportione*. On the other hand, claims that both the Parthenon and the Mona Lisa were designed according to the Golden Mean are not true. In modern times, Le Corbusier (1887–1965) was attracted to the ratio and used it as the basis for his modular system of architecture.

See also: *Perspective* on page 128; *Composition* on page 44

1 According to Jan Tschichold (1902–74) in his *The Form of the Book*, many medieval prayer books used the Golden Mean. Here, the page ratio is 2:3 and the text proportion is the Golden Mean.

2 Albrecht Dürer (1471–1528)
Proportions of the Female Body,
c. 1512, Woodblock print,
$11\frac{5}{16} \times 7\frac{15}{16}$ in (28.8 × 20.2 cm)

Dürer explored many ideas about the proportions of the human body in his 1528 treatise Four Books on Human Proportion.

1

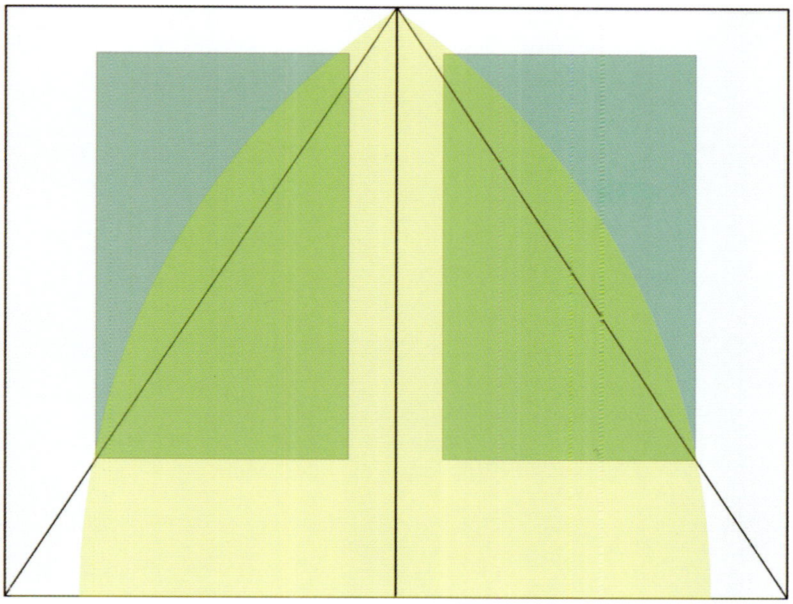

2

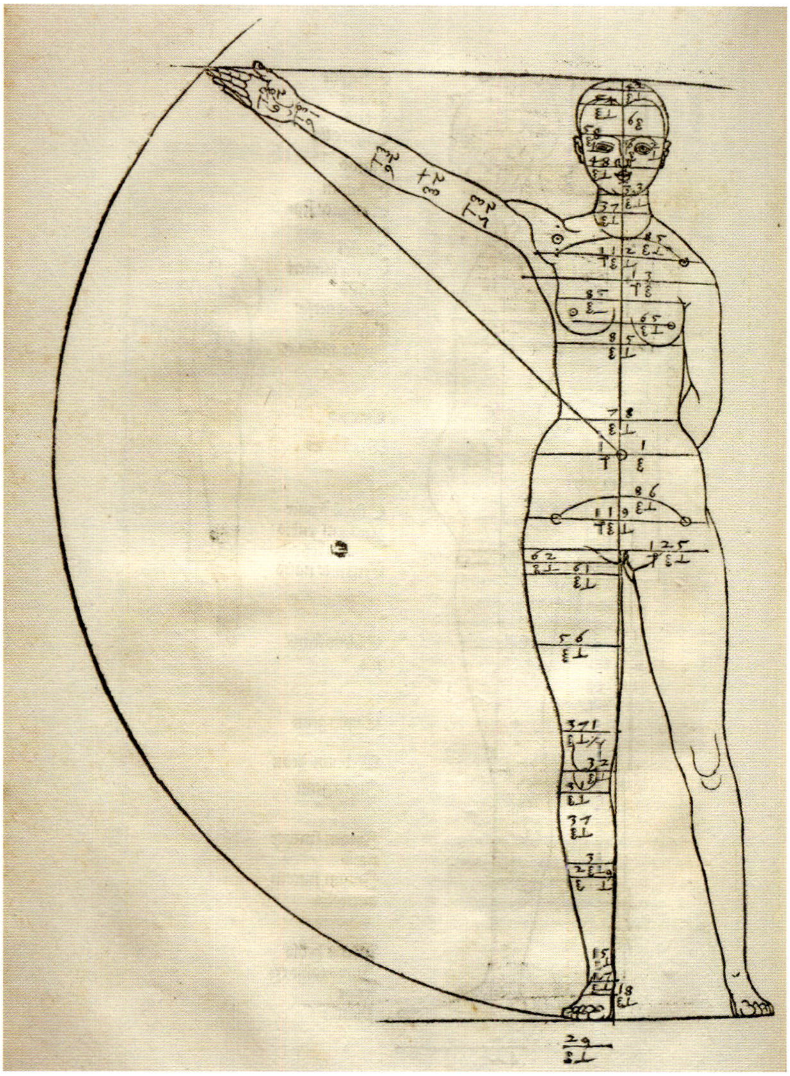

67 QUALITY

ASSESSING THE RELATIVE VALUE OF ARTISTS AND ARTWORKS

When we look at a work of art, we not only experience it, we also often pass judgment on it. We deem it to be good or bad, better or worse. We compare it favorably or unfavorably to other works of art by the same artist and to those of other artists. In other words, we make a judgment as to the quality of the work of art we are looking at. The basis on which such a judgment is made can be hard to define or pin down. It will also be somewhat different for each work of art we look at.

The judgment of quality is, therefore, something of a moving target. It can shift depending on the understanding and selective framework of the viewer, and it can shift with the fashions and collective judgments of the day. The history of art is strewn with reputations that were once elevated and are now all but forgotten.

What is it, then, that we are really doing when we say that one work of art is better than another or one artist is better than another? Perhaps we are recognizing that some works of art function far better than others. They deliver on what they set out to do in ways that are more imaginative, more surprising, and more satisfying.

Although there is obviously considerable subjectivity involved in a judgment of quality, it does appear that at any given time a community of taste will coalesce around a particular view. Most people agree today that Vincent Van Gogh was a great artist, a view that was not apparent during his lifetime. Over long periods of time, judgments of quality concerning individual artists tend to settle into a broad consensus. The pantheon of great artists from Massacio, to Michelangelo, to Monet seems unlikely to be changed in the future in any radical way. Meanwhile, the reputations of thousands of lesser artists will continue to rise and fall with the shifting tides of taste and context.

1 Paul Gauguin (1848–1903)
Parau na te Varua ino (Words of the Devil), 1892, Oil on canvas, 36 1/8 × 26 15/16 in (91.8 × 68.4 cm)

2 Paul Sérusier (1864–1927)
Farmhouse at Le Pouldu, 1890, Oil on canvas, 28 3/8 × 23 5/8 in (72 × 60 cm)

History has judged Gauguin to be a better painter than his contemporary Sérusier.

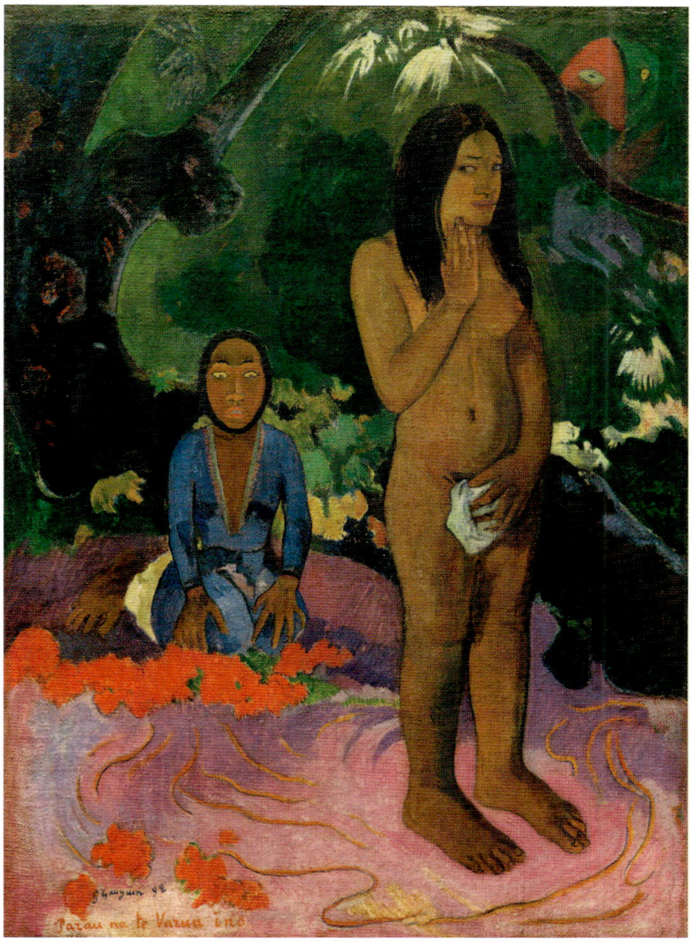

1

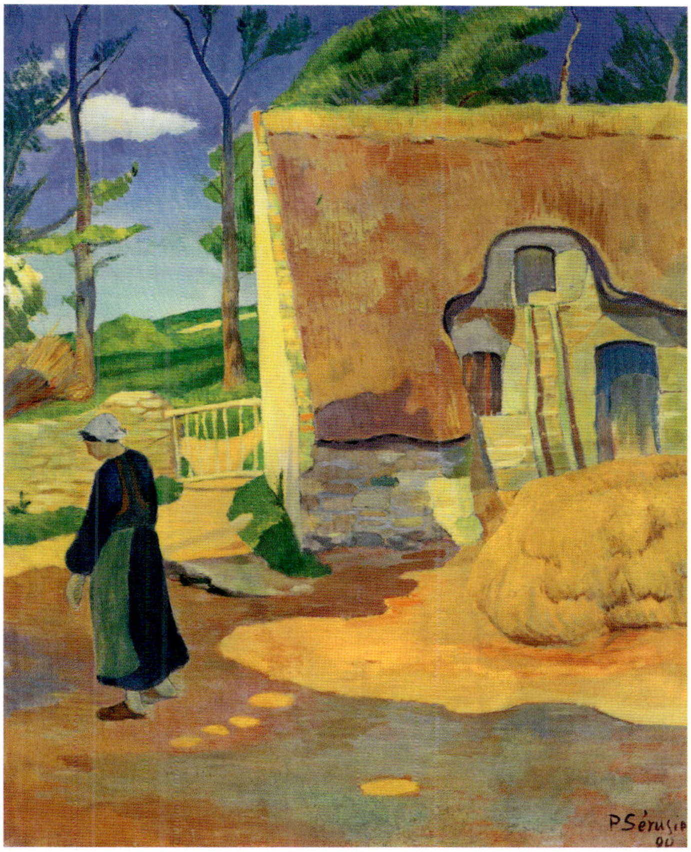

2

68 QUOTING

REFERRING TO ANOTHER WORK OF ART ALLOWS FOR REFINEMENT OF MEANING

Quoting another work of art can lead to more precise and nuanced meaning as well as richer expression. Quoted images can be adjusted or reworked in a variety of ways in accordance with a wide range of possible intentions.

- **Ironic**
  Changing the appearance and context of a quoted image in order to lampoon or otherwise undercut its meaning.
- **Humorous**
  The reworking of a famous image, preferably one that has gravity, can be extremely amusing.
- **Subversive**
  Using an iconic image in such a way that it subverts the social and political constructs of the day.
- **Supportive**
  Quoting another work of art can imply a closeness of intention and spirit with the artist making the quote.
- **Theoretical**
  The artist making the quote may wish to explore the way in which the quoted image operates in a contemporary setting. This is part of the strategy of the Appropriationists, a contemporary art movement (see *Appropriation* on page 16).

1 Marcantonio Raimondi (1480–1534)
The Judgment of Paris, 1515, After Raphael, Copper engraving, 11 11/16 × 17 3/16 in (29.7 × 43.7 cm)

2 Édouard Manet (1832–83)
Le Déjeuner sur l'herbe, 1862–3, Oil on canvas, 82 × 104 in (208.3 × 264.2 cm)

The central group in Manet's painting is a direct quote of a famous image in a painting by Raphael as transcribed in an engraving by Raimondi. The fact that Manet is using a classical quote to make a contemporary image reinforces the transgressive nature of the subject matter.

1

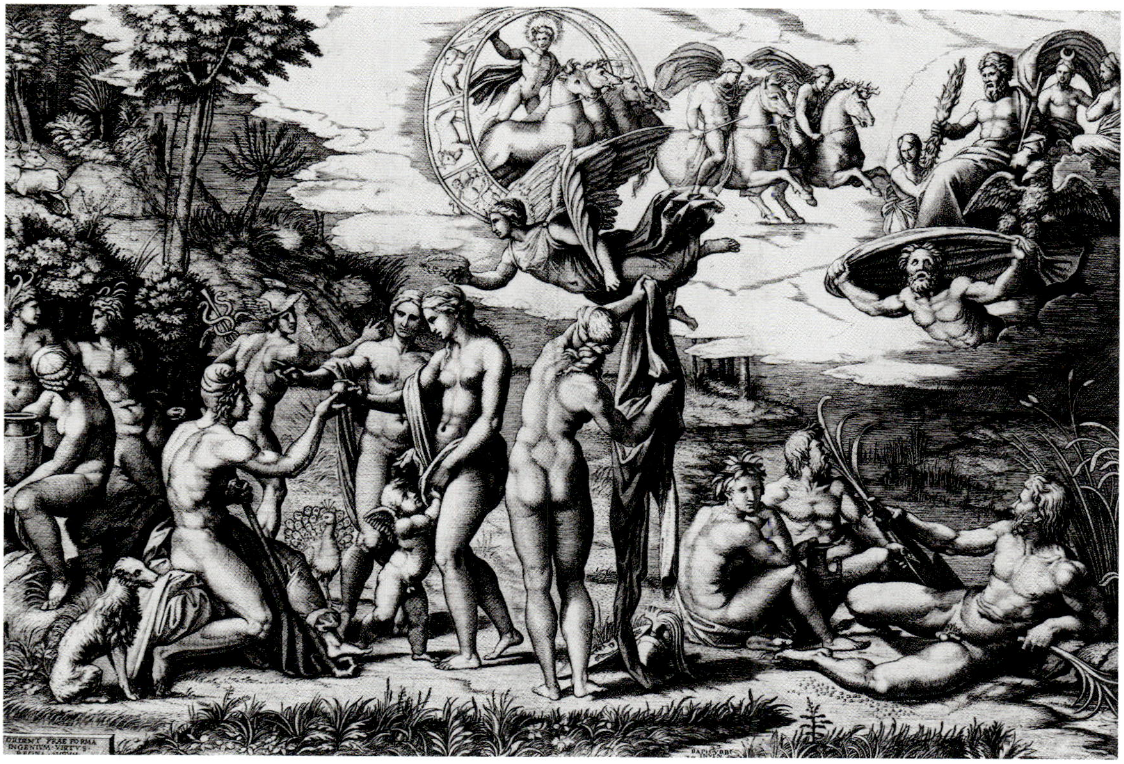

2

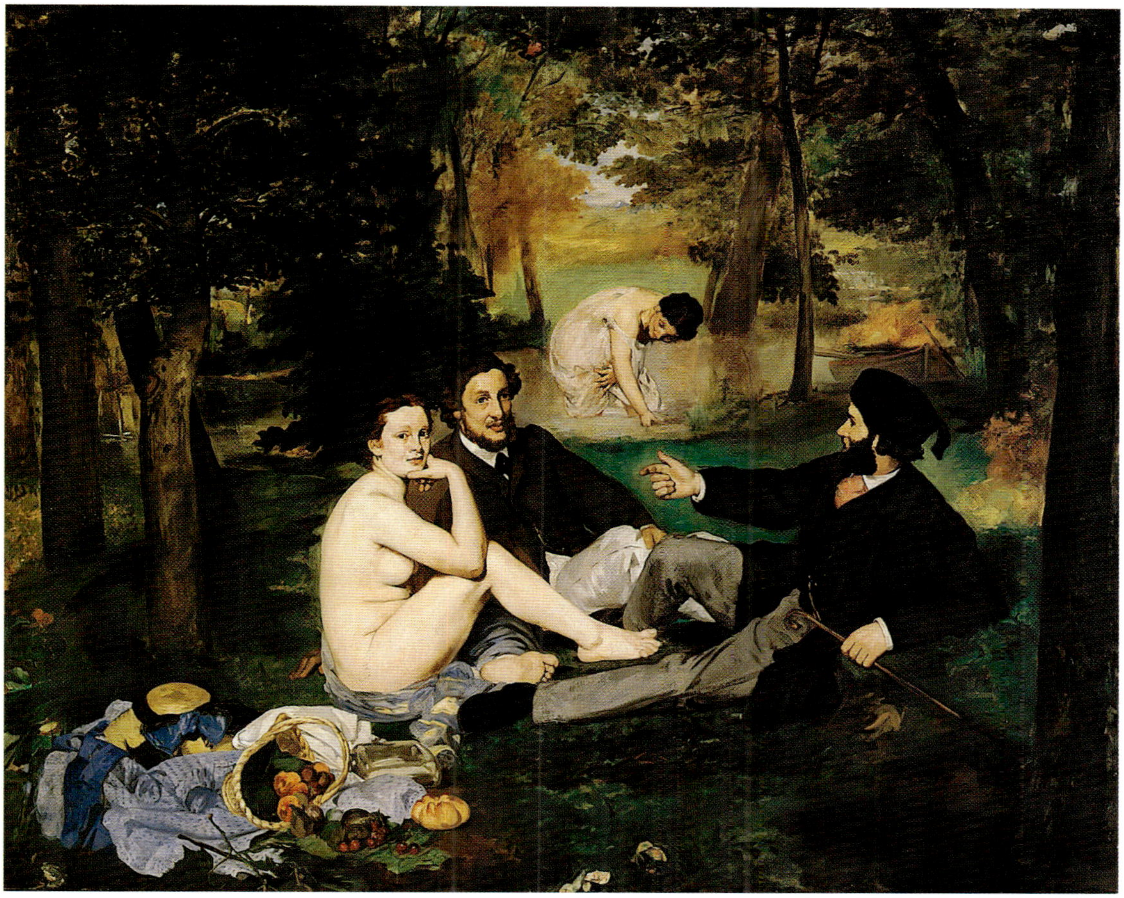

69 READYMADES

DESIGNATING AN OBJECT AS AN ARTWORK

Although an artwork is usually defined as a product of human agency, a number of modern artists have contended that any object whatsoever can be presented or designated as a work of art. Such objects are known as "readymades."

The first appearance of this idea occurred in 1917, when Marcel Duchamp (1887–1968) famously exhibited, or tried to exhibit, a porcelain urinal as a sculpture. The occasion was an exhibition of the Society of Independent Artists in New York, and the sculpture was submitted under the pseudonym "R. Mutt." Even though Duchamp sat on the selection committee of the society, the work was rejected. Duchamp resigned in protest. The work was subsequently photographed in the studio of Alfred Stieglitz and became something of a cause célèbre when the New York Dadaist magazine *The Blind Man* published an editorial making a compelling case for the new art form: "Whether Mr. Mutt made the fountain with his own hands or not has no importance. He CHOSE it. He took an article of life, placed it so that its useful significance disappeared under the new title and point of view—created a new thought for that object."

In general, this is the rationale used ever since by practitioners of this kind of art. For them, the intellectual act of recognition and designation is the making of the art. The form of readymade continues to have currency, most notably in the British artist Tracey Emin's infamous 1998 work *My Bed*, which consists of the artist's unmade bed and various artifacts and detritus from her bedroom.

Readymades are often combined within artworks, providing a bridge to the art of assemblage, the sculptural version of collage.

The very openness of the genre of readymades is also a considerable weakness. When anything or everything might be designated an artwork, the line between what is and isn't art becomes confusing, and the means by which a viewer might engage and enjoy the art can become unclear.

See also: *Conceptual Art* on page 46; *Dada* on page 58

1 Marcel Duchamp (1887–1968)
Fountain, 1917, Porcelain urinal,
24 × 14 × 19 in (61 × 35.6 × 48.3 cm)
Photographed by Alfred Steiglitz

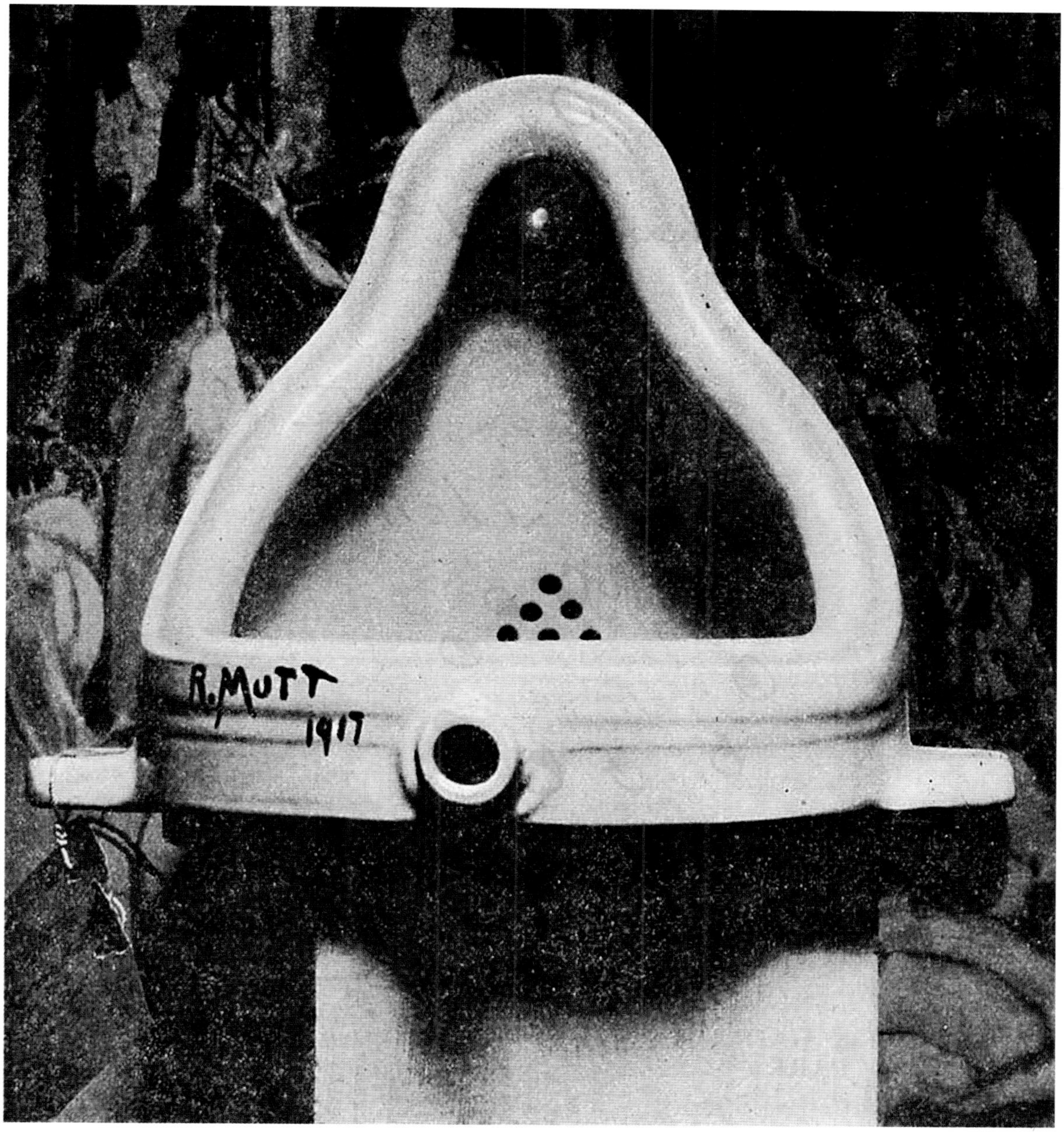

1

70 REALISM

CLAIMING AN OBJECTIVE VIEW OF THE WORLD

More than simply representation, realism is the idea that the artwork presents a neutral and inclusive view of the world. The viewer is persuaded that he is being shown the world as it actually is. This is an idea that emerges perennially in art. In the late sixteenth century, Caravaggio (1571–1610) shocked and galvanized his viewers by using common people as models and including such realistic details as dirty fingernails and soiled clothing. Realism emerged again in the mid-nineteenth century as a powerful antidote to the foregoing Romantic movement. Artists such as Gustave Courbet (1819–77) began to paint the life of French peasants in an unadorned and matter-of-fact manner, belying previous idealized stereotypes and, to some extent, shocking their audience. The advent of photography in the latter half of the nineteenth century gave a new authority to the idea of a neutrally "real" image of the world.

The adoption of a realist stance was particularly strong in American painting in the late nineteenth and early twentieth centuries, a time when many artists began their careers as illustrators for newspapers and magazines. Winslow Homer (1836–1910) covered the Civil War for *Harper's Magazine* before launching on a career as a painter in which he projected a new sense of clarity and unfiltered seeing. Early twentieth-century artists such as John Sloane (1871–1951), Everett Shinn (1876–1953), and George Bellows (1882–1925) began as newspaper illustrators and went on to paint the life of common people. Dubbed the "Ashcan School," they used realist techniques to further the idea that art could be used as part of the political and social discussion about poverty and the conditions under which the poor were obliged to live.

Realism again appeared powerfully in the late 1960s and early '70s with the emergence of so-called "superreal" painting. Inspired by the foregoing Pop Art movement, painters such as Richard Estes (1932–), Malcolm Morley (1931–), and Chuck Close (1940–) made pictures that sought to outdo the dazzling richness and specificity of large-scale color photographs.

The idea that realist art presents a non-selective, non-filtered view of the world is rarely borne out in fact. Choice of viewpoint, subject matter, scale, and medium, allow an artist considerable opportunity to skew the sense of an image, promote a particular point of view, or orchestrate other expressive qualities. As such, claims of neutral realism are often deceptive.

1 Caravaggio (1571–1610)
Judith Beheading Holofernes,
1598–9, Oil on canvas, $57^{1}/_{8} \times 76^{3}/_{8}$ in (145 × 195 cm)

2 George Bellows (1882–1925)
New York, 1911, Oil on canvas,
42 × 60 in (106.7 × 152.4 cm)

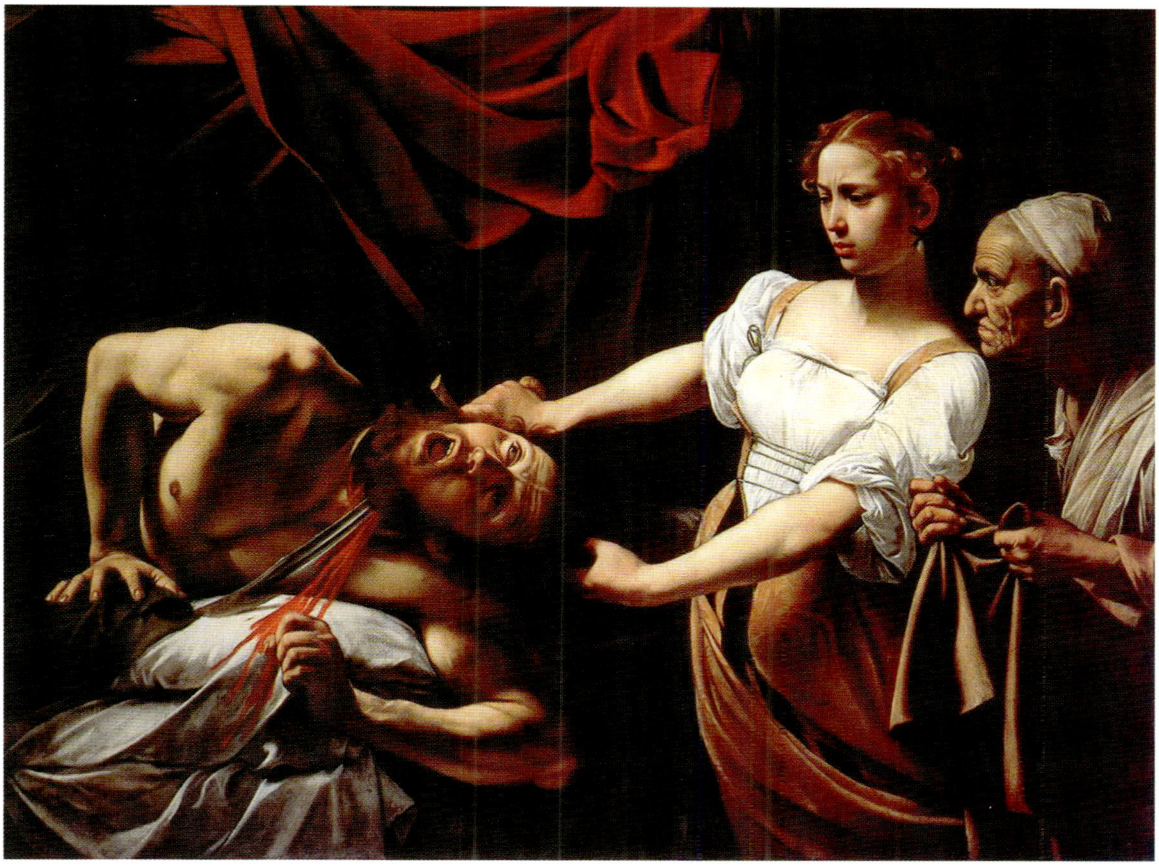

1

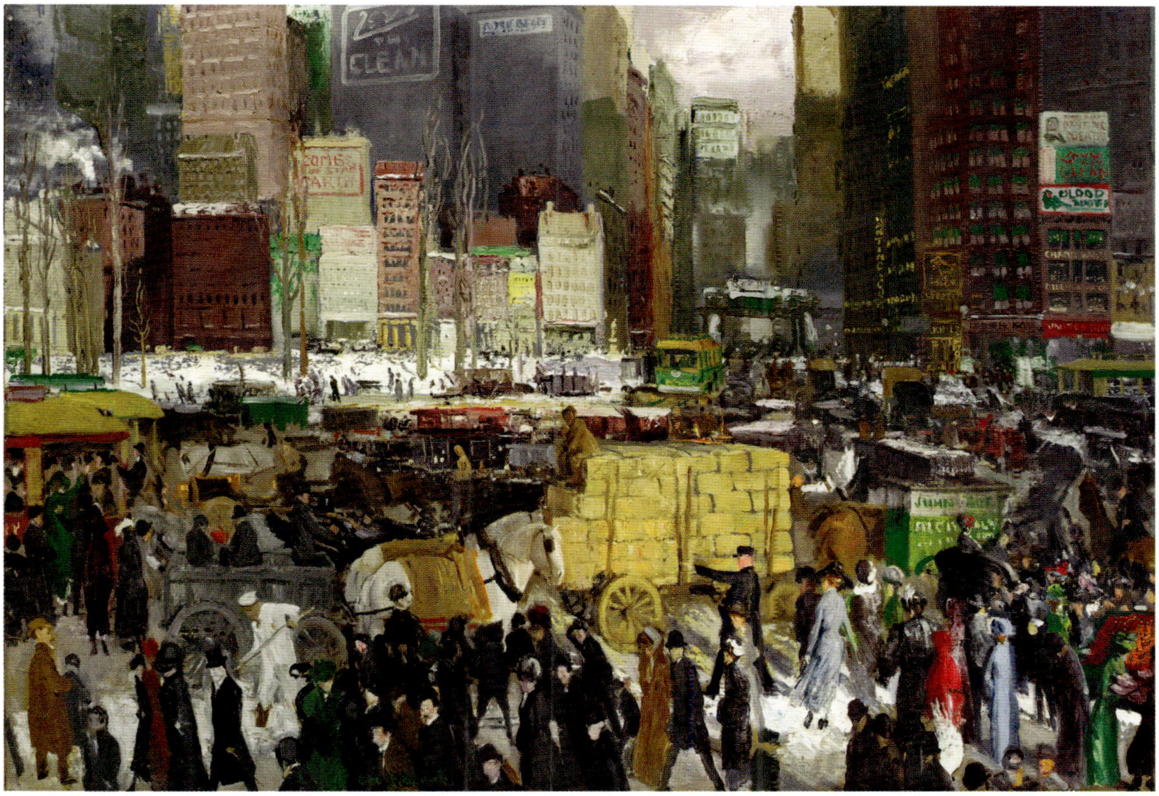

2

71 RELIGIOSITY

BELIEF IN THE SUPERNATURAL AS A SOURCE OF INSPIRATION

The religious impulse has been the motivating factor for a vast number of works of art. Most tribal art appears to have a religious or devotional intention, and much ancient art revolves around religious practices. Western art was largely religious until the Renaissance and wasn't dominated by secular art until the nineteenth century. Indeed it might be possible to argue that the respect that is accorded to artworks in the contemporary world is part of the legacy of artworks as a focus of devotion. We might infer, therefore, that the making of images in tribal societies is an expression of a universal human drive to externalize and thereby control forces that remain mysterious and perhaps threatening.

In some cases, religious images become so closely identified with their subjects that the popular audience has difficulty separating the two. Thus the intense veneration of some works of art, including many Christian icons and sculptures, that become objects of worship in their own right. Such works are sometimes associated with miraculous cures, visions, and other supernatural occurrences.

Religious imagery often tends to the iconic and the symmetrical. The colossal heads of Easter Island, the beautifully simplified sculpture of Cycladic art, the Great Sphinx of Giza, or the myriad statues of the Buddha exhibit symmetry or near symmetry. Clearly humans infer a quality of presence from symmetry that relates to our own symmetrical construction. The quintessential Christian image of Christ on the Cross is also close to symmetrical.

In more sophisticated art, religious imagery often concerns itself with the depiction of the stories and myths associated with a particular religion. In Western art, artists of the Baroque era, particularly those associated with the Counter-Reformation, found new ways to project religious feeling. Carravagio (1571–1610) deployed highly theatrical lighting and a stark realism to draw his viewers into well-known biblical scenes. Sir Peter Paul Rubens (1577–1640) deployed scale, movement, and spectacular rendering to project a sense of dazzling richness and splendor to make his altarpieces compelling for a popular audience (see page 93).

See also: *Symmetry* on page 187

1 ***Christ the Saviour (Pantokrator)***, 6th century, Encaustic on panel, 33 1/16 × 17 7/8 in (84 × 45.5 cm), Saint Catherine's Monastery, Mount Sinai

2 Emil Nolde (1867–1956) ***The Burial***, 1915, Oil on canvas, 38 3/16 × 45¼ (97 × 115 cm)

In an increasingly secular twentieth century, some artists were still motivated by religious feeling. Here Nolde deploys the newly-forged language of Expressionism to re-imagine one of the key scenes of the New Testament.

2 ***Gandhara Buddha***, 1st to 2nd century CE, 43 in (110 cm)

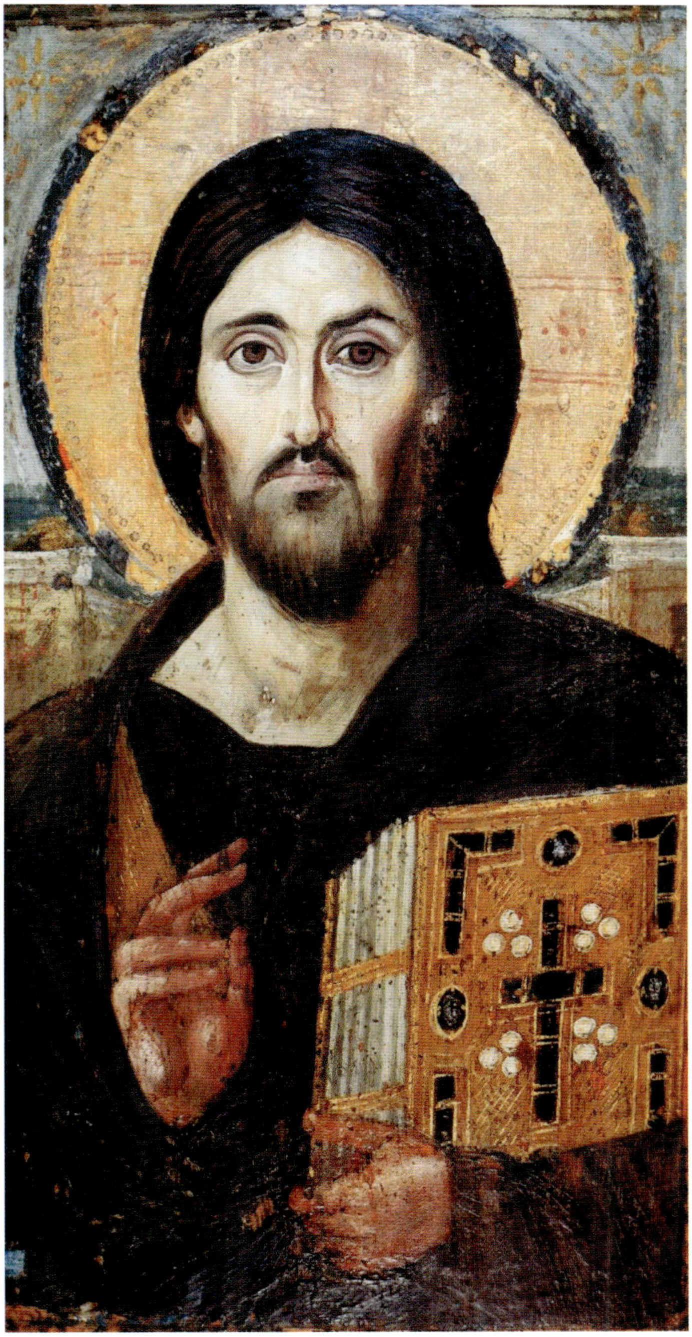

1

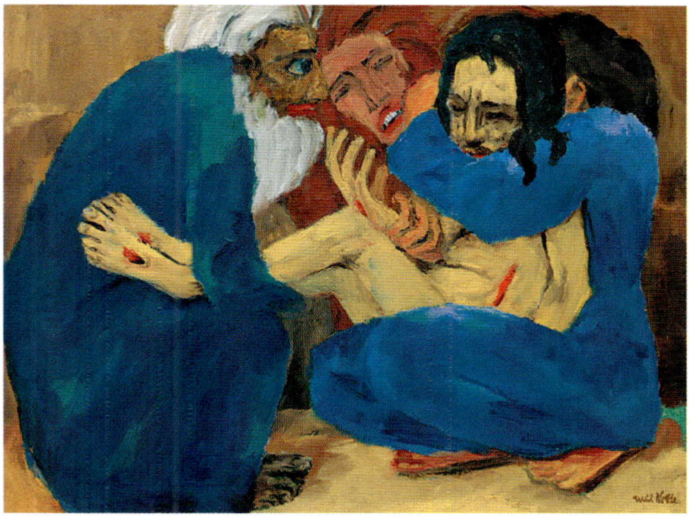

2

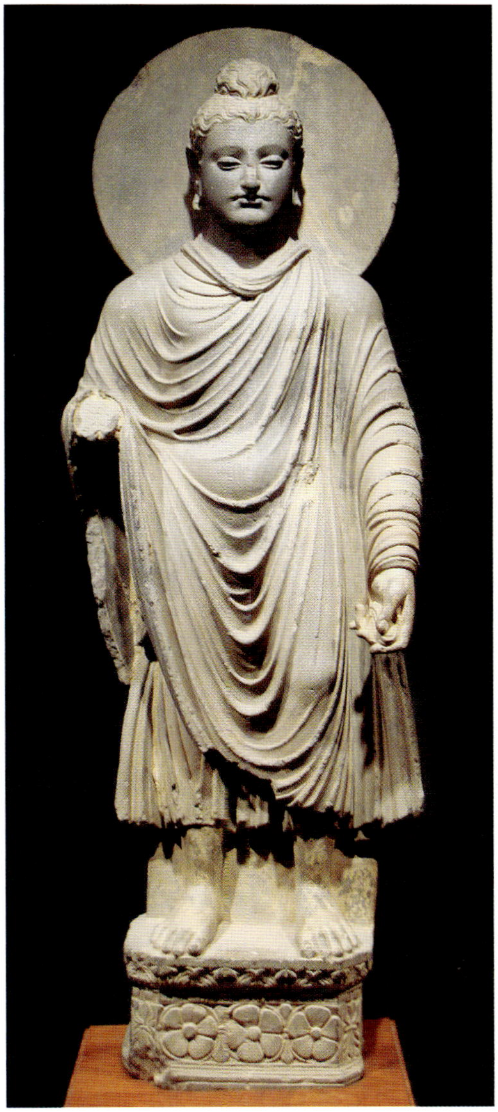

3

72 REPETITION

REPEATING IMAGES CREATES NEW AVENUES OF EXPRESSION

Repetition of images or elements within images can endow them with new authority, sense, or meaning. Although repeated images have always been used in decorative enterprises, repetition as an option for expression in the fine arts emerged with modernism, beginning perhaps with the series paintings of Claude Monet (1840–1926). Using a variety of motifs, including poplar trees, haystacks, and water lilies, Monet explored the play of light on the same subject under varying conditions and times of day. The resulting paintings shift the viewer's attention from an appreciation of the subject as remade by the artist to a concentration on the technical and perceptual work of the artist as he proceeds with the series. These works presage twentieth-century abstract art in which the artwork becomes its own subject. Repetition has since been taken up by many artists, including Andy Warhol (1928–87), Arman (1928–2005), Damien Hirst (1965–), and others.

STRATEGIES

- **Redundancy**
  Repetition is often effective when it suggests redundancy. In Andy Warhol's flower paintings, the repeated image of a desirable object undermines that very desirability, suggesting that it is endlessly available and essentially vacuous, merely another consumer item capable of infinite manufacture.
- **Decorative**
  Repeated images can readily become decorative.
- **Disposability**
  Repetition is strongly associated with modern printing and manufacturing techniques and, therefore, often carries a sense of transience, cheapness, and disposability. The Cuban artist Félix González-Torres (1957–96) made a number of works in which he heaped cheaply manufactured items, such as wrapped candies, in museum spaces and invited visitors to take them if they wished. It was a strategy that undermined the "sacredness" of the art object and the idea that quality and aesthetic value are invested in an object.
- **Breaking the repeat**
  Deploying repeated images and then breaking the repeat by introducing variation is a strategy that operates by undermining the viewer's expectations.
- **Repetition as power**
  The repeated image or element can take on a sense of power or omnipresence. The British artist Antony Gormley (1950–) has made works where many copies of bronze figures are placed in an environment, taking on an uneasy quality of omnipresence.
- **Formal motif**
  Repeated images can provide a predictable and stable structure to support the exploration of other variables available to the artwork.
- **Transformation**
  It is possible to repeat images in such a way that they become entirely transformed. The artist Arman has made many works in which he takes numbers of identical objects and welds them together, entirely transforming their appearance and undermining their original use. Here, the act of repetition brings into question the identity of the object and the relationship between appearance and purpose.

1 Andy Warhol (1928–87)
Nine Jackies, 1964, Acrylic and silkscreen on canvas, 65 × 53 × 2 in (165.1 × 134.6 × 5.1 cm)

At first glance this work presents a banal repeat of the iconic image of Jacqueline Kennedy in which the principal interest is the break of the repeat color in the last two images. The work takes on a more portentous quality when we realize that it shows a photograph taken just minutes before the president was assassinated. He is visible in the background, particularly in the last two images.

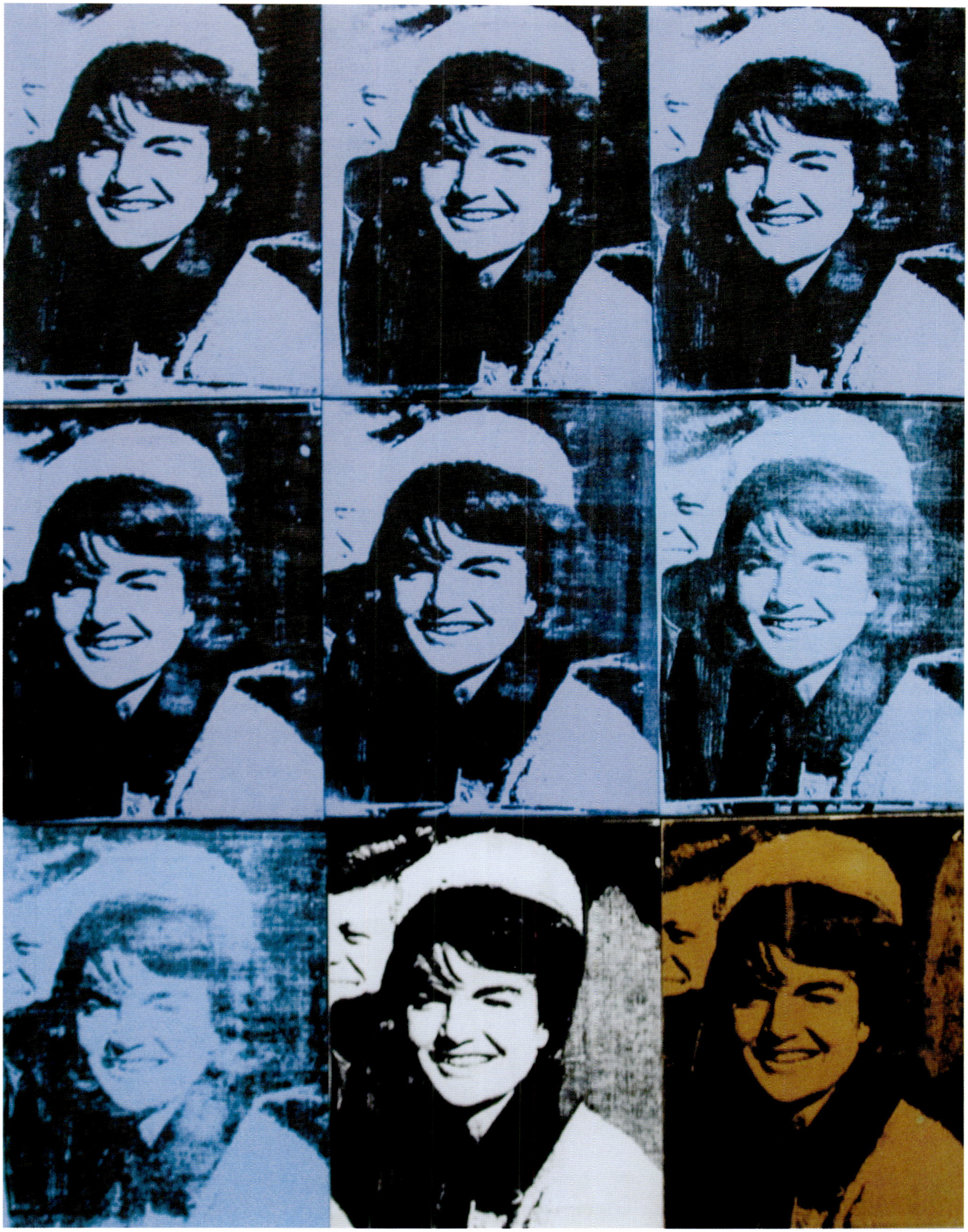

1

73 REPRESENTATION

THE IMAGE STANDS IN FOR THE REAL THING

Representation is a convention in painting and sculpture whereby a flat image or a three-dimensional form is understood to stand in for a visual experience of something in the real world.

Translating a visual experience is central to the activity of representational art. The nature of the translation and how it affects the viewers' perception of the subject becomes a powerful way in which expression may be achieved. Subjects may be simplified, distorted, or rebuilt in various ways. The viewers' comparisons of their experiences of the real world with their apprehension of its representation in a work of art provides the ground for a wide variety of meaning and expression.

HISTORY

The origins of representational art extend back into prehistory with cave paintings and simple sculpture. With the emergence of more advanced cultures, representations became more elaborate. Egyptian art developed complex iconography based on flat designs in which humans, supernatural beings, and physical objects could be shown and manipulated. More comprehensive and naturalistic representations of the human form appear in Greek culture and reach a level of unparalleled sophistication around 400 BCE. Roman art in general pursued a taste for naturalism, particularly in sculpture. Medieval art saw a return to flatter and more linear representation, while the Renaissance ushered in an entirely more comprehensive set of tools, including perspective, to enable a much fuller representation of the world. Contemporary artists deploy a wide variety of representational approaches, from crude and primitive expressions to flawless photographic realism.

PHILOSOPHY

Both Aristotle and Plato discussed representation. Aristotle considered it to be natural to human beings and necessary for their comprehension of the world. Plato, on the other hand, asserted that representation involves the creation of illusions that may or may not say truthful things about the world. As such, representations have the capacity to lead the viewer astray. The potential deceptiveness of representation and its ability to mold perception has emerged as a perennial issue in the modern world. Advertising, propaganda, and the fine arts are areas in which both visual and verbal representations are manipulated to shift the perception and understanding of the viewer.

See also: *Realism* on page 148

1 ***Willendorf Venus***, c. 20,000 BCE, Limestone, 4½ in (10.8 cm) high

One of the earliest surviving artworks, the Willendorf Venus may have had a role as a ritualistic symbol of fertility.
Photo: Don Hitchcock

2 Amedeo Modigliani (1884–1920)
Chaim Soutine, 1917, Oil on canvas, 36⅛ × 23½ in (91.7 × 59.7 cm)

Modigliani deploys the new visual language pioneered by Cubism. He dispenses with perspective and rendered form using instead a flattened space and stylized outline.

3 Praxiteles
Hermes Carrying the Infant Dionysius, 4th century BCE, Marble, 7½ ft (2.1 m) high

The Greek sculptor's comprehension of the nuance and complexity of the human form remains a high point in representational art.

4 Raphael (1483–1520)
The School of Athens, 1509, Fresco, 16 ft 5 in × 25 ft 3 in (5 × 7.7 m), Apostolic Palace, Vatican City

By 1500, artists had mastered both perspective and elaborate rendering of three-dimensional form, enabling extremely comprehensive representations of the visible world.

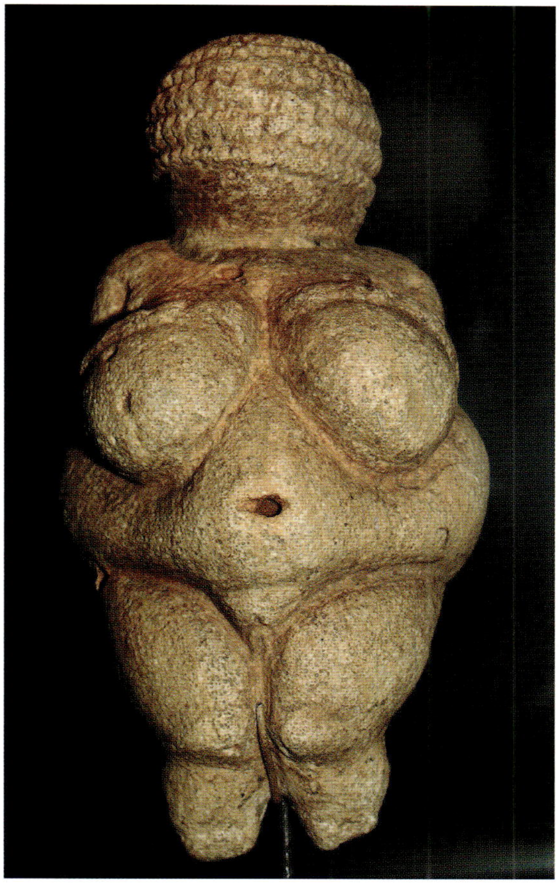

1

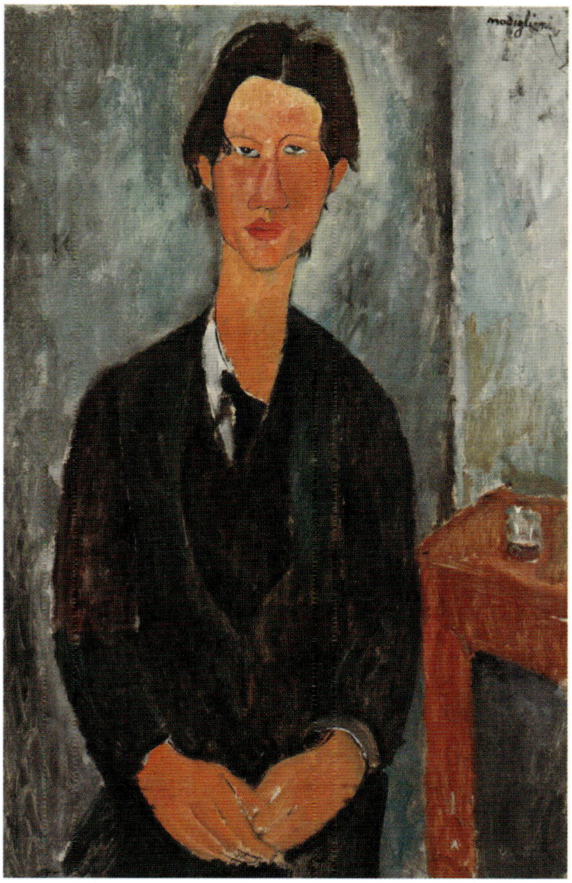

2

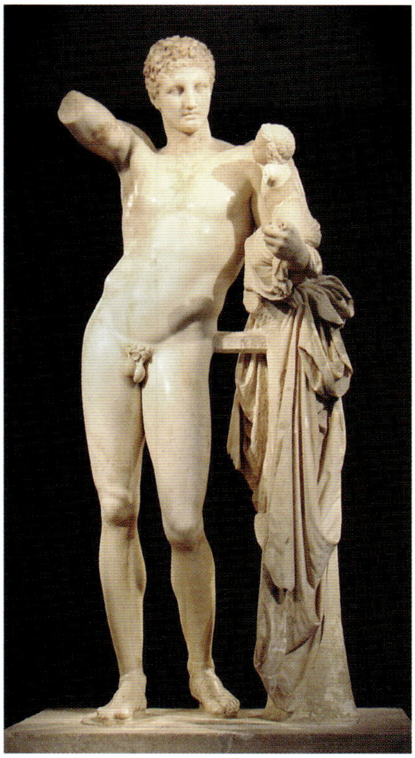

3

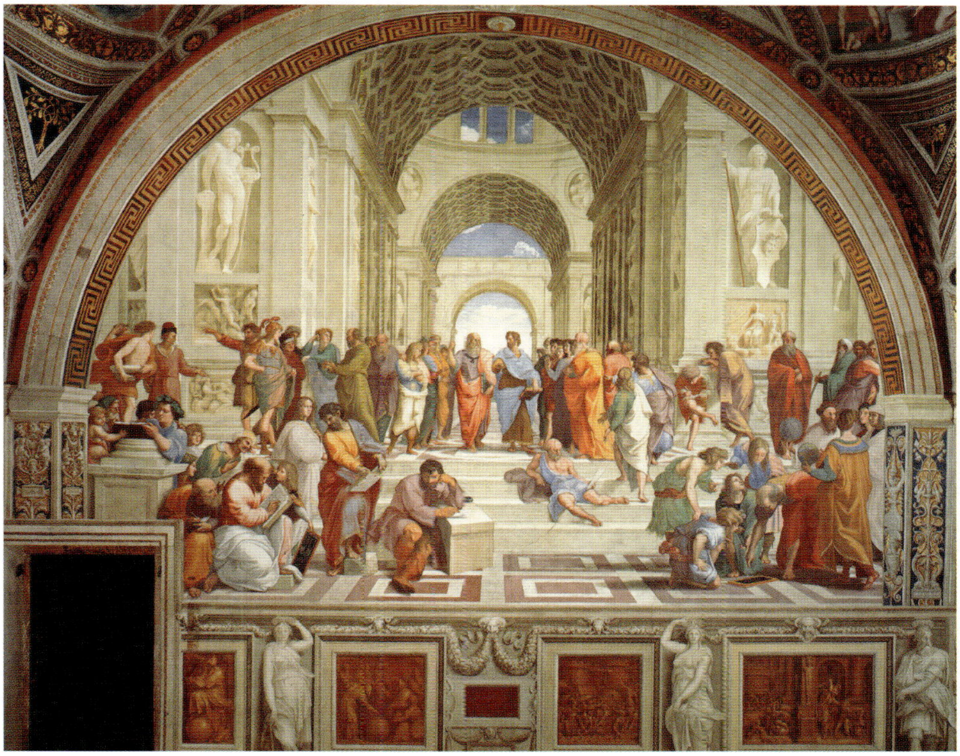

4

74 RESTRAINT

THE POWER OF HOLDING BACK

Restraint can be a very powerful idea in painting and sculpture. Unlike film or illustration, which often seek to entertain and dazzle, fine art can work well when the viewer feels that something is withheld or understated. This can involve simplifying forms, omitting details, or simply being suggestive.

The power of restraint can be seen in the work of the French artist Eugene Carriére (1849–1906), who adopted a style in which he worked in monochrome, sketching heads in loose brush marks with soft edges in such a way that the image almost dissolves into the space around it. The results evoke a sense of mystery as viewers strain to reconstruct the subject from the minimal and somewhat imprecise information they are provided. Similarly, James McNeill Whistler (1834–1903), particularly in his *Nocturnes*, painted his subjects with a limited set of information and clues. Again the results are atmospheric and suggestive, while the somewhat ethereal qualities of his work, combined with elegant proportioning, convey considerable aesthetic pleasure.

Restraint also worked well for the English painter Gwen John (1876–1939), who made pictures using a subimpressionist approach in which a very limited color palette was deployed in small, fairly even, paint strokes. The resulting paintings acquire a feeling of reticence and thoughtful contemplation.

A sense of restraint undoubtedly plays a role in the aesthetic pleasure afforded by much minimal art.

APPROACHES

- Severely pared-down information and stripping-out of detail.
- A limited palette forcing a few colors to do the work of many to convey a sense of quiet.
- Non-showy, quiet execution, such as evenness of brushing and avoidance of showy technique.
- Choice of subject matter that avoids considerable visual drama.
- Introduction of deliberate ambiguities in the form of disguised edges or the selection of shapes that are not readily readable.

See also: *Color as Limit* on page 40; *Minimalism* on page 112; *Simplification* on page 172; *Ambiguity* on page 14

1 Eugène Carrière (1849–1906)
Alphonse Daudet, 1893, Lithograph
$15^{5}/_{8} \times 12^{3}/_{16}$ in (39.7 × 30.9 cm)

2 Gwen John (1876–1939)
The Convalescent, 1923–4,
Oil on canvas, 16¼ × $13^{5}/_{16}$ in
(41.3 × 33.8 cm)

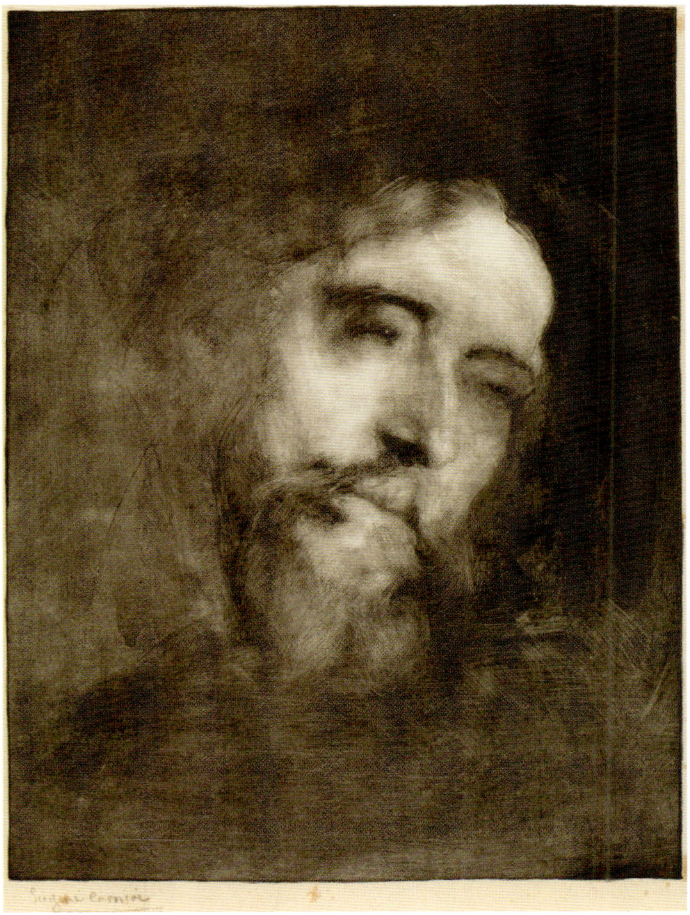

1

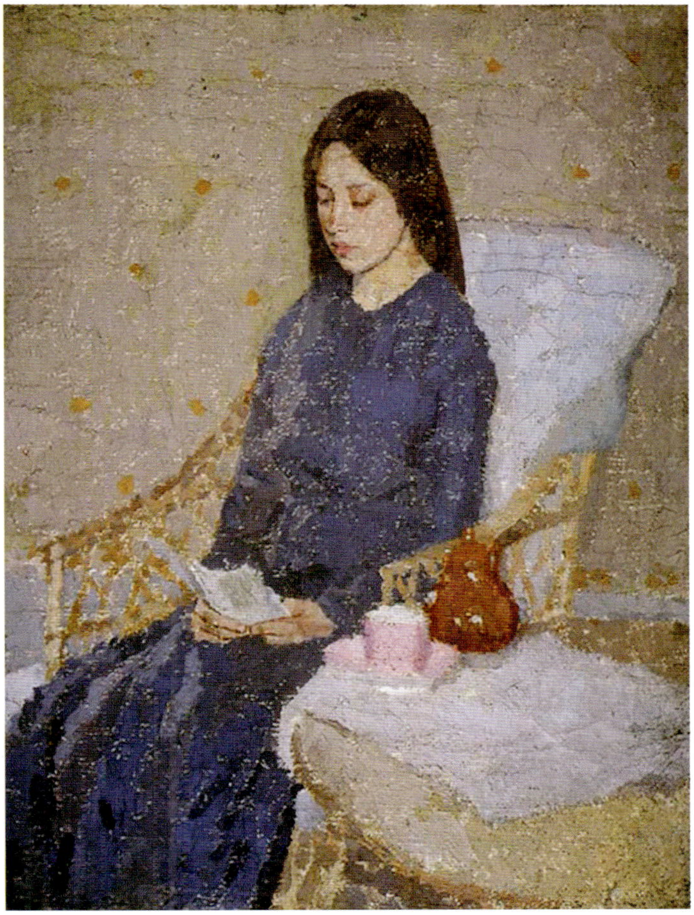

2

75 RHYTHM

THE VISUAL COUNTERPART OF A MUSICAL ATTRIBUTE

Usually a musical concept, rhythm has strong visual counterparts and can sometimes be central to a work of art. A sense of dynamic movement working rhythmically across a surface can be compelling on its own or can provide an underpinning for a more complex work. Rhythm in visual art is generally a linear quality. In Michelangelo's *Last Judgment*, the linear organization proceeds in a rhythmic fashion from top to bottom, carrying the viewer's eye down toward hell. In purer form, rhythmic motifs can be found in many tribal artifacts and is sometimes used in a decorative fashion to embellish objects.

While rhythm was usually only a secondary consideration in much art before the modern era, a number of twentieth-century artists explored rhythm as a central concern. Henri Matisse (1869–1954) made many paintings in which the composition is built on rhythmic linear statements (see page 183). Hans Richter (1888–1976) produced a large body of work in which he explored visual counterparts for musical structures, using abstract elements in both painting and film. His 1921 film, *Rhythmus 21*, is considered to be one of the first abstract films. Rhythmic movements also interested the Abstract Expressionists, and both Jackson Pollock (1912–56) and Willem de Kooning (1904–97) used the word in the titles of paintings. The close association of Abstract Expressionism and jazz certainly inspired this crossover. Rhythm is also a feature in the Op Art paintings of Brigitte Riley (1931–), Victor Vasarely (1906–97), and others.

STRATEGIES

- **Conformation**
  A linear rhythmic movement is established and elements within the work are drawn or sculpted to conform to it.
- **Compositional**
  Elements are placed so that they set up a sense of regular movement or rhythm throughout the work. Often this involves repetition of some kind, with rhythm emerging from the way the elements are sequenced.
- **Illusional**
  Closely packed formations of lines or geometric shapes can be organized to create an optical illusion of movement or rhythm (see *Op Art* on page 122).

1 Melissa Meyer (1947–)
Dassin, 2012, Oil on canvas,
80 × 78 in (203.2 × 198.1 cm)

Rhythmic patterns run through a loosely repeated motif to contribute a lively movement to the image.

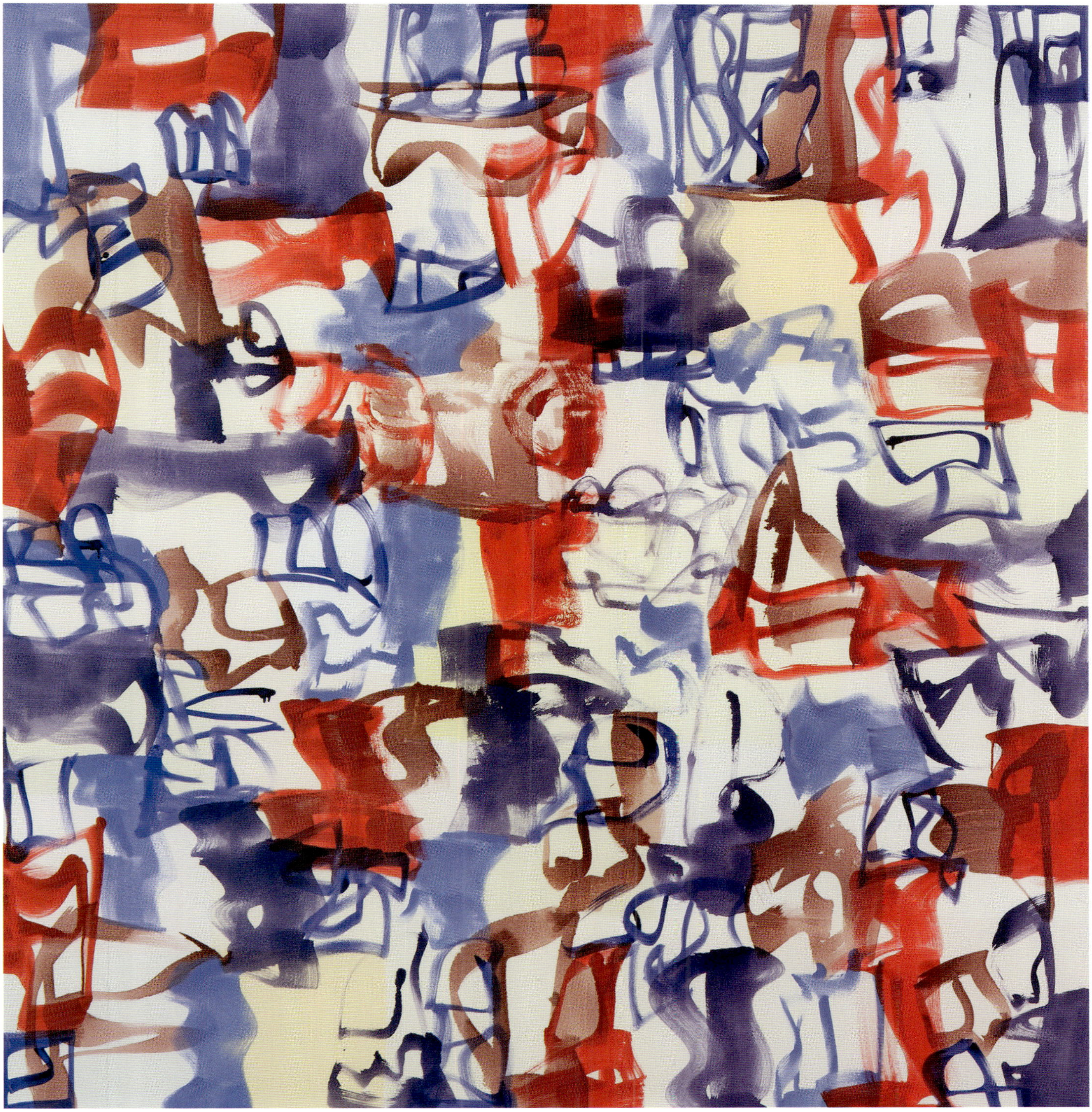

1

76 ROMANTICISM

SPONTENAITY, FEELINGS, IMAGINATION, AND GENIUS

Romanticism was a broad intellectual and artistic movement that swept over Europe between the 1770s and the 1850s. Essentially a reaction against the rationalism of the Enlightenment and the harsh realities of the Industrial Revolution, it championed an art that was driven by the emotions and generated from the personality, feelings, and imagination of the artist. It was particularly interested in the heightened emotions to be experienced in the presence of untamed nature: fear, awe, and transcendental wonder. The great poet of the era, William Wordsworth, said that poetry should be "the spontaneous overflow of powerful feelings." Unlike the classicists, who delighted in order and clarity, the Romantics opposed rules and measurement and embraced the free reign of the artist's spirit. They prized originality and spontaneity and cultivated the notion of the artistic genius, the ideal of an artist working alone and producing extraordinary and revolutionary work. The great painters of the movement were Joseph Mallord William Turner (1789–1862), Francesço Goya (1746–1828), Théodore Géricault (1791–1824), and Eugène Delacroix (1798–1863).

STYLISTIC FEATURES

- **Composition**
  Fluid and dynamic compositions favoring motion rather than repose.
- **Technique**
  Direct brushing and fast execution generated from spontaneous energy.
- **Drama**
  Powerful lighting, strong contrast, and active movements of figures.
- **Nature**
  Romantics prized the experience of strong emotions in front of nature. Turner, for instance, reputedly strapped himself to the mast of a ship in a storm so that he could later paint the experience. He also sought out highly dramatic views in the Alps to obtain the greatest sense of awe and wonder.
- **Emotive subject matter**
  Subjects that would engage the hearts of the audience were favored. Géricault's masterpiece, *The Raft of the Medusa* (see page 133), dramatizes a human disaster for maximum effect.
- **Exoticism**
  Part of the program of Romanticism was the desire to escape the then nascent industrialization, with its crowded cities and filthy air. Delacroix, in particular, sought out exotic subjects, traveling to North Africa and making many paintings of traditional Arab life.

See also: *Creativity* on page 52; *Imagination* on page 88

1 Eugène Delacroix (1798–1863)
Liberty Leading the People, 1830,
Oil on canvas, $102^{3}/_{8} \times 127^{15}/_{16}$ in
(260 × 325 cm)

With its powerful diagonals, heroic poses, sense of action, and dramatic subject matter complete with corpses and smoke, this work is a quintessential product of the Romantic era.

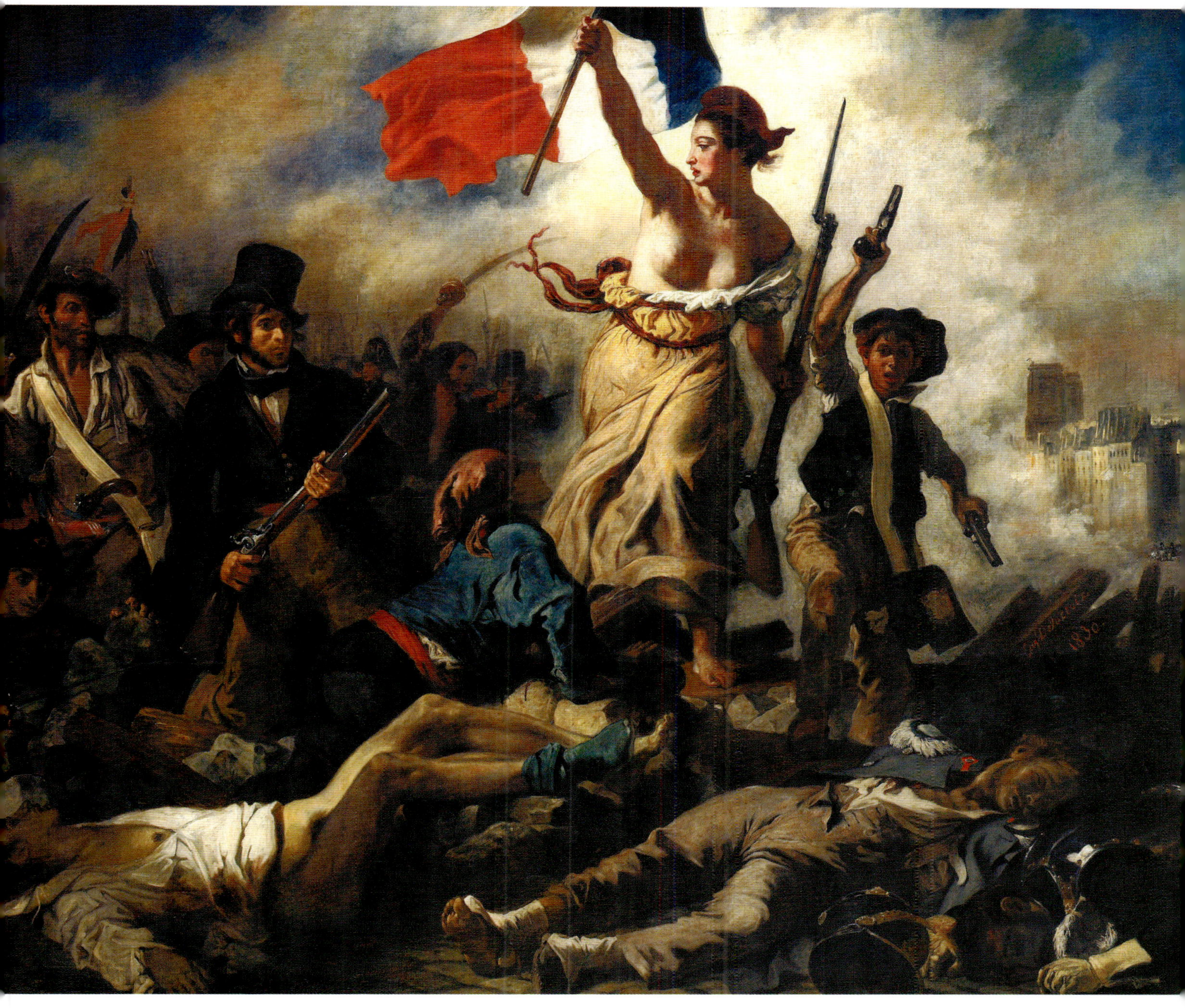

1

77 SCALE

SIZE AFFECTS MEANING AND EXPRESSION

The choice of scale can greatly affect the way that a work of art is experienced. Scale plays a considerable role in the kind of expression, feel, or almost any other intention that the artist is attempting to realize. Some scales are more appropriate to certain kinds of expression.

- **Miniature**
  Very tiny works can exhibit qualities of compression, delicacy, and refinement of technique, as well as considerable intimacy. The presentation of an image on a small scale can itself feel magical. Miniature works also offer portability, a quality prized by portrait miniaturists since the Elizabethan era.
- **Small**
  Works of a modest scale invite intimacy. They can also present the touch of the artist very well since the scale of mark to that of the whole work is usually somewhat larger. For artists with a delicate touch, a modest scale can be a good choice.
- **Medium**
  As the size of a work increases, its physical presence becomes more of a factor. Heavier paint and more theatrical subject matter may work better at a medium scale. Figure paintings or sculptures will tend to feel more present the closer they get to the actual size of a human being.
- **Large**
  Here, the physical presence of a work can become its most overwhelming feature. Yards of color on canvas or a sculpture that is much larger than the viewer can be imposing and may elicit a more powerful and physical response. The artist claims authority merely by adopting such a scale. If the artist is inclined to rhetorical flourishes or theatrical effects, they may be most effective at this scale.
- **Gargantuan**
  A number of artists, mostly working in variations of land art, have pushed the idea of scale to improbable boundaries. Robert Smithson's *Spiral Jetty*, a construction on the shores of the Great Salt Lake, involved moving thousands of tons of rock. Here, art intersects with engineering, pushing the limits of what can be conceived as an art object.

See also: *Land Art* on page 100

1 ***Colossal Head of Constantine***, c. 312 CE

The original sculpture stood some 40 feet (12.2 m) high. Here, the enormous size was used to project imperial power.

2 Nicholas Hilliard (c. 1547–1619) ***Self-Portrait***, 1577, Watercolor on vellum put down on card, 1 5/8 in (41 mm) diameter

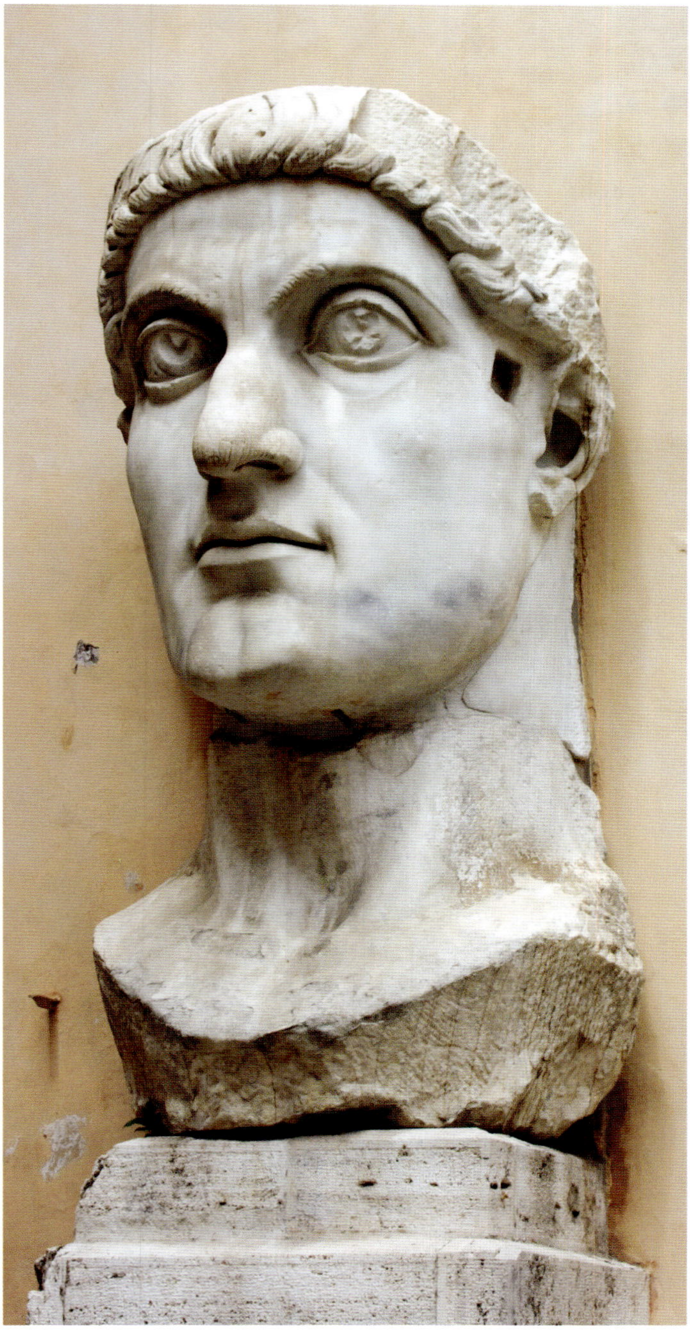

1

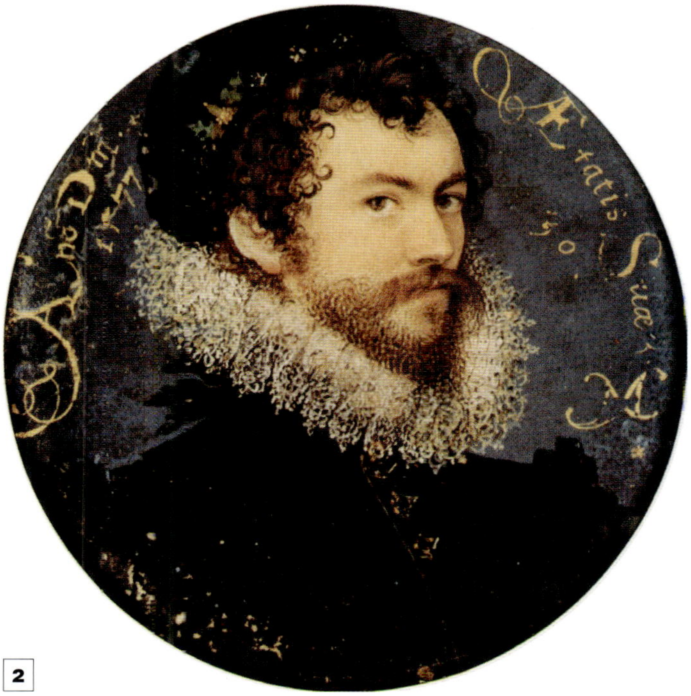

2

78 SEMIOTICS

A MODERN THEORY OF MEANING

Modern philosophy has given birth to a theory known as semiotics, or the doctrine of signs, which has developed a sophisticated set of ideas about the nature of meaning and representation. Semiotics is essentially a broadening of linguistic philosophy to encompass means of communication other than language, including visual artifacts. The principle exponents of this approach include Ferdinand de Saussure (1857–1913) and Charles Sanders Peirce (1839–1914).

Semioticians hold that all thought takes place in terms of signs, which may only be interpreted accurately within the broad cultural context in which they are manufactured. They assert that meaning in art is not held within an individual art object but is shared between all the signs and products of a culture. In order to understand a representation, the viewer needs to have an experience of the subject or similar subjects and an experience of the world of signs particular to that culture. In the extreme view, some philosophers hold that all human intercourse is simply the exchange of signs within a culturally determined system. Signs are the means by which we experience meaning, and individual signs only acquire meaning in so far as they stand in relation with other signs. As the French philosopher Jacques Derrida (1930–2004) put it, "there is nothing outside the text" ("*il n'y a pas de hors-texte*"). Here the word "text" refers to any cultural artifact.

The philosopher and critic Roland Barthes (1915–80) used a semiotic approach to reveal what he called secondary signs, or connotations, in cultural imagery. Thus a representation of a bottle of wine might be attached to an image of good health and conviviality. This would ignore the negative connotations of inebriation and potential societal damage.

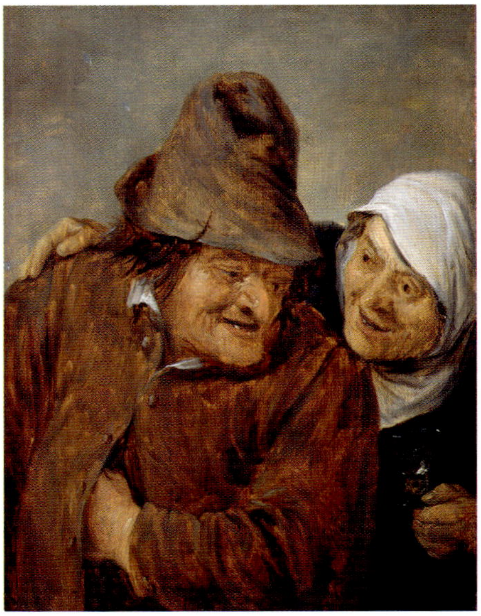

1

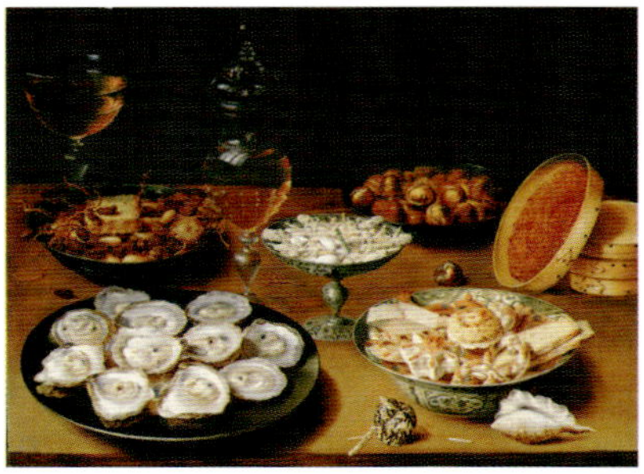

2

1 David Teniers the Younger (1610–1690) ***Two Peasants with a Glass of Wine***, c. 1645, Oil on panel, 9 1/8 × 7 1/8 in (23.2 × 18.1 cm)

2 Osias Beert the Elder (1580–1624) ***Dishes with Oysters, Fruit, and Wine***, c. 1620–1625, Oil on panel, 20 13/16 x 28 7/8 in (52.9 x 73.4 cm)

In these two seventeenth-century Flemish paintings, a glass of wine is seen in very different contexts and therefore takes on different meanings. In the Teniers, it is an agent of inebriation, part of the cheerfully colorful peasant life that Teniers is presenting for our entertainment. In the Beert, the wine glass forms part of an elegant presentation of high-quality food. It has become an accessory of the good life, and an agent of high-class pleasure.

79 SEMIOTICS 2: DECONSTRUCTION

A CRITICAL TECHNIQUE EXPOSES THE MANIPULATION OF MEANING

Semiotics has come to have great influence in the art world by providing a new critical tool known as "deconstruction." Jacques Derrida asserted that all "texts," by which he meant any cultural artifact, create meaning by projecting opposites, such as body-soul, passivity-activity, sensible-intelligible, or receptivity-spontaneity. Derrida maintained that such values were not, in fact, true opposites, but constituted instead what he called a "violent" domination of one of the two values. Their dynamic opposition invites the apprehension or acceptance of what might be called a false "middle value." As such, they are used, in some sense surreptitiously, to impose the normative cultural and political values of the time upon the reader or viewer.

The task of the philosopher, and presumably also the critic, is to undertake what Derrida termed a process, of "deconstruction." In this process the critic engages in exposing the nonrelevant nature of the assumed opposites within the text and substitutes other signs that provide a new and more useful meaning. In other words, the critic exposes the connections between signs that function to distort or shift meanings in directions desirable to those who use them. For example, a seventeenth-century Flemish still life laden with food and fine glassware might be "deconstructed" as an assertion of the values of the era's newly wealthy middle class, promoting the desirability of abundance over scarcity, high quality food over simple food, luxury items over coarse and cheap items. The deconstructionist critic might assert that the piece ignores other possibilities, such as modesty, efficiency, restraint, and the desirability of sharing wealth to include the poor and needy.

Although useful, deconstruction as a critical method has severe limitations. In seeking to identify signs, and through them explore meaning, it ignores aesthetic qualities that lie at the heart of much art and its appreciation. Deconstruction cannot address the idea that the function of a work of art is often not to convey meaning at all, but to provide an experience of pleasure.

3 Gerret Willemsz Heda (1625–1649) ***Still Life with Ham***, c. 1650, Oil on panel, 38¾ × 32½ in (98.5 × 82.5 cm)

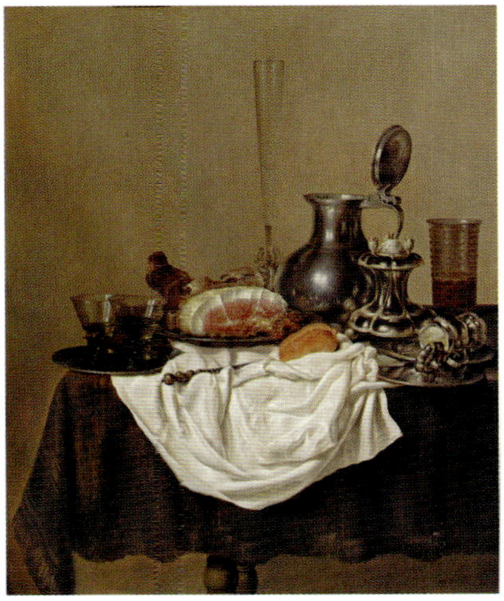

3

80 SENSITIVITY AND SENSIBILITY

A DESIRABLE QUALITY AND A USEFUL PERSONALITY TRAIT

One of the most powerful things that art can do is to communicate sensitivity. The artist alerts the viewer to fine distinctions in the perception of various features of the world. These can include color, texture, line, tone, touch, and atmosphere. Jean Auguste Domnique Ingres's graphite drawings are exquisitely sensitive to nuances of shape and form and also display a great sensitivity to more narrative qualities, such as carriage, posture, and character. The paintings of Pierre Bonnard (1867–1947), with their delicate, hesitant touch and richly graduated color, display an extraordinary sensitivity to color interaction and surface touch. The conté crayon drawings of Georges Seurat (1859–1951) (see page 195) display a refined sensitivity to minute changes in tonal value. In looking at such works, the viewer shares in a state of heightened sensitivity and is thereby enriched and pleasured.

"Sensibility," on the other hand, is a word that refers to that quality in an individual that allows him or her to respond with feeling to people, the world, or works of art. An artistic sensibility is a quality that allows you to appreciate works of art and perhaps to make them. Similarly, a poetic sensibility would allow one to appreciate poetry and perhaps have the ability to write it.

1 Antoine Watteau (1684–1721)
A Man Reclining and a Woman Seated on the Ground, c. 1716, Red, black, and white chalk on brown laid paper, 9½ × 14⅛ in (24.1 × 35.9 cm)

Watteau's drawing displays exquisite sensitivity to line and touch, using chalk with delicacy and liveliness. In addition, he is supremely alert to the nuance of posture and movement. The tonal distinctions across the white dress are also very fine.

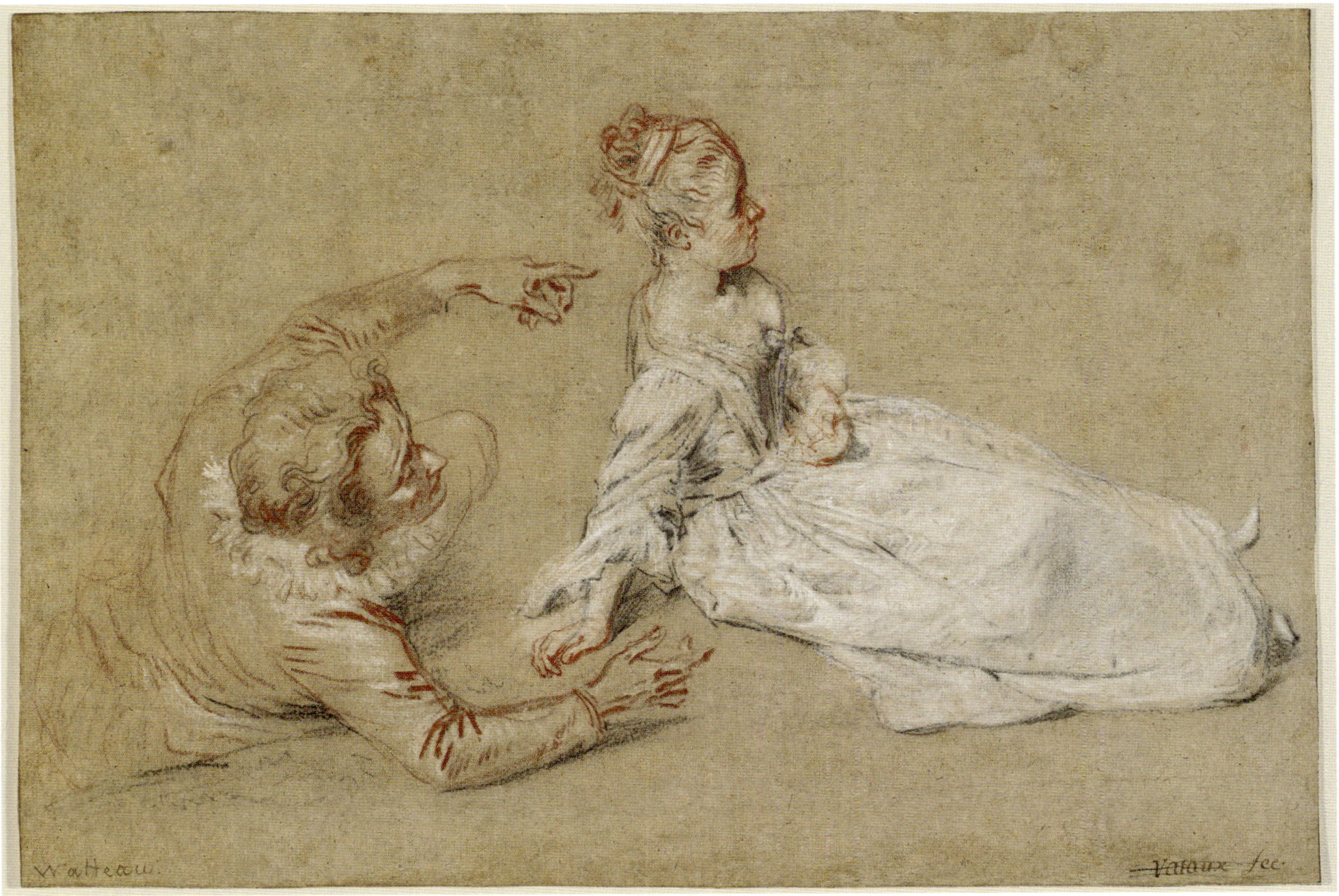

1

81 SHAPE

A PRIMAL CONCEPT

Shape is one of the basic building blocks of our visual world. A shape is a discrete or separated formation of edges that is perceived as an individual element. Part of our makeup as humans is that we apply our powers of recognition to shapes we are presented with. We are prone to find shapes that have meaning to us, such as faces, figures, and animals. We are also sensitive to geometric formations and regularities. Our proclivity to try to attach recognizable referents to indeterminate shapes is used in psychological practice in the famous Rorschach test in which individuals are asked to describe what imagery they can find in a series of ink blots.

OPTIONS

- **Silhouette**
  This approach was named after Étienne de Silhouette (1709–67), a French finance minister whose austerity budget made his name synonymous with things cheap. Making shadow portraits was becoming popular as a cheap way of securing a likeness in the second half of the eighteenth century. In a conventional silhouette, the subject is presented as a flat black shape on a clean white background. This form presents a number of advantages. While the outside of the shape is very specific, its interior is unmodulated and therefore always somewhat mysterious and suggestive.
- **Geometric abstraction**
  The presentation of geometric shapes, sometimes in rigidly formal compositions, allows for the creation of paintings that explore the relationship of shape and color. This is particularly true of art that came out of the Bauhaus, a German art school active between the world wars that championed the relationship of art and design. Joseph Albers's long series of paintings *Homage to the Square* repeated the same composition of nested squares over hundreds of pictures in which a plethora of color ideas were explored.
- **Formal minimalism**
  The presentation of a single shape became a hallmark of some minimalist work. Here, the completeness of a single shape, the idea that it is simply a single thought, no more and no less, gives such work an intriguing authority. The work of the American painter Ellsworth Kelly (1923–) is a prime example.
- **Decorative**
  The ability of flat shape to provide pleasing and engaging decorative design has sometimes invaded the world of painting. Artists such as Raoul Dufy (1877–1953) and Henri Matisse (1869–1954) made pictures in which fluidity of shape, stylishness, and suggestiveness were combined in ways that were elegant, sensual, and entertaining.

1 Unknown artist
Goethe facing a grave monument, 1780, Cut paper, 9 13/16 × 6 11/16 in (25 × 17 cm)

2 Don Voisine (1952–)
Tilt, 2013, Oil on wood panel, 16 × 12 in (40.6 × 30.5)

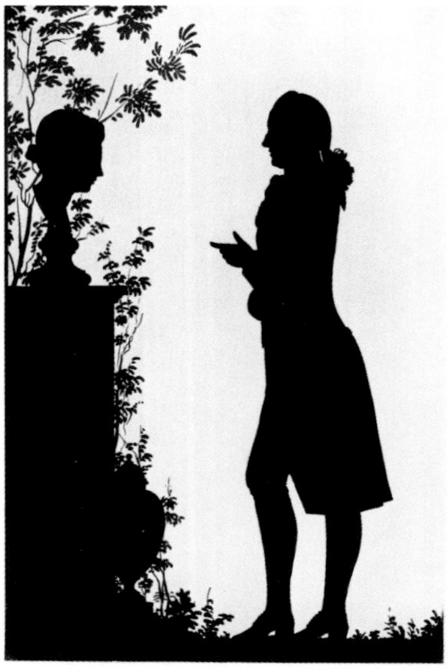

1

2

82 SHOCK

SHAKING UP THE STATUS QUO

One of the potential strengths of a work of art is its power to shock, a feat that is usually accomplished by flouting a social convention or breaking a taboo. The artwork transgresses the cultural norms of the community or culture in which it is made and therefore faces ostracism. It may go on to garner support, in which case it will have functioned to shift the culture's conception of what is acceptable to its members. Otherwise it will soon be consigned to oblivion. Shock art has the added potential of making the artist notorious and sometimes very famous.

A classic example is Manet's *Olympia*, of 1863, a nude portrait of a well-known courtesan painted in a manner that had previously been reserved for classical subjects (see *Composition* on page 45). Here, Manet was exposing the mores of the wealthy, removing the scrim that polite society placed between itself and its vices. Similarly, in 1913 the French artist Marcel Duchamp exhibited *Nude Descending the Staircase* at the Armory Show in New York (see *Movement* on page 118). Painted in a loose version of the Cubist style, the work shows a naked woman in stop-action poses as she walks down the staircase. Society at the time found the idea of a nude in motion uncomfortably suggestive.

In the late twentieth century, there was something of a vogue for artists who set out to deliberately shock the public. In 1999, the Sensation exhibition at the Brooklyn Museum in New York included a work by Andres Serrano (1950–) entitled *Piss Christ*, a photograph of a crucifix placed in a container of the artist's urine. In the same exhibition, British artist Chris Ofili (1968–) exhibited *The Holy Virgin Mary*, an image of the Madonna fabricated from elephant dung and including images of female genitalia torn from pornographic magazines. Both artists enjoyed enormous publicity. Whether their works will retain any lasting interest remains to be seen. The inherent problem with shock as a strategy in art is that it wears off very quickly, leaving the work exposed to more thoughtful examination.

1 Andres Serrano (1950–)
Piss Christ, 1987, Cibachrome print mounted on Plexiglas, 40 × 37¾ in (101.6 x 96 cm)

This photograph of a plastic crucifix submerged in the artist's urine appeared at the Sensation exhibition at the Brooklyn Museum in 1999. The show elicited a lawsuit from the mayor of New York.

1

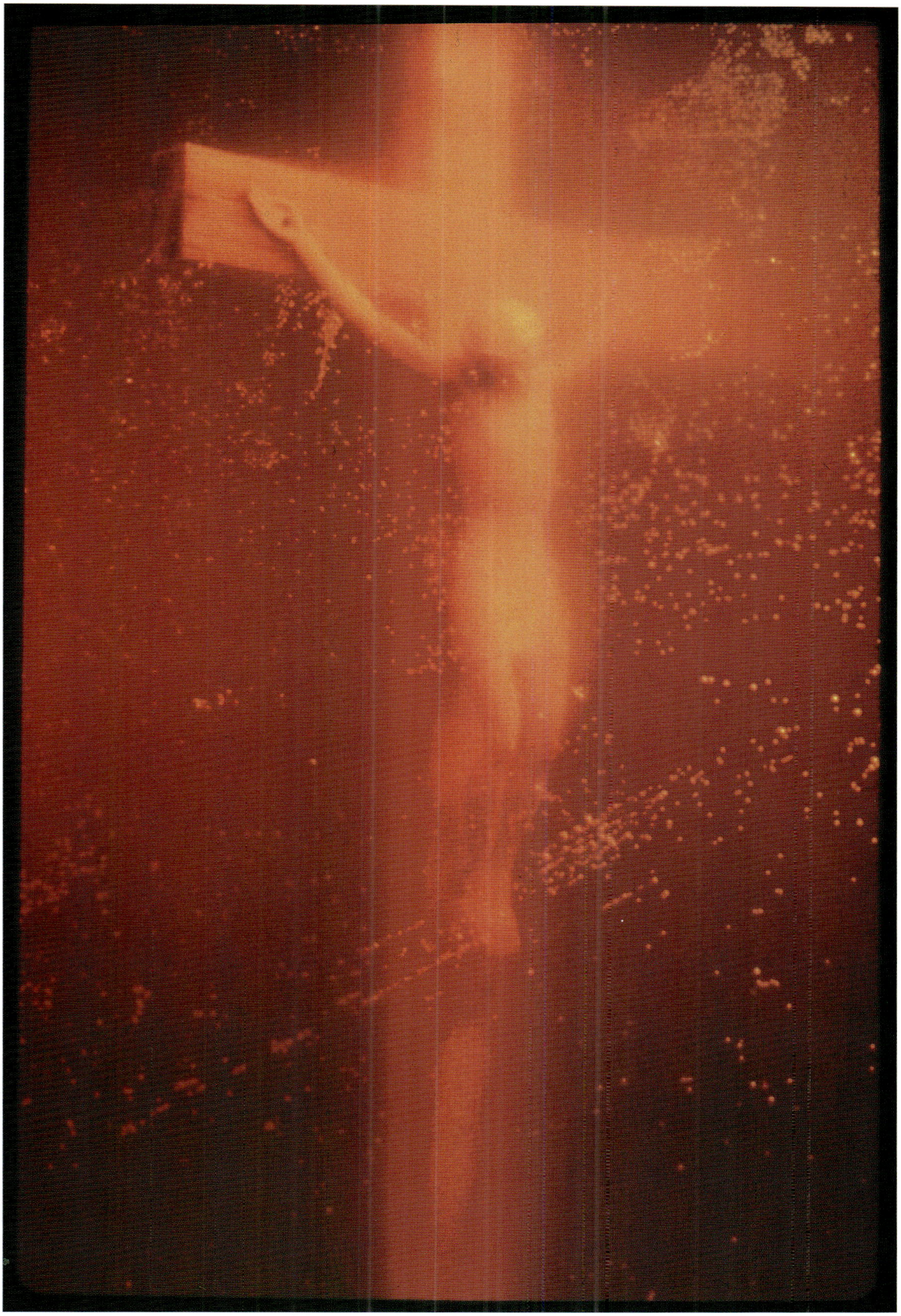

83 SIMPLIFICATION

REDUCING A STATEMENT TO ITS FUNDAMENTALS

Simplifying form, or editing complex situations into a readable set of forms or ideas, is one of the foundational strategies of art. Many tribal cultures pursue an art based on severe simplification, and ancient civilizations generally rendered figures and settings as simplified formations. More sophisticated simplification occurred in the Renaissance, particularly in the work of Piero della Francesca (1415–92), whose deep interest in Euclidean geometry led him to reduce forms towards the condition of geometric solids. A great deal of modern abstract art involves the reduction of appearances to sets of simple forms. For example, the French artist Fernand Léger (1881–1955) reduced both human and machine forms to highly simplified motifs, which he then built into almost entirely flat compositions.

The process of simplification can be broken down into four stages:

- **Objective**
  The subject is examined carefully.
- **Analytic**
  The central and distinguishing features of the subject are identified.
- **Reductive**
  Extraneous, unnecessary, confusing, and distracting information is stripped away.
- **Synthetic**
  The remaining information is combined to make a new image that exhibits clarity and coherence.

Simplification can be applied to any element or feature of an artwork. Color can be simplified, as can form, shape, mark, and line. The process can be applied equally to a contemporary video installation as it can be to an oil painting or a monumental sculpture.

The kind of expression that emerges from a process of simplification can vary. Constantin Brancusi (1876–1957) made sculptures based on natural subjects that were reduced to simplified shapes of great beauty, projecting a kind of purity of insight and sensual warmth. On the other hand, many Expressionists, such as Max Beckmann (1884–1950), simplified motifs to reveal a vision that was disturbing and at times brutal. Other artists, such as the Italian painter Giorgio Morandi (1890–1964), deployed a process of simplification in order to yield a quiet and suggestive vision. Rather than dictate any one point of view, simplification allows the artist to reveal his vision and present it in a concentrated, persuasive, and accessible fashion.

See also: *Sufficiency of Means* on page 182; *Abstraction* on page 10; *Minimalism* on page 112

1 Cycladic female figurine, c. 2300 BCE, Marble, 6 13/16 in (17.3 cm) high

2 Piero della Francesca (1415–92) ***The Baptism of Christ***, c. 1450, Tempera on panel, 65¾ × 45 11/16 in (167 × 116 cm)

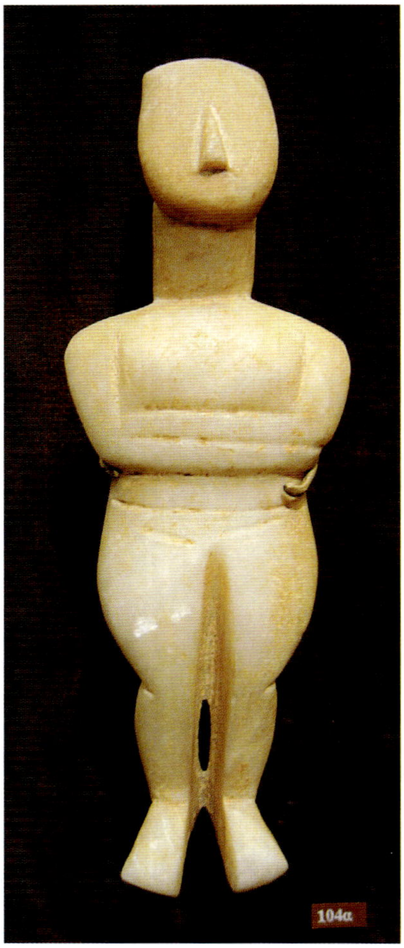

1

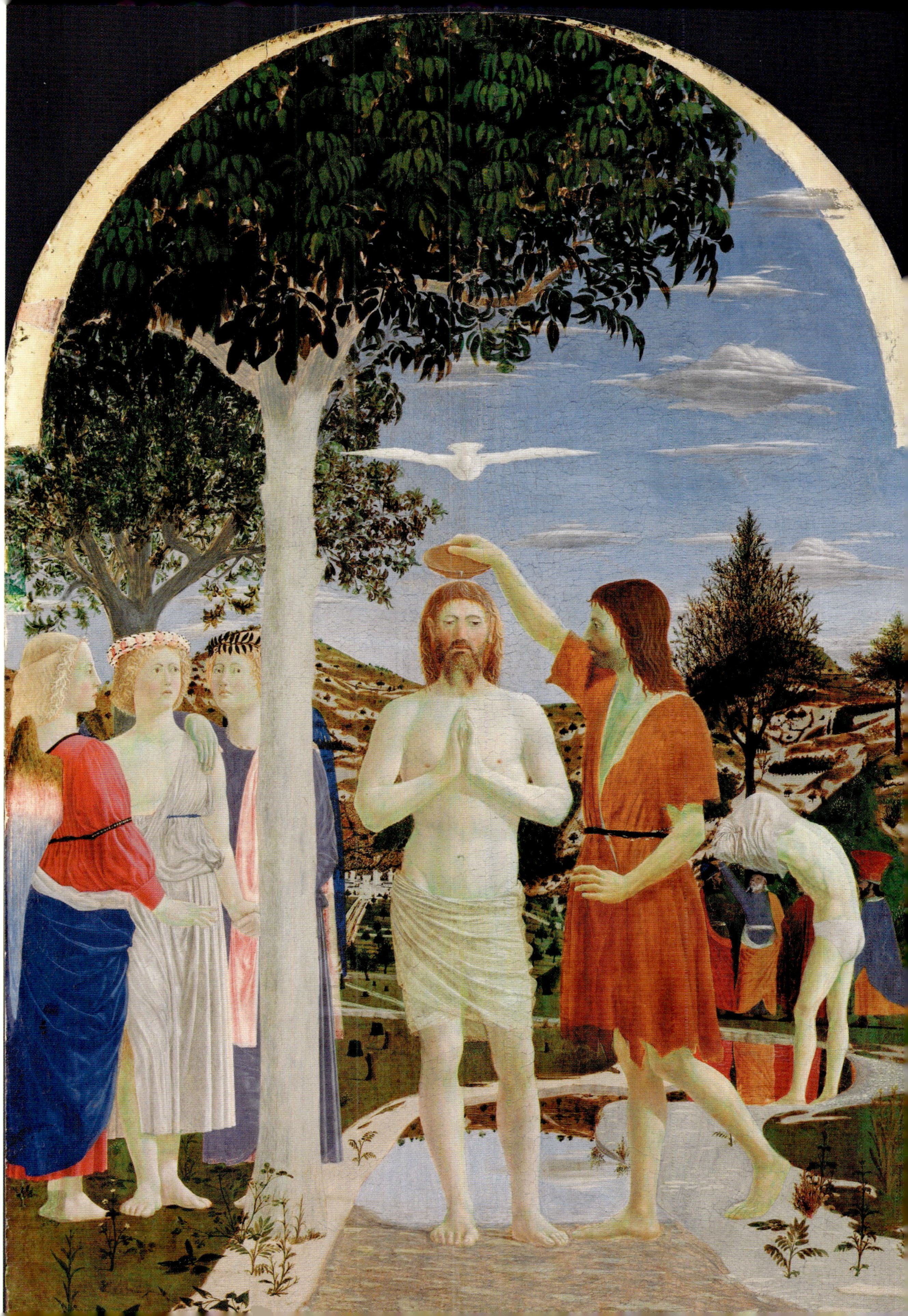

2

84 SPACE AND VOLUME

AN INVISIBLE ELEMENT CAN BE MANIPULATED, CONTAINED, AND DEFINED

The control of space and volume is central to much Western sculpture and is fundamental to the art of architecture. The idea that space can be manipulated so that its presence and shape become expressive is seen in the art of sculptors as diverse as Michelangelo (1475–1564) and Alberto Giacometti (1901–66). The representation of space and volume on a two-dimensional surface has also been a primary concern in painting over many centuries.

Beacuse volume and space are largely invisible, we comprehend them through the arrangement of surfaces, points, and colors. The manipulation of these elements allows the artist to control the viewer's experience of space.

Sculptural concerns with volume undoubtedly begin with figurative sculpture. Renaissance artists strove to achieve an apprehension of clarity in volume and space while understanding some of the expressive possibilities inherent in controlling these elements.

Modern sculptors, freed from the requirements of naturalistic description, have been more adventurous in exploring these possibilities. Space can feel squeezed, open-ended, curved, structured, oppressive, vast, or indeterminate. The English artist Henry Moore (1898–1986) made many sculptures in which he abstracted the human form in such a way that an inordinate amount of spatial volume is made palpable for the viewer. The Minimalist artist Sol Lewitt (1928–2007) made sculptures that were nothing more or less than simple frame structures of cubes that defined space and volume in a quasi-scientific and deliberately banal fashion. More spectacularly, the American artist Richard Serra (1939–) has made works in which narrow volumes of space are contained within monumental curving walls of steel, creating a sense of oppression and even danger.

In architecture, control of volume is the immediate result of designing even the simplest building. The long tradition of religious architecture has bequeathed a large vocabulary of ways in which space can be managed and effects of hierarchy and theatricality can be achieved. The tall, narrow volumes of the naves of gothic cathedrals, for instance, with their soaring arches, contrive to make the viewer look upwards and heavenwards. Meanwhile, domestic spaces can be designed to feel elegant, cozy, quaint, calming, inviting, or many other qualities. In public and business settings, modern architects control space to convey everything from splendor and opulence in an opera house foyer to a utilitarian business atmosphere in cubical office space.

See also: *Mass* on page 108

1 **Ely Cathedral** (Interior), Cambridgeshire, England

The space is designed to move the viewer's eye upward, creating a sense of awe and wonder.

2 Giovanni Paolo Panini (1691–1765) ***Interior of the Pantheon***, Rome, c. 1734, Oil on canvas, $50^{3}/_{8}$ × 39 in (128 × 99 cm)

The artist distorts the perspective to provide a heightened experience of space.

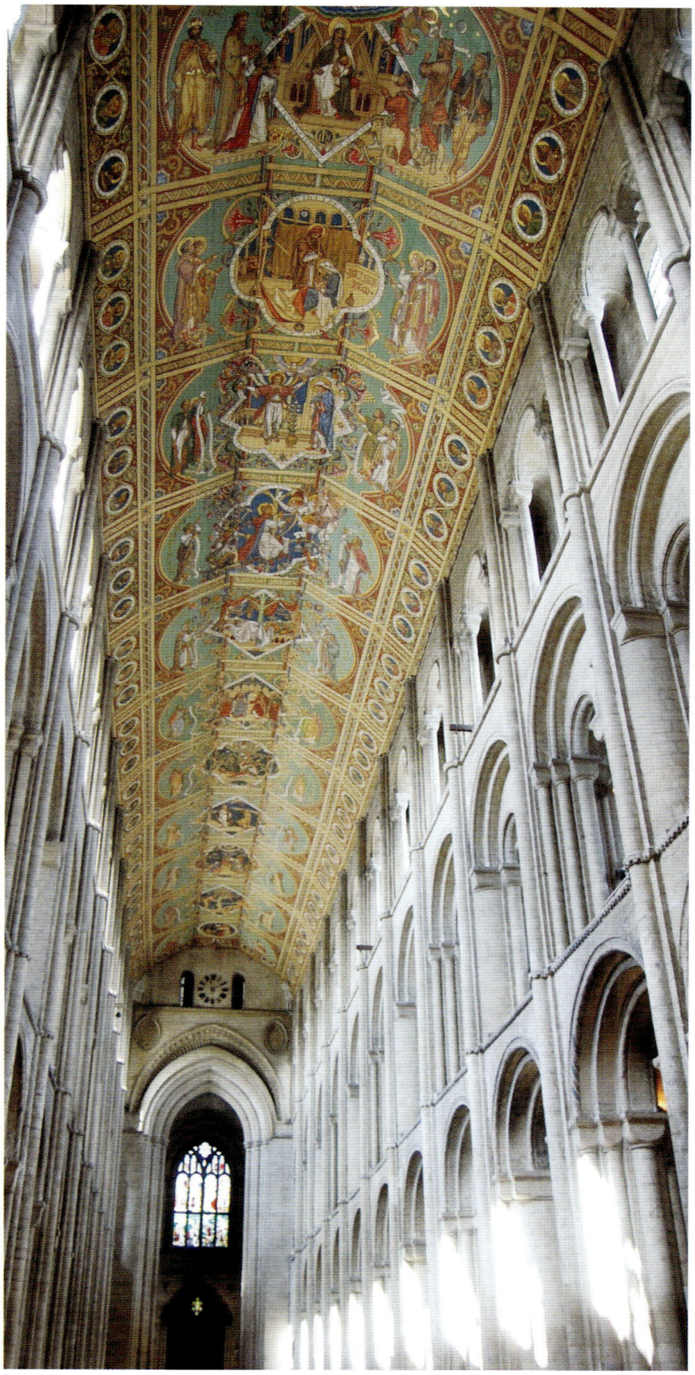

1

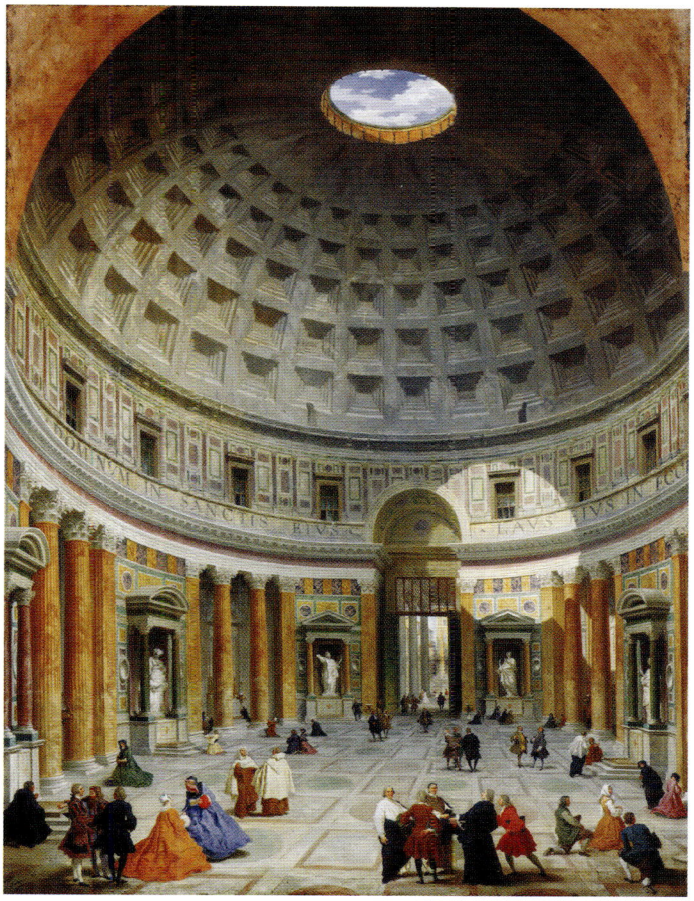

2

85 SPECTACLE

KNOCKING THE VIEWER'S SOCKS OFF

Art can sometimes become spectacle when it seeks primarily to bedazzle, entertain, or overwhelm the viewer. This has generally been the province of religious art and occasionally secular public art. The interiors of many religious buildings, including mosques, Indian temples, and Western churches, are adorned with decorative or narrative imagery, amassed and displayed in a way intended to dazzle its audience. This kind of theatricality reached a zenith in Europe during the Counter-Reformation, when the Catholic Church instituted a policy of using alluring decorative schemes to attract and maintain its congregation. Rubens (1577–1640), in particular, became adept at creating spectacular altarpieces in which dynamic compositions, dramatic lighting, and powerful rendering were united to make an extraordinary impression on those who saw them (see page 93). Church decoration later in the Baroque era, such as that undertaken by the Tiepolo family, engaged in trompe-l'oeil and perspectival distortions to create images that attempted to transport the viewer to an entirely different spatial realm (see page 200).

The strain of modernism that embraced abstraction generally avoided spectacle in favor of quieter forms. In recent years, however, new endeavors in installation and land art and new technical possibilities in multimedia and interactive art have spawned a greater interest in spectacle as art. The architecture of Frank Gehry (1929–), particularly his Guggenheim Museum, Bilbao, Spain, presents the building as a spectacle of undulating and curving metallic roof lines. Enormous outdoor sculptures, such as *Puppy* by Jeff Koons (1955–), a giant steel framework shaped like a dog and festooned with thousands of flowers, are designed to engage and overwhelm the immediate attention of the viewer. Other examples would include Rudolph Stingel's 2013 installation at Venice's Palazzo Grassi, whose every surface was covered with enormous photo prints of a Persian carpet. Many of the artworks of Christo (1935–), involving wrapping whole buildings or natural areas, invite consideration primarily as spectacle.

The problem with spectacle as art is that its impression on the audience is all too often very short-lived. Once viewers become acclimated to the scale and splendor of the production, they will look for more lasting interest or else simply turn away.

1 Jeff Koons (1955–)
Puppy, 1992, 488 × 327 × 358 in (1,240 × 830 × 910 cm), Steel framework coated with fresh flowers. Installed at the Guggenheim Museum, Bilbao, Spain.

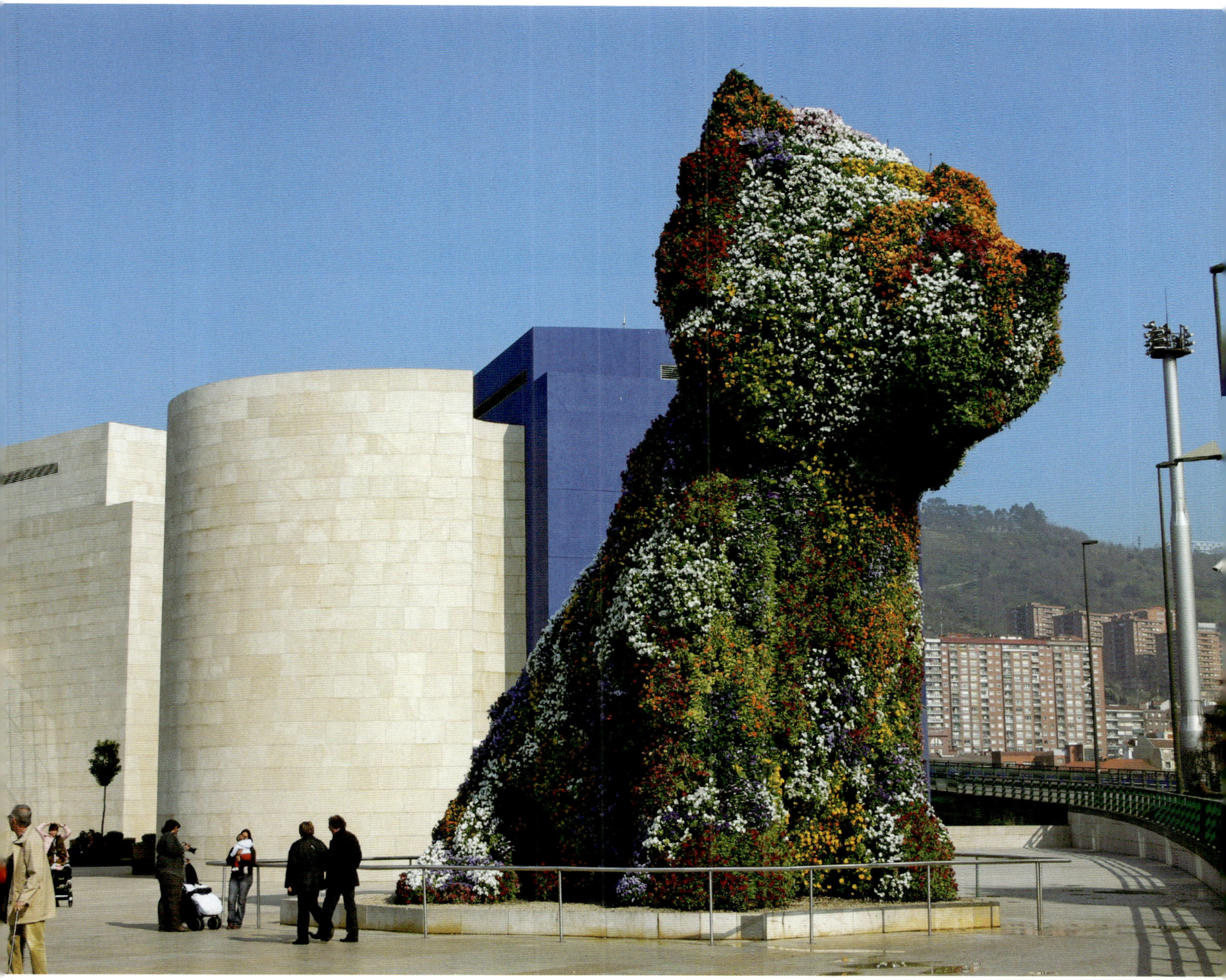

1

86 STYLE AND STYLISHNESS

GROUPING ART ACCORDING TO MANNER AND LOOK

In the art world, "style" essentially means "in the manner of," and applies to the characteristic look and feel of the work of a particular artist or era. For instance, we talk about "Louis XVI style," meaning the look and feel of that monarch's era. Or we can talk about the style of Rembrandt, meaning the look and feel of that master's work. Some styles are not attached to any one artist but refer to a vein of art making that runs through an era. Art historians sometimes like to organize the history of art into distinct movements, each of which exhibits a particular style or group of styles. Thus, we can talk about the style of Mannerist painting or Baroque painting or Romantic painting. Such styles may be further broken down into regional variations or variations within the time frame of the style, such as Florentine Renaissance style as opposed to Roman Renaissance style, or late Baroque style as opposed to early Baroque style.

The emergence of styles in art seems to be a natural result of artists working at the same time, in the same geographic area, and with similar influences and ideas. Styles continually change and mutate as new ideas, concerns, looks, and features are invented or embraced.

"Stylish," has a narrower meaning. A work of art is said to be stylish when it exhibits a fashionable elegance delivered with a seemingly effortless surety and aplomb. It is a quality attached to presentation and is generally thought of as something that doesn't have a lot of substance. Fine artists are not happy to be known as stylish unless it is central to their ambitions. Thus, a society portrait painter might be happy to be stylish, which would imply that his manner is warmly acceptable to those with a taste in current fashion. A "serious" artist might find the sobriquet to be diminishing, implying that his work has merely to do with surface appearance. There are, however, exceptions. A portrait by Van Dyke (1599–1641) might be seen as stylish and also be an excellent painting; likewise a portrait by Whistler (1834–1903) two centuries later. In both cases, these great artists were seeking to reflect the style, dress, and presentation of an upper class that was very much concerned with surface and appearance. They painted their subjects in a way that entered into the sense of insouciance and ease that those classes prized as qualities of behavior and appearance.

1 Antoine Bourdelle (1861–1929)
The Meditation of Apollo and the Nine Muses, 1910–12,
Bas-relief, 11 ft 6 in × 49 ft 10 in
(3.5 × 15.2 m)

An example of the style of Art Deco.

2 Sir Anthony van Dyke (1599–1641)
Charles I out Hunting, 1635,
Oil on canvas, 107$\frac{1}{8}$ × 83½ in
(272 × 212 cm)

3 Aubrey Beardsley (1872–98)
Salome and John, 1892, Pen and ink on paper, 8$\frac{13}{16}$ × 6$\frac{3}{16}$ in
(22.3 × 15.7 cm)

An example of the style of Art Nouveau.

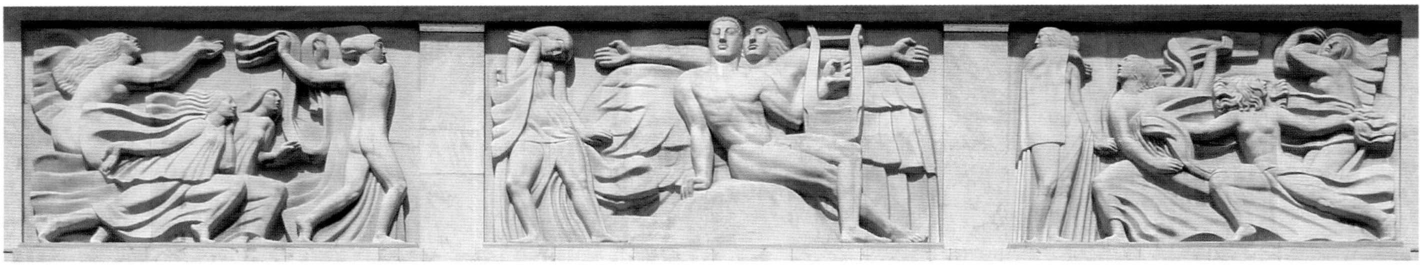

1

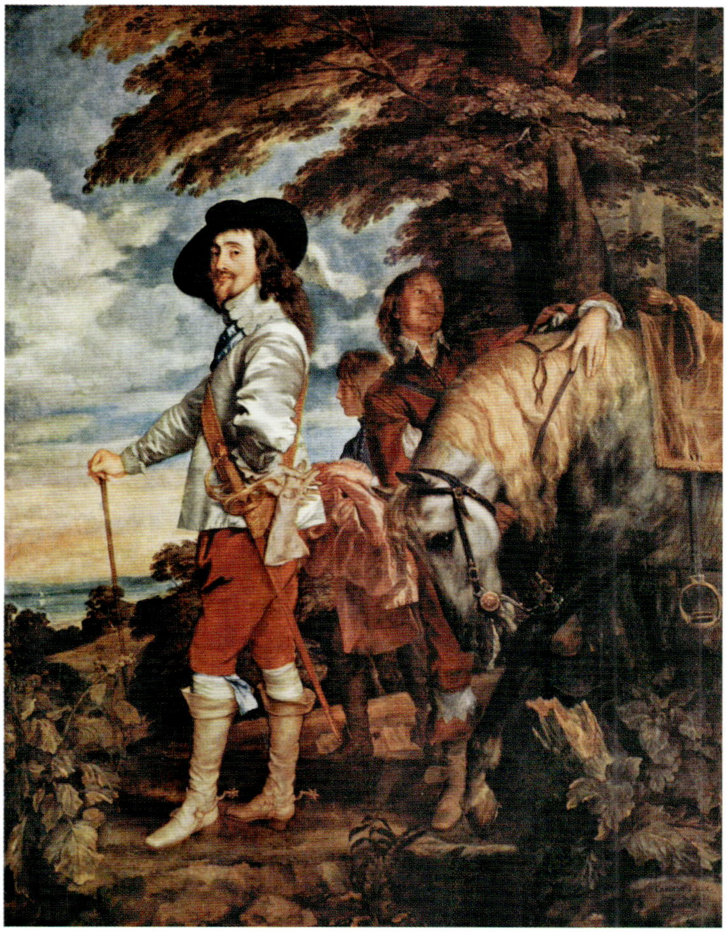

2

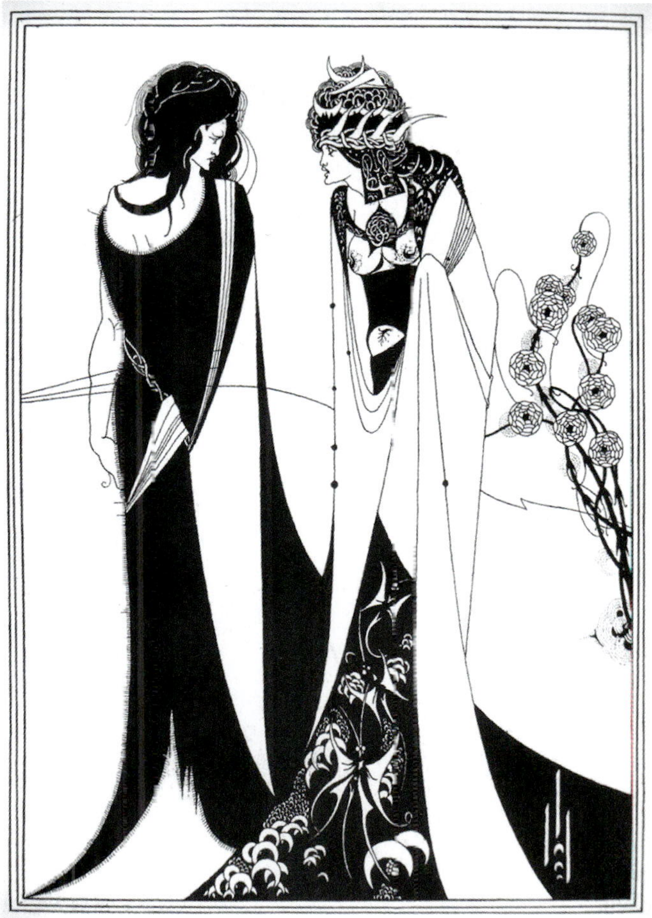

3

87 SUCCESSIVE APPROXIMATION

THE ARTWORK AS A JOURNEY

Successive approximation is a process whereby the artist makes statements that he or she then continually corrects, gradually arriving at the finished statement. The work alternates between creative generation and critical assessment. It proceeds as both a response to the subject matter and a response to what has already been achieved in the work.

This process can be glimpsed in many old master drawings where the artist has launched into the work but then adjusted his first statements in a continuous process. In a drawing by Jean-Honoré Fragonard (1732–1806) illustrating a scene from *Don Quixote*, multiple marks and erasures are visible, recording the struggle of the artist to arrive at a successful composition. Similarly, in many paintings from the Romantic era, by artists such as Joseph Mallord William Turner (1789–1862), John Constable (1776–1837), and Eugène Delacroix (1798–1863), it is possible to see that the artist has made numerous changes during the course of the work as he pushes both drawing and color into position.

Prior to the late nineteenth century, artists would conceal the process of successive approximation in their finished work. The idea that the work of art could incorporate the record of these changes in the final state gradually took hold during Impressionism, with its immediate and fresh technique. The Postimpressionists took things further. In the mature works of Paul Cézanne (1839–1906), the artist stood in front of his subject matter, usually a landscape or still life, and made numerous attempts to record exactly where he perceived the locations of various elements in his composition to be. "Painting from nature is not copying the object," he once observed, "it is realizing one's sensations." As he turned his head or moved slightly, his perception of location shifted. The painting becomes the sum of its attempted approximations.

Similarly, the Swiss artist Alberto Giacometti (1901–66), working later in the twentieth century, made drawings, paintings, and sculpture that engaged in a long process of approximation and correction. For this artist, the process created a gloriously deep and unearthly sense of space in drawings and paintings and a strangely thin and attenuated set of forms in his sculpture. In both cases, the artist saw the works as unfinished. For him the process of successive approximation remained open ended. "That's the terrible thing," he said, "the more one works on a picture, the more impossible it becomes to finish it."

1 Jean-Honoré Fragonard (1732–1806) ***Don Quixote Attacking the Biscayan***, 1780s, Brush with brown and gray washes over charcoal on laid paper, 16 5/16 × 11 5/16 in (41.4 × 28.7 cm)

2 Alberto Giacometti (1901–66) ***Portrait of Annette***, 1961, Oil on canvas, 45 5/8 × 35¼ in (115.9 × 89.5 cm)

3 Paul Cézanne (1839–1906) ***At the Water's Edge***, c. 1890, Oil on canvas, 28¾ × 36 7/16 in (73 × 92.5 cm)

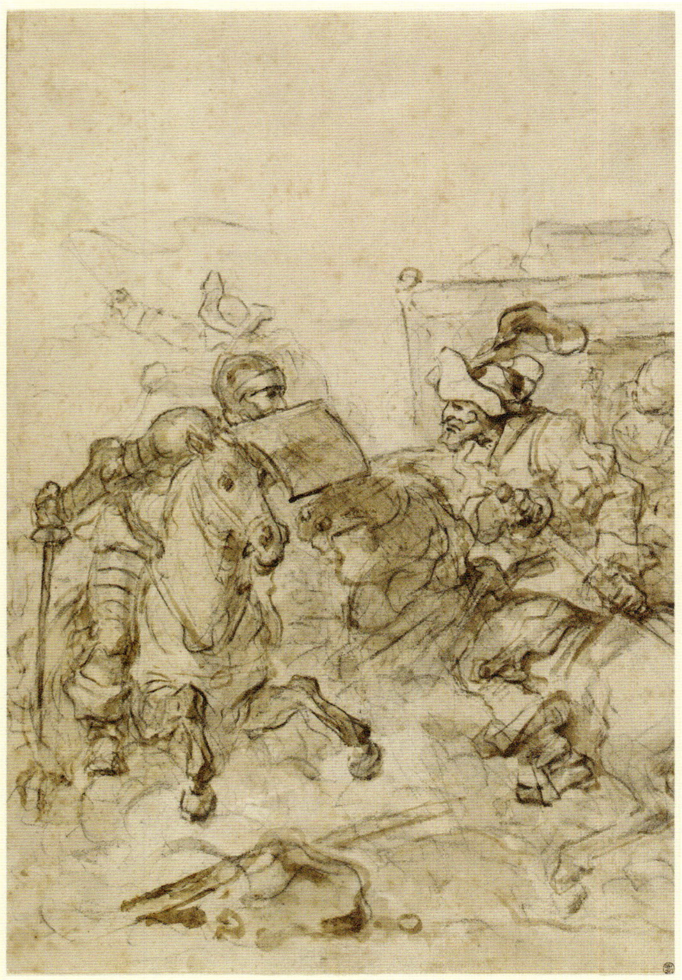

1

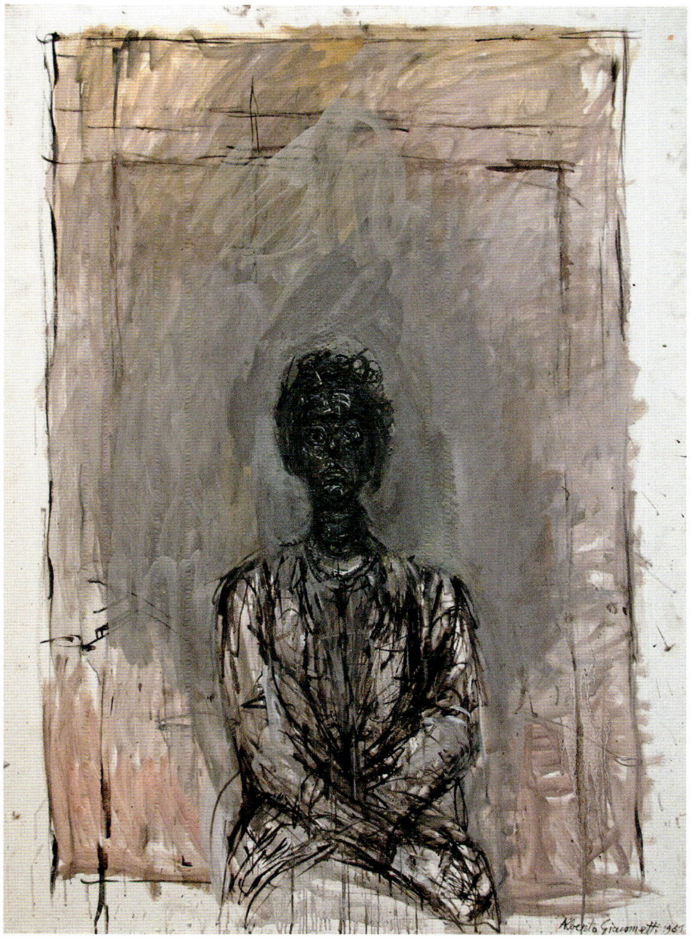

2

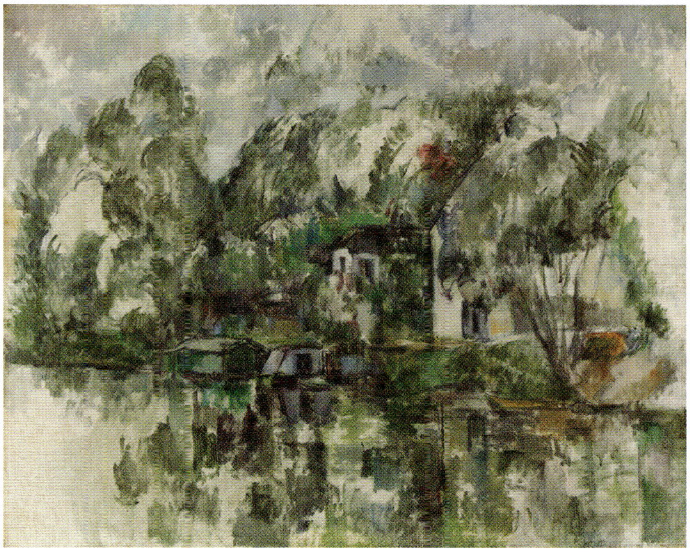

3

88 SUFFICIENCY OF MEANS

ECONOMY YIELDS EXPRESSIVE RICHES

Sufficiency of means is the idea that the work of art is strongest when it achieves its desired result in the most economical fashion possible. Each component, whether it be color, line, layering, or tone, is deployed in a fashion that allows it to simply achieve its task and no more. Often this idea involves considerable editing, the removal of extraneous material that is not germane to the success of the artwork. Unnecessary detail, overplayed drama, excessive elements, tiresome overworking, theatrical flourishes might all be jettisoned so that the primary purpose of the artwork comes to the fore.

This principle is sometimes expressed by the idea "Less is more," a phrase first coined by the English poet Robert Browning in his poem about the Renaissance painter Andrea del Sarto (1486–1530). The opposite is true of the so-called "pompier style" academic paintings of late nineteenth-century France, where painters such as William-Adophe Bouguereau (1825–1905) and Jean-Léon Gérôme (1825–1905) indulged in a surfeit of descriptive drama and showy illusionism to the detriment of the narrative force of their paintings. Compare this to an earlier Neoclassical painting by Jacque-Louis David (1748–1825) (see *Classicsm and Rennissance* on page 34) where every element fulfills an exact function within the composition, or to later modernist works where nonessential description is usually stripped away.

See also: *Restraint* on page 156

1 William-Adolphe Bouguereau (1825–1905)
Nymphs and Satyr, 1873, Oil on canvas, 102³/₈ × 70⁷/₈ in (260 × 180 cm)

2 Henri Matisse (1869–1954)
La Danse, 1909, Oil on canvas, 102¼ × 153⁹/₁₆ in (259.7 × 390.1 cm)

Two paintings separated by thirty years address similar subject matter in very different ways. The Bouguereau is tediously rendered and over described, while the Matisse brilliantly reduces the subject to its essence.

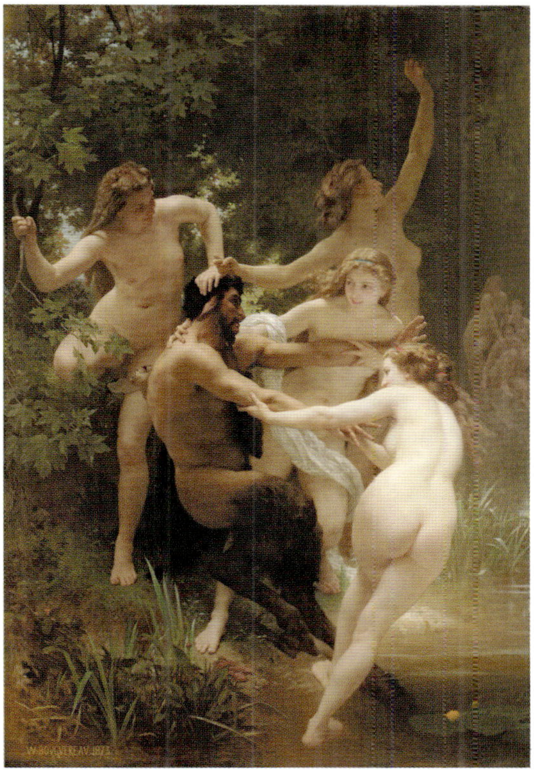

1

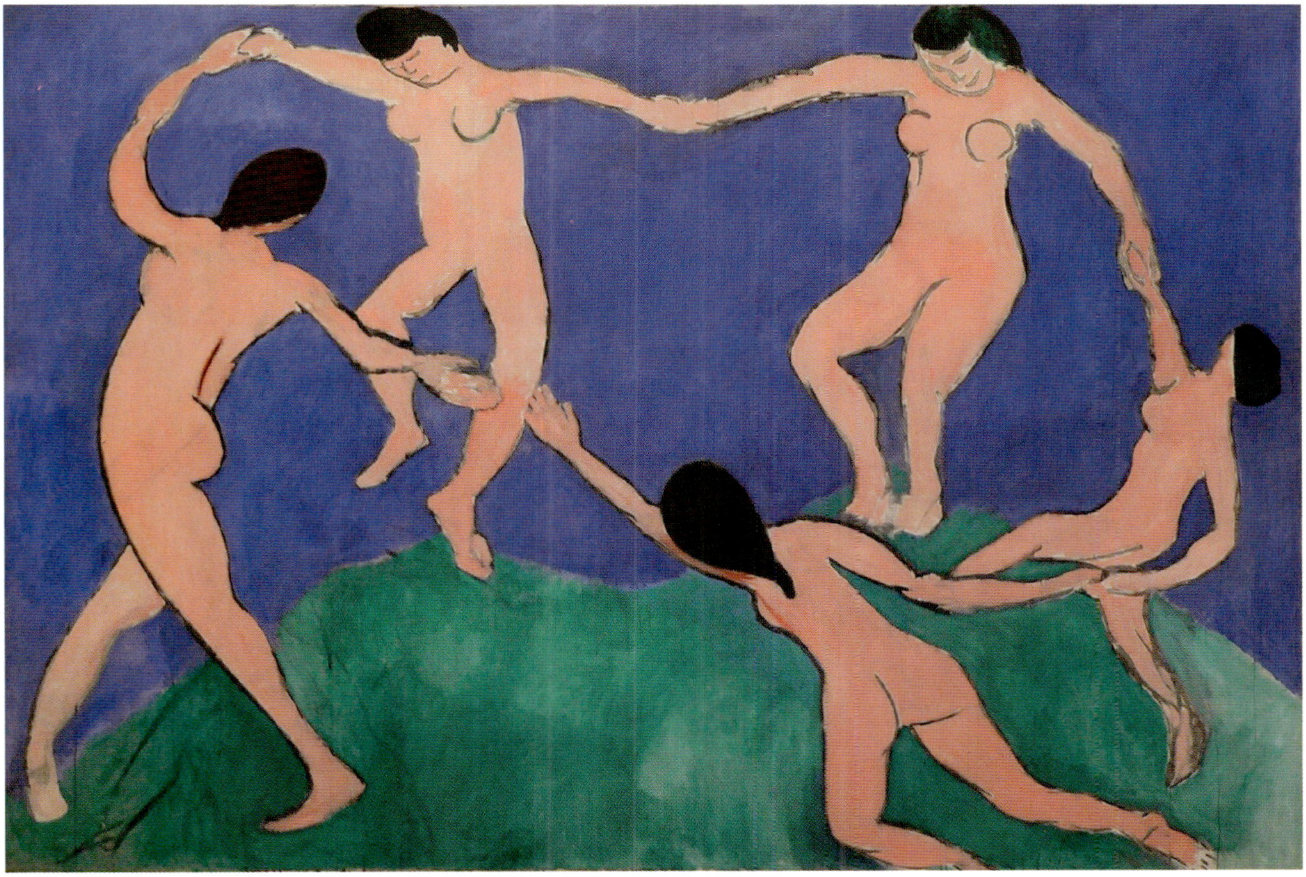

2

89 SURREALISM

MINING THE UNCONSCIOUS

Surrealism, a European art movement that developed in the years after World War I, promoted the idea that the unconscious, nonrational mind was the appropriate guiding force in art. The movement's leader, André Breton (1896–1966), was inspired in part by his role as an army psychologist during the war where he used some of the ideas of Sigmund Freud in his work with shell-shock victims. Freud regarded the dream as a means of access to the subconscious mind. The Surrealists also found other ways to make the unconscious accessible. For the writers, this involved "automatic writing," and for the visual artists, techniques such as frottage and decalcomania allowed for similar results.

Whether Surrealist artworks do actually reveal the subconscious mind is an open question. The movement did, however, expand the range of what is possible and acceptable in art and explored new vocabularies in visual production.

METHODOLOGY

- **Automatic writing and drawing**
  A technique in which the artist puts himself into a sort of passive trance and allows his hand to move without control on the paper. This was a practice first used by "spiritists" in the nineteenth century.
- **Frottage**
  A technique in which the artist places a sheet of paper over a textured surface and makes a rubbing. She then looks at the image and allows it to suggest shapes and images which can then be worked up. The word "frottage" was appropriated by the Surrealists from its traditional use in French as a reference to sexual rubbing.
- **Decalcomania**
  A technique in which paint films are built up on paper and then pressed onto canvas. Once the paper is pulled away the paint is left on the canvas in often surprising formations. The artist then works to discover images suggested by these chance formations of the paint.
- **Juxtaposition**
  The idea that unlikely combinations of images can yield subversive and poetic meanings. André Breton described it in 1924 as "a juxtaposition of two more or less distant realities. The more the relationship between the two juxtaposed realities is distant and true, the stronger the image will be—the greater its emotional power and poetic reality."

See also: *Juxtaposition* on page 96

1 Max Ernst (1891–1976)
The Antipape, 1941–42, Oil on canvas, 63¼ × 50 in (160.8 × 127 cm)

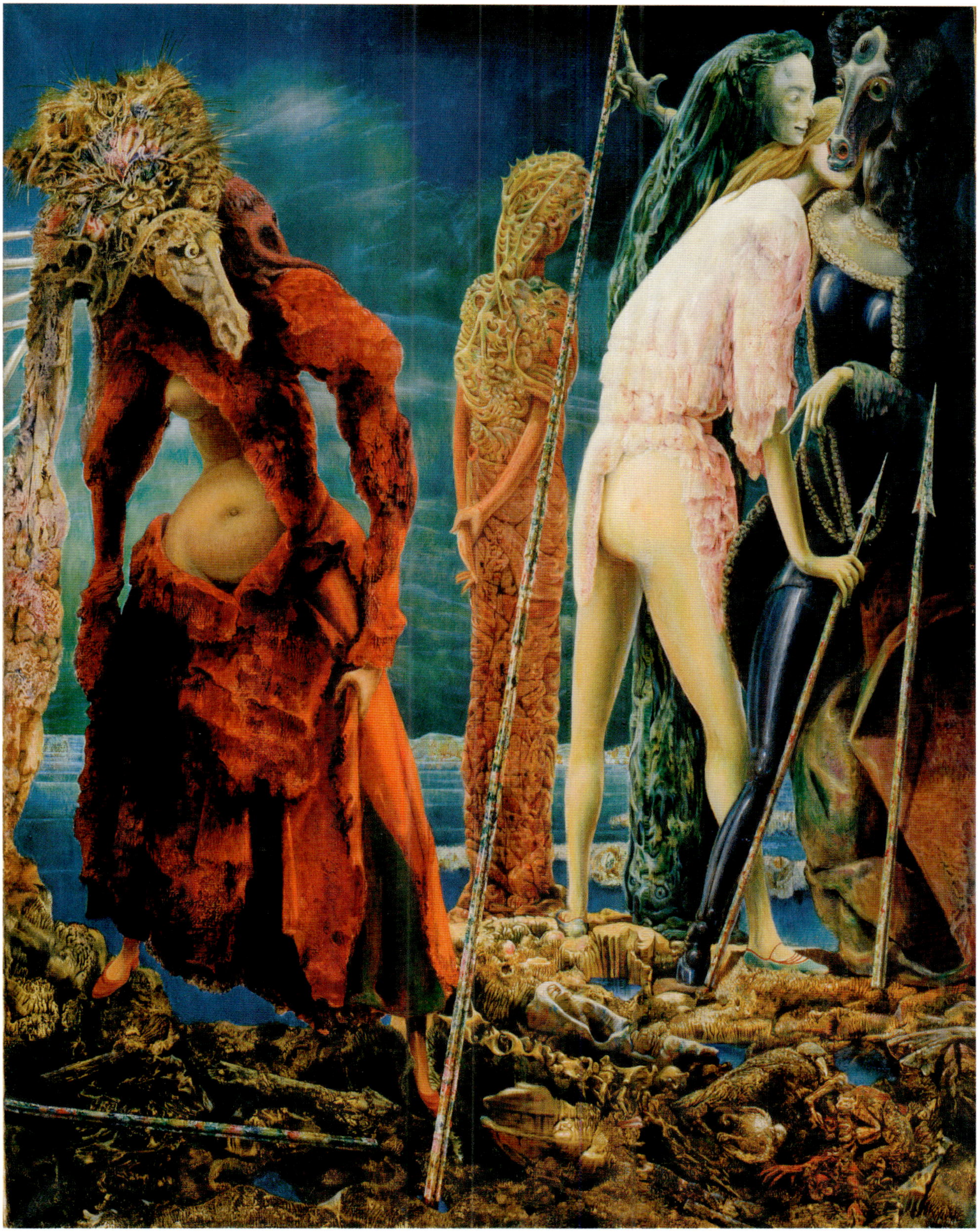

1

90 SYMBOLS

BROADLY ACCEPTED REFERENTS

A symbol is a visual element that stands for something else. It may depict the thing that it represents, but this is not a requirement. It is merely necessary that there is an understanding within the culture in which it is produced as to the meaning of the symbol. Almost anything can be symbolized, including ideas, the elements, danger, groups, or nations. For example, a yellow triangle often symbolizes a road hazard, a linear representation of a fish symbolizes Christianity, and a hammer and sickle together symbolize Communism. Religious symbols, such as the cross or the Star of David, readily communicate their meaning to a wide audience, while national symbols, in the form of flags, are used throughout the world. Internationally recognized symbols for poison, radioactivity, and quarantine are immensely valuable.

In the visual arts, the manipulation of symbols allows artists to convey meaning in many ways. Symbols are sometimes placed within otherwise descriptive or narrative paintings to clarify and reinforce their meaning. Thus, in Raphael's *Saint Catherine of Alexandria* (page 45), the wheel on which the saint is leaning is symbolic of her death. She was broken on a wheel. A more complex example is found in *The Ambassadors* by Hans Holbein the Younger (1497–1543), painted in 1533. A portrait of two prominent ambassadors to the English court, the work includes a wealth of symbols relating to scientific and religious ideas and includes an anamorphic (stretched out) representation of a skull, the traditional symbol of death.

When a painting functions primarily as an interplay between various symbolic elements, it is known as an allegory.

Symbols can be used in a more basic fashion, as letters or numerals, to refer to sounds, intellectual constructs, or language systems. There appears to be a close relationship between the development of symbols and the emergence of written language. Egyptian hieroglyphs, for instance, began with pictographs—collections of representations of objects and simple ideas—then gradually became less descriptive and more symbolic as they were incorporated into the syntax of language.

A number of modern painters have played with the possibilities offered by simple and even primitive symbols. Keith Haring (1958–90) evolved a visually potent series of symbols that he often deployed as graffiti in public places.

See also: *Allegory* on page 112

1 Hans Holbein the Younger (1497–1543)
The Ambassadors, 1533, Oil on oak, 81½ × 82½ in (209.5 × 207 cm)

2 Keith Haring (1958–90)
Tuttomondo Wall Painting, 1989, detail, Pisa, Italy

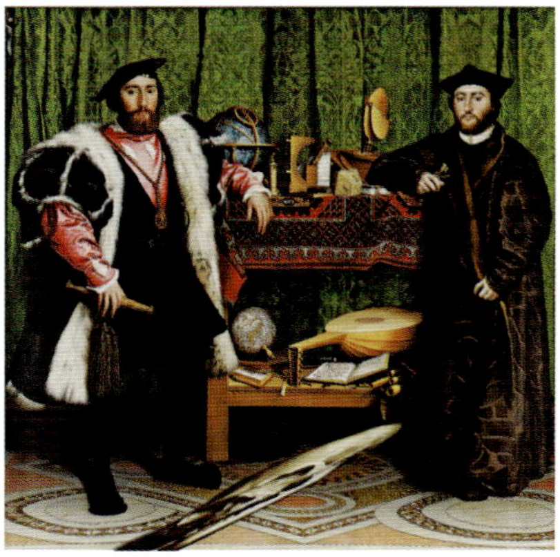

1

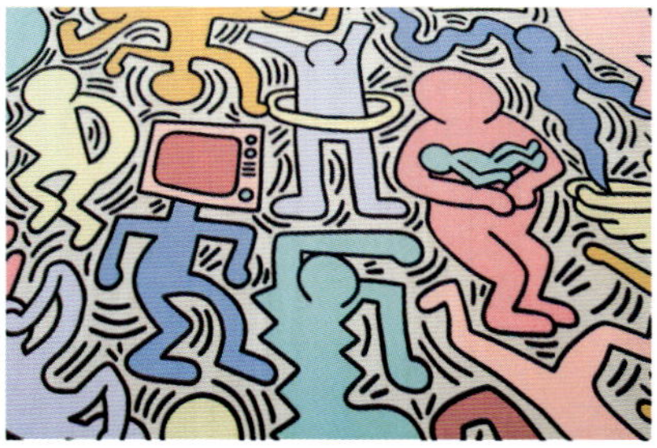

2

91 SYMMETRY

THE JOYS OF PERFECT BALANCE

Symmetry is a quality of ideal balance, where each half of a picture or sculpture is a perfect mirror image of the other. In art, symmetry is generally vertical, which is to say that the central axis runs from top to bottom of the artwork. This is known as "bilateral symmetry."

Symmetrical images convey a sense of frontality and stability and can be particularly powerful in creating a sense of presence. Because the human body is more or less symmetrical, we perhaps associate symmetry with the presence of another being.

This quality of presence conveyed by symmetrical images has been used over the millennia in religious art. There are many examples, ranging from Byzantine, medieval, Renaissance, and Baroque paintings, where a religious figure or part thereof is presented symmetrically. The central image of Christianity, the cross, is a symmetrical image, as is the Star of David. Similarly, in tribal cultures, masks, costumes, and sculpture are often symmetrical, suggesting and conveying presences both human and supernatural. This quality was exploited to great effect by the American painter Mark Rothko (1903–70), whose abstract paintings presented soft-edged rectangles in vertically symmetrical arrangements.

The downside of symmetry is that its very stability can lead to a lack of drama. The eye can be somewhat bored looking at an exactly balanced image that repeats the same information on either side of an axis. This sets up the possibility of exploring near-symmetry, the idea that the eye is interested in an image that promises symmetry but then delivers subtle differences between the two sides of the image.

Symmetry plays a larger role in the decorative arts and in architecture and furniture design. The advantages of symmetry in decorative schemes is self-evident, while the construction of buildings around a central axis offers opportunities for balanced aesthetics and ease of use. In the design of religious structures, the sense of presence offered by symmetry clearly plays a role.

See also: *Balance* on page 24; *Religiosity* on page 150

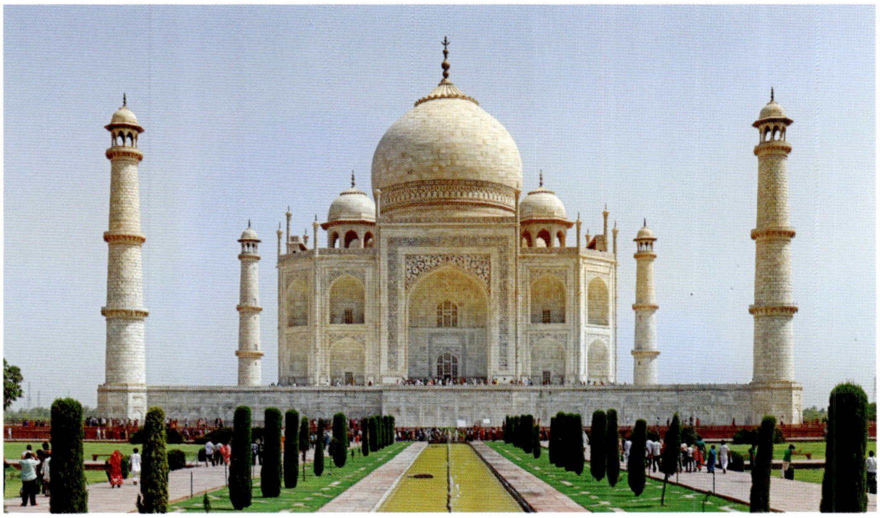

3

3 **The Taj Mahal**, 1632–53

An essay in quiet presence based on exact symmetry.

92 TEMPORARY ART

IGNORING POSTERITY

Temporary, or ephemeral art, is designed to last for a limited period of time. Over the centuries, artists have often made temporary or occasional works, but in general, artworks have been regarded as precious objects and constructed with an eye toward permanence. In the twentieth century, however, some artists made works that were designed to change, decay, or collapse altogether in relatively short periods of time. The impetus for this approach grew out of anti-art movements such as Dadaism in the early twentieth century. It gained new strength from the Land Art and Conceptual Art movements in the 1960s and '70s, whose adherents subscribed to the notion that the most important component of an artwork is not an object but rather an idea.

VARIETIES

- **Works that undergo a process of natural decay**
  The German artist Dieter Roth (1930–98), for example, made a number of biodegradable sculptures using foodstuffs ranging from cheese to sausage meat.
- **Works that can only be entertained at a location for a limited period**
  The French artist Christo (1935–), for instance, made many site-specific works that were announced to run for a specific period before being dismantled. His *Gates*, in 2005, was a construction of 7,503 gates draped with saffron fabric spread over 23 miles (37 km) of pathways in New York's Central Park. It was allowed to be in place for only two weeks.
- **Works that are constructed in natural environments that will eventually obliterate them**
  Many practitioners of land art pursue forms that are ephemeral. The English artist Richard Long (1945–) has made many pieces out of local materials, piles of stones, and shapes drawn into the earth that will have a relatively short lifespan.
- **Works that are designed to actively self-destruct**
  The artist Jean Tinguely (1925–91) made a number of kinetic sculptures that physically destroyed themselves. In a rather different approach, the Swiss artist Urs Fischer (1973–) has made elaborate figurative sculptures from candle wax. Wicks are placed in them and lit, allowing the sculpture to slowly melt and disintegrate.

See also: *Conceptual Art* on page 46; *Land Art* on page 100

1 Steven Siegel (1953–)
New Geology #2, 1992, Newsprint, 5 × 10 × 10 ft (1.5 × 3 × 3 m)

The artist amasses a simple and massive geometric form from layered newspapers. The sculpture then decays over a number of years and is slowly subsumed into the natural environment.

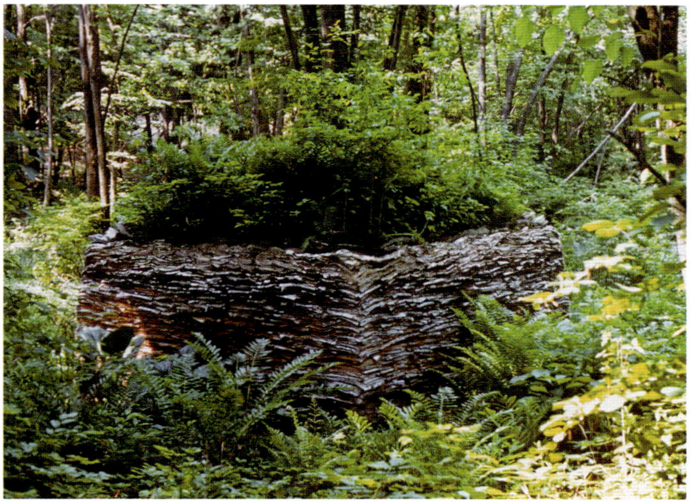

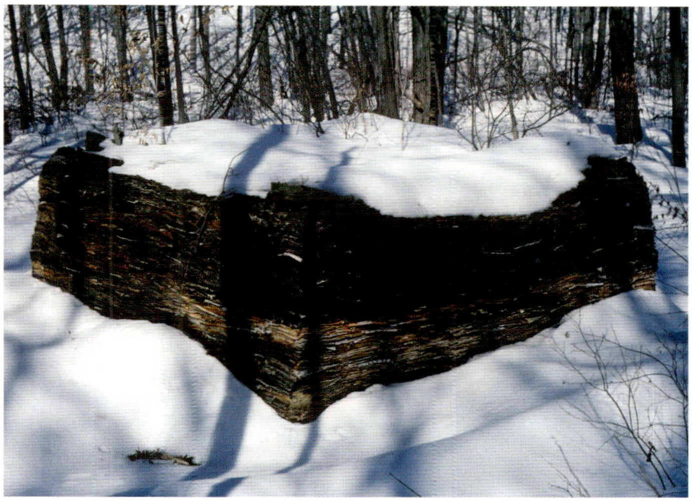

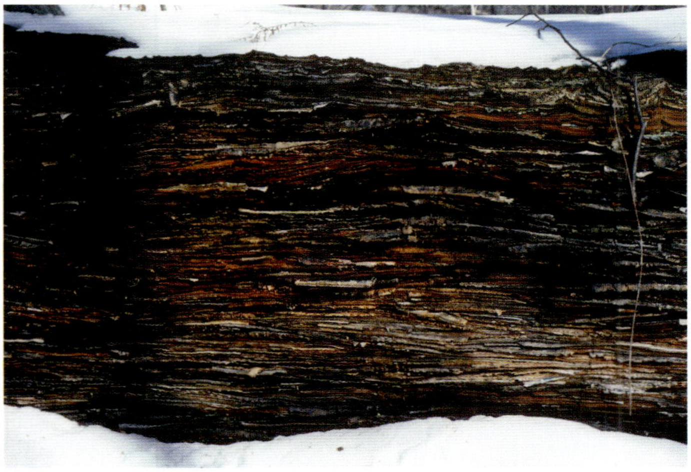

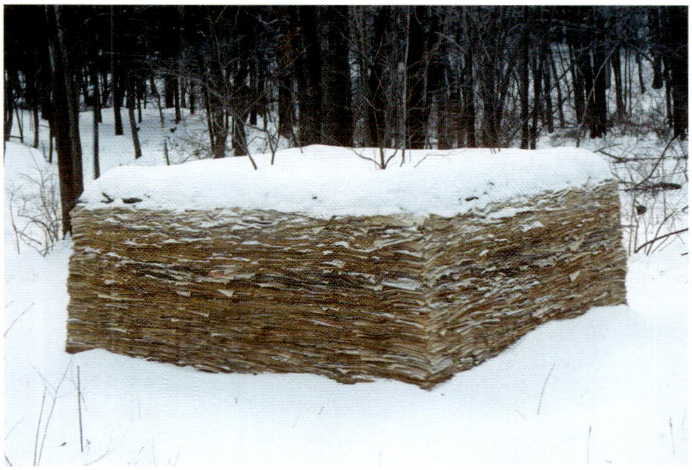

1

93 TEXTURE

AN ESSENTIAL ATTRIBUTE AS AN EXPRESSIVE ELEMENT

Both sculpture and painting allow for the creation and use of texture, a feature that can be central to the sense of an artwork. In addition, the art of painting allows for the depiction or reproduction of textures. The sensual excitement afforded by texture, whether real or perceived, is increased by the presence of multiple textures. The experience of variety, of moving from one texture to another, allows for the comparison of rough with smooth, shiny with dull, granulated with grooved.

Sculpture offers the greatest opportunity in deploying texture as an expressive element. David Smith (1906–65), for example, would often use a handheld grinder to create a highly dramatic and sometimes brutal texture on his works in steel.

Painting offers the opportunity to manipulate both real texture on the surface of the painting and depicted texture within the picture. Prior to the late nineteenth century, the prevailing convention in Western art was to make paintings with smooth surfaces. Many artists, however, embraced texture as a subject. The eighteenth-century French painter François Boucher (1703–70) used multiple textures in his *Toilet of Venus*. Satin, silk, velvet, flesh, polished metal, and stone are included, making a great contribution to the sensual nature of the work.

The manipulation of the surface texture of painting begins with Impressionism, when thick brushstrokes of broken color make a more assertive surface than traditional techniques. The Postimpressionists, in particular Van Gogh, began to deploy much heavier paint, displaying an entirely more physical brushstroke than previous painters.

In the twentieth century, abstract painters quickly recognized the creative possibility of texture. Both Picasso and Braque built textures into their Cubist works, through techniques of collage and through texturing areas of paint by combing it or otherwise working it. In postwar art, many of the American Abstract Expressionists incorporated texture in their work both by building heavy surfaces and by deploying additives, such as sand or other materials. In recent years, perhaps the most dramatic use of texture has come from the German artist Anselm Kiefer (1945–), whose large-scale works have deployed everything, including poured lead, rocks, stone, and tree branches, to create immensely powerful textured surfaces.

1 Anselm Kiefer (1945–)
Dein aschenes Haar Sulamith, 1981, Oil on canvas with collage, $51^{5}/_{8} \times 66^{7}/_{8}$ in (131 × 170 cm)

2 François Boucher (1703–70)
Toilet of Venus, 1751, Oil on canvas, $42^{5}/_{8} \times 33\frac{1}{2}$ (108.3 × 85.1 cm)

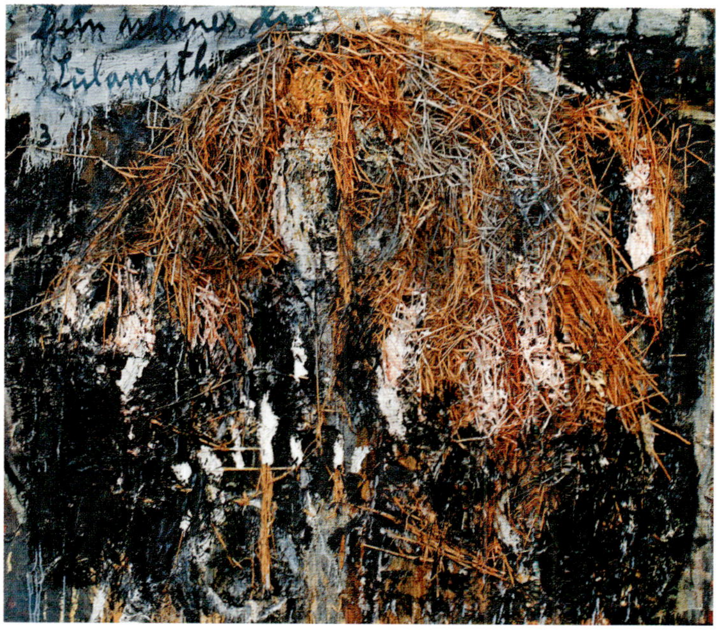

1

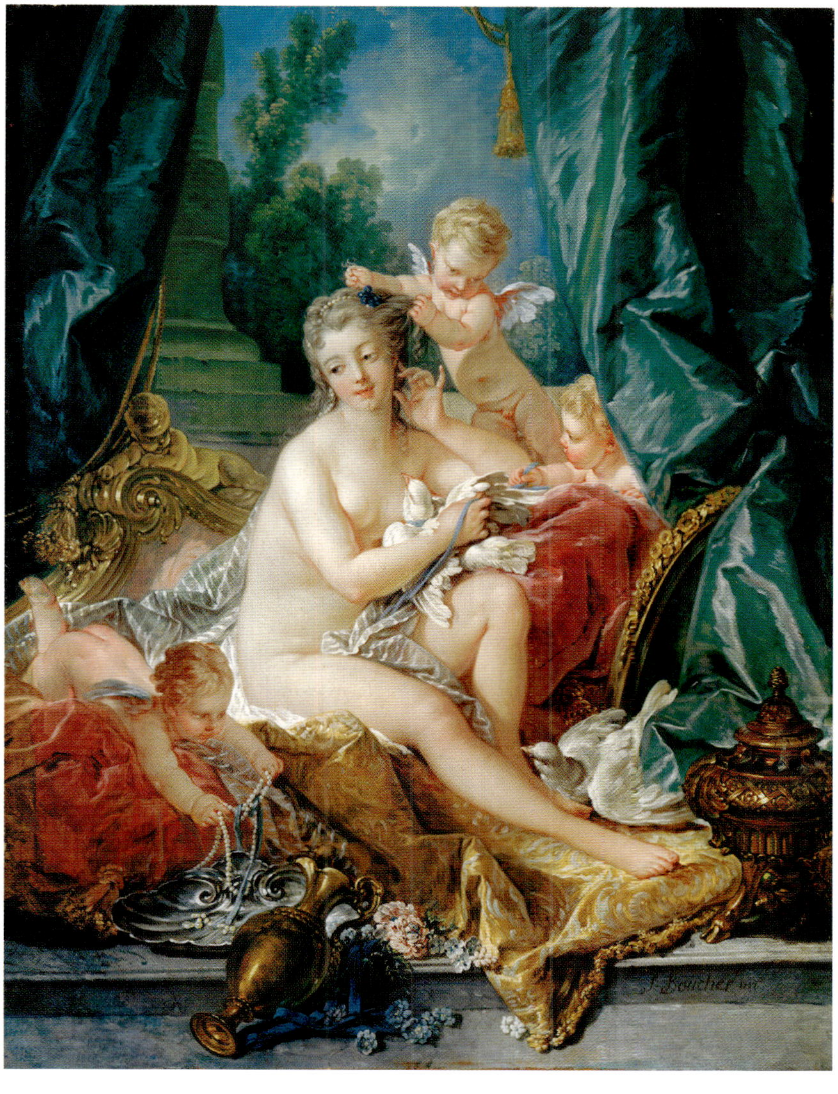

2

94 THEME

PURSUING AN IDEA

A theme is an overall idea that carries through a work or a series of works. The expression and elaboration of the theme may be the goal of the artist in producing the work. In other cases, themes emerge as the artist pursues other ideas or ambitions. Themes are often supported by motifs, repeated elements that can have both symbolic and structural value. (See *Motif* on page 116.)

APPROACHES

- **Philosophical**
  The artist pursues a theme to convey an idea. For instance, in *The Disasters of War*, (see page 133) a series of etchings by Goya (1746–1828), the artist pursues the theme of the senselessness of violence brought about by human conflict. Each image shows an instance of the theme in action or in some way that relates to the theme.
- **Abstract**
  A visual idea is carried through a number of works and explored through multiple variations. Robert Motherwell's series of paintings, *Elegy for the Spanish Republic*, explores variations on a series of abstract visual motifs in the context of an overall comment on the demise of the democratic movement in Spain. The artist called it "a funeral song for something one cared about." An even more abstract example is Joseph Albers's series *Homage to the Square*, in which the artist explored the theme of color interaction within a single geometric composition over several hundred paintings.
- **Narrative**
  A series of works forms a narrative that displays a theme and variations. Domenico Tiepolo (1727–1804) produced a series of more than a hundred pen and ink drawings on the theme of Punchinello, a rather hapless, but amusingly clownish, stock character in the Commedia dell'Arte. The narrative is extremely loose, but each image presents a dramatic situation that reveals and elaborates on the nature and behavior of the central character.

See also: *Narrative* on page 120; *Motif* on page 116; *Politics and Polemics* on page 132

1 Domenico Tiepolo (1727–1804)
Frontispiece, 1797, Pen and ink with wash on paper, 16 × 11½ in (40.6 cm × 29.2 cm)

Punchinello's Father Brings Home the Bride, 1797, Pen and ink with wash on paper, 14 × 18 13/16 in (35.5 × 47.7 cm)

Two of the more than a hundred drawings that the artist made on the theme of Punchinello. The inscription in the frontispiece means "An entertainment for children."

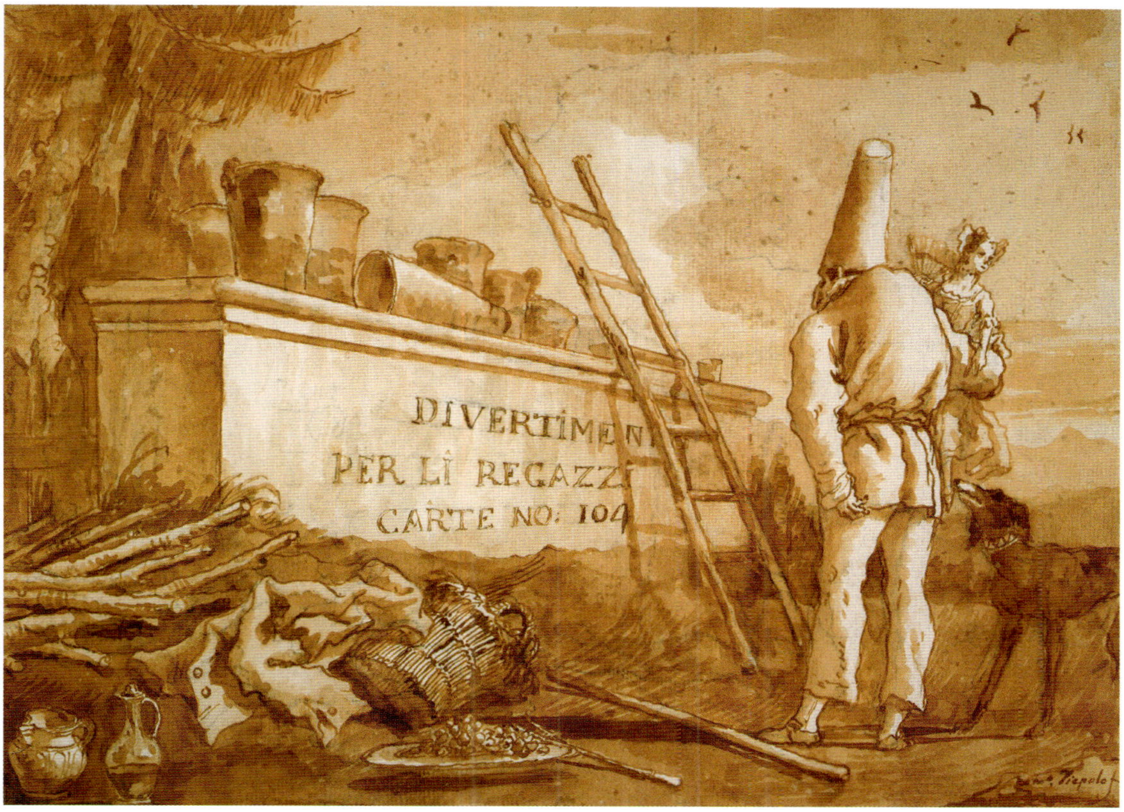

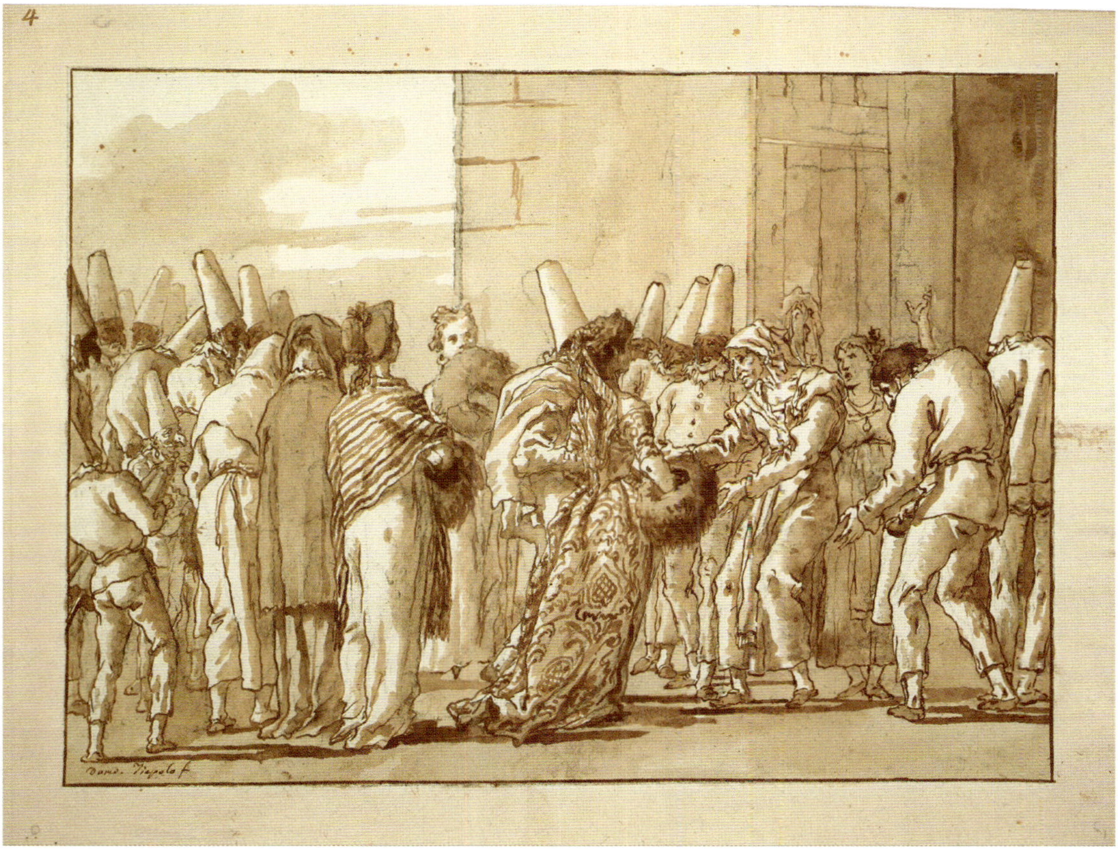

1

95 TONE AS STRUCTURE

TONAL RELATIONSHIPS IN REPRESENTATIONAL ROLES

Tone is the property of relative lightness or darkness of an object. The human eye has an extraordinary sensitivity to tone, which is registered by an array of sensors on the retina called rods. Each eye contains approximately 94 million rods, each of which is capable of recording light levels down to a single photon.

In painting and drawing, tonal values can be used for a variety of purposes:

- Tone can be used to distinguish between elements.
- Tone is employed to create form and secure the illusion of consistent light throughout a painting or drawing. The artist creates a range of tones from light to dark that correspond to the range that is displayed in the subject matter. As long as the tones in the painting are established in the same order as they are in the subject, then the illusion will work.
- To make a tonal illusion function, it is not necessary to re-create the absolute value of the tones in the subject matter. Rather it is only necessary to create the same relationships. The range can therefore be extended or reduced by the artist for particular effects. For instance, a subject that has little contrast can be painted with much higher contrast using lighter highlights and darker darks.
- Tone can be manipulated to considerable expressive effect. Caravaggio (1571–1610) was probably the first artist to fully exploit the theatrical qualities of tonal rendering. Rembrandt (1606–69) often dramatically illuminated key elements within a painting, as did Velázquez (1599–1660), Eugène Delacroix (1798–1863), and many others. Conversely, in the late nineteenth century, James McNeill Whistler (1834–1903) often reduced contrast to create a sense of elegant calm and wistfulness. Extreme contrast is often deployed in expressionist works where drama and emotive response are required.

Tonal relationships can be established independently of color as a gray scale. Similarly, monochrome color can be used in a purely tonal fashion.

1 Gray Scale

2 Monochrome Tonal Scale

3 This pixelated image shows the power of tone to secure an illusion. In the second image, the tonal range is narrowed but the image remains intact. The tones remain in the same relationship to each other.

4 Rembrandt (1606–69)
The Night Watch, 1642, Oil on canvas, 141 11/16 × 173¼ in (360 × 440 cm)

The massing of areas of deep tone allows the artist to guide the viewer's attention to the illuminated figures in the foreground.

5 Georges Seurat (1859–91)
The Artist's Mother, 1882–3, Conté crayon on laid paper, 12 × 9 3/16 in (30.5 × 23.3 cm)

The artist builds a drawing that is entirely tonal—no lines are used at all. This is an example of the suggestive power of tone.

6 James McNeill Whistler (1834–1903)
Symphony in White #1, 1862, Oil on canvas, 84¼ × 42½ in (214 × 108 cm)

Whistler uses a background that is tonally very close to that of the girl's dress to create a delightfully gentle effect.

1

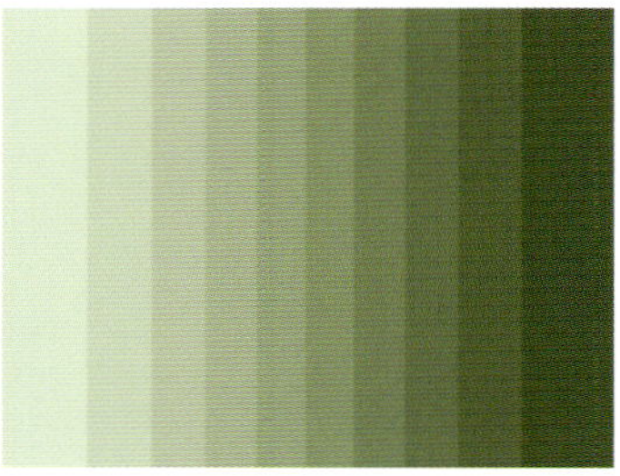

2

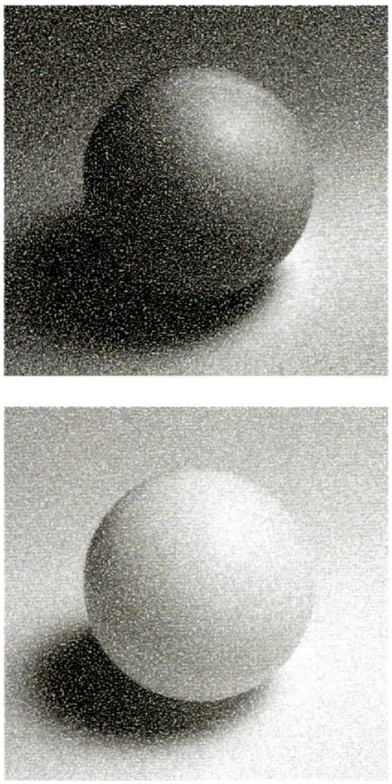

3

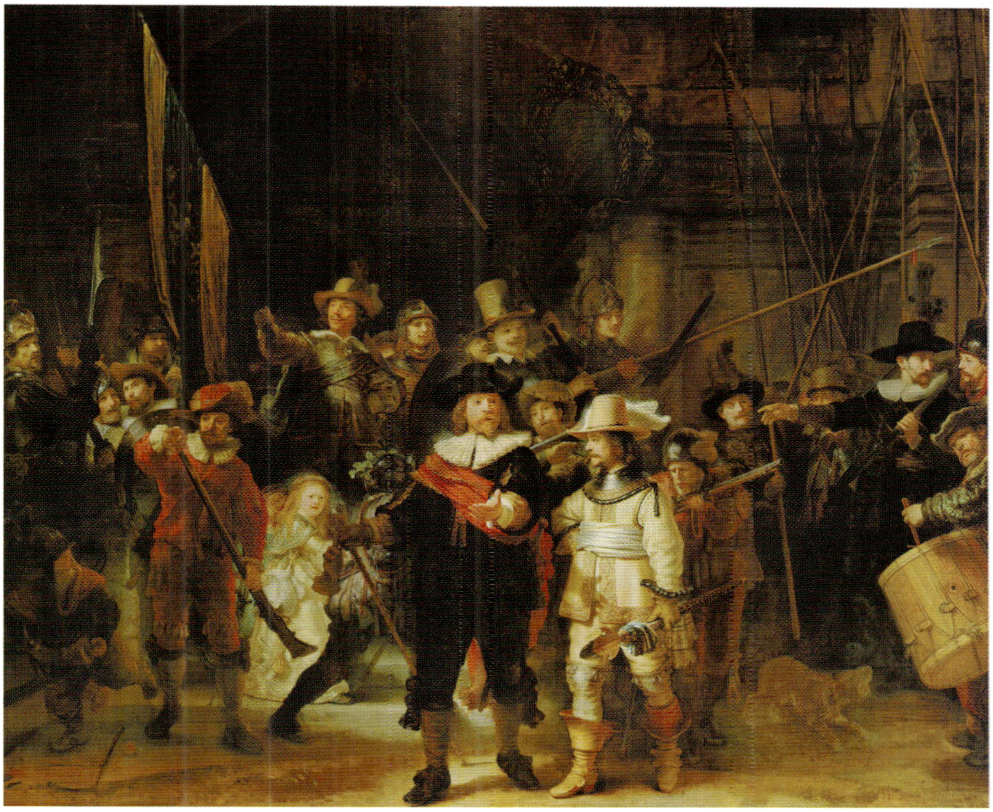

4

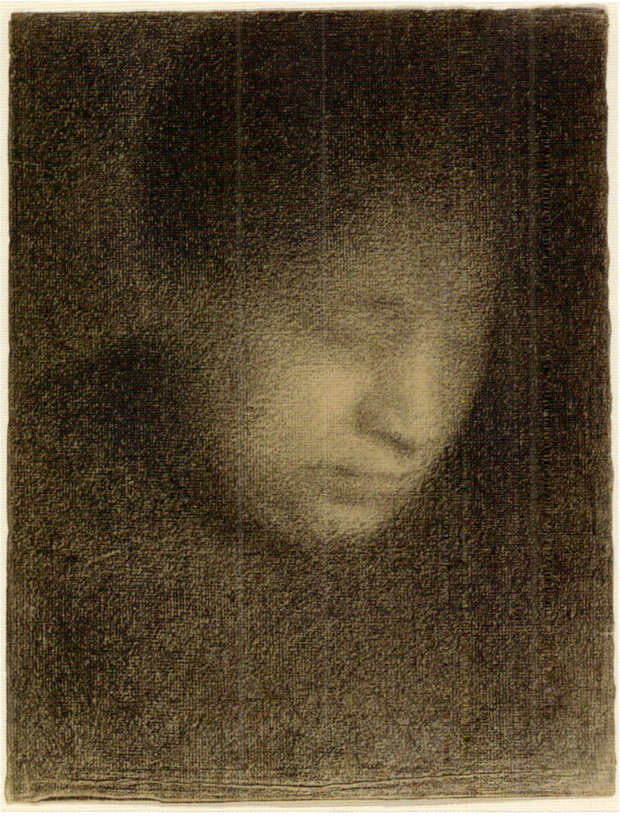

5

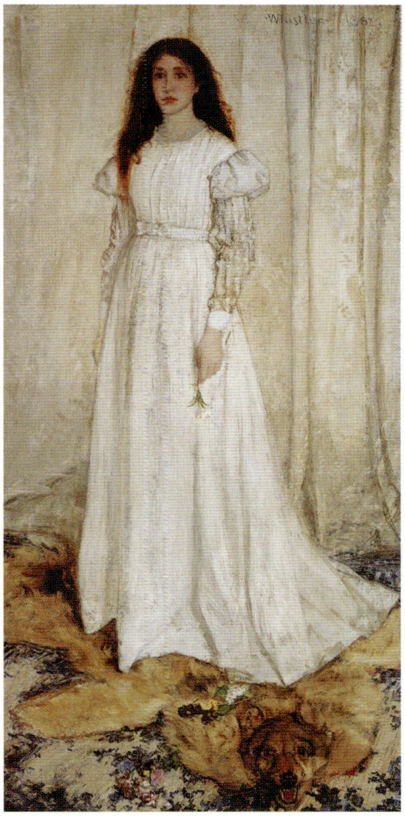

6

96 TOUCH COMMUNICATES

A PHYSICAL CONNECTION WITH THE ARTIST

Many artworks present traces of the physical touch of the artist in the form of brushstrokes, fingermarks, chisel marks, and so forth. The nature of the marks made by an artist establish a strong bond with the viewer and provide a conduit for expression. In looking at a painting, the viewer empathizes with the kind of stroke made and understands immediately whether it is firm, angry, tender, delicate, rough, strident, or forceful. Similarly, in certain kinds of sculpture, the touch of the artist is revealed as clay is pushed around or stone surfaces are carved and chiseled.

Usually the artist's touch is a secondary feature of a work of art, something that is displayed while the artist goes about his or her business. In a painting by Rembrandt (1606–69), the artist is generally working to secure form by building tonal and color relationships. The display of his brush mark is to some extent a byproduct of the process of placing and layering paint. Similarly, in an Impressionist painting where small brush marks laden with color are being carefully amassed throughout the painting, the artist's touch and feel will be left visible on the surface, an almost inevitable result of his or her endeavors. This allows the viewer to appreciate the minute physical movements involved in making the work and thereby to connect in a visceral way with the artist.

The communication of this fundamental, almost biological, information about the artist comes to the fore in much expressionist art, where the marks made often appear to carry a sense of the artist's state of mind. Qualities of urgency, obsession, frenetic energy, and exquisite delicacy, for instance, can be readily conveyed by a sense of touch. Likewise, negative qualities such as heavy-handedness, clumsiness, thoughtlessness, and weakness can also be apprehended through touch.

See also: *Brush Techniques* on page 30

1 Frans Hals (1580–1666)
Portrait of a Member of the Haarlem Civic Guard, c. 1636–38, Oil on canvas, 33 7/8 × 27 3/16 in (86 × 69 cm)

Hals's warm and sure touch is revealed as he places successive layers of paint.

2 Vincent van Gogh (1853–90)
The Olive Orchard (Detail), 1889, Oil on canvas, 28¾ × 36¼ in (73 × 92.1 cm)

The energetic, speedy, and intense quality of Van Gogh's attack is matched by his heavy and luscious touch.

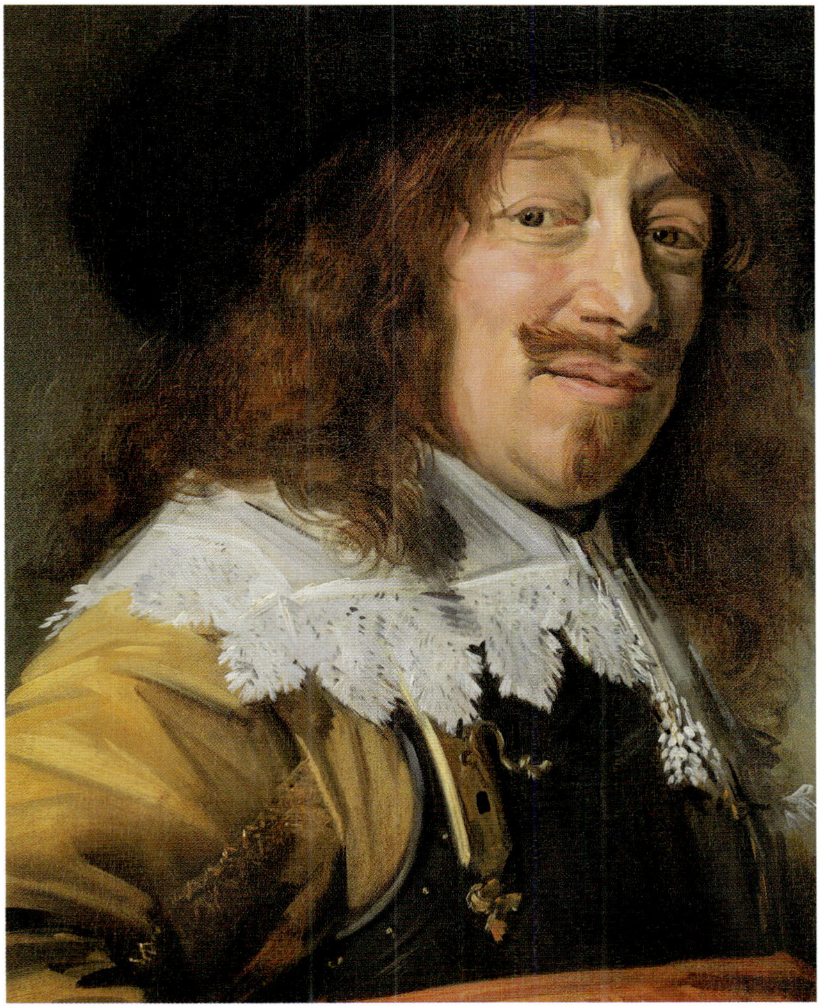

1

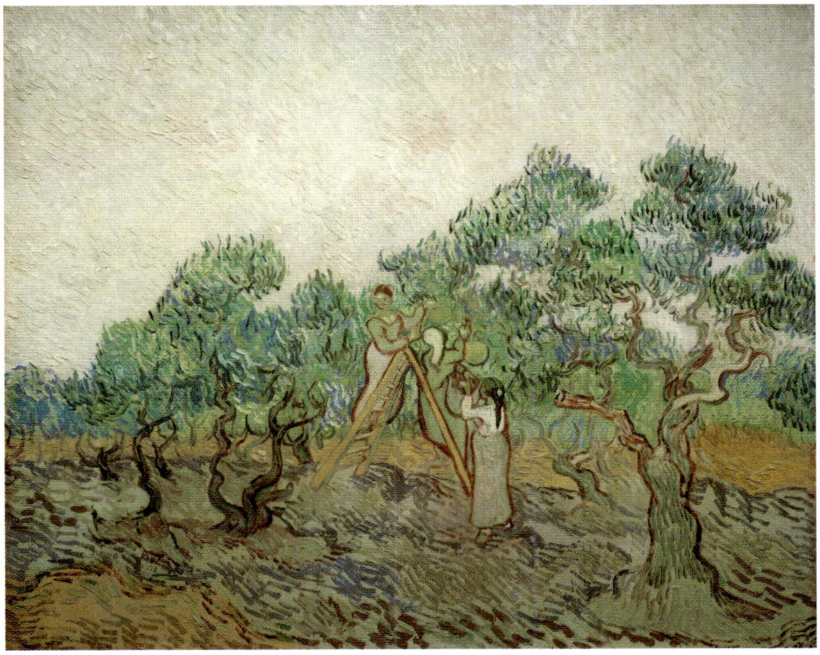

2

97 TRIBAL ART

AN INTEGRATED ROLE FOR ART

"Tribal" art refers to art made by people living in communities that are cut off from, or only recently acquainted with, the international community. These cultures are nonliterate, generally organized into small villages, and subsistent on hunting and gathering along with some small-scale agriculture. Europeans first became interested in the art made by such peoples in the second half of the nineteenth century when African and Oceanic artifacts were imported in quantity. Painters, in particular Picasso, were impressed by the stark power of many of the masks and figures.

A question remains, however, as to whether tribal art is actually art at all in the strictly European sense. It may be that our comprehension of it is entirely the result of a Eurocentric outlook that knows little of the context in which it was made or the purposes for which it was designed. Moreover, the artifacts that have been imported are generally of the more portable variety. Left behind are more ephemeral forms, such as dance, body art, or art made from perishable materials.

Most tribal art is integrated into ritualistic practices or otherwise forms a ceremonial role within the community. Anthropologist Alfred Gell suggests that many tribal artifacts have a "magical utility," in which their form and decoration assist with some important task. The decoration on a spear, for instance, may help it to its target. Or a carved head may hold the spirit of some ancestor. Clearly, without knowing this cultural context, an outsider may be hard pressed to fully understand the nature of the artifact. Conversely, other authorities contend that tribal art is readily accessible and that qualities such as rhythm, balance, coloration, and strength are valued as they are in Western art. Artworks are generally made by specialists within the community and are set aside as objects of respect, just as they are in the West. The very large amount of tribal art that represents the human figure, or heads, forms a simple, direct connection with all humans. As the philosopher Dennis Dutton (1944–2010), in his book *The Art Instinct*, points out, "The passionate, imaginative visions of tribal arts, expressing as they often do modes of life and thought which have been abandoned since contact with Western culture, have significantly expanded the West's notion of how art can mean."

1 **Figure with chin resting on his knee**, c. 6th century BCE, Nok sculpture, Nigeria, Terra cotta, 14¼ in (36.8 cm) high

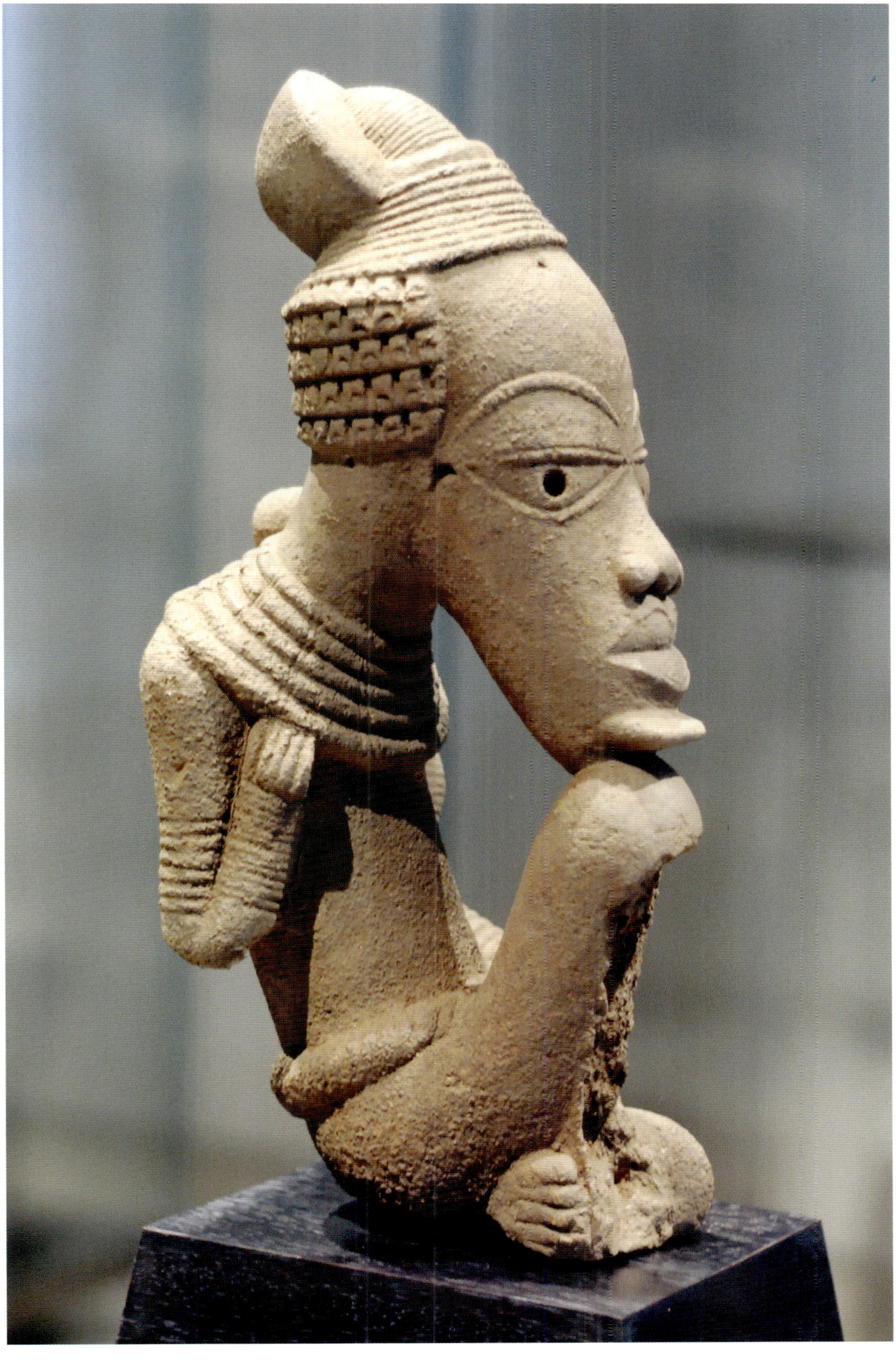

1

98 TROMPE L'OEIL

DECEPTION AS ART

Trompe l'oeil is the attempt to deceive the viewer's eye into believing that a representation is actually the thing itself. This ambition for perfect imitation goes back to Greek art. Aristotle, in *The Poetics*, writes, "The instinct of imitation is implanted in man from childhood, one difference between him and other animals being that he is the most imitative of living creatures, and through imitation learns his earliest lessons; and no less universal is the pleasure felt in things imitated." In his *Naturalis Historia*, Pliny the Elder tells the tale of a contest between two Greek painters, Zeuxis and Parrhasius. Zeuxis painted a bunch of grapes with such verisimilitude that birds swooped down in an attempt to pluck them. He then asked Parrhasius to pull aside the curtain covering his own painting only to discover that the curtain was, in fact, a painted image. Parrhasius was declared the winner. "I have deceived the birds," said Zeuxis, "but Parrhasius has deceived Zeuxis."

Since the mastery of representational techniques achieved in the Renaissance, trompe l'oeil has made regular appearances. In general its use divides into three areas:

- **Architectural**
  Mural and ceiling paintings attempt to convince the viewer that non-existent spaces and architectural adornments are present.
- **Easel painting**
  Creation of the illusion that elements are projecting out in front of the picture plane
- **Diversion**
  An element used as an amusing or diverting addition to another work of art. A highly realistic fly, for instance, might be painted on top of a picture or even on the frame.

See also: *Representation* on page 154

1 Andrea Pozzo (1642–1709)
Fresco, 1703, Jesuit Church, Vienna

The creation of illusionistic ceiling paintings began with Mantegna and Melozzo da Forli in the fifteenth century. By the mid-sixteenth century, artists had discovered how to integrate such illusions into the perspective of architecture. The spectacular theatricality of such effects was well suited to the ambitions of the Counter-Reformation and its attempt to attract congregations with visual splendor. Here a faux dome is created in the ceiling. Such an illusion only works perfectly from a specific viewpoint.

2 William Michael Harnett (1848–1892)
The Old Violin, 1886, Oil on canvas, 38 × 23⅝ in (96.5 × 60 cm)

Harnett specialized in still life paintings in which objects appear to be projected into real space in front of the canvas. He perfected an approach that first appeared in seventeenth-century Dutch painting.

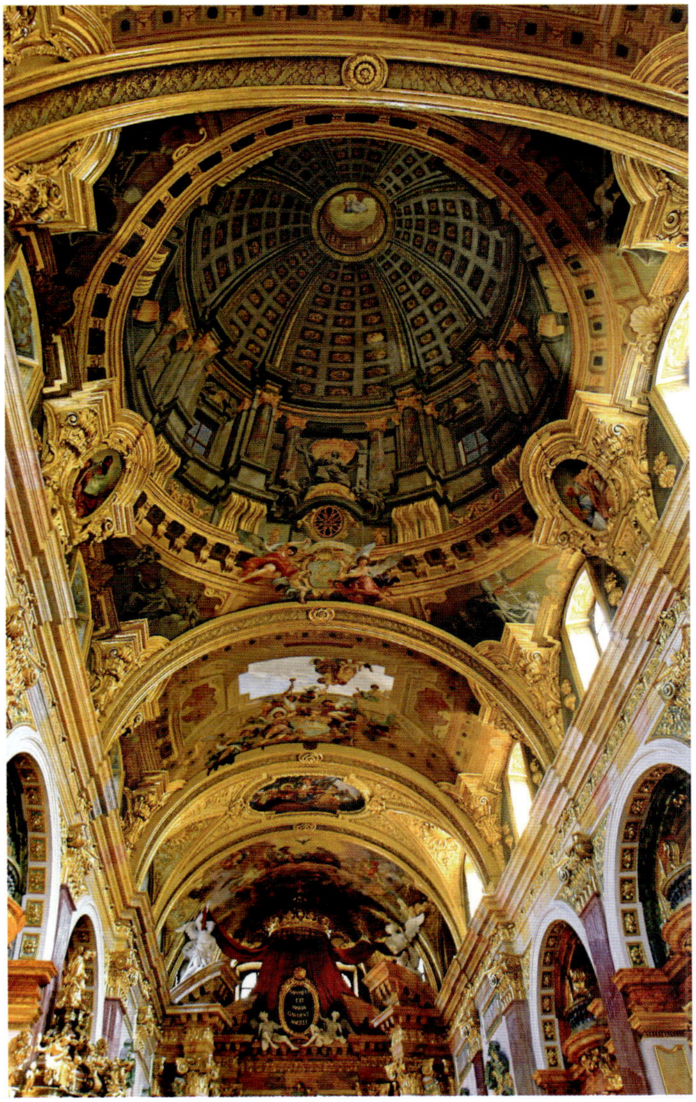

1

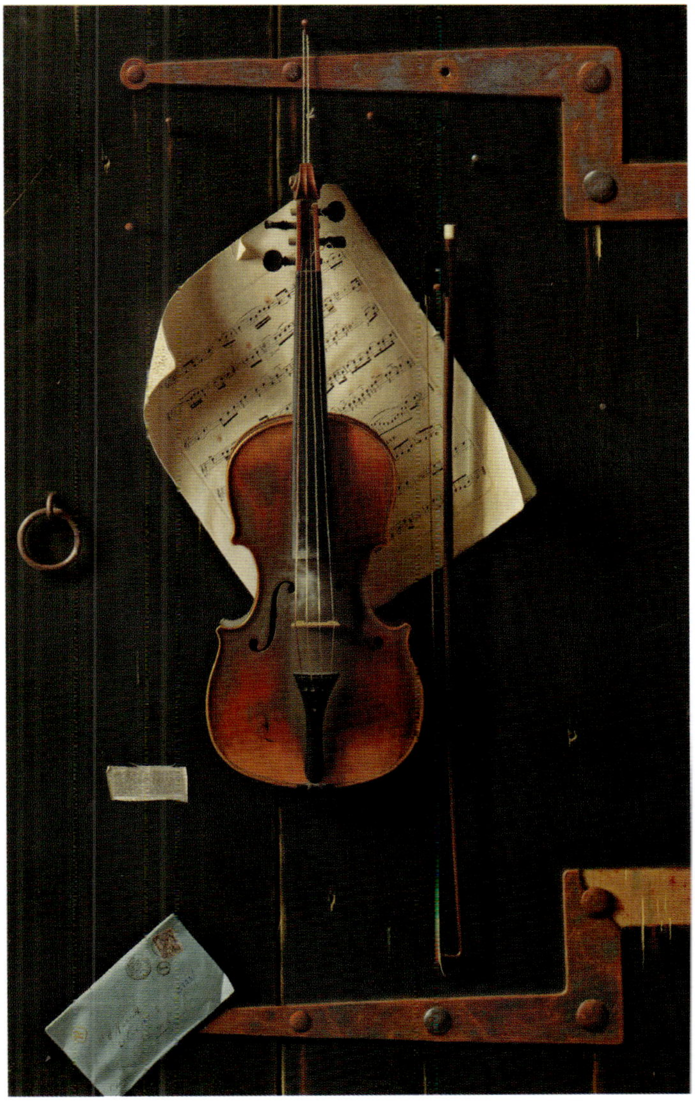

2

99 UNDERPAINTING

A VERSATILE TECHNIQUE BESTOWS DEPTH, RICHNESS OF COLOR, AND SOLIDITY

Underpainting is a technique that allows for the creation of greater depth and solidity in a painting. Although there are many variations, the most common procedure is to execute a monochrome version of an image, usually in a warm brown. Another popular option is simply to use black and white, a procedure known as grisaille. The underpainting may be worked until it is a fairly full account of the image and then allowed to dry. The artist will then build on top of it using glazes, semitransparent layers of paint, or stippled brushing so that the presence of the underpainting layer is at least partially visible through the succeeding layers. As the paint builds, the artist manipulates the color and interaction between the upper and lower layers, creating both an increased sense of depth and added richness of color.

Many Renaissance painters preferred a two-stage underpainting beginning with a thin drawing in a warm earth color followed by a tonal rendering in verdaccio, a mixture of mars black and yellow ochre that forms a dull green hue. This cool layer sitting on top of the warm drawing created color activity that readily mimicked the play of shadows on flesh. A full color layer was then worked on top using glazes or semitransparent paint. This was the technique that Leonardo da Vinci used for his *Mona Lisa*.

Underpainting can also be used to more dramatic and expressive effect by deploying more powerful hues. The American illustrator Maxfield Parrish (1870–1966) would often begin a work with a monochrome rendering in ultramarine blue. Once it was dry, he would work on top of it with multiple layers of glaze so that in the finished work, a blue glow emanated from the piece. The effect was suggestive of magical and otherworldly realms, and perfectly reinforced the artist's imaginative and visionary transformation of the world.

As well as reinforcing the spatial depth of a painting, monochrome underpainting has other advantages. It allows the painter to separate the tasks of drawing and tonal distribution from that of color. This makes the work simpler, increasing the artist's ability to closely control the development of the image.

See also: *Form Rendered* on page 80

1 Nanette Fluhr
Demonstration, Oil on canvas

An initial thin underpainting in a warm brown establishes the drawing and the tonal arrangement. A thicker coat of paint is then applied on top, building heavily into the lights but leaving the shadows a little more transparent.

2 Maxfield Parrish (1870–1966)
The Lantern Bearers, 1908, Oil on canvas on board, 40 × 32 in (101.6 × 81.3 cm). Published in *Collier's* magazine, December 10, 1910

Parrish uses a brown underpainting for the foreground figures but no underpainting for the lamps or sky. This results in increased luminosity for the lamps and sky while the artist builds subtle glazes of muted color in the figures and steps to give them a shadowy density.

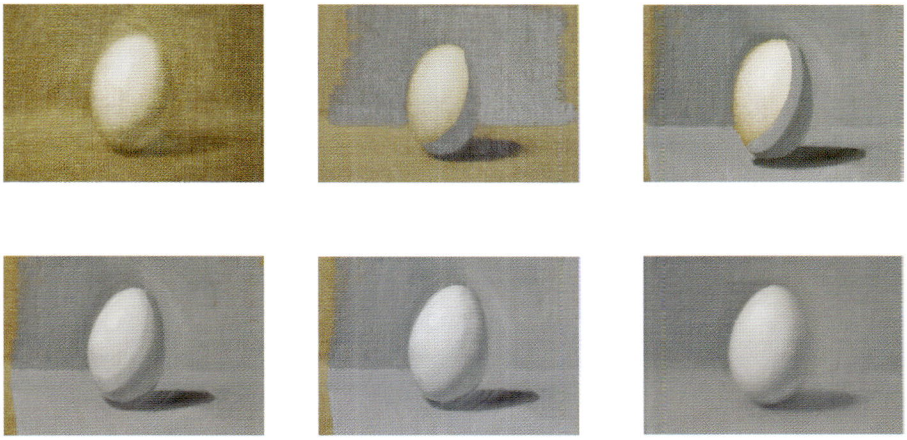

1

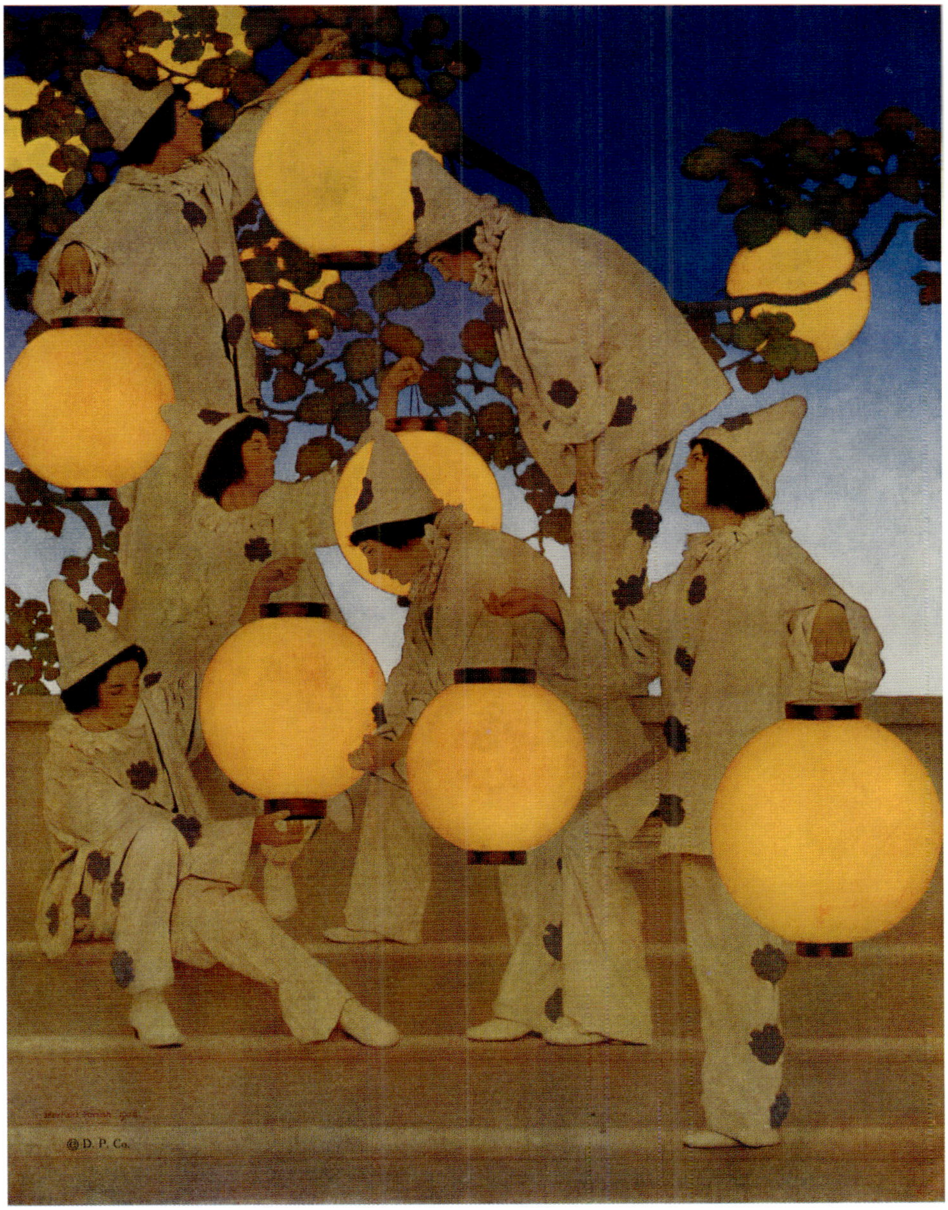

2

100 VIDEO ART

BRINGING THE SCREEN TO THE ART GALLERY

Video art is a genre that came into being in the late 1960s, when consumer portable video cameras were first manufactured. The form is distinguished from film and television by its lack of adherence to traditional expectations of entertainment and diversion. A work of video art may very well not have plot, actors, discernible action, or coordinated sound. It may not even show recognizable imagery at all, or it may deliberately distort or otherwise mutilate the imagery. Early video artists were interested in challenging the viewer's assumptions about what might be presentable on a television screen as well as exploring the expressive possibilities available outside the conventions of commercial film and television.

STRATEGIES

- **Real time**
  Early video artists quickly discovered that video enabled extremely long takes, far longer than a viewer might normally expect. The idea of showing something in real time, however tedious, carried with it a new kind of authority, the possibility of viewing an unedited world. Bruce Nauman (1941–), for instance, left the camera running in his studio overnight, capturing only a few mice and his prowling cat in many hours of footage.
- **Multiple display**
  By 1969, new technology allowed for the screening of coordinated videos on multiple screens. At this point, the video also became an installation work and presaged the onset of multimedia presentations. Early works, such as *Wipe Cycle* by Ira Schneider, concentrated on mixing disparate images and moving them from screen to screen in a more or less choreographic fashion.
- **Abstract**
  Electronic synthesizers and digital graphic software allow for the creation of video images without the use of a camera. Modern computers can generate and animate both imagery and text in almost any way imaginable.
- **Combination**
  Video art can be combined with installation art or even with traditional media, such as sculpture or painting. Nam June Paik (1932–2006), one of the pioneers of video, made a famous piece, *TV Buddha*, in which a bronze statue of the Buddha sits contemplating a small Sony portable TV showing an image of this same Buddha streamed from a camera above the TV.

The advent of much cheaper and more powerful video and editing hardware and software in the 1990s and 2000s gives contemporary artists unbounded possibilities in manipulating imagery and sound. The growth of multimedia technology in which video, audio, large-screen projection, and live action can be mixed has, to some extent, subsumed video art as a form.

1 Nam June Paik (1932–2006)
Self-Portrait. c. 1982, Video installation with sculpture

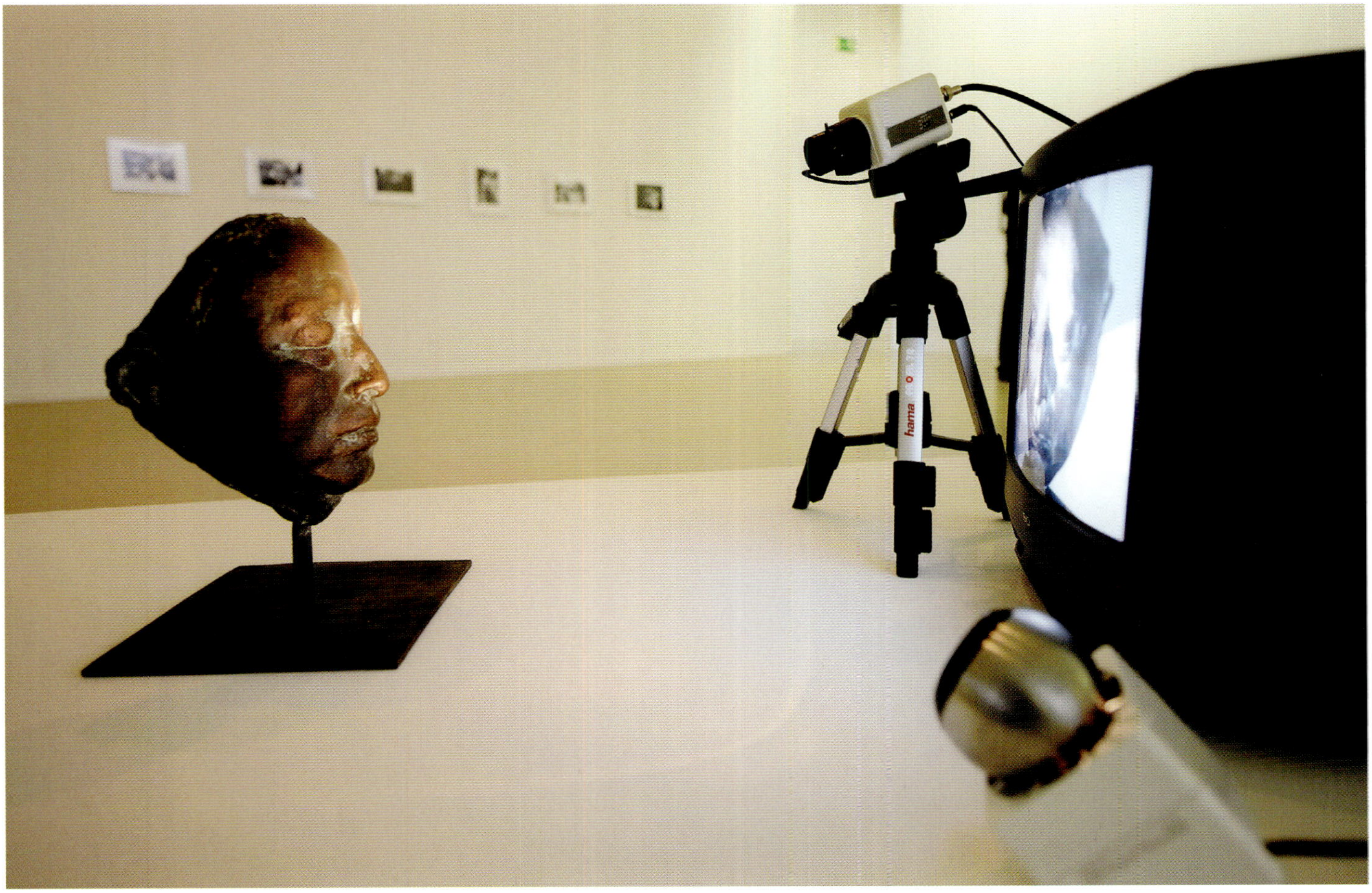

1

CREDITS

AMBIGUITY

The Mountain, Balthus. Photo: © Alfonso Vicente / Alamy

APPROPRIATION

Andy Warhol Flowers, Richard Pettibone.
Photo: © Presselect / Alamy

AUTHENTICITY AND OUTSIDER ART

Henry Darger image courtesy of the American Folk Art Museum.

COLLAGE AND ASSEMBLAGE

Man with Pipe, Georges Braque. Photo: © SuperStock / Alamy

Specific Hungers, Kathy Bruce. © The artist.
Photo courtesy the artist.

Dream, Reginald Case. Photo courtesy of Bonnie Case.

COLOR AS LIMIT

The Zorn Palette. Image and photograph courtesy of Michael Lynn Adams.

CONCEPTUAL ART

No Secret Painting XI. Art and Language. © The artist.
Photo courtesy of Lisson Gallery, London.

CONSISTENCY OF VISUAL LANGUAGE

Idyll, Francis Picabia. Photo: © ACTIVE MUSEUM / Alamy

DISTORTION

Fang Mask, Gabon. Photo. Marie-Lang Nguyen.
Released into public domain.

EROTIC ART

Kiss Painting, Betty Tompkins. © The artist. Photo courtesy of Galerie Rodolphe Janssen, Brussels. Private Collection.

EXPRESSION IN THE ABSTRACT

Rosy-Fingered Dawn at Louse Point, Willem de Kooning.
Photo: © Peter van Evert / Alamy

GENDER

Abundance: Shoes, Claudia DeMonte. © The artist.
Photo courtesy of June Kelly Gallery, New York.

INSTALLATION

Installation at the Rose Art Gallery, Brandeis University.
Judy Pfaff. Photo: Boston Globe / Getty Images

INTERACTIVE ART

The Gift, Birthe Blauth. © The artist. Photo courtesy of the artist and 532 Gallery Thomas Jaeckel, New York.

JUXTAPOSITION

Son of Man, René Magritte.
© Heritage Image Partnership Ltd / Alamy

KINETIC ART

Trigger Fish, David Beck. © The artist. Photo courtesy of Hackett Mill Gallery, San Francisco, CA.

LAND ART

Mapping Arcadia, Cazenovia and the Topography of Place, Alastair Noble. Photos courtesy of the artist.

LAYERS

Yangon, Joan Thorne. © The artist. Photo courtesy of Sideshow Gallery, New York, NY.

MATERIALS AS ART

Kitchen, Liza Lou. © The artist. Collection of the Whitney Museum of American Art, New York. Photo by Bruce Osborn provided by the artist.

MINIMALISM

Untitled, Donald Judd. Photo: © Presselect / Alamy

OP ART

Zephyr, Bridget Riley. Photo: © Daily Mail/Rex / Alamy.

Vassarely paintings at auction. Photo: © Press2000 / Alamy

PERFORMANCE ART

BEBECHY, Krzysztof Zarebski. Courtesy of the artist. Photo: Zosia Zeleska-Bobrowski.

Zero Gravity, Nadja Verena Marcin. Courtesy of the artist. Photo: Violetta D'Agata. Sponsored by WARP & Aurora Aerospace.

POLITICS AND POLEMICS

F-111, James Rosenquist. Photo: © Peter Horree / Alamy

PROCESS AS MEANING

Autumn Rhythm Number 30, Jackson Pollock. Photo: © Peter Horree / Alamy

Untitled, Robert Morris. Image courtesy ARS.

REPETITION

Nine Jackies, Andy Warhol. © Peter Horree / Alamy

RHYTHM

Dassin, Melissa Meyer. © The artist. Photo courtesy of Lennon, Weinberg Gallery, New York. Private Collection.

SHAPE

Tilt, Don Voisine. © The artist. Photo courtesy of McKenzie Fine Art, New York.

SHOCK ART

Piss Christ, Andres Serrano. © The artist. Photo Bridgeman Archive. Many thanks to the artist for waiving his rights fee.

SUCCESSIVE APPROXIMATION

Portrait of Annette, Alberto Giacometti. Photo: © Peter Horree / Alamy

SURREALISM

The Antipope, Max Ernst. Photo: © Heritage Image Partnership Ltd / Alamy

SYMBOLS

Tuttomondo Wall Painting (detail), Keith Haring. Photo: © age fotostock / Alamy

TEMPORARY ART

New Geology #2, Steven Siegel. Photo courtesy of Marlborough Gallery, New York NY.

TEXTURE

Dein aschenes Haar Sulamith, Anselm Kiefer. Photo: © Peter Horree / Alamy

UNDERPAINTING

Demonstration, Nanette Fluhr. Photos courtesy of the artist.

VIDEO ART

Self-Portrait, Nam June Paik. Photo: AFP/Getty Images

ABOUT THE AUTHOR

A highly-regarded painter and widely-published writer on art and art techniques, John A. Parks trained at the Royal College of Art in London in the 1970s and subsequently pursued a career in New York, exhibiting his work with several of the most renowned art galleries in the city. His painting has received considerable critical acclaim. In *The New York Times*, John Russell dubbed him a "true poet in paint," and *Times* critic Roberta Smith recently described his work as a "treat to discover." Parks' paintings are represented in a number of museum collections, including the Victoria and Albert Museum in London, and the Museum of the Rhode Island School of Design.

Parks has been a member of the faculty at the School of Visual Arts in New York since 1979, where he has taught courses in painting and drawing at every level, from undergraduate to post-graduate. He began writing about art in the early 1990s. His published work has explored a very broad array of subjects, ranging from profiles of contemporary artists such as Lucien Freud and Wayne Thiebaud, to historical figures such as Rubens, Raphael, and Whistler. His writings on art technique also cover considerable ground, including a major article on the painting technique of Velázquez as well as pieces on quill pen drawing, watercolor, and gouache techniques. Parks makes his home in Dutchess County, New York.

ACKNOWLEDGMENTS

I would like to acknowledge the generous help and support from everyone who has contributed to this project. In particular, I would like to thank Steven Heller for suggesting my involvement in the first place. I also owe a considerable debt to my editor, Emily Potts, for her highly professional and thoughtful guidance. The coordination of the all the reproductions and rights could not have been accomplished without the work of Renae Haines and all the folks at Rockport Publishers. The staff of the libraries of the School of Visual Arts and Bard College could not have been more helpful. Nanette Fluhr was extremely kind to do a demonstration of underpainting technique, and Michael Lynn Adams was generous in providing his immaculate color chart of the Zorn palette. Thank you to all the contributors for being so forthcoming with reproductions. My gratitude is also due to the staff at Lisson Gallery, London; Lennon, Weinberg Gallery, New York; and Thomas Jaeckel Gallery, New York, for coordinating contact with their artists and providing high-quality reproductions. Lastly, many thanks to my wife, Melanie Marder Parks, for her careful first reading of the manuscript and her many suggestions and corrections.

JOHN A. PARKS